WE WERE ILLEGAL

Uncovering a Texas Family's Mythmaking and Migration

JESSICA GOUDEAU

VIKING

VIKING
An imprint of Penguin Random House LLC
penguinrandomhouse.com

LIBRARY OF CONGRESS CATALOGING-IN-PUBLICATION DATA
Names: Goudeau, Jessica, author.
Title: We were illegal: uncovering a texas family's
mythmaking and migration / Jessica Goudeau.
Other titles: Other uncovered truths: my family's migration and mythmaking in Texas
Description: New York, NY: Viking, [2024] | Includes bibliographical references.
Identifiers: LCCN 2023047038 (print) | LCCN 2023047039 (ebook) |
ISBN 9780593300503 (hardcover) | ISBN 9780593300510 (ebook)
Subjects: LCSH: Goudeau, Jessica—Family. | Reese family. | Texas—Biography. |
Texas—History. | Texas—Race relations—History. | Slavery—United States—History. |
United States—Relations—Mexico. | Mexico—Relations—United States.
Classification: LCC F385 .G66 2024 (print) | LCC F385 (ebook) |
DDC 976.4009/9 [B]—dc23/eng/20240220
LC record available at https://lccn.loc.gov/2023047038
LC ebook record available at https://lccn.loc.gov/2023047039

Printed in the United States of America
1st Printing

Book design and family tree illustrations by Daniel Lagin

To Jonathan, who is writing a better story with me,

and our children, who bring us so much joy.

I love y'all the most.

About the difficulties of Texas: Love does not require taking an uncritical stance toward the object of one's affections. In truth, it often requires the opposite. We can't be of real service to the hopes we have for places—and people, ourselves included—without a clear-eyed assessment of their (and our) strengths and weaknesses. That often demands a willingness to be critical, sometimes deeply so.

—ANNETTE GORDON-REED,
ON JUNETEENTH

CONTENTS

PART 5
J. C. REESE
(1881–1930)

237

PART 6
FRANK PROBST
(1905–1990)

297

CONCLUSION | 349

ACKNOWLEDGMENTS | 357

NOTES | 363

WE WERE ILLEGAL

INTRODUCTION

I have loved Texas my whole life. Even when we moved away, my family has a long history of boomeranging back to this state, over many generations and for my entire childhood. Some of my earliest baby pictures are orange-tinted snapshots of me on a blanket on dry buffalo grass in West Texas, near where my father grew up. When I was a toddler, we moved to Iowa, where I jumped in leaf piles and trekked through snowdrifts. I left Texas before my grandmother did; the first time my mother's mother, my Nanny, traveled out of the state in her entire life was to come to Iowa when my sister was a baby. It wasn't long before we moved back to Texas, this time down south, near where my mother grew up. My parents bought a house based mostly on the trees for our growing family—my brother was born a Texan. I spent the majority of my early elementary years in one of the huge live oak trees in our yard, usually with an apple, always with a book.

Like most San Antonio schoolkids, I went on multiple field trips to the Alamo, the mission turned historical landmark in the center of our city. We shuffled through in long lines, listening to guides shouting over the din of dozens of rowdy kids in a small close space. I remember very little from those tours of the Alamo: mostly that James Bowie, William B. Travis, Davy Crockett, and other brave heroes of Texas died fighting for their freedom against the evil general, Santa Anna; that their sacrifices spurred Texans on to win the war for independence from Mexico; and that's how Texas became its own country. I remember that when I got home, my father sang "Davy, Davy Crockett, king of the wild frontier" for the rest of the day, and now I can't even type his name without that song running through my head.

I remember nothing about the border tensions rollicking the region during my childhood in the 1980s. For me, the border was something we crossed for a day trip, to buy crepe flowers and twirly dresses and elotes so hot, the butter dripped down our fingers while we walked. One of my best friends today grew up only a few miles from me; her family were some of the estimated three million people to receive a path to citizenship when one of the most conservative presidents in modern history put an amnesty program in place that seems impossible now at a time when we struggle to talk reasonably about immigration. That act changed my friend's life; I only learned about it years later.

Growing up in Texas means growing up in the tensions of who controls the border, who has the right to be here and who does not. Those frictions are one of the few constants in the history of this state. I grew up thinking those conversations about the border were "issues" to be learned about from school and books, and that they had nothing to do with me.

When I was nine, we left San Antonio for my dad's job, and I spent a miserable school year in Tennessee. On the first day at my new school, my classmates cornered me, asking where my boots were (I didn't have any), where I left my horse (I'd ridden twice in my life, both times in a circle at the rodeo), and if I knew any Texas Rangers (it turns out, I did). We didn't stay gone long. Less than a year later, we were back in West Texas, with twisted mesquites and tumbleweed instead of the live oaks and wildflowers I missed so fiercely. An awkward, bookish kid in a town where it seemed like every other girl was a basketball player or cheerleader, I had a hard time fitting in for years; that's probably why it took me some time, but eventually I fell in love with that part of Texas too.

I stayed here for college. In my literature classes, I learned more about the state and my place in it than I had ever known. A handful of lines I read in *Borderlands/La Frontera* by Gloria Anzaldúa burst open a truth about Texas I'd been stumbling toward but hadn't yet been able to put into words. Her memoir sections were about growing up in South Texas not far from my mom's hometown of Pleasanton. The first time I read Anzaldúa, I wanted to position myself as I always had in books: alongside the plucky young protagonist, as an underdog setting out against the odds. Anzaldúa, through her writing, firmly and clearly picked me up and placed me on the other side of the line—we "the Gringo" were "locked into the fiction of white superiority."

Perhaps embarrassingly, that book was the first time I read a history of Texas that did not center people who looked like me: "In the 1800s," Anzaldúa wrote, "Anglos migrated illegally into Texas, which was then part of Mexico, in greater and greater numbers and gradually drove the *tejanos* (native Texans of Mexican descent) from their lands, committing all manner of atrocities against them." Reading those lines made me uncomfortable. It made me want to put the book down, to justify myself, to explain that I wasn't like *those* Anglos, but I kept reading; by the end of the book, I felt a new understanding opening up in my mind. For the first time, I heard voices from the same land in Texas I had always loved but who had very different experiences from my own. It was only a start, the smallest of steps, but when I moved away from Texas as a young adult, I was beginning to view the layered stories of my home in a new way. Leaving gave me valuable clarity.

At the time, I thought—like so many of my family members before me—that I was never coming back to Texas. I taught English in Southeast Asia and South America, learning to sleep in rickety hostel beds and gaining a forever craving for spicy street food. I married a man who also loves to travel; Jonathan and I spent most of our twenties adventuring. We fished for piranhas in the Brazilian Pantanal while jabiru storks flapped giant wings over the water. We bunked on overnight Soviet-era trains from Slovenia into Italy to avoid paying for hotel rooms. We woke to the lazy roar of lions at the zoo next door in Guadalajara, Mexico. We felt the thrum of the discotheques beneath us through the floor of our cheap apartment in Santiago, Chile. In those years, I consciously dropped my Texas accent, tried to stop saying "y'all," and got by with faltering but improving Portuguese and Spanish.

I had almost convinced myself by my late twenties that I had no desire to move back to Texas. Which is why I was unprepared for the surge of pure longing I felt when I walked on the campus at the University of Texas, where I was interviewing for the English graduate program while visiting our families for the holidays. A future unfurled before me in an instant: me on the quad outside of the English department, reading a book between classes beneath enormous, sprawling live oak trees like the ones I climbed as a kid. Photo sessions with yet-to-be-born small children in fields of bluebonnets to match the ones my mom had in photo albums of my sister, my brother, and me. A soundtrack of cicadas lulling us to sleep. The smell of sunscreen and chlorine lingering on our damp skin. Watching the sun set on a flat Texas horizon where I could see every gradation of crepuscular color.

The day the acceptance letter came, I was ecstatic. There was a catch in my voice when I called our families and said, "We're coming home." As we drove into Austin with our scant worldly belongings in the back of a dented U-Haul, I said to Jonathan, "I love the geography of other places more. I'd rather have mountains and lakes and leaves that change in the autumn. But I can breathe in Texas like I can't anywhere else."

I still feel that way.

IMMEDIATELY AFTER WE MOVED HOME, THE CHILDHOOD LOVE I HAD felt for Texas deepened into a chosen love for a state that surprised me with the depths of its hospitality. I started class at the University of Texas the third week of August 2005. On August 23, Hurricane Katrina hit New Orleans.

My memories from that month are hazy snapshots. Standing beside a childhood friend, outside of the Austin Convention Center, wearing Red Cross vests. She was the brand-new volunteer coordinator suddenly in charge of thousands of volunteers in a massive displacement event; I was one of the friends who came when she called.

Setting up a call center with business leaders in suits in a strip mall to help facilitate the enormous community response.

Picking up books at the university co-op: Aimé Césaire, James Joyce, C. L. R. James, Nella Larsen, Salman Rushdie, Zora Neale Hurston, Paul Gilroy, Gabriel García Marquez.

Threading my way through rows of sleeping people in orderly cots, leading recently arrived chaplains of all different faiths to find coffee before their long days began.

Sitting in hard brown chairs in a 1980s-era mint-green classroom while students elaborated at length on theoretical ideas I barely understood.

Holding the hand of a woman in her eighties as she named all the children and grandchildren who had been evacuated, none of whom she could find, while I sat beside a computer bank set up to connect separated families. Her tears splotched our joined hands.

It was a chaotic way to return home. I fell in love completely. Over the next few years, I sought out that hospitable side of Texas with more and more frequency, pairing my academic education with community involvement. I taught a rhetoric class filled with DREAMers—young adults who came to the US as undocumented minors—and read with them *The Devil's Highway* by Luis Alberto Urrea. Prompted by discussions in that class, Jonathan and I went to pass out health-care pamphlets in Spanish at a community event in North Austin with our baby. I assumed we would meet asylum-seekers and people without documents. Instead, I got to know a group of former refugees from Myanmar.

That day changed my life completely. Those friendships grew into English classes for women trying to make ends meet in a bewildering new country, and then a nonprofit helping weavers and sewers and jewelry makers turn their skills into sustainable incomes they could use to support their families. For years, I saw Texas hospitality at its best at Catholic sanctuaries, Jewish community centers, Baptist gyms, and Muslim cultural centers, through English teachers and community partners, jewelry designers and graphic designers, seamstresses and tutors, medical appointment drivers, lawyers, surrogate grandmothers, interpreters—all of us bridging thousands of gaps in our lovely, unlikely community.

My education about borders and Texas and my place in this state— that began with those pages by Anzaldúa in college—expanded in those years, both outside of the classroom and through my studies. I had applied to UT to study US and Brazilian poetry because it has one of the best libraries of Latin American literature in the world. I immersed myself in 1950s newspaper archives from Rio de Janeiro; studied translations of poetry from all over the Americas; learned about immigration policies; took classes on surrealism in Central and South American novels. Conversations about borders were all around me in those years.

Jonathan and I decided to stay in Texas. We had three children through birth and adoption. Most of our family moved here too, and we made friends that felt like family. We bought a house with magnificent live oaks like the ones I climbed as a girl and my mother climbed before me. The largest one in our backyard is probably two hundred years old. Beneath it, we held family gatherings and birthday parties, the evening sky lit by twinkle lights. We say "y'all" unapologetically, welcoming everyone with one short word. We are raising our kids in the kind of place we always wanted: a diverse community that gives them an expansive sense of the world while still being rooted in our past.

That is the Texas I love now, as I have loved it for more than four decades, as I will love it for the rest of my life. I believe in the strength of this Texas, with wide-open skies and room enough for all kinds of people.

I describe this Texas so that you can understand what is at stake and why it has felt necessary to write a book that has personally been so difficult for me. As we have been many times in our past, we are at a precarious moment in our state. I believe firmly in our ability to find a way forward.

But we have to face some hard truths together first.

I FIRST NOTICED THINGS STARTING TO CHANGE IN TEXAS IN 2015. A friend who had been here for a few years messaged me; someone had spit on her on the bus, gesturing at her hijab before walking away. A few weeks later, a co-worker screamed at another friend that she should go home—which my friend would gladly have done, if home were not a war zone far worse than here. Newcomers who had once enjoyed a warm Texas welcome were increasingly becoming the objects of public anger and antagonism. All over the news, the governor, the attorney general, and our senators began referring to refugees as "terrorists" rather than the victims of terror. They accused refugees of trying to game the long, intensive vetting system for "free tickets" into the United States—rather than recognizing that resettlement was a yearslong process designed only for the direst cases, and that people accepted to the program had long ago proven that they were the victims of persecution, not the perpetrators of it. Eventually, this anti-refugee language spread on a national scale, but I noticed it in Texas first.

The vitriol turned to violence. There was a knife attack at the Presbyterian church in Austin where many refugees learn English; some quick-thinking men from Burundi thwarted it before anyone was hurt, but the refugee community in Austin was shaken. One day soon after the attempted attack, I was sitting with Kying, one of the artisans working with our nonprofit. She felt like it was a matter of time before the violence escalated, like it had in other cities around the US. Kying asked me what I was planning to do about it, whether I would write and tell other people her story like I had done with the artisan profiles on our nonprofit's website. In the highest compliment I can pay her, Kying is a strong advocate for herself and her family. I tried to tell her no; I had concerns I wasn't the right person to take on that role. She cut me off impatiently: "You're saying, you know how to write, you can tell people what my kids and I went through, and you're just . . . not going to? We've been friends for a long time. Why won't you help me when I'm asking you to?"

That exchange with Kying was a catalyst for me. I left academia and moved into journalism, eventually writing a book about resettled refugees' experiences in Texas.

Through that work, I began to investigate what was changing in my state. In my interviews, undocumented people and longtime advocates gently but firmly pushed back on my questions: some part of Texas has always been like this, they told me. The fact that it felt new to me said more about *me* than the state; perhaps these views had once been buried, but they had strong precedent.

But still, the fervor of this moment felt different from the Texas I had grown up with. I changed my questions. I became obsessed with understanding this very public turn in rhetoric, moving from hospitality to open hostility in a matter of months. I kept hoping the antagonism toward newcomers would pass. It only deepened.

Childhood friends started refusing to speak to me after reading social media posts or articles I wrote about immigration. Neighbors who had once waved in friendliness gave me side-eyes after seeing women in hijabs leave my home. The political ground shifted drastically beneath my feet—in supporting refugees and talking about commonsense immigration reform, I held what were once considered moderate, uncontroversial views. Now many people in my life seemed to think that these ideas—born out of love for people I know who were affected by these changing policies—made me suspicious. To me, it just felt like I was doing what I had been taught in my years of growing up in churches in Texas: caring for people who had been made vulnerable by catastrophes beyond their control. I hovered on the edge of a widening political chasm I could do nothing to bridge.

The discourse ratcheted up. The language from state leadership took on tones I had never heard in all my years of living here. Politicians in Texas framed the debates using aggrandizing stories that flattened complicated individuals into one-dimensional roles: all newcomers became threats from whom faithful, law-abiding Texans had to protect their homeland. The myths about the border passed down over generations in Texas made it clear, even when the politicians used coded language and indirect phrases, who the "good guys" were—who was "legal" and who was right.

Though I noticed it first with immigration, the scope widened: Vigilantism became official Texas policy, with large bounties offered to those willing to tattle on their neighbors' medical decisions. School board meetings took on the fervor of saloon shootouts from centuries past. Books were banned, teachers' language and lessons constrained, neighbors took to social media to lambast each other. It wasn't just one-sided; no matter their political affiliation, it seemed like neighbors and friends suddenly saw each other only with outrage and suspicion and distrust. People from all walks of life portrayed those with differing beliefs as buffoons or villains. Real people were collapsed into caricatures.

What was more bewildering to me was that sometimes, it seemed like Texas had always been this way. As if the generous, generative nature of the Texas I grew up in and had rediscovered as an adult never existed. Perhaps the fault lines had always been this pronounced. Perhaps I was the one misremembering my own history.

One day researching in the library at the University of Texas, I found four seventh-grade textbooks; all schoolchildren take Texas History in fourth and seventh grades, a fact I did not realize was unusual until I moved away from the state. One of the textbooks was the one my school used when I took Texas History—the photo of bluebonnets on the cover is distinctive. During my childhood, control of the state pingponged between the two political parties, ending when George W. Bush beat Ann Richards for the governorship. As I thumbed through those textbooks adopted across the state in the late 1980s through the late 1990s, I assumed I would find views that seem more and more common in Texas today—a desire to hide the unsavory parts of our history to focus only on a heroic past.

But that wasn't what I found at all. One textbook stated that the reason the Texas Revolution started was because Anglo settlers "worried that the Mexican government would end slavery, and many settlers believed they had a right to hold slaves." Another featured a pullout section about the "overlooked" history of Black soldiers who fought against Mexico: "Most of their names are not listed on the muster rolls of the Texan Army since only a few were enlisted soldiers." Over and over again, the textbooks addressed Texas history with nuance and a frankness that was invigorating.

I took those books home and read them almost like novels, blown away at the lack of today's partisanship in many of the depictions of Texas. I knew then—and have confirmed later through my extensive research and interviews—that I was not misremembering my own past in this state. What is happening is not about the necessary balance between differing views that is a hallmark of a thriving democracy—one of the highest values inherent in both Texas and the United States. Something new is happening, an extremism that deeply concerns me and many others. It is not happening only in Texas, but Texas has—like Texas always has—its own unique spin. We are in a period of discord and disconnection that has precedent in our history but is unique to our time. Like it has in other similar eras, our language is driving our fears.

The origins of that language are in the stories of our past.

I AM NOT A POLICY PERSON. I AM A RHETORIC PERSON, A STORY PERSON. My scholarly work and my journalism have all focused on the stories we tell ourselves. This began as a book about immigration and Texas myths. As I dug, I found that this is a story about stories: how they were formed, how they were passed down, where they came from, what they reveal about identity and values and fears in every age.

The Texas myths began like gossip passed down to the next generation, fluid and changing. The stories shifted with each telling, becoming a little more colorful each time. Those received narratives reveal the culture and values of a particular place and time—plucky underdogs who came out on top, good men in white hats who stood their ground for what they believed, distasteful acts of violence justified for righteous reasons—more than they told the straightforward details of what happened.

Meanwhile, the real facts became buried as the layers of myths solidified over time like sandstone. Over generations, those stories hardened into cultural views about who is allowed to hurt others and what kind of violence is acceptable in a society, whether on a small or large scale. Those layered stories became history and law and policies here in this land along the border. I had to go back four hundred years to fully understand the scope of how those ideas came to Texas, but in tracing their route, I learned more about the country, the state, and myself than I ever anticipated.

THE MYTHS I GREW UP WITH ABOUT MY FAMILIES' PLACE IN TEXAS ARE the backdrop of the histories of my family I am telling. I knew that I was at least a fourth-generation Texan from all of my grandparents' families— Perkinses and Probsts on my mother's side, Reeses and Munses on my father's. All four of my grandparents spent the vast majority of their lives in Texas. Our generational roots in Texas gave me a sense of pride growing up, a feeling that I belonged here and that this place would always be mine.

My mother's family were all members of the Churches of Christ, a faith tradition shared by my father's parents as well—which taught, like most faiths, that caring for others is a key religious tenet. But the idea of "helping" also implied a slight but critically important social hierarchy in Texas that was crucial to the Perkins and Probst clans. It was the only sense of superiority my mother's family possessed in their spatchcock home on the wrong side of the tracks in Pleasanton, Texas. As she put it, "We were poor, but we were better off than those people, and we should help them." In his 1935 book, *Black Reconstruction*, W. E. B. Du Bois refers to that feeling as a "sort of public and psychological wage"—a phenomenon after the Civil War, when poor white people felt that they now competed against newly freed Black laborers. They might receive the same low pay as their Black co-workers, but they also gained "public deference and titles of courtesy because they were white." During the Jim Crow years, they could still go to parks and public events and attend schools. In a line that would be especially telling for my families' stories in the Reconstruction era and after, Du Bois said the "police were drawn from their ranks, and the courts, dependent upon their votes, treated them with such leniency as to encourage lawlessness." The Probst side of my mother's family passed down the story that they had once been rich but had lost their wealth—a loss that rankled and that gave many of them a sense of resentment and of always being above their circumstances. For many of the Probst men in Nanny's family, it gave an added incentive to be cruel as a sign of their superiority. For many of the Probst women, but especially Nanny, that family myth called them to charity even when times were tight—and times were always tight.

My father's family myth, according to my dad, was that the Reeses were "exceptional but overlooked," a story shared by generation after generation of seemingly underappreciated and aggrieved underdogs. There was a secretive edge—positive things were passed down, the less flattering things tucked away, hopefully to be forgotten within a generation or two. I was able to trace this family line the furthest by several decades—the secrets go back almost as far as the United States, along with the sense that they were being ignored for honors they deserved. There was also a Reese family myth that somehow the family was outside of, and therefore unimplicated by, their time periods. As my dad put it, the loyalty in the Reese clan before his parents' time was not to Texas: It was first to the Churches of Christ, a denomination the family joined in the 1830s. Then it was to the Church of Christ university they helped form; because that university was in Abilene, they felt loyalty to the town. Finally, their loyalty was to Texas only as the place which held all of those things.

Both sides of the family shared that crucial sense of distance, what I'd call a great blankness in our knowledge of how we contributed to history in this state and this country. I certainly don't think I'm alone in having a family history that was hardly talked about except as a story of "faith on the plains." To be "in this world, not of this world," to quote a Bible verse that defined my own denominational heritage, meant that many of us across several Christian subcultures never grappled with the legacies of how we got to this land in the first place. That is at least partially why I think my childhood views of Texas had more to do with cowboy hats and bandanas than border tensions, why those felt like "issues" that were separate from my own life and experiences.

I had no idea until I began the research for this book about my family's real history in Texas—that my relatives were here from the very beginning, shaping the history of this state at almost every turn. Members of my father's family have been in Texas at almost every pivotal moment since the first US settlers started coming in the 1820s; my mother's family arrived in Texas only at the beginning of the twentieth century.

Over the course of three years of research, I found hundreds of stories about my families' pasts that filled in the gaps I had never known about how we came to be on this land. Of those stories, six in particular emerged because they hold parallels with what we are grappling with today. They show the generational consequences of the kinds of rhetoric that comes up often in our ever-churning news cycle, but that we rarely look at more critically—about displacement, migration, mass violence, voting, education, and individual rights. They prompt questions about what is legal and what is right, what our laws show about our societal values, and what they reveal about our cultural fears.

These six different relatives lived through periods of extremism that resonate with our current moment in Texas. For the purpose of this book, I am defining those as time periods—days, months, years, or decades—of profound disconnection within a place or community. Often, fiery rhetoric and dehumanizing narratives advertently or inadvertently led to extreme acts of violence that injured or killed innocent victims. Defining one of these time periods in a small town, one writer talked about the "rigid righteousness" that had "an awful political odor, an emotional stench as if something in the town had died."

I recognize that definition could be vague or overly broad; you could say, rightly, that all of slavery or any war is, by this definition, an example of this kind of period. Times of extremism vary the way dust devils and tornadoes do—they share common qualities but differ greatly in size, scale, and degree of damage. It is easy to trace the destructive path of super tornadoes; I want to examine the dust devils too. From each of these stories about my ancestors who lived through such times, I learned something valuable I hope to take forward into the future.

The stories begin with Sally Reese, the daughter of a suspected traitor during the American Revolution, whose opportunities and constraints in slavery-era Virginia would shape the rest of the Reese family stories to come and the myths they brought to Texas later—a fact hidden by an only recently revealed family secret.

Next is Robert Leftwich, one of the first land grant agents and a friend of Stephen F. Austin, whose role in the earliest days of Anglo migration to Texas helped frame the later stories—which lives would be recorded and preserved, which would be cropped out entirely, and what kind of language would become the hallmark of Texas myths moving forward.

After Robert is Perry Reese, a soldier in the Texas Revolution, whose journey to Goliad as a result of an early public relations campaign made him—like others whose stories I tell—a victim of myths intentionally fabricated by desperate, indebted men with something to sell and something to hide.

In the decades after Juneteenth, Sam Houston Reese and his family in Colorado County helped make Texas one of the most murderous states in the nation; the killers in my family show what happens when a community plunges into violence, and how people with moral courage can change the story, though there might be great personal cost.

The last two stories are the most personal to me: My great-grandparents moved to Abilene, Texas in the 1920s, and in writing about that ancestral pivot, I build on the work of my father, my uncles, and others I deeply respect in uncovering the quiet, complicated foundation of the town I grew up in and the university my great-grandfather, J. C. Reese, helped found—this story reveals what happens in the years after extremism in a community dissipates but the ideas don't go away, and how the legacy of that time shapes the future for generations.

And finally, my mother's family, who came to Texas later than many of my other family members. My great-uncle, Frank Probst—the grandson of an undocumented economic migrant—was a Texas Ranger who stayed behind during World War II. As an expert witness in the trial of a notorious sheriff of Bee County, Uncle Frank would play an essential role in whether justice was served for a family of murdered farmers. But the heroes of the community are the united citizens of Bee County who banded together; their choice to take a stand finally put an end to the brutal reign of an out-of-control sheriff. And the heroes are the descendants of those involved, who never forgot what happened.

I found examples in each of those stories about how periods of extremism end—some only after devolving into further violence, others stopped by community members who had had enough. Each of them helped me understand fundamental truths about where we are in Texas today, and what it looks like to move toward a future where everyone thrives.

In the process of researching and writing these stories, I fell in love again with a Texas that is not defined by politicians or pundits but by its complicated, wonderful, courageous people, including my own family. I found the names of people I had never known about—some in my family, and some whose stories are as much a part of mine as the people I'm related to. I framed the questions that guided me in this book: What can I take from the past moving forward, and what do I want to leave behind? What are the foundations of my values and beliefs about myself, about the world and my place in it? What should I change? What can we learn from this difficult time period? What would it take for everyone—not just some people—in Texas to flourish? What kind of ancestor do I want to be as I help shape the future of this state that I love?

Through writing this book I found, unexpectedly, a profound sense of hope. It is the hope of someone who knows that Texans have never shied away from doing hard things. And who learned that facing our past will teach us important lessons for the future. With all my heart, I believe in the strength of Texans to have difficult conversations when it's necessary. I believe it because we've done it before, multiple times throughout our history. I believe in our ability to do that now, in this complex time when it feels like tensions are fissuring the very foundations of our state. I believe that what happens in Texas matters to the rest of the United States because I've seen—both through my lifetime and through my research for this book—that often, where Texas goes, so goes the nation.

I write this book with the unyielding hope of someone who sees signs of change in Texas already bursting forth, irrepressible and uncontainable, like bluebonnets in the soft rain of spring.

AUTHOR'S NOTE

This is a book as much about absences as it is presence. As often as possible, I've included the names of the people my family enslaved, or who bore the consequences of our actions, or who were otherwise mostly lost to recorded history. I would love to center these stories more fully but was often left only able to acknowledge the gaps for stories that should be included that I could not recover.

I have primarily used the terms for groups that indigenous people used for themselves rather than the names they were given by colonists. I use "Tejano" and "Hispanic" rather than other terms like "Latinx," "Mexican American," and "Chicane" because those are the preferred terms of the people I spoke with for this book, particularly in part 6, when the Rodriguez family chose how I describe their family and community.

In order to make the narrative easier to follow, I have kept some names consistent even if they were spelled in various ways in official documents. Since many of the people in this story have the same handful of last names, I almost always refer to my relatives by their first names.

My wide-ranging investigation into my family's past has helped me expand my definition of what it means to be an ancestor. It is not just the people from whom I'm actually descended, but the people who were in their communities, who informed their thoughts, who taught them their values, who transformed their lives. When I use the word "ancestor" in this book, I am widening it from the usual Western definition of biological or genetic relative to include the broader idea that the actions of people who came before me have an impact on my life whether they were related to me by blood or not. That assumption also carries forward, since a person does not have to be a parent or grandparent to care about the well-being of people younger than them.

In part 1 in particular, but in a handful of other places throughout the book, I am piecing together a story based on scattered documents and dozens of unconnected resources; Colonial and Revolutionary War–era research in Virginia is notoriously tricky. Where I could, I have indicated in the endnotes that my story is an educated estimation or that I rely on plausible theories to weave together narrative possibilities.

The endnotes are organized in the back of the book by page numbers and by phrases to which the notes refer. As often as possible, I have attributed my sources, provided insight into issues surrounding the history, or given opportunities for further reading in the notes for each chapter. I am deeply grateful to the historians, journalists, genealogists, and others whose work I relied on in building this narrative.

Finally, the research required to first unearth and then contextualize each of these six stories about my ancestors was extensive; I could have spent years on each time period. I have been as careful as possible, but in moving across more than four centuries of history, I am confident I have missed details and nuances. Any mistakes are my own.

PART 1

SALLY REESE

(1765–1854)

. . . Virginia is the mother of Texas. We never knew who the father was, but we kinda suspected Tennessee.

—TEX RITTER

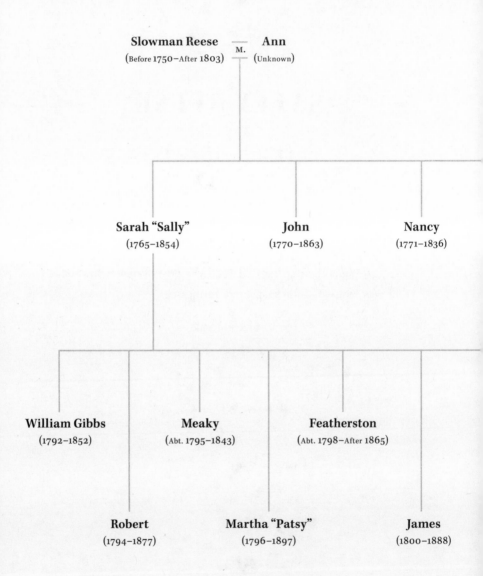

Slowman Reese
(Before 1750–After 1803)

M.

Ann
(Unknown)

Sarah "Sally"
(1765–1854)

John
(1770–1863)

Nancy
(1771–1836)

William Gibbs
(1792–1852)

Meaky
(Abt. 1795–1843)

Featherston
(Abt. 1798–After 1865)

Robert
(1794–1877)

Martha "Patsy"
(1796–1897)

James
(1800–1888)

Polly Leftwich — Jordan   Rhoda
(1779–1857)   M. (1772–1830)   (Abt. 1774–
                               After 1823)

Nancy   Fleming   Two daughters
(Abt. 1805–1838)   (1810–1870)   and two sons

Parthenia   Wilkerson
(Abt. 1804–1871)   (1807–1899)

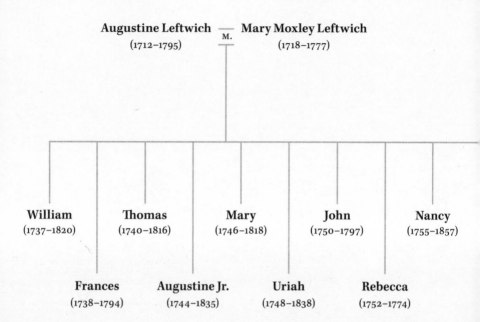

Augustine Leftwich
(1712–1795)

M.

Mary Moxley Leftwich
(1718–1777)

William
(1737–1820)

Frances
(1738–1794)

Thomas
(1740–1816)

Augustine Jr.
(1744–1835)

Mary
(1746–1818)

Uriah
(1748–1838)

John
(1750–1797)

Rebecca
(1752–1774)

Nancy
(1755–1857)

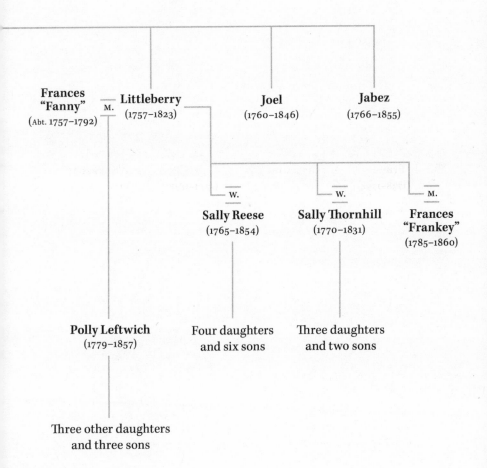

Frances "Fanny"
(Abt. 1757–1792)

M.

Littleberry
(1757–1823)

Joel
(1760–1846)

Jabez
(1766–1855)

W.

Sally Reese
(1765–1854)

W.

Sally Thornhill
(1770–1831)

M.

Frances "Frankey"
(1785–1860)

Polly Leftwich
(1779–1857)

Four daughters
and six sons

Three daughters
and two sons

Three other daughters
and three sons

CHAPTER 1

I drove up switchback roads tunneled by greening trees to find the grave of my great-great-great-great-great-grandmother Sarah "Sally" Reese. Golden flowers and lush, layered grass carpeted fields on the way to Old Mt. Hermon Cemetery in rural Tennessee, where Sally had been buried seven generations ago. As my car wound higher and higher up the mountain, the air became cooler, weighted with the delicate humidity of growing things. I rolled my windows down and turned my music off. It felt—after a day and a half of driving from Texas to Tennessee, more than a year of research, and almost two centuries of not knowing her story—as if the journey to see Sally for myself were sacred.

I knew most of my life about Sally's children and their descendants. In 1931, Sally's great-grandson and my great-great-uncle, Sloman Brooks Reese, wrote out a family history he called *Corinth and Its Kinfolk*. Uncle Sloman handwrote the narrative on yellow legal pads, and someone typed it up and xeroxed copies for the family, and my father showed it to me when I was young. It became one of the most formative stories of my childhood.

As Uncle Sloman framed the story in *Corinth and Its Kinfolk*, my relatives first arrived in Tennessee in an "axle tar wagon" to land "rich with blue grass growing everywhere" where "cold spring water ran out of most every hollow." The story did not mention where they arrived *from*, as if they burst into being on those wagons. I didn't know her name at the time, but that early caravan into Tennessee would have included Sally.

A generation later, Sally's children and grandchildren left Tennessee, heading south to Texas. They arrived near Christmastime, either in 1845 or 1846. They stayed less than a week.

After stopping somewhere near Paris, Texas, "the rolling plains held no appeal for the weary travelers and before unpacking, someone suggested, 'Let's go back to Tennessee!' This was met with jubilant approval from all, and the caravan turned back east, retracing their journey." On their way back to Tennessee, they camped near a spring in Arkansas. They liked it enough to stay. That landing spot came to be the small town of Corinth, Howard County, Arkansas, populated by many of Sally Reese's children and grandchildren and their relatives in a tight-knit, clannish community whose tangled relationships Sloman Brooks Reese tried to straighten out years later for their many descendants. Two of the kinfolks were my great-grandparents, my father's father's parents.

Corinth and Its Kinfolk is not a story in the traditional sense. It is a community history. I received the narrative as it was intended when I first read it as a girl. Uncle Sloman begins: "I have been requested by a number of people to write up a history of the church and the people that made it what it has been, and is yet." The church was established a few years after the caravan headed back from their week in Texas in 1850. They founded a small community because they wanted a place to practice the new sect of Presbyterianism they had joined called the Stone-Campbell movement. Eventually, we would call the denomination the Churches of Christ.

The lack of plot in *Corinth and Its Kinfolk* did not bother me. I nestled into the story, lulled by Uncle Sloman's chatty tone: "Well, I guess I had better get back to my text as to what kind of country that was. It was a hilly country, nearly all of it, covered with the finest poplar timber ever grown in any place." I relished the old-fashioned names: Minerva and Tacie and Bula ("a fine specimen of womanhood") and Sloman, a name passed down to multiple men in our family that I've never encountered outside of the Reeses. I loved to imagine the Reeses and the Joneses and the Womacks and the Bacons, all intermarried and interrelated. I read *Corinth and Its Kinfolk* dozens of times as a teenager. I was a misfit bookworm in a sports-loving small town in West Texas; *Corinth and Its Kinfolk* gave a roosting place for my imagination in those often-lonely years, a sense of being part of a shared past that extended generations.

I wondered often where the family came from before Tennessee, and I imagined a history for myself that mattered a great deal to me when I was growing up. One day in middle school, I was alone at the university library waiting for my dad to finish teaching when I discovered a book about Wales that referenced a line of kings named Rhys—the original spelling of Reese. I ran my hand over the image of a Rhys crest featuring a red lion, turned the page to see a Rhys castle. I knew with the instant certainty of a girl who almost exclusively read books about kids uncovering secrets in libraries and attics and dusty old trunks that I had found a clue to my heritage: somewhere in the murky years before the *Corinth and Its Kinfolk* family, I was descended from royalty.

It made perfect sense to me. Like the protagonists I loved, I was misunderstood in my hometown. I held that myth to myself for long, dark years of being made fun of for having skinny legs and big feet, for reading huge tomes, for shoving my bifocals up my nose with my index finger—"Six Eyes," they called me, or "Dictionary Breath." It was fine, I told myself; I am a Welsh princess, descended from a long line of misunderstood Reeses.

Later, as I began my genealogical research, I found a Howard County Heritage Club book that recounted the stories of some of Sally's children and grandchildren in Corinth. That book confirmed that what had seemed like a clue to my family heritage was roughly true—the Reeses who came to the United States had come originally from Wales. Whether or not we were royalty centuries ago is anyone's guess; the records from the years before the American Revolution, during which my family members immigrated to the British colonies, are hopelessly lost. But in addition to confirming the tie to Wales, the Howard County Heritage Club finally shed light on one question I had always wondered

about, the origin of those Tennessee-bound axle tar wagons that Uncle
Sloman wrote about: our family came to Tennessee from Virginia.

That knowledge itself feels almost miraculous to me. The fact that I
am able to trace my paternal grandfather's family back seven generations
so easily is a sign both of their relative wealth and of their education
levels. I have nothing like those kinds of records for any of my other
grandparents' lines. Though not rich, the Reeses had land that they
bought and sold with deeds in record books. Some of them enslaved
people—something I always knew, though I did not know the extent of
it. There are court documents and family Bibles and *Corinth and Its Kinfolk* and recorded memories in various family stories and dozens of obit-
uaries in local newspapers—a veritable flood of information about that
side of the family's history.

It felt, in the beginning of my research, that tracing Sally's line was
an indulgent side project. Or maybe it was a chance to finally solve one
of the private mysteries of my family's past that had meant so much to
me as a girl. I had no idea that, in uncovering the details about Sally and
her family in Virginia, I would gain crucial insight into my research
about how we arrived where we are in the state of Texas today.

Virginia is one of the headwaters of Texas. In the streaming migration patterns that took my family and so many others westward through
the future United States, those immigrants who arrived first in the
South pieced a set of values and beliefs into a discrete worldview that
their descendants would carry whole and unchanged to Texas a few generations later. The story of Sally Reese and my family in Virginia coin-
cides, in many ways, with the origin story of Texas. I was tracing a river
of ideas and hopes that had shaped and watered the terrain of the state
I love back to the trickling tributary where it all began.

CHAPTER 2

When I pulled up at Old Mt. Hermon Cemetery in Tennessee, I found Sally's grave almost immediately; it was one of two in the middle of a clump of headstones protruding like snaggled teeth. The light stone was covered in muck from birds. I wet some napkins and cleaned off the stone so that I could see the words clearly:

In Memory of

SARAH REESE

Who Died Dec. 31th
1854 Aged 89 Years
Blesed are they Who di
e in the Lord hencefor
th they rest from their
Labors and their Works
do follow them.

The secret of Sally Reese's life might have been lost if not for the excellent stone carver her family hired when she died, even if spelling and spacing were not his strong suit. Most of the other markers around hers are faded, but the depth of the letters on hers allowed them to survive the harsh Tennessee weather.

Sally's "Works" did not follow her, at least not in the typical way that is meant by that phrase. I knew so little about Sally and what she had gone through. I was on my way to research and reconstruct the barest outline of her life.

For more than an hour, I wandered the graveyard, scribbled names in my notebook, meandered back to sit in front of Sally's headstone. I reflected on how many women in my past had records kept of "their Labors and their Works." How many were denied educations that could have changed their lives or provided them careers they would have found meaningful and fulfilling. How many died and were mourned by the people they loved and then forgotten within a generation or two. Most did not have Sally's grave marker, or Sally's descendants' educations. The women of the Woodford, Jones, Farley, Muns, Owens, Nelson, Lawson, Ball, Grant, Foster, Massey, Holloway, Ward, Ford, Moore, Nickolson, Riggs, Tuck, Embry, Howard, Brown, Zeizlei, Kappi, and Probst families are mostly lost to me.

And if those foremothers are gone, how many more names am I missing—the people whose lands they moved onto, the people off whose labor many of them would profit. Tens of thousands of names and faces and voices and dreams, blown away by the harsh wind of time.

I found myself reluctant to leave Sally's grave. I stayed long after I told myself I would go. She had no husband to join her. Nothing on her grave said "Beloved wife."

I ripped out a piece of notebook paper and made a rubbing of the headstone next to Sally's, where the letters were barely legible. I knew, because someone had already identified the grave, that it belonged to her grandbaby Granville—the only one of Sally's huge family to be buried near her.

I would think of the scratch of my pencil on paper for the next week of researching. I will never be able to see the whole of Sally's life, but in filling in as many details as I can—in coloring widely on the page—

patterns emerged nonetheless. Perhaps I am reading those patterns correctly; perhaps I am not. The etching is all that remains.

Before I left, I gathered a bouquet of wildflowers growing by Sally's grave—purple, yellow, and white—and pressed them into my notebook. Keeping the flowers felt silly to me, something a sentimental young girl might have done. But, in that moment, I was brought back to the bookish little Jessica reading about Welsh royalty and Uncle Sloman's memories of the community in Corinth who always wanted to know the truth about her family. Gathering those flowers felt like a sacrament, uniting past and present, preserving the small blossoms before they wilted and died.

When I drove down from the mountain, I turned east for the long trek toward the second stop on my research trip: Bedford County, Virginia. I was on my way to meet the cousin who had, several years ago, uncovered a critical part of Sally's story—who Sally was and where she had come from. Together, we were going to research in the county archives in hopes of uncovering how Sally ended up in a highly unusual situation and what the Reese family myth about those axle tar wagons headed to Tennessee left out about Sally's real constraints and options and opportunities.

As I drove to the mouth of this story, there were connections to Texas everywhere. I passed the birthplace of Stephen F. Austin, the "Father of Texas"—who brought many of the first Anglos when it was a Mexican colony. The first president under the new republic, Sam Houston, was born seven months earlier than Austin and less than sixty miles away; Sally's grandson would bear his name, Samuel Houston Reese. Martin Parmer and Davy Crockett and James Fannin and dozens of others who would change the fate of Texas in the 1820s and 1830s, whose names would be part of my story later, also traced their family roots to Virginia.

My trip felt like it was not just in space but in time—into the past, to the origins of the myths and stories that would shape Texas, the ideas of right and wrong that would resonate across several generations, and the choices that would transform the future.

CHAPTER 3

When it was officially founded in 1782, they called the village where Sally Reese grew up "Liberty." Though it would later be renamed Bedford, in those years as a new country emerged, its name was a battle cry.

Just a few years earlier, Virginians had led the charge toward independence. Virginia declared itself a free commonwealth at the state convention in May 1776. The British commander, Lord Dunmore, and his troops evacuated from Virginia in June and weeks later, Virginian Richard Henry Lee initiated the call for independence, which the new American Congress would pass after weeks of debate on July 2. On July 4, they passed the Declaration of Independence, written by Virginian Thomas Jefferson. Publicly, Virginians' fiery rhetoric and staunch support for the Patriot cause was legendary.

When we first began to research that week in Bedford, I expected the major turning point of Sally's story would be that war. I thought it would be the time that marked her life into before and after. Instead, we discovered that the moment when everything changed in Sally's life came later—in 1792, when she was twenty-seven and already a spinster by her society's standards.

I DROVE INTO BEDFORD TO SPEND THE WEEK AT THE COUNTY GENEA-logical museum and the next-door county courthouse with an experienced researcher—and also a direct descendant of Sally's—Sherry Finchum. I encountered her early on while tracking down information about Sally. Sherry calls all of us she encounters in this kind of research "cousins." Though we only met on Zoom before this trip, it felt within minutes of both of us arriving in Bedford County as if we were, in fact, close cousins, and that we'd known each other all our lives.

Sherry is a bit of a genealogical rabblerouser, though you'd never know it by talking to her—she is the kind of mother and grandmother who always has an umbrella in case it rained (which it did) and a pack of nuts in her car in case you get peckish (which I usually was). And she was as eager as I was to spend hours digging through archives—my exact kind of nerd.

Over several days of researching in Bedford County, as we found papers in the back of dusty boxes and began to compile a list of court dates and bankruptcy filings and witness testimonies, a sketch emerged of Sally as a woman who was young by our standards and old by her society's, facing increasing, unsustainable pressures. We gained some insight into what it meant for Sally to walk through minuscule, insular Liberty, Virginia as a member of the Reese family, trying to keep her head up high despite everything her neighbors knew.

To understand the momentous choice Sally faced in 1792, and what she did next, you first have to understand the settlers' profound motivations that forged early Virginia and later the Westward Expansion all the way into Texas: debt, greed, and fear.

Perhaps no man in Virginia more clearly showed the effects of those motivations than the man we confirmed that week was Sally's father. His name was Slowman Reese.

SOMETIME BEFORE 1750, SLOWMAN REESE WAS BORN INTO A TUMULTU-ous, indebted Virginia that was still very much on the frontier of the colonies. I grew up, probably like most white school children in the United States, assuming my ancestors were oppressed believers who fled persecution and finally found freedom in a new land. That idea was planted in my mind by years of school textbooks and pageants and gloppy-glued paper sack costumes for Thanksgiving. I liked that imagined origin story. It was not true for me.

Like the other early settlers to Virginia, Slowman's parents or grandparents or great-grandparents came as economic migrants. Colonialists settled first in Jamestown in 1607—thirteen years before the *Mayflower* landed at Plymouth in Massachusetts. At some point between 1607 and 1750, Sally's ancestors came from Wales seeking wealth in the new colony.

Virginia began as a corporate enterprise. The Virginia Trading Company, chartered by King James I, was a joint stock company where investors in England pooled their money to provide the funds to send the first colonizers to Virginia. The word "capitalism" would not emerge as a philosophical concept until the 1770s, but as an Early American historian wrote, the capitalists arrived "in the first ships." No matter what language they might have used, those colonizers arrived with a clear directive—to make money for the stakeholders.

That created an all-consuming problem my ancestors and others needed to solve upon arrival, in addition to their concerns with basic survival: They were in debt. And that debt only expanded, hydra-like, as each debtor went into more debt to pay off the first debts, a monstrous tangle of determined people joined through a shared appetite for more than what they had and a fear of losing it all.

They needed the colony to be wildly, ridiculously profitable—immediately. Until they found some resource—gold, maybe, like the Iberian colonists sought across two continents—the settlers were willing to try just about anything to see if it could generate an income. They made silk, blew glass, harvested lumber, manufactured soap. But while those projects made their lives a bit easier, none could begin to turn the kind of profit that would make a dent in their debts.

By the early 1610s, it became clear that the solution to their dilemma might be large-scale farming. The temperate climate of Virginia offered a chance to innovate with different types of crops that the British market was eager to receive. In 1610, a farmer named John Rolfe spent ten months in Bermuda. While there, Rolfe acquired tobacco seeds from the Caribbean; when he finally arrived in Virginia, he brought those seeds to the colony and planted them. He and others began experimenting to find a version of the crop that would grow best in the colony. Within a few years, this particular strain of tobacco emerged as the potential answer to the colonists' economic woes.

It was the first idea that was really scalable: It was a relatively easy-to-grow crop that shipped well and found a market of European smokers who liked the "sweet and stronge [sic]" flavor of the Virginia brand. All they would need were large amounts of land and plenty of workers.

THE LAND THEY ARRIVED ON WAS ALREADY NAMED TSENACOMOCO. AT the time, the land was the home of more than fifteen thousand people, possibly as many as twenty-five thousand, made up of dozens of groups who gave allegiance to Wahunsonacock, their primary leader. The English called him Powhatan.

Wahunsonacock tried to negotiate with and then—when that failed—to defeat the intruders to Tsenacomoco. The ensuing conflict paused only briefly, in 1614, when his daughter, Pocahontas, married John Rolfe.

In 1616, Rolfe left his crops and took his indigenous bride and their young son back to England, where she was an instant sensation. Their passage was paid for by the Virginia Trading Company, who used the young bride as a marketing tool to convince new settlers to join their enterprise. She moved in exalted circles in England; she went to court and met King James I. You could call her the first brand ambassador for the colony.

She contracted a terminal disease there, likely tuberculosis or pneumonia, and died in 1617 at the age of twenty-two. She was buried in England, far from the rolling hills where she had lived all her life.

A year later, in 1618, her father Wahunsonacock also died; his brothers became rulers after him. The conflicts began again and continued for the next three decades, until 1646, when the people who had lived for generations in Tsenacomoco were effectively defeated. The colonizers signed treaties they wrote. Then they took over the land almost completely.

NOW THAT THEY HAD SECURED THE LAND ON WHICH TO GROW TO-bacco, the British colonists needed people to farm it. In the first half of the seventeenth century, most of that labor came from indentured servants. At first, the Virginia Trading Company paid for the transportation of people who indentured themselves for four to seven years in exchange for their passage, a place to live, food to eat, and clothes to wear. The initial investment, however, was steep for the cash-strapped company, so beginning in 1618, they started the headright system, which offered fifty acres of land for anyone who settled in Virginia or paid the transportation expenses of another immigrant. In return for tracts of land, indentured servants worked grueling, exploitative hours by today's standards, often enduring cruel masters, poor work conditions, and fatal diseases.

For those of us who grew up learning about US history, using land as an incentive for immigration might not seem revolutionary. But in the trial-and-error years of the first British colonies, it must have felt like an ingenious solution. It was the enticement that would become the basis for almost all Anglo settlement in Texas almost two centuries later.

Immigrant indentured servants in seventeenth century Virginia and other colonies still had some rights. And eventually, after several years, most would be free. But the well of workers dried up quickly as the economic situation improved in England and lower-class people decided it wasn't worth leaving everything they'd ever known to work in some backwater colony across the sea.

The only way to turn a profit in Virginia was if landowners and investors could eliminate paying their laborers completely, if they could extract more work from them, if they could bind them to the job for life. The settlers tried enslaving indigenous people, but this land was theirs and they knew its secrets; the ham-handed colonizers could not lure or oppress the indigenous people into the kind of decades-long labor arrangement they needed in order to make money off the big farms. And so, the British colonists turned to the economic system that was already maximizing profits for investors in the Caribbean.

Within twelve years of the British settlers stepping foot in the colony, the first enslaved people arrived in Jamestown, Virginia.

CHAPTER 4

From its earliest days, slavery in the colonies was not a cold, fixed system. It was molten, shaped by the hammer of public opinion over centuries into an ever-more torturous institution.

Slavery was an integral part of Slowman Reese's life in Virginia. Though we know very little about his life before the American Revolution, there are two facts we are certain of: first, in 1774, he was listed as one of fifty-eight men at a church that enslaved four people to pay their minister's salary—the church where Sally grew up. And second, Slowman was a slave overseer.

Without being able to know much more about Slowman in those years, I'm left with generalizations about his job: In a series of interviews with former enslaved people from Virginia, they describe slave overseers as notoriously cruel. White overseers were generally feared and hated by the people they controlled. They were also often despised by the people who employed them. Thomas Jefferson once wrote that "overseers, the most abject, degraded and unprincipled race" were "feculum of beings" guided by "their pride, insolence & spirit of domination."

Overseers like Slowman served a hated role in a society built on contradictions—the most passionate language about freedom came from a place where a growing portion of the population was deeply oppressed. In eighteenth-century Virginia, the population of enslaved people exploded. In 1700, there were thirteen thousand people who were enslaved, about a sixth of the overall population of Virginia. By 1750, there were more than one hundred thousand enslaved people—almost half of the colony. As the number of enslaved people in their society grew, so did enslavers' fears that Black people would tire of being subjugated and revolt.

By the time Slowman was an overseer, the importance of the tobacco industry in the colony could not be overstated. Tobacco crops backed Virginia's currency. Slave overseers were the frontline workers of the oppressive system off which enslavers were finally turning the tide on their debt.

Several Virginia laws in the seventeenth and eighteenth centuries attempted to regulate the complicated, precarious arrangement on which the settlers built their lives and livelihoods. Those laws give us further insight into what the enslavers valued, what they feared, and what slave overseers were expected and allowed to do. Many of the stories that began in Colonial- and Revolutionary-era Virginia would later form the worldviews of the settlers in Texas.

IN EARLY VIRGINIA'S SOCIETY WITH SLAVES, BLACK PEOPLE COULD BE freed—many even arrived as indentured servants. Some Black masters enslaved white or Black people. There was social mobility in the Virginia colonial society that seems wild to those of us who grew up only picturing slavery as the huge Georgia plantations of the *Gone with the Wind* era. The first enslaved people had some tiny, granular levels of movement that would be vehemently denied later generations.

When I was a schoolgirl learning about the history of the United States, I imagined laws came about because white men in powdered wigs had long discussions while holding quills—an interactive John Trumbull painting. But in truth, the laws were reactive—ideas formed not only from philosophical discussions in genteel drawing rooms but the reality of living in an agitated society. Every few years, the legal humanity of Black people was stripped away layer by layer as the Virginia legislature tried to restrict and control people who continued, with each generation, to audaciously assert that they were human.

The history of that collective act of dehumanization matters because white colonizers meticulously crafted over time a legal narrative of Black people as less than human. Virginia society did not begin with these views; it was an intentional and communal act, a choice made again and again over decades.

THE BRITISH SETTLERS FEARED FREE BLACK PEOPLE. ENSLAVEMENT AS a life sentence first appeared in the law in 1641, when John Punch, a Black man, was sentenced to serve his master for life. It was only the beginning; within a couple of generations, slavery would be widely understood to be a lifelong state.

They feared Black fugitives—losing their labor, losing the financial investment, losing the power over their persons. In 1661, a law passed that legislated punishment for Black people running away from masters.

They feared Black families as a social unit and Black people with rights. In 1662, a landmark law declared that children's status as free or enslaved would be dependent on the status of the mother. In England, legal status, even for servants, was determined through the father's line. By declaring that it was the mother and not the father whose societal status the children shared, the Virginia law essentially treated all Black children, even the ones born of marriage or in committed partnerships, as legal bastards. The law essentially incentivized raping Black women in order to produce more enslaved Black people. As one encyclopedia put it, "The act enabled the reproduction of one's own labor force." That law only increased the colonizers' framing of Black women as threats to patriarchal order and as sexualized temptresses whose seductive wiles blameless white men could not resist. The law opened the door for centuries of rape and coercion and widespread abuse of Black women.

They feared Black religion: As an end of itself. As a means to the awakened consciousness of Black people, revealing the hypocrisy in their faith and society. As an avenue to freedom. In 1667, the Virginia legislature declared baptism did not exempt Black people from enslavement. One of the theological arguments to justify slavery was that the enslaved people were heathens. Clever slaves had started getting baptized, either from true belief or a righteous desire to leave their bondage. If Black people were their spiritual brothers and sisters, then oppressing them was especially evil. Enslavers had to tell themselves narratives that emphasized made-up racial differences in order to live with the cognitive disconnect of harming God's fellow children—sometimes the enslavers' literal, biological sisters and brothers or nieces and nephews. This law had been in effect for more than a century before Slowman's name would appear on the roll of a church that enslaved people.

They feared Black men's bodies, worrying constantly about rage and reprisal: white settlers in Virginia lived in a state of panic that the violence they meted out would be repaid to them. Legalized murder of oppressed people passed in a 1669 law that declared if an enslaved person should "chance to die" when being punished for resisting their white master or overseer, it would not be considered a crime.

Colonists would also be haunted by the fear of Black enslaved people organizing an uprising. This fear would come up again and again over the years as occasional rebellions and revolutions only heightened the fright that systemic change might overtake white communities. In 1680, Black people arming themselves to resist enslavement was outlawed. In particular, the revolution in Haiti from 1791 to 1804, when Toussaint L'Ouverture led enslaved Haitian people to independence from France, lay heavy on white enslavers' minds. In Virginia, a man named Gabriel led an uprising in Henrico County in the summer of 1800. White people would justify violence for centuries based on rumors of these types of revolts.

And they feared intermarriage as a threat to the "purity" of the white race. In 1682, the Virginia assembly decided that all non-Christians— "whether Negroes, Moors, mulattoes, or Indians"—would be considered enslaved. And in 1691, that it was illegal for any free white men or white women to marry outside of their race as a "further prevention of that abominable mixture and spurious issue." Rape and murder were legally permitted; marriage was not.

This fear of "abominable mixture," perhaps more than any other, would drive policies and foment violence over the next several centuries.

The racial purity rules would be legally codified in several laws across the United States, and in 1924 in Virginia, in the "one-drop rule."

Less than a hundred years after the first British colonists stepped foot in Virginia, they had gone from silk-making, glassblowing, soap-manufacturing indebted peons of the Virginia Trading Company to top-of-the-hierarchy members of a growing enslaving society. For most of the century, the Royal African Company in England were the sole traffickers of human beings from Africa to the United States. They were efficient and effective at their horrific trade, transporting almost one hundred thousand people from 1672 to 1690. In 1690, the English parliament ended the company's monopoly, and the slave trade exploded: from an average of almost thirty thousand people a year being trafficked out of Africa to slaveholding colonies along the Atlantic Ocean in the 1690s to an estimated eighty-five thousand a year by the 1790s.

By 1705 the Slave Codes of Virginia passed by the House of Burgesses obliterated what few freedoms Black people held in the colony. They declared that every Black or indigenous person who came into the colony after 1705, and who was not a Christian before their arrival, "shall be held to be real estate." With those slave codes, indentured servitude effectively ended. The slave code enacted harsh punishments—hanging for murder or rape; sixty lashes and their ears being cut off while held in stocks for robbery or other crimes. The law allowed masters to whip, brand, or maim Black enslaved people for even minor transgressions. Enslaved people had to carry with them written permission to travel off their plantations.

A much harsher era of enslavement in Virginia was only beginning. In 1723, Black people in Virginia were forbidden to keep weapons or have meetings, and individual enslavers could emancipate enslaved Black people only with the consent of the Commonwealth governor and council. In 1724, even Black people who were legally free were denied the right to vote.

We do not have records of his treatment of the people he oppressed, but by the time Sally's father, Slowman, became an overseer, there was little to no incentive for him to hold back on violence.

―――――

AS I RESEARCHED THE STORY OF SALLY REESE, I KEPT COMING BACK TO the slave-owning church in which she grew up. In 1774, fifty-eight members of the Peaks of Otter Presbyterian Church filed a petition with the Virginia House of Burgesses, asking for permission to pay a minister's salary by enslaving Kate, Tom, Jerry, and Venus, who worked backbreakingly for profits they would never see. And what happened to Kate, Tom, Jerry, Venus, and their children, as well as the church's minister, David Rice, reveals the tension I am wrestling with in writing this history of my family.

It can be easy to dismiss these kinds of stories by saying something like "Well, things were different back then." But these questions aren't clear-cut. What does it mean to acknowledge that someone did what everyone else did, was "of their time," if there *were* people in their time— maybe even people they knew—who realized the injustice inherent in oppressive systems that benefited them and therefore changed their lives completely? How does each culture—on a widespread scale, like the colony of Virginia, or a small scale, like the village of Liberty or the Peaks of Otter Presbyterian Church—collectively decide what is acceptable? And what is the role of individuals within the larger decision-making process?

At what point should we look back and recognize that a person with at least some level of power knew their actions hurt other people and did nothing to stop it?

I am wrestling with these questions as I write this book in a time that feels as turbulent as the eras I am researching. I'm also turning them on myself: What am I missing in this day and time that will seem obvious to future generations? What will feel like morally urgent truths in fifty or a hundred years that I am not aware of, or that I currently ignore? It is easy to criticize from the vantage point of the future, but these are crucial questions now too.

Because, unlike his parishioner and my ancestor, Slowman, the preacher at the Peaks of Otter Presbyterian Church, David Rice—the one whose salary was paid by enslaved people—changed his mind about slavery.

Something shifted for Rice in the years in which Kate, Tom, Jerry, and Venus worked tirelessly for the salary he and his family lived off. In 1783, the church added ten more names to their roster of enslaved people: Nance, Ishmael, Sall, Mopes, Herod, Cyrus, Pharaz, Jenney, Charles, and Milly, probably the children of the original four. Rice clearly had a relationship with the families. One historian said that, as a preacher in Virginia, Rice had been "more successful among the blacks than the whites in the congregation."

Rice left the Peaks of Otter Presbyterian Church and became a controversial preacher as a "gradual emancipationist" and abolitionist, one of dozens of antislavery preachers who stayed in the South and preached against the way of life that was growing more and more popular every year. There was a financial and cultural cost for Rice; after leaving Bedford County, he would never make as much money again. He was poor, often overlooked, a known "troublemaker" in the slave-owning South, where he lived and preached all his life. He also influenced a generation of abolitionist preachers. The views that made him scandalous in his time made him prescient later—that he saw other people as humans.

Slowman Reese decidedly did not make the same choices as his preacher. His actions during critical years in Sally Reese's life reveal a man who was increasingly desperate, presumably violent, and possibly a traitor to his colony and his new country.

In a tumultuous time in Virginia, the consequences of Slowman Reese's actions landed squarely on his daughter Sally.

CHAPTER 5

The early years of Sally Reese's childhood coincided with increasing tension in Virginia and the other British colonies that had been brewing against England's King George. The debt that had been a hallmark of those early colonies had exploded to new international heights. The French and Indian Wars had ended in 1763, just two years before Sally was born. Great Britain was in debt because of its many wars; Virginians remained in debt to the Crown and to investors. When King George tried to cash in on those debts through the Sugar Act and Stamp Act in the 1760s, the colonies retaliated with nonimportation agreements boycotting English goods. During the economic conflict preceding the war from 1765 to 1775, some of the fiercest speeches came out of the Virginia House of Burgesses—including Patrick Henry's famous "Give me liberty, or give me death!"

When Sally was seven, in 1772, an international financial panic and credit crisis along the Atlantic rim shook the unsteady economic foundations of the colony. The credit bubble that fueled the colonial experiment burst. Virginia bore the brunt of the financial hit.

In the spring and summer of 1775, war with England officially broke out. Virginians did not see much overt military action in the early days of the war. There were small battles and several conflicts. Mostly, though, Virginians supplied George Washington's army and wrote rousing speeches and sent sons and husbands off to war and tried to prepare for the worst.

The Revolutionary War did not follow clean divisions. American colonists who did not support the separation from England—called Tories, Royalists, or Loyalists—often worked seditiously on the side of the British troops.

The Virginia assembly decided they needed a way to signal who was on their side at a time when most of the white men of fighting age were British or of British descent. They passed an act that declared that all men who were free and above the age of sixteen had to swear loyalty to the revolutionary cause before the justice of the peace in their county.

On August 9, 1777, "Slowman Reace" is the eighth name on a list of Bedford County men who swore such an oath. Officially, that signature made Slowman a Patriot. Whether he really supported the fledgling independent government or not is impossible to know, but signing the oath was certainly most prudent in a small community that five years later named its village Liberty, Virginia.

In November 1778, barely a year later, Slowman filed a promissory note in the Bedford County Courthouse, signaling that he was in debt to a neighbor. It was the first of several debt filings for Slowman. If the highest classes of people—wealthy even by European standards—lost economic footing during the American Revolution, poorer families like Sally's had no hope.

Political tension in the region ratcheted up as the war moved closer. In May 1779, the British general in New York launched an attack in Virginia and disrupted the supply chain. In later court documents, Slowman revealed that he offered to serve in a neighbor's place for six months as a soldier for forty pounds. Figuring he was about to leave, Slowman rented out the land their family farmed, which records show probably belonged to his wife, Ann. Then, at some point in 1779, they sold the land. It was a short-term decision that would cost them dearly in the long run; they forever lost the earning potential that cultivating the land might have given them.

The neighbor was never called up—Slowman didn't get his cash. In the same year he sold his farm, Slowman sued the neighbor he was going to be a substitute soldier for—accusing the man of cheating him, despite the fact that the man had no control over the direction of the ongoing war. The suit would go on for years. It was the beginning of a swift downward trajectory for Slowman Reese and his family.

BY 1780, RUMORS RAN RAMPANT THAT THE LOYALISTS WERE PLANNING to attack the Patriot militia from within their own ranks. Constantly on the lookout for Tories among them, in the summer of 1780 in Bedford County, Patriots discovered a Loyalist plot to attack the nearby lead and saltpeter mines supplying Washington's troops, free British prisoners of war, and implement a coup against the Virginia government. Militia leaders in the area rounded up seventy-eight suspected Tories.

One of those men was Slowman Reese.

Then governor Jefferson had ordered the mine manager to send anyone suspected of helping to instigate the plot against the Patriots to Richmond to face trial. But the manager refused, preferring to punish the men right then and there. Things were too urgent to wait, the manager reasoned. Better to try the men while they were in custody—transporting them would have been not only cost prohibitive but complicated, since they could flee or fight at the first opportunity. He would just have to explain himself later.

The manager's family's plantation in Bedford County became the site of raucous, spur-of-the-moment trials. The mob became the jury. Punishments were imposed immediately. Slowman Reese was held for four days.

The exact details of what happened to the Loyalists "convicted" in these illegal trials, which lasted for several days, is unknown. Persistent rumors remained for generations that the mine manager and the other militia leaders meted out vicious punishments. Some "convicted" men were hung by their thumbs to black walnut trees. Others were severely flogged with a whip made up of multiple knotted cords called the "cat o' nine tails." At least some of their relatives did not believe justice was being served.

There is no way to know if Slowman genuinely supported the British or whether he was set up, perhaps by one of the many men to whom he owed money. If he was a Loyalist, he was obviously not one of the bigger players in the conspiracy. There is no record of whether he was punished or exonerated after his short detention. He was released; nothing else is known.

Governor Jefferson was not initially pleased that the mine manager defied his order to send the prisoners to Richmond. But the manager's gamble paid off—he was not just exonerated but praised. Jefferson personally wrote him: "Your activity on this occasion, deserves great commendation. . . . The method of seizing them at once which you have adopted is much the best." The Virginia government declared the manager's actions retroactively legal in a December 1782 law that indemnified his response as "justifiable" because of the urgency of the times.

The mine manager broke the law, took matters into his own hands, and convicted people outside of the court. The legal system declared after the fact that extraordinary circumstances justified this violence and retribution—formally praising a type of vigilantism that would be repeated thousands and thousands of times throughout United States history.

The manager of those lead and saltpeter mines was Charles Lynch. He called what he did "Lynch's law." Later, the vigilante, outside-of-the-law, trial-like mob tactics would be called simply "lynchings."

Sally Reese's father was one of the first seventy-eight men to endure Lynch's law in the soon-to-be United States. Unlike most later lynching victims, those men survived the experience. Sally Reese's grandchildren would adopt lynchings—in the way we now mean the word, as crowd-fueled, hatred-driven public killings—as one of their primary control-keeping strategies in Texas.

CHAPTER 6

The year Sally Reese turned sixteen, US forces finally defeated the British army at Yorktown, Virginia. On October 19, 1781, Lord Cornwallis surrendered to George Washington. The decade that followed in Virginia, as across the rest of the new nation, held a precarious peace.

For alleged Tories like Slowman and his family, tensions did not disappear with the end of the war. As the country tried to pull itself out of the economic hole caused by an expensive war following an international credit crisis, there was little sympathy left for those who had been suspected of loyalty to the enemy.

The 1780s were marked by lawsuit after lawsuit bearing Slowman's name—some he filed, many more filed against him. He was quick to countersue—in one instance because he said his suer's "actings and doings are contrary to equity and good conscience." That speech recorded in the court filing provides a portrait of a family in dire straits and demonstrates an aggrieved fieriness that is the only insight into Slowman's personality.

By piecing together information from various records, Sherry and I were able to verify that Slowman and his wife, Ann, probably had at least five living children—Sally was the oldest. Two of her brothers, Jordan and John, would play a critical role in Sally's story in later years.

Slowman leaned on almost all of the children as witnesses in his lawsuits over the years, though none more than Sally.

But it's the story of Sally's younger sister, Nancy, and how their father's increasing indebtedness impacted her life, that gave us an important clue about what might have motivated Sally over the next few years.

ONE OF SLOWMAN'S MOST CONTENTIOUS SUITS IN THE BEDFORD COUNTY records went back and forth for nine years. Guarantors were often listed on promissory notes that Slowman filed as well, as he went into debt in order to pay off other debts in a spiraling cycle. In December 1786, Nancy Reese filed charges against one of those guarantors for trespassing in their home and attacking her with staves and knives. She asked for two hundred pounds in damages. A few months later, that guarantor filed a countersuit for the same amount. In the same court filing, someone filed a Bastardy Bond against Nancy Reese. Though we cannot know for sure who filed it, the timing of the bond indicates it was possibly the retaliatory guarantor. If we're piecing the evidence together correctly, the man attacked Nancy since her dad owed him money, she sued for damages, and he got back by legally naming her as a burden to society.

Bastardy Bonds were ostensibly filed to protect the community in a parish from having to care for a child born without a legal father. Often, the mother would post the bond if the father refused to support the child. The court would issue a warrant and sometimes the father would be required to pay for the care of the child or pay a fine. If the father was not named, then the punishment fell to the mother, who would be forced to pay a fine; she could also receive a jail sentence or a whipping. Because neither Nancy nor a father are named in the bond, it is clear she did not post it herself. The age of the child is unknown. All that is clear is that, in March 1787, someone tried to make Nancy Reese either pay a fine or receive lashes for having a child out of wedlock.

Eventually, a judge ordered in court that the guarantor had to pay five pounds, and Nancy had to pay two pounds. After all of the stress, the family came out only three pounds richer—a drop in the bucket of their debts. But that time period might have significantly impacted Sally.

When she found herself in a similar situation to her sister, Sally made very different choices—ones that would change the trajectory of my family forever.

FIVE YEARS LATER, IN 1792, ALMOST ALL OF SALLY'S SIBLINGS WERE married, and Sally was already twenty-seven—a veritable spinster in that society. In an unknown month in 1792, my great-great-great-great-grandfather William Gibbs Reese was born to Sally.

William Reese was given his mother's last name, which meant he was a known bastard. But unlike Sally's sister Nancy, no Bastardy Bonds were filed for William, indicating Sally's son was financially taken care of and the father was not shirking his duties.

The father of Sally's son was a mystery to her descendants for almost two centuries. It was not a mystery, of course, in the small town in which they lived. No one would have been in the dark about Sally's situation. But the story that I received generations later, the one William Gibbs Reese passed down to his children, grandchildren, and great-grandchildren, was that the Reese family was originally from Wales and that our line descended from "two brothers from Tennessee," making it sound like those brothers were the only forebears of many of the Corinth kinfolks.

William knew the truth, but he covered up his family's past with his cousins' tale. Those two brothers were John and Jordan—Sally's younger brothers and William's uncles—who would lead the axle tar–wagon exodus out of Virginia to Tennessee that included Sally and her family. William essentially erased his parents from his story. He must have thought he left the truth of his parentage behind in Virginia.

How could they have anticipated anything like DNA research, which can reach back over the centuries to uncover the secret they thought long buried?

That's how we found out William's father was a man with the nursery-rhyme name Littleberry Leftwich.

CHAPTER 7

On the opposite end of the economic scale from the Reeses were the Leftwiches—one of the richest, most powerful clans in the region. In tiny Liberty, Virginia, everyone knew them. The patriarch and matriarch of the clan, Augustine and Mary, had been in the area—at the time, the western frontier of Virginia—since the 1750s. Over decades, the Leftwiches acquired thousands of acres of land and enslaved dozens, if not hundreds, of people.

Littleberry Leftwich was the tenth of twelve children—in total, four daughters and eight sons. Almost all of the twelve Leftwich siblings lived long lives—another sign of their wealth given the access to nutritious food and medical care available in that era. By my count, the next generation of Leftwiches consisted of more than a hundred known grandchildren.

In Bedford County in the last half of the eighteenth century, the twelve adult Leftwich children and their grandchildren were an economic force. They snapped up land, married well, expanded Augustine's wealth, and took their place in the highest society available in Virginia at the time. The plantation of one of Littleberry's sisters, called "Trivium," was very near Thomas Jefferson's Poplar Forest, the retreat where the second president spent a great deal of his time in the last years of his life. Members of the Leftwich clan probably socialized with the taciturn former governor and president on the few occasions he consented to be out in the neighborhood.

One local history book—like *Corinth and Its Kinfolk* but more sophisticated and with a broader scope—details the lives of each of the brothers, listing many of their accomplishments and relationships. Through sibling after Leftwich sibling, the writer measures their lives by land and marriages and military rank and civil careers. Two of the brothers were justices of the peace and representatives in the Virginia legislature. One of the brothers led the rear guard at the Battle of Camden and owned a vast plantation named Mt. Airy. One was a captain in the Revolutionary Army. Among the eight brothers, there were three captains, three colonels, and two generals. Military service was a critical part of their family legacy.

In the midst of this high-achieving, pillar-of-the-community family, Littleberry stood out—for his lack of accomplishments. The family historian's entry for Littleberry, set in the midst of long paragraphs about his brothers, is brief and succinct: "Littleberry m. Fanny Hopkins: was famed as a foot racer, and never beaten."

IN THE YEARS THAT SALLY REESE WAS WITNESSING HER FAMILY BE BURied under her father's debts, Littleberry Leftwich married his first wife, Frances "Fanny" Hopkins, in 1778. She was eighteen and he was twenty-one. After their first daughter was born a year later, Fanny had a baby like clockwork every two years, mostly in the spring. Four girls in a row came first, then three boys.

Despite his lack of accomplishments, Littleberry's holdings provided a comfortable living for the family. The nineteen people he enslaved—including at least eight who worked in agriculture—kept his family from having to perform manual labor in order to earn a living. Littleberry was free to pursue other ways of spending his time.

While there is no recorded medical information available to understand what happened to Fanny, I have to assume birthing seven children took a toll on her body. In September 1792, almost exactly a year to the day after her last son with Littleberry was born, Fanny Leftwich died.

That was also the year Sally had Littleberry's son William.

IT IS NOT THE FACT THAT SALLY HAD A CHILD OUT OF WEDLOCK WITH Littleberry that is itself so scandalous from the vantage point of centuries later—there are many such examples on both sides of the Reese and Leftwich families. It was the life they set up together on Littleberry's land after William was born that was so unusual. The historians I spoke with said they had never heard of a similar situation.

One illegitimate child might be an accident or an assault. Ten children are a life.

After William's birth in 1792, Sally gave birth to five more children, one every year or two, until 1800. During those years, we know that Littleberry remained active in the local militia. But we know very little about how Sally spent her time, or what her daily life was like. It would have made sense if Sally Reese were a kept woman on the mountain, hidden from society's sight while Littleberry fathered children with her. That was a known and moderately accepted practice in slave-owning Virginia, especially if the kept woman were the daughter or granddaughter of an enslaved woman and if the relationship were never publicly acknowledged; the most famous historical example was Thomas Jefferson's longtime relationship with Sally Hemings. When I first encountered the story of Sally Reese, I assumed she was the biracial daughter or granddaughter of an enslaved woman, but the same kind of targeted DNA research among her descendants that confirmed Littleberry was the father of her children also revealed that she was not biracial.

Revolutionary-era Virginia was not Puritan Massachusetts; there were more complex views about sex and children out of wedlock than those of us who grew up reading *The Scarlet Letter* might assume. Still, even accounting for that relative liberalism, the apparent openness of Littleberry's relationship with Sally was unusual for its time.

One historian I spoke with called what Littleberry offered Sally a "circle of protection." I assume—and might be wrong—that this was a mutually beneficial relationship in some way to both Sally and Littleberry. He offered her a kind of security Sally clearly needed enough to stay with him for years in an openly acknowledged sexual relationship. We don't have any letters between them or any other clues to their motivation. All we can discern comes from the deed books and court orders.

But even those make it clear that Sally was not hidden away at all. Littleberry was publicly close to her family members. In fact, in 1796, Littleberry's oldest "legitimate" daughter, Polly, married Sally's younger brother, Jordan. This could not have been an advantageous match for Polly—Jordan came from the same indebted household that Sally did and had been arrested two years before their marriage for biting the ear off a man. Jordan's charges were dismissed by the local judge—Littleberry's older brother. It seems entirely possible Littleberry made an appeal to his big brother for Sally's sake. There are other records that link Littleberry's name with Sally's brothers—including a 1797 charge against all three of them for breaching the peace together.

Whether they considered each other brothers-in-law, or how they explained their relationship publicly, is unknown. All we know is that around 1800—three years after Littleberry was arrested, the year Sally's sixth child was born—things on Littleberry's plantation got more complicated.

LITTLEBERRY TOOK UP WITH ANOTHER MISTRESS, ALSO NAMED SALLY. They never married, and her children carried her last name, Thornhill, making them also legal bastards. In 1801, her first daughter with Littleberry was born; she gave birth to a son two years later.

Then Sally Reese had two more daughters in 1804 and 1805.

Sally Thornhill also had a girl, born five months after Sally Reese's daughter.

Sally Reese had a boy in 1807.

Sally Thornhill was next with a girl, probably in 1810.

Sally Reese had her final child with Littleberry Leftwich on February 20, 1810. Fleming Reese, the youngest of her ten children, would live to have an extensive clan of his own and move to Texas not long after the Texas Revolution.

A year later, Sally Thornhill had her last known son with Littleberry.

LITTLEBERRY KEPT GOING. WITH TWO BABIES IN ARMS BORN TO TWO Sallys within the last two years, in December 1811, Littleberry legally married again at fifty-four to a woman—bizarrely, almost humorously—with the same name as his first wife: Frances. His new wife went by "Frankey." She was younger than some of his oldest daughters.

He and Frankey never had any children. For the next twelve years, Frankey lived near Littleberry's two large families with the two Sallys. As was often the custom at the time, Frankey presumably shared a house with at least some of Littleberry's children. She possibly even lived with Polly and Jordan, who would often have interacted with Sally and the Reese children—who were Polly's half-siblings, Jordan's nieces and nephews, and the children of Frankey's husband's mistress.

It had to have been a deeply knotty situation, at the very least.

Littleberry, black sheep of the powerful Leftwich clan, collected Franceses and Sallys—and possibly other women we don't know about, including women he enslaved—on his plantation while his brothers and sisters were building the community of Liberty in Bedford County.

LITTLEBERRY DIED IN 1823. IT IS IMPOSSIBLE TO KNOW HOW HE WAS mourned by the children, lovers, siblings, enslaved people, in-laws, nieces, nephews, and neighbors he left behind. Compared to his family, he was the least successful of all of his illustrious siblings. No obituary remains to understand how they framed his life. His legacy was at least twenty-two known living children by three different women, and a

handful of descendants named "Berry" who would pop up over the next
few generations.

But when he died, in his will, he not only provided for his widow,
Frankey, and for his oldest children with Fanny. He also left the "children of Sally Reese" and the "children of Sally Thornhill" the land on
which their mothers lived—which is how we know where they lived and
that he acknowledged them. Sally's acreage was "on the Northeast side
of Wolf Creek supposed to contain one hundred & ninety odd acres."

That line in Littleberry's will marked a profound turn for the family
line of Sally Reese. Almost forty-five years earlier, in a time of war, Sally
Reese's mother, Ann, had released the dowry on some land. Sally's father had probably sold it to pay off debt; certainly, by the time Slowman
was mired in lawsuits in the 1780s, the land was gone. Ann and Slowman Reese eventually disappeared from the Virginia records; I have no
idea where and how they died, only that for Slowman it was sometime
after 1803. I also do not know how much choice Sally had in the years
she lived on Littleberry's land and gave birth to his children—whether
she had the ability to walk away, whether she would have taken that option if it were available to her. Sally's motivations, dreams, hopes, and
beliefs were intangible and lost to time.

All that remains are the bones of her story. If she played a long
game, Sally succeeded. When her children became owners of valuable
real estate in Virginia, Sally Reese reversed their family's fortunes completely.

CHAPTER 8

One morning in Virginia, after several days spent poring over deed books and Bastardy Bonds, Sherry and I set out to track down the land where Sally lived. The boundaries of land were often given by references that changed later, when markers like singular trees and big rocks and neighbors' names no longer gave us clues to where one property line ended and another began. We'd spent days mapping out any information we found mentioned in land grants, bills of sale, or wills to make our best guess as to where Littleberry might have built a home for Sally and her children.

We used sketched notes and our phones to navigate to Wolf Creek along Dickerson's Mill Road, crossing the creek at a narrow bridge the length of two cars. We parked on the side of the road and walked back to gaze down at the creek; I took pictures of Sherry, her silver hair striking against her dark purple jacket, as she overlooked the water, then joined her. Neither of us spoke much.

Wispy birch and hornbeam trees leaned over brown water, which flowed with the alto resonance of an oboe. It was overcast after a late April cold front. A bird made a repeated chittering sound that devolved into chatter and then song. The air was cool, and I could feel, as I breathed, the freshness of air created by days-old leaves. One small tree flowered, feathering white against the green.

Like I had been at Sally's grave, I was surprised at how emotional I felt. Sally was too far removed for me to feel any real connection to her as a person, but the idea of her—after days of tracking down her life in yellowed documents—had become powerful to me.

I had given up the name Reese a few years after I left Texas. My parents raised me as a feminist, and I've considered myself one since I could pronounce the word, probably around the age of four. I wrestled with the choice of whether to take my husband's name when I got married, and I know many people have made different decisions than the one I did. For years, I kept Reese as a middle name that I used for scholarly publications. I finally dropped it completely when my parents got divorced when I was an adult. At the time, I liked how being simply Jessica Goudeau let me loosen some painful connections with my past and slip into a new identity. It matters much more that I'm married to someone with whom I share an equal life than it does which name I use, and I've always liked Goudeau. But now I felt a new connection to Sally's last name, a desire to reclaim it.

Sherry walked down the hill to take a phone call. I walked in the other direction, up the hill, away to where the forest thickened, and the tone of the creek deepened slightly. I tried to picture Sally Reese in her home, and wished that there were fewer centuries between us. The only images I could conjure were actors in Colonial Williamsburg, women with modern haircuts pulled back into buns, churning butter or weaving on looms or cooking over an open fire.

More than I wanted to picture her, however, I wanted a connection with her as a person. None of the documents could tell us her thoughts. There were entire decades in which she was having children, nurturing them as they grew, creating a home with them. Was she resentful? Was she happy? Was she frustrated? Was she grateful?

If she could move forward in time, what would she have wanted to do with her life? Was having so many children something she would have repeated, given access to health care and contraception and a means of providing for herself through her own career? Or would she have made different choices if she had the options I did, to balance a career and motherhood, to choose a vocation that aligns with her passions and interests?

I was in high school when my mother finished her doctorate, the first on either side of her family to achieve that educational milestone. I thought of my mother the whole time when I was getting my own PhD, how she modeled for me what it was like to pursue her own goals. I almost didn't walk at my doctoral graduation, but decided at the last minute I would, mostly so that my young children could have the memory of their mother wearing regalia on a stage and realizing her dream. I have carried with me my whole life a sense that my career choices are, in some way, a culmination of all of the strong women before me who never had the opportunities I do.

Standing by the stream on land where Sally once lived—perhaps she washed laundry in the small pool eddying upstream, or pulled her skirts up to wade in the shallow water, or called in laughing children with disheveled hair and grass-stained knees for dinner—I was in awe of what she had done with the very limited choices in front of her. Sally had raised ten children as a single mother. The details of how she co-parented with Littleberry are gone. Though he acknowledged them as his children, their last name made it clear that they always belonged, in the eyes of society and probably in their home, more to their mother than their father. The youngest was a toddler during the War of 1812, when Sally once again found herself living in a war zone in her commonwealth—this time with ten children.

Of the very few things I am certain of about Sally, one of them is this: she cared about her children and wanted them to flourish. I can see this in the way they traveled with her to Tennessee, in the strength of their family connections, and in the fact that her children gave her such a loving grave marker to commemorate her life.

The first period of extremism during Sally's life culminated with her father being one of the first victims of a new vigilantism codified into law. The first calls for war and the decision to break from their homeland must have been deeply shocking for many colonialists. It's hard for those of us who grew up in the United States, who recited the pledge of allegiance and sang "The Star-Spangled Banner," to recognize how scandalous those years must have been. It's easy to look back on Slowman as a traitor because the rebels won, because they wrote the history we study. Had England won, perhaps Slowman would have been seen as more prudent than desperate. It's impossible to know what Sally's opinions were of her father; we don't even know what her father's views were, only the suspicions his community held of him. All we know is the level of tension that must have existed in the tiny village named Liberty. Extreme views would have surrounded Sally, and they only subsided when the Patriot army birthed a messy, complicated republic.

Sally Reese lived as an oppressed woman in a hierarchical society—certainly not the most oppressed, as the enslaved people her father oversaw and who worked Littleberry's land could certainly have attested. Still, the social hierarchies of her time could not have been comfortable for her. Though a life dependent on Littleberry was somewhat freer than life as suspected-traitor Slowman's daughter, it was not a life that was completely hers.

When Sherry finished her call, we got back into the car and drove on, up the mountain, windows down. We came to a clearing in the woods as we wound north and uphill. It held mobile homes, similar to those down the street from where my mother grew up in South Texas. Some were well-maintained double-wides with lush lawns or sprawling porches or wheelchair ramps. Others were beige or tan singles with sagging siding and rusting exteriors. The homes were set in what once might have been farmland—the trees in the park had obviously been planted in the last couple of decades. The homes were a winding, inconvenient drive up the mountain from town. But the views were spectacular: from the clearing on the mountain, we could see nearby hills in the Blue Ridge Parkway and the Peaks of Otter several miles due north.

We got out of the car and stood, looking at the mountains that were dazzling in the midafternoon sun. I wondered what it might have meant to Sally, to know that two of her descendants—educated women with families of our own—had found her. That we had walked the land where she lived. That we were trying to piece together what clues she left. That we cared that she had lived—where she lived, how she lived, with whom she lived.

Before I went to Virginia, Sally Reese had been only a name to me. I knew she had been alive in a turbulent time. Creating a new nation out of war, building a society where almost half the population was enslaved—those could not have been easy days to live through. Before, though, that time period felt academic to me, removed from my experiences.

Standing on a field looking at the unchanging mountains in front of me, I felt a many-times-removed granddaughter's desperation for wisdom and answers.

I wanted to sit down with Sally in the view of those mountains, maybe on her front porch, to grab her hand, look her in the eye, and ask: How did you raise your kids well? How did you let them go into a village that still remembered your father as the enemy? Did you worry they would be bullied or harmed? Did you worry the war would come closer when it began again in the 1810s? How did you help them calm their—probably sometimes-legitimate—fears? How did you teach them about kindness and hospitality in a time of such high suspicion between neighbors? Do you have any regrets? Is there anything you wish you had known? Did you raise them to keep secrets, or was that all their own decision?

How did you instill in your children confidence? Or security? Or hope?

EVENTUALLY, WE HEADED BACK TO THE HOTEL. AS WE ROLLED DOWN the shaded mountain road, so similar to the one in Tennessee on the mountain where Sally was buried, I wanted to imagine Sally living a good life here, on land Littleberry gave her while she had his children. I wanted to imagine that the whole thing was her choice, that he made a proposition she gladly accepted even if they never married. Sally was a mother who raised ten children through difficult days; I am a mother trying to guide my own children through difficult days. I wanted to think that she had some control in the midst of the chaos of two wars and two men—her father and the father of her children—whose actions constrained her life choices. I wanted to know that she learned some things along the way, gained wisdom she could have passed along to me if we could have met over the centuries. I wanted to imagine her happy, at least for a time.

I wanted those things for her, knowing the truth was probably darker and more complex. How often it is.

The details of her life are lost to time. But we uncovered the truth of her legacy. She gave a very different life to her children than the one she had. Against all odds, Sally Reese made an ancestral pivot that changed the future for generations of Reeses—including me.

CHAPTER 9

After Littleberry's will in 1823 gave the land near Wolf Creek to Sally Reese's children—though not to her—they retained ownership of it for eight more years. By 1831, it was clear that the Reese clan's future was no longer in Virginia. Two of Sally's sisters and three of her daughters ended up in Logan County, Kentucky, near many of their Leftwich cousins—including Littleberry's nephew, Robert, who became the first of our relatives to head to Texas. The rest of Sally's family would go to Tennessee.

Sally's brothers, John and Jordan Reese, went to Tennessee first—they were the two brothers in William Reese's stories passed down over generations, the ones in the axle tar wagons that fascinated me so much as a kid.

Sally's son William didn't leave with that first group to Tennessee. He got married and had a number of children mostly named after Sally and her relatives, including a John and a Jordan. William's son Sloman Woodford Reese would have his own John and Sloman among eleven children. I'm descended through that John Wiley Reese, whose son was the first of my own line of the family to move to Texas. And that later Sloman was the self-styled Uncle Sloman who wrote *Corinth and Its Kinfolk*. There are Slomans, Sarahs, Johns, Jordans, and Berrys scattered throughout the Reese generations. The names of Sally's immediate family lived on in my Reese clan long after she was forgotten to us.

When they finally sold the land in 1831, Sally's name appeared on the document first: "Sally X Reese," followed by the names of most of her children and many of their spouses. That bill of sale was the year Sally turned sixty-six and William—whose birth had changed her life forever in 1792—turned thirty-nine. That document represented the end of a profound chapter in Sally's life and the beginning of a new one—through an extraordinary one-generation turn.

AS I PACKED UP AT THE END OF OUR RESEARCH TRIP, SAID GOODBYE TO Sherry—who had become not just a trusted research partner but a good friend—and got in the car to begin the nineteen-hour drive back to Texas from Bedford County, I thought of Sally leaving Virginia for Tennessee. I wondered if she felt sad at leaving the home where she had raised her children, or if she felt relief to have left behind that small village. I wondered if the Tennessee mountains where she spent the last quarter of her life felt like her own pursuit of happiness.

When they left Virginia, like many pioneers pouring west, the Reese clan believed they had a right to the land they encountered. Sally's generation, like many in the Virginia Commonwealth, were not as religious as their children would be. Whether Sally believed it or not, her children certainly thought their right to the land—on which thousands of indigenous people had lived, as they had for hundreds or thousands of years— was God-given. In 1845, the year that Texas became a state, the idea of Western expansion and American colonialism as a providential directive would get a concise name: an editorial published in *The Democratic Review* called it "Manifest Destiny."

Across the South in particular, those westward-pushing settlers carried with them the idea that white supremacy was not a scandalous phrase or a debatable issue, but an unquestioned hierarchy based on cultural stories so ubiquitous, few questioned their veracity. Those stories accompanied the same specific fears that fueled the tightening laws in the 1600s and 1700s meant to control the lives of Black people and uphold slavery: among them the fear of the white race being made less pure by mixing with other groups, especially Black people, and the possibility of uprisal of oppressed Black people. When the Leftwiches and Reeses left for Tennessee, they brought those ideas with them.

On the frontiers, and especially in Texas, the people raised with the stories of Lynch's law still fresh in their ears loaded up the idea that good white men could mete out justice without worrying about legality as long as times were urgent enough. They would call it vigilantism, extralegal activities, private justice. When it was an organized group, it became a militia. But it would remain a core value of my relatives, and the people who came with them to Texas, that violence was acceptable and justifiable for US citizens.

Many of those bound for Texas would also bring along our families' propensity for debts. For most of its early years, only Texas rivaled colonial Virginia in the desperation of its indebted settlers. Texas was known as a haven for tax fugitives and bankrupt runaways. Greed—the kind that led to high-risk, high-reward gambling—often went hand in hand with those debts.

In the years in which Sally's clan moved into Tennessee, Littleberry's bankrupt nephew, Robert Leftwich, was already doing everything in his power to secure himself land and a new home in Texas—driven by his own combination of fear and greed.

He also carried what I would identify—after years of reading writings by and about him—as a singular sense of insecurity and an aggrieved air of being wronged. I wondered if that was a Leftwich trait Robert shared with his Uncle Littleberry—who alone among his brothers was recorded in family history not for his military or civic achievements but for foot racing, who was known in the community not for his judicial wisdom or legislative accomplishments but for breaching the peace and siring children. I have tried not to speculate too much about Littleberry and what motivated him in the years when he fathered children with two Sallys while marrying one Frances and then another.

Littleberry was nineteen when, in 1776, Thomas Jefferson lifted John Locke's phrase and added it to the Declaration of Independence in what would become a quintessentially American philosophy: "We hold these truths to be self-evident, that all men are created equal, that they are endowed by their Creator with certain unalienable Rights, that among these are Life, Liberty, and the pursuit of Happiness." Even without much more speculation, it feels fair to think that the "pursuit of Happiness" might have been Littleberry's personal mantra. Without direct evidence of Littleberry's thoughts, I cannot confirm this. But from letters between Robert and his uncle Joel Leftwich—who was Littleberry's next-youngest brother—I sense a combination of self-centeredness and self-doubt that plagues Robert. He refers to himself as the black sheep of his father; I wonder if Littleberry also viewed himself as a Leftwich black sheep.

I will probably never be able to know what personal characteristics Slowman, Littleberry, and Sally possessed that they passed down to their descendants. But even the broadest sketches of their past show a very American start to the clan's movement across the southern US that eventually ended up in Texas.

The Reeses packed with them specific ideas they had learned in the crucible of Revolutionary War Virginia from the two generations before them—about debt and greed and power. They reinvented themselves in Tennessee, as many on the frontier were wont to do; the Reeses' reinvention—as legitimate descendants rather than illegal bastards—was relatively tame, especially in comparison to the reinventions to come in Texas. Underneath it all, Sally's and Littleberry's children carted with them the idea that their children should have a better life than the one they had lived and that they were justified in taking what they needed to ensure their families would thrive.

ON THE SECOND DAY OF MY LONG ROAD TRIP HOME, I MADE THE FINAL stop on my research trip, following my ancestors' journey from Virginia, through Tennessee and Arkansas, and finally to Texas. I had arrived at another small cemetery. This one was near old Corinth, Arkansas, the one in *Corinth and Its Kinfolk*, where Sally's son William and his family were buried.

As I got out of the car and meandered among the stone markers of so many Reeses and Joneses and Hales and Womacks, I thought again how remarkable Sally's grave marker was at that other cemetery in Tennessee. These tombstones were decades newer than hers, and yet most of the names of her grandchildren and great-grandchildren were almost completely eroded away. None of the letters were as clear as Sally's.

I have one deep fear that has always been with me. I put it into words as a little girl; it is part of what haunts me about the unnamed people from my family's history. It is the fear that my name will be lost—that in a few generations, no one will remember me.

I think about it at every funeral. I told Jonathan years ago that part of why I'd always wanted to be a writer was simply because leaving a legacy of books would be proof I had once existed. It's a way to scrawl on the wall of the world "Jessica was here."

I have no way of knowing whether Sally shared my fear. Perhaps she did and it might have brought her comfort to know that it would take two hundred years, but Sherry and other researching cousins and I would piece together the details about her life and what she went through. Quite possibly I was projecting my own fears onto her. There would never be any way to know.

I moved to stand by the stone fence around the cemetery. The fields beyond were dotted with tiny yellow flowers, flecks of sunshine scattered under an overcast sky. In the distance I could hear cars on a highway, but around the graves, the only noises were birds and rustling grass. Like I had been at Sally's grave, I was reluctant to leave this place. I sat down on the low wall around the cemetery, the sharp edge of the gray stone cutting into the back of my legs. I thought of what it must have been like for each generation born and raised here, burying their parents and a few of their children, knowing they would also rest here one day. I thought of the people who left Corinth behind to scatter around the country, including my great-grandparents who ended up in Texas. How they told stories about their family past so that future generations would recall where they had been, what they valued, what they endured. How, eventually, all that remained were a handful of family myths, a xeroxed document on a few family shelves about *Corinth and Its Kinfolk*, official records, and their headstones.

Sitting there, an awareness rose up in me: To strive to be the person who is remembered is selfish. I cannot carve my own grave marker. If I am always angling so that I can have a legacy that ensures that I live on after my death, then my love for others becomes self-seeking. But to be the person who remembers—that is a sacred role.

When I was young, I worried about my own legacy, but as an adult, I want to be like the person who made sure that Sally Reese would never be erased by inscribing her name with such intention.

This epiphany put into words an idea I have felt instinctively in the years in which I have done so many difficult, earnest interviews with former refugees, asylum seekers, and other people made vulnerable by catastrophes. The people I interview are often talked about as if they are political issues, but they never view themselves that way. For them, the conversations always end up being about existence: "I am here, and it feels like the world has forgotten me. My family deserves to be healthy and free. I just want to be safe and loved."

I recognize in those conversations that most human of motivations, the same thing that drove me as a little girl—to live. To be remembered. To be understood.

Unknowingly, all of my life, I have carried the name of a woman who refused to be constrained by her impossible circumstances; I will not let that be forgotten by her great-great-great-great-great-great-grandchildren. And alongside her name, I will record a few others, as many as I can find. There are so many people whose stories are intertwined with my families' whose lives I wish I could chronicle more fully. Most often, all I have is a gap—a knowledge that there are people left out of the frame of history, or names with little context or history. It is not enough, but to place their names in this story is at least a start.

As I got in my car at the cemetery in Corinth, Arkansas, my mind felt as clean as the air that cool morning by Wolf Creek, on the mountain where Sally Reese raised her children. In understanding the Reese name differently, I was returning to the strong, subversive roots Sally gave me and all of her descendants. I had gone to the mouth of the river in Virginia and traced many of the myths that shaped Texas. Along the way, I had gained the hope and purpose I needed to do the work ahead.

As I crossed the border into Texas, driving home to my family, I felt a phrase rise up in my mind. It was both a direction and a directive for the stories left to write, the names yet to be uncovered, and the truths yet to be told. The loving, authoritative voice in my mind sounded like my mother's and my grandmothers', and maybe the voices of all the other women in my family who came before me.

Carve the letters deeply.

PART 2

ROBERT LEFTWICH

(1778–1826)

I had an ignorant, whimsical selfish and suspicious set of rulers over me to keep good natured, a perplexed and confused colonization law to execute, and an unruly set of North American frontier republicans to countroul [*sic*] who felt that they were sovereigns. . . . Added to all this, I was poor, destitute of capital.

—STEPHEN F. AUSTIN ON THE DIFFICULTIES
OF BEING AN EMPRESARIO, APRIL 24, 1829

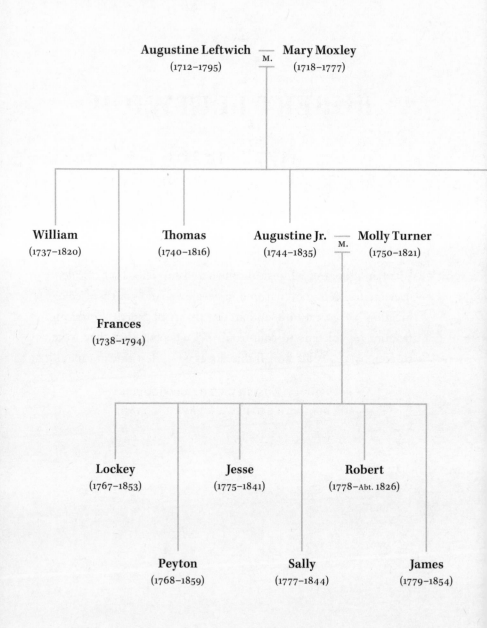

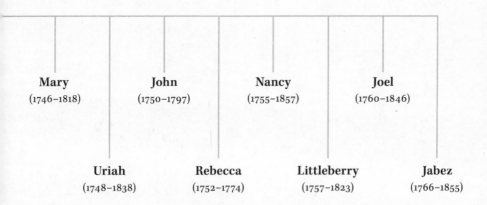

Mary
(1746–1818)

John
(1750–1797)

Nancy
(1755–1857)

Joel
(1760–1846)

Uriah
(1748–1838)

Rebecca
(1752–1774)

Littleberry
(1757–1823)

Jabez
(1766–1855)

CHAPTER 10

When my mother was a little girl growing up in South Texas, live oaks were her sanctuary. They were shade in the summer when their house had no air conditioning, and they were a place to hide and get away. My mother—a scrawny, perceptive bookworm—escaped up a tree whenever she could. The live oaks on their ten acres of land were centuries old and palatial. The knobby trunks gave her footholds as she climbed barefoot with a book under her arm and tightrope-walked across broad branches to nooks where she could hide from the world below. But it was more than that. Her family was too poor to travel, rarely had reason to go to a big city; when she was young, she had never flown in an airplane or been in a skyscraper. Held in the swaying branches yards above the ground below her, my mother could breathe and dream and see the world in a new way.

When I was a little girl living in San Antonio, she taught me to love live oaks too. For my sister and me (our brother was too young then), the trees in our front and backyard were playgrounds rather than the refuges they had been for Mom. But we inherited our mother's knobby knees and propensity for barefoot climbing. The house where we lived was not large but might have been a mansion compared to my grandparents'. It was a 1980s-style ranch home that my parents bought in part because there were more than thirty live oak trees crammed into a typical suburban-sized yard. The trees grew so closely together we could climb one and jump to another without coming back down to the ground. We often spent much of the day in our personal forest. I read in those branches as my mother had—for hours, being rocked gently by the wind.

We left that house in San Antonio when I was nine. A generation later, I wanted to raise my children to play among the same kind of trees. When we were looking at houses in Austin, I fell in love first with a massive gnarled live oak at the house we eventually bought.

I had no idea that, in buying that home, I was entering back into my own family story. The tree that reminded me of some of my mother's and my favorite childhood memories was growing on land that once had been owned by the nephew of my great-great-great-great-great-grandfather.

IN 1825, ROBERT LEFTWICH WAS ONE OF ONLY A HANDFUL OF ANGLO empresarios, agents given land grants by the newly independent Mexican government. It was an ad hoc system that grew from the machinations of desperate men trying to make a buck and get ahead—Robert fit right in. After a lifetime of trying to prove himself to a wealthy, exacting father, Augustine Leftwich Jr.—Littleberry's distinguished and overshadowing older brother and the third son of the large, respectable family who had been pillars of Bedford County, Virginia—Robert would end up the owner of almost 1.5 million acres of some of the best cotton-producing land in the North American hemisphere. It was land he got by lying through his teeth. His triumph lasted less than four months, from April 15 to August 6, 1825. He had no idea the first time he rode into Texas the dramatic events that would follow, events with generational consequences for Robert, his son, Grandison, and one of the families he enslaved—Polly and her three sons, Lewis, John, and James.

As far as I know, Robert never journeyed to the part of the land he owned that I now live on. But I often sat under the shade of that tree, with roots in what had once been "Leftwich's Grant," as I researched and read about the man I had never known was part of my own family.

Our connection had been hidden by Sally's secrets.

CHAPTER 11

Long before Robert Leftwich or any other Anglo-American settlers from the southern United States became part of its history, the land in central Texas he would own had been politically complicated territory for centuries.

At the end of the seventeenth century, Spanish colonizers began wresting away the land that would eventually be called Texas—ironically, a bastardization of the Caddo word for "friendship"—from the indigenous people who had lived there for thousands of years. The land was well populated with dozens of groups already, including people who were Caddo, Acoma, Waco, Comanche, Tonkawa, Tigua, Potawatomi, Karankawa, Kickapoo, Coahuiltecan, and Apache, among many others. Ignoring that fact, European colonizing nations often referred to the region as "sparsely populated" or "savage" or "untamed." In the centuries they tried to move settlers into Texas, Europeans faced a tenuous narrative balance—it was a hard sell to convince their citizens to move to a place where they were so spectacularly unwelcome. But colonizing nations wanted to populate the land in order to profit from it, and for that they needed loyal settlers willing to live on the front lines of a combative frontier.

Despite the difficulties, most of the governments who scrabbled over colonial land in the Americas like seagulls over Gulf Coast crabs wanted a bite of the land now known as Texas. Spain was the dubious winner, occupying parts of the region since 1690. They established a mission at San Antonio in 1716. Their hold on the land lasted more than a century but was always shaky.

Spain had other issues to deal with. Their colonial forces were already spread too thin. As with all colonized places, what happened in the seat of the empires affected the territories they controlled, and in the eighteenth and early nineteenth centuries, European empires were in absolute turmoil. The United States successfully routed British forces in the fight for independence in 1776 and again in the War of 1812. The years of the Napoleonic Wars, with shifting alliances pushing long-term enemies Britain, Spain, and Portugal into an uneasy coalition against the encroaching French, also led to lack of colonial oversight in the Americas.

US citizens got much closer to Spanish territory in Texas in 1803, when Napoleon Bonaparte sold a huge chunk of land to the Leftwiches' sometime neighbor, President Thomas Jefferson, to fund France's losing war against the British. The "Louisiana Purchase" extended across the middle of the country in what is now Louisiana, Arkansas, Oklahoma, Missouri, Kansas, Colorado, Nebraska, Iowa, Minnesota, North and South Dakota, Wyoming, and Montana. The land exchange marked a new threat to Spanish rule; as French and British power in the Americas diminished, the might of the United States grew.

By 1810, as the US was gearing up for their second war with England, Spain essentially lost all control of the northeastern edge of their territory. Those places that were not held by indigenous groups became lawless areas ruled by American smugglers and fugitives—all immigrants to Texas illegally. US farmers defaulting on loans from land around the Mississippi River figured out they could flee bank collectors and start over in Texas because Spain did not extradite fugitives. Many of the Anglos stayed away from settlements hoping to avoid notice by authorities, which left them largely unprotected by raiders of all types who stole horses or food in order to survive or get ahead economically.

Just like the early days in the Virginia colony, many of the early

Anglo settlers in Texas were indebted and desperate. Had Sally's family not had Littleberry's land to sell, during the years when they were settling in Tennessee, they too might have ended up debt-ridden fugitives in Texas. The Reese family were exactly the kind of people who otherwise would have had no choice but to risk it all by coming to this haven for the desolate.

Spanish authorities spent a great deal of time tracking down the Anglos building a shadow economy in the region, but they did not really have the resources to focus on illegal Anglo economic migration to Texas.

By then, Spain was already fighting a war in Mexico.

IN 1810, REVOLUTIONARIES IN MEXICO DECLARED INDEPENDENCE FROM Spain, launching a bitter rebellion. Catholic priest Padre Miguel Hidalgo y Costilla issued a tract called the "Grito de Dolores." In it, he laid out a plan for the redistribution of land to provide greater equality for people in the ruled classes. The values of that revolution slowly led to widespread support for ending the institution of slavery completely in Mexico. Those changing views on class, caste, and justice in Mexico would have a significant impact on the political haggling about land in Texas for the next twenty-six years.

Mexico had a long history of slavery. Primarily, Spanish colonizers enslaved indigenous people as part of the encomienda system that started in the 1500s. When the government granted Spanish citizens land in payment for political or military service, they enslaved indigenous people in order to labor on that land. The colony of Mexico also enslaved African people like the other countries in the region; from 1580 to 1640 there were more enslaved people from Africa coming to Mexico than any Central or South American colony other than Brazil. By the early 1800s in Mexico, there were still places where people were forced into labor or coerced into situations against their will. But the economic incentives for enslaving others were not as high as in the southern United States; the climate in most of Mexico wasn't ideal for big plantations.

In Mexico in the 1810s till the 1830s, the question of what to do about slavery was hotly debated in newspapers and letters, in congressional chambers and homes. Many of the elite Mexicans were global citizens of the region—they had seen slavery not just in the US but in the Caribbean and Brazil. They knew there was money to be made for those willing to enslave others and work them to death to profit off the land. Yet the cultural, religious, moral, familial, or economic narratives that Anglo farmers told themselves to justify slavery in the United States had never fully taken root in Mexico. From the earliest days of the revolution, it was clear that a large number of Mexican leaders would work tirelessly to eradicate slavery from the country all together.

By the end of the 1810s, as Spanish authorities still wrestled for control of Mexico and worried about an invasion of Anglo settlers from the north, the issue of how to manage immigration along their northern border and what to do about slavery became one central, churning national question.

THAT WAS CERTAINLY NOT THE CASE IN THE UNITED STATES. THE LOUisiana Purchase opened up land along the Mississippi River Valley at a time when cotton was changing the economy of the country forever. Eli Whitney patented the cotton gin in 1794 and other inventors built on that first patent, soon making large-scale cotton production feasible and profitable for farmers who could get enough land and workers.

Profitable cotton production required the same three things tobacco had in Virginia: First, the right strain of crops. Second, large tracts of land in a temperate climate with access to water (for the fields) and to roads, rivers, or the ocean (to ship the harvest efficiently to be processed). And third, many, many laborers—cotton could often produce multiple crops per season, making it fast-paced and lucrative.

By the turn of the nineteenth century, farmers in the southern United States had established an entire economic system built on slavery as they cultivated tobacco, rice, and wheat for worldwide consumption. Cotton was especially easy to grow, store, transport, and market. The

English port in Liverpool had risen to international dominance, providing one central location for cotton sales to the insatiable European market. There was a moment when it seemed like abolitionists were making strides to eradicate the institution; US Congress abolished the foreign slave trade in 1807. But within a few years, the influence of abolitionists somewhat dissipated in the new nation. The major concern in the 1810s for many would-be plantation farmers was how to get more land.

The Louisiana Purchase had seemed to be the answer. With many of the cotton-growing areas in the Mississippi River Valley already divvied up, settlers pushed west, hoping for choice acreages to start plantations of their own.

Then, in the late 1810s, a frightening economic downturn only ratcheted up settlers' desperation for cotton land. After losing to the US but beating France in war, England's financial wells ran dry, vaporizing the many connected economic tributaries running through the United States. It hit at the worst possible time: To pay for the 1803 Louisiana Purchase, the Jefferson White House had gone into $11.25 million in debt, which would come due by the end of 1818. Beginning in New York in the late 1810s, the damage spread down from the northeast region of the United States first, moving from New York through Pennsylvania and into the Ohio River area, arriving finally in Kentucky and Tennessee, culminating in the Panic of 1819.

It desiccated almost every industry in the United States except one: cotton production.

Suddenly, the immigration pattern for Anglos coming to northernmost Mexico changed significantly. Before, the Anglo immigrants had been embattled farmers and smugglers, trying to scrape by off the grid, as it were. But now a whole class of would-be immigrants rose up from the southern United States. They were white slaveholders who knew that land in Texas near the Gulf of Mexico—so similar to those hugely prosperous plantations in Louisiana, Alabama, and Mississippi—would be perfect for them. They watched the roiling political situation of the Mexican Revolution with the piercing eye of birds of prey.

Those free-for-all years only increased the already astounding violence in Texas. Many indigenous groups made money selling stolen horses, donkeys, and mules to planters in the US South. The demand for animals was almost as steep as the demand for enslaved people to labor on their farms; smuggling animals was almost as lucrative as smuggling people. Few slaveholding farmers asked questions about the provenance of the animals or humans that they bought.

It was a cycle of bloodshed that seemed unbreakable. For indigenous people, the violence was truly one of survival—of individuals and families, of entire ways of life that had existed for centuries. For enslaved people, it was also about survival—if they could fight to free themselves or their fellow enslaved people, they would, though very few succeeded.

But for Anglo farmers, the brutality was less about surviving than it was about taking.

That is not how the story of Anglo immigration was presented to me growing up. When I learned about Texas history in school, at museums, and from my reading as a kid, Anglo farmers' motivating need was always presented as one of survival. The unspoken question underneath the historical framework was, what choice did Anglo enslavers really have? The cotton economic equation only worked if they enslaved the people who worked their land—were they just *not* supposed to take other peoples' land and profit off slave labor?

THE ANGLO SETTLERS' LAND CONUNDRUM IN THE 1810S MIGHT HAVE continued indefinitely, with groups squabbling and squalling over the dubious right to squat or scrabble for survival. But in 1821, two things changed: First, Moses Austin showed up at an outpost at the mission in San Antonio with what he framed as an elegant solution to the land dilemma. And second, Spanish troops finally succumbed to the Mexican revolutionaries.

Moses Austin journeyed to Texas with a singular proposition to connect Spanish authorities and eager US would-be investors. His idea was based on his previous experiences living in Spain-controlled territory in what is now Missouri. Like he had been in the past, he wanted to be a middleman, a mediator between settlers he would recruit and bring over to the territory, ensuring they could then be easily vetted by Spanish officials. Having a trusted mediator could be critically important in a Catholic country concerned that Protestants and other migrants they viewed as undesirable would encroach on their territory, and it benefited the settlers because they come as part of communities working together to build a shared space with well-regulated defenses and civil rules. It was a win-win for Spain and for would-be immigrants— and of course, an extra win for Moses Austin, who would make money off the whole endeavor.

Moses struggled to convince the officials in San Antonio to give him the first Texas land grant. A grifter from Holland interceded on his behalf. He was an old friend of Austin's from New Orleans whose real name was Philip Bögel. Bögel had fled to Louisiana around 1795 after embezzling money as a tax collector, leaving a wife and five children behind in Holland. When he got to Louisiana, he told everyone his name was Felipe Enrique Neri, el Baron de Bastrop. That alias became the name by which he was known in Texas history; a county southeast of the city of Austin is named Bastrop after his pseudonym.

Bastrop was glad to see his old friend and able to convince the governor that Austin was trustworthy. In early 1821, the governor approved Austin's proposal, making him the first Texas land grant agent—an empresario. But on his journey back to the United States to recruit his first settlers, Moses took ill. He died in June 1821.

Weeks later, his son Stephen F. Austin received word of his death and went to Texas, determined to continue his father's legacy.

THAT SUMMER, THE POLITICAL SITUATION IN TEXAS CHANGED ABRUPTLY. On August 21, 1821, Mexico wrested its independence from Spain. Conservative royalists turned away from the Spanish crown and aligned themselves with the lower-class revolutionaries who had been fighting for a decade. These new upper-class revolutionaries had deeper pockets and more military strategizing. They helped transform the ragtag insurgency into an effective army that ousted one of the most successful colonial powers in history.

The army thrived under the leadership of the general who led them to victory, Agustín de Iturbide. He rose to power on three promises: that Mexico would become independent; that it would unite across political divisions; and it would remain firmly Roman Catholic. The pillars of his victory promises set up the battles for Anglo settlers—many of whom were not Catholic and who would certainly not unite the country—for the next many years.

The treaty signed by the two countries was fundamentally different from the US Declaration of Independence. The US had rejected British rule and with it, monarchy altogether. For the first months after independence, Mexico faced the critical question of whether the Mexican government would be one elected by the people (republican) or under the rule of a new emperor (imperial). On September 27, 1821, Iturbide rode on a black horse at the front of an army to the convent of San Francisco and received the golden keys to Mexico City on a silver platter.

In December 1821, Stephen F. Austin was already in Texas receiving the first colonists to the Austin land grant. A few months later, with the government in chaos, Austin went to Mexico in March 1822 to ensure there were no legal hang ups with his father's documents. By virtue of being first, and because of the relationships he developed with Mexicans and Anglos alike, Austin would remain central to the land grant process in those years—earning him the nickname the "Father of Texas."

Perhaps Austin's first few colonists wrote letters to relatives in Tennessee, or the news made it to Nashville another way. In those days of slow travel, it could take weeks or months for news to travel thousands of miles. By February 1822, as Austin was preparing for his journey, news about the government change that had happened in Mexico almost six months earlier was finally moving upward through the southern United States.

Land-hungry slaveowners across the US South had been eyeing the coastal land in Texas for just such a moment. Many of them had missed the window to snag the huge plots of land in Georgia and Mississippi that would become the plantations memorialized forever in American imagination. They were ready to snatch the land in Texas the minute it was available.

None of them were more eager than Robert Leftwich.

CHAPTER 12

To understand what motivated Robert in the years in which his actions helped shape the future of Texas, you have to first know how he grew up in the heart of the wealthy, respected Leftwich clan in Bedford County, Virginia. Robert's father, Augustine Jr., was one of the oldest, most established sons in the clan by the time Robert came along. Robert and his five siblings grew up not far from his uncle Littleberry's twenty-two children and their homes with the Franceses and Sallys.

As an adult, when Robert left home and began to travel, he regularly wrote letters to his Uncle Joel, who was a general in the Virginia militia during the War of 1812, a state legislator, a justice of the peace, and Littleberry's younger brother by three years. Joel was married to Robert's mother's sister, making them doubly close—they often wrote back and forth to give and receive news about both sides of his family. Joel's descendants kept copies of his papers and later donated them to a university library. Those letters give us a remarkably intimate portrait of Robert's state of mind. There are also three encyclopedic books—published in the 1970s and 1980s as part of a series of eighteen exhaustive books chronicling the history of a large parcel of land in central Texas—containing hundreds of pages of documents, many of them about Robert. And they are only a starting place; there are dozens of sources that give me information about the actions and thoughts of Robert Leftwich. I know things about Robert I could only guess about Sally, Littleberry, and Slowman.

What I do not know are some of the most basic details of his life, including which year he was born. In later letters to Joel, he seems to be lying about his age. Because in other places Robert proves to be an un-reliable, un-self-aware narrator of his own life, I'm going to assume his birth year is the one most historians agree on, 1778.

Robert left Liberty, Virginia as a young man near the turn of the nineteenth century. He worked in and then owned mercantile businesses in other counties in Virginia and then in North Carolina. He married his wife, Priscilla, in 1806, the year he probably turned twenty-eight. His letters from those years show he was still in good standing with his fam-ily. One letter, about a stud horse his father and brother wanted to buy, also reveals the kind of disposable money the Leftwich clan had: Robert recommended his father spend eight hundred dollars on the horse, about eighteen thousand dollars today.

At some point after those letters, something happened between Robert and his father. Robert never states the specifics, but his letters to his Uncle Joel reference their estrangement. The tone of those letters reveals a critical aspect of what motivated him in those later years too: Robert felt he always deserved more than he got, and that, if he were neither rich nor powerful, it was because the world had done him wrong. His indignance, combined with the shame of his father's disapproval, would drive Robert ever deeper into a quicksand of debt—which is how he would get involved a few years later with a group of men with their eyes fixed on Texas.

IN ALL OF THE DOCUMENTS THAT REVEAL INFORMATION ABOUT ROB-ert's life, two people are often left outside of the frame: his only son, Grandison, and a woman he enslaved named Polly. Their stories, which are intertwined so thoroughly with Robert's, are evident mostly in their absences. Only at the end, when Robert himself is gone from the story, do we get a sense for how his decisions over the years impacted the people closest to him.

Grandison was born to Priscilla and Robert, probably in North Carolina, possibly in 1811. By 1813, the small family had moved to Logan County, Kentucky, where they intended to set up their life. Several of Robert's cousins had relocated to the area from Bedford County, Virginia—including two of Sally's daughters with Littleberry. Robert was doing well: by 1818, he had purchased expansive and expensive plots of land in the country and in the biggest nearby town, Russellville.

At some point in those years, Robert acquired at least three enslaved people—Treacy, Garry, and Polly. I know virtually nothing about Treacy and Garry.

According to later court documents, Polly was born around 1805. Polly's oldest son, Lewis, was born in 1814—probably when she was about nine. Even if her birthdate and Lewis's are off by a few years, she was clearly very young when she had her first child. Even in those days, her age at pregnancy would have been scandalous. That means that early in her life, Polly was raped and gave birth to a son who would be highly valued by her white master primarily because he could be sold when he was old enough. Two years later, when she was probably eleven, Polly gave birth to John. And then for a long time, she had no more children. The records I uncovered never name the father of Polly's boys.

Robert was still involved in the mercantile business. In the 1810s, Robert became friends with Amos Edwards, whom one historian calls the "Big Operator" in the area, a tax collector and tavern owner. In January 1819, the Russellville *Weekly Messenger* announced Robert's partnership with Edwards and another man starting a new frontier store—Russellville had become an important stop for farmers heading farther west and they needed supplies. Robert traveled frequently to nearby cities and New Orleans, and then a fateful trip to New York in 1819.

On that trip, Robert journeyed back to Kentucky by way of the Ohio River, just ahead of the news about the depression in England that spread into the interior of the United States along the well-used trade route. That economic downturn was catastrophic for Robert. Their mercantile business failed spectacularly in less than ten months. In his role as business agent, Robert had acquired an admirable amount of merchandise for a store targeting a frontier community that turned almost instantly from flush to cash starved.

The Panic of 1819 razed the fledgling national economy, devastated entire market systems, and demolished what financial security Robert had built for his wife and their son and their household. Robert and his business partners had convinced investors to give them exorbitant sums; the investors, facing their own financial difficulties, did not wait long to call in the balance. The only option for Robert and his partners was to essentially declare bankruptcy, though the legal process differed in the 1810s.

On November 6, 1819, Robert filed four documents in the Logan County Courthouse in Kentucky showing a total debt (of everything he listed, at least) of $20,372.35—nearly half a million dollars in today's currency.

At the end of each document, Robert itemized which of his possessions would be compensation for each batch of creditors. The lists included big tracts of land with storybook descriptions ("200 acres on the Big Whipperwill, near Mosley's Pond"); town lots in Russellville and Elkton; horses; two large trunks; and numerous smaller items, like two double flint quart decanters, Liverpool Porcelain chinaware, and six Windsor chairs. At the very end were the names of the people he owned.

These documents are the first times Polly and her children are listed by name in legal papers, at least that I have found.

Once those documents were filed, the clock started ticking. He had two years after the first filing before four of his creditors could split the horses and the trunks. A year after that he would release the two lots in Russellville, the tracts of land on the Big Whipperwill—and Polly and her boys. Everything else he would keep for another year. By November 1, 1823, if he didn't figure out something big and quick, he would lose everything, and two other people would be displaced, Treacy and Garry—though apparently that happened anyway, because neither Treacy nor

Garry are ever mentioned in any Leftwich records after those documents were filed.

Robert had four years to manufacture a reversal of fortune so profound, it would feel as miraculous as turning away a hurricane at the edge of landfall.

BACK HOME IN VIRGINIA, THOUGH, HIS FATHER'S WEALTH INCREASED. According to the 1820 census, Augustine Jr. owned seventeen Black men and women whose intensive forced labor made him a very wealthy man. By 1830, he'd augmented the number to twenty-six. How many people he enslaved is not a unit of measurement I am comfortable using as a way to accurately understand Augustine's personal wealth. And yet, to ignore the immediate connection between the capital that Black laborers were forced to create and the benefit that capital gave to the people who enslaved them is to ignore the truth of the past.

A few months after his epic bankruptcy filing in 1819, Robert wrote a letter to his Uncle Joel on March 7, 1820 about the hard times he was enduring. In the letter, he mentioned that his father considered him the "black sheep of his flock as he has done more for every other child he has." Robert's grievance against his father, at least in part, seemed to be that Augustine Jr. was uninclined to help Robert out of his financial predicament. It seems reasonable to think that Joel said something to Augustine, or that someone else in their tight-knit clan did. Maybe Robert also wrote to his father and the letter did not survive the centuries.

On April 6, 1820, Robert filed another indenture document—his fifth—in the Logan County Courthouse, this time with eight hundred dollars of debt to two people to be repaid by December 1, 1823.

Three weeks later, a month after Robert sent his "black sheep" letter, Augustine seemed to have sent a response not by post but through the deed of a gift—to Robert's son, Grandison. If it was a response, then the short, efficient deed document was deeply passive aggressive. Augustine wanted "all men by these presents" to know that he was giving this gift "in consideration of the natural love and affection which I have and bear to my Grandson Grandson [sic] son of Robert Leftwick [sic]." Like many of the court documents of the time, the deed was dictated to someone who did not spell names correctly, but the repetition of "Grandson" as a mistake for "Grandison" seems to emphasize—this gift was definitely not for Robert. Augustine made no mention of any love or affection for Robert. Instead, he filed the deed in the courthouse so that the official document would "hereby warrant and defend the right and title" against any claims—he made sure Robert's debt collectors could not touch the "gift." The document was a major slap in the face to Robert, a sign that Augustine would protect and enrich his grandson but make no move to help his son.

It was also a rupturing, traumatizing document. The "gift" was a child named Winston. He is described as "a certain negro Boy (Slave)." No other information is given about this child whose life was suddenly upended by Augustine's whim. It was not uncommon at the time for enslavers to give children away from their parents—and it was a horrifically cruel thing to do to them and their families. If my reading of the situation through their documents is correct, then in giving Winston to Grandison, Augustine focuses on the wealth of his grandson and on sending a clear-cut message to his estranged son. There is no mention made in any official records of how it affected young Winston.

When he was separated from his family and displaced to Russell-ville, Winston joined Lewis, John, and Garry in living in Robert's home. Grandison would have grown up with these boys, probably cared for by Treacy and Polly and others. Most of their fates are lost to history. We don't know what life was like for the enslaved people in that home as the financial pressure built, but we can only imagine it was intensely stressful.

THE BLOWS FOR THEIR HOUSEHOLD KEPT COMING. IN ROBERT'S MARCH 1820 letter to Joel, Robert mentions the illnesses of his wife, his mother, and one of the women he enslaved, possibly Polly or Treacy. They thought Priscilla might be pregnant ("the nine month fever"), but instead, it proved to be a condition that continued with no pregnancy.

At some point in 1820 or early 1821, Priscilla died. In September 1821, Robert's mother died. In November 1821, the first and smallest of Robert's debts came due. The due dates of the others loomed closer and closer as each day passed.

His business partners faced mounting financial trouble of their own. In addition to the enormous debt racked up in their mercantile business, Amos Edwards had apparently not turned in all of the money he gathered as a tax collector for the US Treasury. In February 1821, the Treasury sued him for $4,052.98—more than one hundred thousand dollars today.

By early 1822, Robert Leftwich was a desperate man with desperate friends.

And then he was handed an opportunity so risky, with the possibility of such an enormous payout, that it seemed feasible he might reverse his fortune completely. By February 1822, Robert had left Russellville for what should have been a short trip, a few months at most. He took with him an enslaved man who presumably acted as a valet or "body servant" who would remain unnamed despite the prolific documentation about the trip. Grandison and presumably Winston went with him too.

The locations of everyone else in Robert's household remain mostly unknown as his careening adventure began. Treacy and Garry disappear from official documents. Polly, Lewis, and John, who were supposed to be sold in November 1822, were not; they either stayed in Kentucky or possibly went with Grandison and Winston. At some point in 1822, Polly gave birth again—to a third son named James. But how they spent those years is forever forgotten.

The focus of recorded history stayed firmly on Robert Leftwich who—in traveling from Kentucky to Tennessee—had no idea he was about to suddenly, unexpectedly enter the future history of Texas.

CHAPTER 13

O n March 6, 1822, almost six months after Iturbide's triumphant
ride through Mexico City, the Nashville *Whig* published the news
that Spain had finally been defeated. On that same day, several miles
upriver, the Russellville *Weekly Messenger* announced that the "President,
Directors, and Company of the Bank of Kentucky" had filed a bankruptcy
suit against Robert, Edwards, and others involved in the failed mercantile business. Now that the lawyers were involved, it was just a matter of
time before collectors tracked down Robert and Edwards in Tennessee.

For Robert, at least, it would be too late—by March 6, he and his com-
panions were hell bound for Mexico, hot on the heels of Stephen F. Austin.

A LAND-HUNGRY GROUP OF SEVENTY SLAVEHOLDING WOULD-BE INVESTORS
from Kentucky and Tennessee calling themselves the "Texas Association"
had been waiting for news that Mexico had a new government. They
were some of the best-connected leaders in Tennessee society, including
an up-and-coming young lawyer named Samuel Houston. Having followed the rumors of political unrest in Mexico, the group had evidently
been preparing for a while. By the time the news hit the Nashville papers,
they had already implemented their plan.

The Texas Association needed a delegate to represent their interests in Mexico: Ideally someone with experience as a mediator who could doggedly pursue their goals and endure the tedium and bureaucracy of pushing paperwork through a newly formed government. Someone with few family ties who could be gone for an indeterminate amount of time. Someone desperate enough to go with only a few days' notice into a war zone with a contested government to try to talk newly minted politicians into granting a group of Anglos in questionable financial situations tracts of land in exchange for the promise to become good Mexican citizens. Someone who could subtly imply they would be non-slave-owning Catholics, even though they had zero intention of emancipating their slaves, or changing their religious views.

They found that smooth-tongued, just-reckless-enough representative in Robert Leftwich.

The first step of their campaign for land in Texas was an open letter to the Mexican government asking for a large grant of cotton-growing land that they called "the Memorial." Like the loyalty document Slowman Reese signed to prove he supported the Patriot cause, it was a pledge committing the men to an investment in the hopes of securing the grant.

The letter was written in the typically florid language of the time. The Texas Association wanted to make sure Mexican government officials knew they were always on the side of the rebels against Spain. And now that the rebels had won, they hoped the Mexicans would open up Texas, which they called "an unappropriated and extensive wilderness"—in spite of the fact that Texas had many occupants, though few of European descent—to "an industrious, honest, and agricultural people." In page after page, they effusively praised the new government, positioning themselves as humble farmers, coming—hats rhetorically in hand—to ask for a chance to be virtuous and free in Mexico. It is unclear whether or not the Mexican officials read between the lines and knew that, when the would-be-landowners extolled the "virtues" of industrious farming, they planned to rely on enslaved laborers for that work.

They were Virginia Trading Company–level capitalists dressing themselves up in freedom-seeking-Puritan tropes.

Robert and another delegate, Andrew Erwin, would have to walk a fine narrative line. On the one hand, they would have to obfuscate the truth enough that Mexican officials did not suspect that the group had no intention of giving up their slaves. On the other hand, as the delegates reported back home about their mission in Mexico, they had to convince the investors waiting in the US that the government was not a threat to the institution of slavery—otherwise the enslavers would refuse to move, and their business endeavor would fail. Any hints of political unrest in Mexico could prompt skittish investors to pull out, potentially leaving the leaders on the hook if the land grants did come through.

The delegates had to tell each group exactly what they wanted to hear in order to be successful, ideally without either side fully recognizing what they were up to. This kind of language, what George Orwell called over a century later "doublespeak," would prove to be Stephen F. Austin's specialty.

But in those early days before they met Austin, Robert and Erwin were the Texas Association's brand managers, the keepers of these dueling narratives. They had a strict means of communicating—Erwin wrote their official letters to his son, who remained in Nashville. Erwin's son then passed them around as circulars. All other correspondence was forbidden so that no individual could profit or learn more than the rest of the group. They signed the circulars "D.T.A."—Delegates of the Texas Association—and Robert kept copies of all of them in his private diary. A hundred and fifty years later, the diary would be turned into one of the encyclopedic books about the land.

IN THE FEW DAYS BEFORE HE LEFT, ROBERT WROTE HIS UNCLE JOEL HE had been "taken captive by a little fascinat[ing] girl." She was seventeen and she lived in Nashville. Assuming my dates are correct, he was around forty-four at the time; his wife had been dead a year or less, and his son was sixteen. Robert calls this young woman "handsome" and "highly accomplished"—and he tells Joel that "by the by" she has "a little fortune of fifteen thousand dollars which in these hard times no man would refuse."

The "little girl" was almost the exact age of Polly.

With nothing but exorbitant debt to his name, Robert had little chance in persuading the young woman's family he would be a good husband. Her income would have provided some financial stability for him, but not enough for him to make a large dent in what he owed. But if he could convince Mexican officials to give the Texas Association the grant, come back in a few months with money and the grateful respect of Tennessee's leading men, and secure the fortune and attachment of a young woman—the future glittered for Robert in early March 1822.

The delegation left Nashville for New Orleans possibly as early as March 3 with the documents and presumably enough funds to cover their few months of travel. Before they left, Amos Edwards privately entrusted Robert with an exorbitant amount of cash—$6,500, the equivalent of more than $160,000 in today's currency. By giving the money to Robert, Edwards later indicated he hoped to invest heavily in Texas land. But he also successfully kept the cash out of the hands of the debt collectors.

In turn, Robert left Grandison with Edwards and his wife to attend school in Nashville. There is no mention of what happened to Polly and her boys, or anyone else in Robert's household. Whether they stayed behind in Kentucky—free from their capricious master, though unsure about his fate—or stayed near Grandison in Tennessee is unknown. Because Polly remains a part of the family's story, it is clear that somehow, Robert was able to keep her and her sons away from his debtors.

Robert pulled out of town with the Memorial—and Edwards's cash—in the nick of time. The debt collectors could not touch Robert in Mexico. He had pockets full of cash, the pull of powerful friends, and the vision of an idyllic Texas—where he could make a windfall, get the girl, and finally gain his father's respect—to spur him forward.

ON MARCH 8 OR SOON AFTER, THEIR STEAMBOAT ARRIVED IN NEW OR-leans. They secured other investors for their grant. They began collecting reference letters supporting their cause from well-connected business-men. They presumably gathered what supplies they needed for their trip. They left within days, setting out not through Texas, but around.

At the end of their voyage across the Gulf of Mexico, they docked in Veracruz, one of the last strongholds in Mexico controlled by Spanish forces. The new leader of the country, Iturbide, had already declared independence in Mexico City, gotten his golden keys, and had his pompous parade. But his rule was highly disputed and, with a harbor packed full of Spanish ships waiting to take their soldiers back to Europe, the port was a tinderbox.

It took weeks to sort out who was in charge and get permission for the Delegates of the Texas Association and the people traveling with them to enter the country; it took them longer to leave the port than to journey from Nashville to Veracruz. During their delay, a friend of Stephen F. Austin's wrote in a letter: "There is every probability that Mr. Robert Leftwich will receive a Grant of Land . . . In my Opinion the Austin Grant will have as much to fear from the encroachment of new grantees as from any other cause."

As it turned out, that analysis was right: By the end of the year, there would be nearly a dozen petitions to the new Mexican government for settling on Texas land, including petitioners from Ireland and Germany who many government officials were more inclined to work with because of their Catholic faith and because their countries didn't pose the same kind of political threat as US, British, and French citizens.

On April 13, Robert, Erwin, and the people they traveled with were finally allowed to leave Veracruz and began their journey into the interior. Their circular letter to John Erwin, dated May 11, 1822 and published in the Nashville *Clarion* later that summer, barely mentions the weeks languishing at the port. The letter designed to be their first circular is essentially an advertisement for other investors about the adventures and promises ahead for the Texas Association.

In the style of visiting dignitaries, they wrote that they passed through an "open sandy barren country" where they "suffered from the dust and heat," but soon "ascended the mountains on one of the best paved roads we ever travelled." Erwin and Robert rode on litters slung between the saddles of two mules, allowing the men to "sit or lie at perfect ease," all the way into what would soon be called Mexico City.

And then, at the end of the letter, what seemed like throwaway lines would later haunt them: "We expect to return home . . . through Texas, unless detained longer than we expect. We [hope] to be home in August. It is uncertain whether this government will be Imperial or Republican."

THEY REACHED THE CAPITAL CITY ON APRIL 26, 1822. WITHIN DAYS, Austin arrived from Texas to protect the initial land grant his father had been granted by the Spanish government—the one that he already had colonists living on. The Delegates of the Texas Association met Stephen F. Austin at the US consul's house party on April 30. A little more than a week later, Austin was the delegates' "room companion" at a hotel at No. 26 Calle de los Cocheros and they were planning the route of their return trip through Texas. The various Anglo delegates in Mexico shared goals in common; there was plenty of land in Texas to go around and, in those heady early days, the groups easily combined forces.

In the weeks after they arrived, getting permission to colonize Texas seemed like it would be simple enough. In late March, the Mexican Congress had formed a committee to begin hammering out the stipulations of a new colonization law. Robert and the other delegates called on Congressmen and well-connected officials to explain who the Texas Association was and persuade them to support their petition when the law came to a vote. They were prolific and enthusiastic, sometimes calling on as many as three Congressmen per night.

News had just arrived that the government of the United States had officially recognized the independence of Mexico. Many members of the Mexican Congress were eager to receive American delegates. One of the officials was so interested in meeting with the Texas Association that he came to Robert's suite when Robert took ill and couldn't leave his room for a few days.

The Delegates of the Texas Association certainly encountered some resistance from Mexican officials too—Catholic groups from Ireland and Germany had special pull with some members of Congress over the groups from the United States. And there were factions within Mexico who did not want enslavers to move into Texas at all. But that resistance did not seem strong enough to the delegates to stop the colonization process; as Robert wrote in May, "little doubt remains" that the grants would be passed quickly. The Delegates of the Texas Association sent their petition to the government committee on May 18.

It was all right there at their fingertips, waiting only on a couple of discussions and a few signatures, and then they would set out for Texas with papers in their pocket that ensured they were going to be very rich men. Instead, that very night, all hell broke loose in the city.

There had been a sharp uptick in tensions between the ruling general, Iturbide, and several members of Congress. He accused eleven Congressmen of being a part of a plot to turn Mexico back to Spain. Congress retaliated by removing Iturbide loyalists and spreading word that they were thinking about limiting the size of his ruling army. The country seemed poised to become a republic, which would have meant that Congress had the power over Iturbide.

On the same day that the Texas Association petition made it to the committee's office, a mass demonstration erupted after darkness fell. Shouts shattered the nighttime silence in a resounding—critics later said, a suspiciously well-organized—chorus: "Viva Agustín I, Emperador de México!" The demonstration spread throughout the city, as growing crowds called for Agustín Iturbide to be declared the first of his name— the new emperor of Mexico. Iturbide feigned reluctance, but within two days, he accepted the role. The government had become an imperial one.

As one historian put it, "That shout delayed the colonization of Texas for three years."

CHAPTER 14

The weeks following Iturbide's declaration as emperor were an exhausting combination of chaos, confusion, and tedium. The circulars the delegates sent that Robert copied in his diary gave postcard-like highlights of their trip: Negotiations were not easy, but they continued their dogged lobbying of members of Congress. A group bribed Mexican officials for the same land the Texas Association wanted and—after a lot of tense negotiations—the Delegates of the Texas Association changed the boundaries on their request. Iturbide moved into his new role as emperor. Political tensions ratcheted up. Mexican officials who had been receptive now seemed increasingly repulsed by American requests. The delegates had to walk a fine line; as Robert put it, "frequently all was lost from grasping at too much."

On July 28, 1822, Robert wrote he was too ill to leave his room. On July 31, Andrew Erwin—who had only committed to staying in Mexico for a short time—left for the United States, riding through Texas hoping to see the land for which they were petitioning the government. After that, Robert was left alone in Mexico.

His tone became querulous. He was one of fifteen Americans invited to Iturbide's coronation—the only memorable moment in an otherwise wearisome summer. The waiting and cajoling and partying—what we might now call networking—wore on him. His illnesses (which he never explained) came and went, taking a toll on his health. His money was running low fast and would not last long in an environment where political decisions favored the highest bidder. "Such is this uncertainty in their progress in business, that those who are waiting on them shoud. [*sic*] have a great share of patience and his purse well lined with gold," Robert wrote on June 2, 1822. He was neither patient nor rich.

By the end of the summer, three new colonization bills out of Congress quashed the hopes of the Anglo delegates. It was clear Congress preferred the land to go to native Mexicans. If Americans or other foreigners did get the land, all three bills required that they had to be Catholics. And most importantly, all three mandated the abolition of slavery. As Austin put it plainly, "The principal difficulty is slavery."

Colonization wasn't the only thing in front of the new congress, of course. They were trying to write a constitution. The country was dead broke, and they needed to build financial systems to run the government. They also had to contend with an increasingly out-of-control new emperor. Iturbide had a low tolerance for dissent; he shut down newspapers that criticized him and jailed his political opponents. He argued with congressional leaders on everything. In October 1822, Iturbide took a radical step and dissolved Congress completely, imprisoning several Congressmen, including those Robert had called some of "our greatest friends."

Robert's letters grew more and more aggrieved. While the Texas Association threw Erwin a thank-you dinner in Nashville, Robert was left alone in Mexico trying to do a job that was becoming increasingly impossible. He decided it was time to cut his losses and leave.

Iturbide sent Robert a personal message, telling him to hold on, that soon Robert would get a grant and find "satisfaction without the least delay." As good as his word, Iturbide replaced the jailed Congressmen with his own handpicked junta and, in November, the new junta passed a colonization bill. Robert was elated; the bill just required Iturbide's signature to become law.

But things kept coming up. Iturbide had tension with a brigadier general, Antonio López de Santa Anna, which took him away from the

capital for a time. Then there were feasts, processions, and parties in
Iturbide's honor that continued through the Christmas season. Finally,
Iturbide signed the colonization bill into law on January 3, 1823.

The law mandated the slow abolition of slavery in Mexico by ending
the slave trade and ensuring enslaved children be freed when they turned
fourteen; it was not the proslavery law the empresarios had been lobbying for. But it was at least a colonization law after almost a year of
waiting that left the door open for the Anglo settlers to arrive. Robert
decided to get his grant now and worry about spinning a narrative to slaveholders later.

He fired off letter after letter to the Mexican officials he had been
networking with, trying to get his petition approved now that a law had
been passed and signed. On February 2, 1823, he and Austin sat outside
the office of one representative for seven hours. Spanish-speaking Austin was especially effective at convincing officials his settlers would be
loyal Mexican citizens; Robert, who was learning the language, was
right beside him.

They were trying to stay ahead of the next political storm. The country was, Robert wrote, "in a state of anarcky [sic]."

In mid-February, Austin got his land grant officially recognized.
Robert assumed his would be right behind Austin's. They made plans to
leave together. Robert wrote the Texas Association, begging for funds to
make up for spending almost a year of his time representing them.

Two days later, he wrote his Uncle Joel a more hopeful letter than
he'd sent off in months. He'd received word that Grandison was doing
well. And he thought he still had a shot with the "fascinating little girl"
in Nashville; despite probably being closer to fifty than to forty, Robert
wrote, "I shall not be surprised even to pass currently on my return for
twenty-five which is the greatest age that an old Bachelor or old maid
ever lived to see."

He then copied for Joel a line he had written to that young woman
to show "how hard an old colt can love" again. As he apparently told her,
"The impressions made on me by you the lovely object of all my wishes

will remain untill [*sic*] the Catastrophe that launches us into the Ocean of forgetfulness."

ROBERT'S HOPEFUL MOOD WAS SHORT-LIVED. ON MARCH 19, 1823, ITUR-bide abdicated his throne. The republican army led by Santa Anna marched into Mexico City on March 27.

Robert had not officially gotten his land grant yet, and with a new government in power, it might have been worthless paper even if he had. He switched sides immediately, calling Iturbide a "traitor" and Santa Anna "a young but intrepid officer." Now the empresarios in Mexico had to begin again, petitioning a brand-new government for the right to settle in Texas. Robert submitted another request on April 12.

Austin's grant arrived on April 14—the only approval given by the committee under the new government. On April 18, Austin took his grant and went back to Texas. Left behind, on that same day, Robert petitioned the Mexican government again. Nothing happened. Iturbide was exiled to Europe in May 1823.

The weeks turned into months. Robert submitted multiple petitions. With Austin gone, he grew closer to other empresarios who were also waiting. One of them was Haden Edwards, a brother of Amos Edwards, who was Robert's business partner in Russellville and the guardian of Grandison. Possibly at the behest of Amos, Haden Edwards lent five thousand dollars to Robert, who would otherwise have been financially destitute.

By January 1824, Austin was already welcoming the next round of legal newcomers into his colony and writing letters to interested settlers in the United States, enticing more to come. Meanwhile, sheriffs in Kentucky issued an execution against Robert's estate, trying to get back some of the exorbitant debt he owed with his business partners. As Robert bled cash and waited for unmoving bureaucracy, knowing his assets were being possessed back home, Austin sent letters with news of his growing colony.

Robert sank further into depression.

IN THE SPRING AND SUMMER OF 1824, THE MEXICAN CONGRESS DEBATED their border policies as they tried to forge a national constitution. The issues of slavery and immigration to Texas were inextricably linked. These were not philosophical debates, they were political decisions with critical economic, cultural, and moral implications for a new country.

On one side, the argument to curb unwanted immigration was relatively straightforward: slavery was morally wrong and should be outlawed. Many Mexican officials wanted to end the practice in the country completely. In fact, the debate for many of them was not *if* slavery would be abolished in Mexico but *when*—whether it was better to stop the practice completely and deal with the fallout of following their beliefs or live with it as a necessary evil with a mandated end date to give enslavers time to mitigate the effects and enslaved people time to adjust to new lives. For people who held this position, allowing new enslavers to migrate to the territory in Texas made absolutely no sense.

And yet, there were others—even those who opposed slavery—who were in favor of what they positioned as commonsense border policy that allowed well-regulated immigration by Anglo enslavers. Mexico worried about the vacuum of power on their northern border if they did not vet which settlers came to Texas and on what terms. People were already coming, but some Mexican officials argued they would continue to see an influx of fugitives and smugglers, rather than organized communities who would "civilize" Texas. It was not only the age-old European view that indigenous people are "savages," though it was that too—it was also the awareness that unregulated prime farmland with ocean access held a pull in land-hungry times. Plus, they argued, it would be a pragmatic policy: Mexico needed money, and taxing Anglo enslavers in the explosive 1820s cotton market was potentially very lucrative.

On the extreme end of the border controversy were those who wanted much more open borders. The future Anglo leaders of Texas— and their political allies who hoped to profit with them—pushed actively and directly for slavery without limitations. Robert, who enslaved people, clearly had no moral concerns about it; neither did most of the empresarios hoping to work with Anglo settlers. Austin did not necessarily like slavery, but he liked making money from enslavers. The laxer the border policies were into Mexico, the more they stood to gain.

In 1824, politicians in Mexico remained in a quagmire about border control for months. Eventually, their only way forward was to agree to disagree. They kicked the question about slavery to individual states—meaning that those who governed the territory in Texas could choose to enslave people and other Mexican states could choose to outlaw the institution. In August of that year, Congress passed yet another new national colonization law. And on October 4, the national constitution officially passed.

Because Texas did not have enough representatives to be its own territory, it was lumped together with the neighboring territory. The state officially became Coahuila y Tejas, with the capital city of Saltillo. After more than two years of lobbying national representatives in Mexico City, the empresarios now had to start over petitioning new state representatives. The so-called Baron de Bastrop—the Dutchman who had been in San Antonio and originally helped Moses Austin get his land grant in 1821—was in Saltillo. He remained a close friend and ally of Stephen F. Austin, and the other Anglo empresarios. He lobbied tirelessly on their behalf to pass a new state colonization law that would open the door for an influx of Anglo immigrants across the border.

Austin would come back to the Constitution of 1824 often over the next several years. The Mexican government's promise to allow slavery in states like Coahuila y Tejas would be the basis for his legal arguments later that, if the government could change its mind and outlaw slavery and therefore slaveholding immigrants, then the state had the right to fight back. A decade later, Austin and others would even turn that promise from the Mexican Constitution of 1824 into a flag.

You could say that an idea that would become so dominant for the region in later years was born then: that a state could secede from a nation over the right to control its own laws—especially when it comes to slavery. The right to own slaves would consistently be the driving political position of Texas leadership—in Mexico, as an independent Republic, and as a new state in the US—for the next forty years.

BY 1824, WHICH WOULD BE ROBERT'S LAST FULL YEAR IN MEXICO, THE players were all moving into position for the coming conflict. Santa Anna was in power, Sam Houston was getting updates on Texas, Stephen F. Austin was settling colonists, and Mexican politicians were debating federalism and who got to make the decision about whether slavery was legal.

While those debates slowed Robert's professional ambitions, they were life or death discussions for Polly and her sons and the tens of thousands of other enslaved people whose futures hung in the balance. Even as their stories have been lost to history because they were not documented in troves of letters and documents and diaries, I wonder what this time was like for them—whether or how much they knew about the political arguments swaying back and forth, with their whole lives at stake.

Several state-level abolitionists in Mexico fought valiantly to include a provision that any slave was free the minute they stepped foot in Texas, but it was not successful; Bastrop later congratulated himself on keeping that provision from being included. It would have ended the empresarios' plans to bring slaveholders to Texas. As it was, the tension between abolitionists on one side and empresarios and their allies on the other simmered on—even after the state colonization law was finally passed in March 1825.

ON APRIL 15, 1825, AFTER MONTHS OF PETITIONING STATE OFFICIALS IN Saltillo, Robert finally got word he was approved to establish a colony for eight hundred families in Texas on a 1.5-million-acre land grant. The last and final grant petition was not on behalf of the Texas Association, but in his own name. He'd also had a personal windfall of his own: in addition to finally getting his grant, he left Mexico with one-sixth of another large land grant, that of Haden Edwards—Amos's brother. Robert never revealed how he came into such a large stake in someone else's grant. Some historians speculate he might have won it at cards.

After more than three years of waiting, Robert's tone in his letters was euphoric.

When he left Mexico, Robert still didn't go to Texas. He went back by boat through New Orleans, arriving on June 25, 1825. From New Orleans, he wrote his Uncle Joel a long letter telling him several things he must have hoped Joel would spread around. Robert was now a militia leader—"Commander-in-Chief" of his new "colony militia." He said this honor was "received unsolicited," but came about because his years in Mexico had "inspired them with the highest confidence and friendship." In truth, Robert had asked for a title and a leadership role in the militia when he submitted his land grant petition.

Concluding the letter, Robert laid out his plans to Joel—to head back to Tennessee and win the hand of the "fascinating little girl." He made it back to Nashville by mid-July. By then, the young woman had already married someone else.

There in Tennessee, Robert told the assembled Texas Association in their July 23, 1825 meeting that he had not gotten a contract in all of their names, as they expected, but only in his own. Robert felt he had reached the limit of what he owed the investors in Tennessee since they were no longer funding him; instead, he planned to charge them three thousand dollars a year for the time he had spent representing them without pay in Mexico and retain one-seventieth stake in that grant. He told the assembled investors he would sell it to them—for a sum of ten thousand dollars.

The group immediately went into an uproar. One man was appointed to negotiate with Robert. The others put out a call that all investors in the Texas Association had less than a month to pay $250 or else they would no longer have a stake in Texas land.

After so many years of waiting, many of the original seventy signers were not interested in the endeavor anymore—some had moved on, while others might have felt it was not worth the risk of losing the people they enslaved since word of Mexican efforts to end slavery had reached the United States. When they finally got all of the money in, Robert had to take a reduced amount: only eight thousand dollars.

He signed a contract with the investors in August 1825, with one line in the contract reading that the colony would still be called "Left-wich's Grant." Robert officially owned the land for four months, from April to August 1825. He hoped his name would live on in Texas history.

After all the years he spent negotiating land grants, Robert finally made it to Texas in early 1826. But he headed for Edwards's colony and would never step foot on Leftwich's Grant. And his future in Texas would be much shorter and bleaker than he had hoped when he set out from Nashville, full of grit and promise, all those years ago.

AS FOR THE LAND THAT WAS BRIEFLY LEFTWICH'S GRANT, IT WOULD never be called by that name. A group led by Sterling Robertson left for Texas in November 1825 to explore the grant, and it would eventually become "Robertson's Colony." They stopped first in Nacogdoches at Haden Edwards's settlement.

According to some stories, Mexican officials turned them away, saying the only people allowed to cross the border were colonists for Edwards's or Austin's colonies—ones that had the correct paperwork. Robertson and the other would-be settlers were, in the words of one local historian, "undaunted." They went around Nacogdoches, setting a course that others followed.

The first settlers on the land grant Robert Leftwich had spent years trying to secure came without the documents Mexican officials required. As they spread the news back to other economic migrants hoping to come to Texas, they told them exactly which route to take. They gave a name to that illegal entryway across the border into Mexico, where they hoped to set up new lives with better economic opportunities than they could find at home.

They called their route the "Tennessee Road."

CHAPTER 15

From the moment I made the connection that I am living on land Robert owned, I was riveted by his story. His presence gave me a tie to the history of Texas I had never experienced before. A distant relative—a novelist and historian—wrote an unpublished document about Robert called "Our Family's Man in Mexico," and that felt right to me. Robert was a representative of the Texas Association in Mexico City in the early 1820s, but he was also a representative of my family to some of the most seminal moments in Texas history. Even though there are several generations—and his uncle's deeply buried family secret—separating us, it felt from the beginning like Robert belongs to me somehow. Even calling him "Robert" rather than "Leftwich," like a journalist and scholar should, made him familiar to me. In collapsing this distance, I started to feel that I was rooting for him as I discovered the story of his past.

Those feelings of sympathy for Robert and his frustrations in Mexico were instilled in me early on in every history and literature class in my entire education from kindergarten through college. He was genuinely tenacious in the face of political chaos in pursuit of his goals. The history of Texas, like the United States, is full of narratives written by educated men in power either about themselves or about other men like them. Every story has a conflict that the protagonist must face, one they usually overcome; Robert's fits the formula. If you frame the story just right, crop certain details, and cut the eventual awkward ending, Robert gets the grant and has his name in Texas history.

I knew I could have done that, just stopped with "Robert finally made it to Texas in early 1826" and let the story be triumphant—the hero riding into the sunset toward his next adventure.

Actually, Robert could have done that work himself. If he were a better writer than he was—as evidenced by those disastrous "Ocean of forgetfulness" lines he copied for Joel—or if he kept his diary not as a public record for the Texas Association investors but as a private place to explore his own thoughts while in Mexico, he could have written a book that would have made him a figure of national or international interest. It might have become a staple of nineteenth-century travel literature. He had everything he needed to succeed in that genre—time alone in a captivating locale, a space in which to write, and an angsty personality that focused intensely on exactly how and when he had been wronged.

There are dozens of examples of fiction and nonfiction travel books by writers who journey to a foreign place and use their time among people who are different from them to examine themselves and their own place in the world. They question their existence. They face the demons from their past. I have always loved those kinds of travel books. I have also experienced the bureaucratic frustrations of visa applications lost in a labyrinthine process for months. I have stood, lonely and alone, in a foreign country away from every connection I've ever known and faced my own mortality.

The few extant personal letters show that Robert was exploring what Vivian Gornick called "the inviolable self," one of the constant ideas of nineteenth- and twentieth-century memoirs and essays. Gornick frames it as "something we call our real selves." It is the "I" at the center of who we are—our soul or core personality, the part of each of us that is contained and limited and marvelously unique. Memoirs trace the arc of that inviolable self becoming something more, growing into a more enlightened or insightful version of the narrator who began the story. Robert came close to that in some of his letters to Joel Leftwich when he wrote about being a black sheep or missing his father's love; if he were more self-reflective and aware, he might have written a compelling memoir not just recording the details of his time in Mexico but of his own internal growth.

While I was wrestling with how to frame Robert's story—which details to keep and which to leave out, how to balance the volume of information about Robert against the sparse mentions of Polly and her family—Gornick's phrase about the "inviolable self" came up one time in a class discussion with some of my brilliant graduate students. It clicked for me then—why I had such a complicated reaction to Robert, and the implications of his story for this moment in the history of Texas and for me in particular.

In his letters, Robert intensely centers his own inviolable self while actively violating others. And historians have followed his lead in that, writing about Robert's concerns and desires, Robert's disappointments and frustrations. In Mexico, Robert prioritizes what is best for him— what he wants, what he is denied, how he will make money, how he can thrive. To achieve those things, he is willing to intentionally swindle a government, promising to obey their laws about slavery while dashing off letters that reveal every intent to do exactly the opposite. For Robert—and, more broadly, for the Texas Association investors and other empresarios— the ends unquestionably justified the means. And even when he hovered at the precipice of bankruptcy, when it seemed like he had lost it all, Robert and his larger society always viewed his internal self—but also his external body—as inviolable.

His body and his life would remain unviolated by others. No one would sell him to pay off his debts. No one would physically harm him or take away his autonomy. Even if, in his worst-case scenario, he ended up in jail, he had rights and friends with connections and a smooth tongue. He would probably end up just fine.

Robert's story begs a question that feels to me like one of the foundational issues we are debating right now in Texas: Whose selves do we assume to be inviolable? And whose selves do we view as legally, culturally violable?

IN THE 1820S, THE LINES AROUND THOSE QUESTIONS WERE VERY CLEAR.
The fact that many people in my family trafficked and enslaved others
was never a secret from me—*Corinth and Its Kinfolk* mentioned it freely
and my parents talked about it openly and honestly with us kids. I remember one story in particular: the Jones family, who married Sally
Reese's descendants, sold an enslaved family to finance their move out
of Tennessee, but they took a lesser price in order to keep the family together. If the details of the story as I heard them are correct, it was probably the trip in the 1840s where the Reese clan went to Texas first, and
then turned back, staying in Arkansas instead. I remember talking to
my great-aunt about it, though I'm not sure if she's the person who first
told me the story; she felt proud that her ancestors had been willing to
make less money in order to keep a family unit intact.

I was a teenager at the time. When I told my dad what my great-
aunt said later, he pointed out that the sale of people was horrific, full
stop. It bothered him that his aunt felt compelled to mitigate the act, to
point to it and say, "Well, at least they were slightly better than other
people."

My great-aunt's argument that it was a different time with different
values was one that had been passed on to her; before that, it must have
been used by various family members over several generations to mini-
mize the Joneses' sale of an entire family. But my research for these
stories has brought home to me even more fully that, even by the standards of their time, plenty of people who benefited from slavery recognized the moral depravity at the heart of the system. They changed their
viewpoints and their lives completely as a result of their own moral
awakening.

It happened on a widespread scale: In Mexico in the 1820s—and, as
I'll explain more later, in England at the turn of the nineteenth century—
abolition became the predominant worldview. And it happened at the
individual level: the story of David Rice, Slowman's preacher who went

from being supported by slaves in Virginia to preaching abolition in Kentucky, was one of many that I uncovered.

If I want my critiques of the past to serve as a roadmap for the present and future, this feels like a critical framework to wrestle with. Choosing to view our rights as inviolable, but others as violable, is a large-scale choice, but also an individual one: Whose rights do we as a larger society rarely question? Who is centered in mainstream stories? Whose rights are open to legal discussion? Who do we view as less important? Who is expected to give way, to change and acquiesce, sometimes only for the convenience or comfort of others?

Robert Leftwich, in choosing to ignore the humanity of the people who served him and lived alongside him every day, had to intentionally avoid having that kind of moral awakening. He had to cover his eyes and ears to not see the effects of his actions on people with whom he necessarily had an intimate relationship. He may not have recognized that he was actively choosing—it was a choice essentially to do nothing—but especially in Mexico in the early 1820s, he must have lived with the social repercussions of blatantly benefiting off a lifestyle that the people around him found morally repugnant.

For many contemporary slaveholders, travel was the time when they took stock of the system that had become so normal in the US South. Thomas Jefferson—who lived in Paris in the 1780s as a Minister to France with James and Sally Hemings—wrestled publicly and privately there with his role as an enslaver. It would have been entirely possible for Robert to have had a moral awakening in Mexico, as did Jefferson and so many others who traveled and encountered abolitionist ideas. And Robert did not, at least not that he recorded. He never even names the man whose life was as upended as Robert's own by those years in Mexico. Even when Stephen F. Austin had a passport written up for Robert and that man when they thought he might be able to leave, it just said Robert Leftwich and his "servant."

I think that man might have been named Rufus, because that name appears in court documents later, but that is speculation on my part.

There are too many variables to know his identity with certainty. Robert recorded the minutiae of every bureaucratic activity that affected his chances of getting a land grant but never once wrote down the name of the Black man who shared those years with him.

As he moved back to the United States, reunited with his household, and moved them to Texas, Robert never considered whether Polly, Lewis, John, James, and Rufus would not have that same space to explore the motivations, gifts, interests, and desires that Robert so faithfully chronicled in himself. Their selves, in 1820s Kentucky, Tennessee, Mexico, and then Texas, remained legally violable.

I wish I could counter the narrative about his life with the story of how Polly and her boys spent those years without Robert, what Rufus thought about and witnessed if he was indeed in Mexico. But those stories are lost, part of a vast forgotten history of people whose lives were never considered important enough to be remembered, and whose bodies were unquestioningly considered violable by the people in power who captured the narratives to pass on to future generations.

CHAPTER 16

In February 1826, Polly left for Texas on board the steamboat *President* with her three sons and Rufus, accompanying Robert; it was the first time Robert would step foot in the territory he had spent so many years writing, thinking, and strategizing about. Before going to Texas, Robert returned to Tennessee and Kentucky briefly. While he was in Logan County, he sold what little land he had managed to keep from the hands of creditors: the Whipperwill land for $1,200. Probably Polly had to nurse Robert back to health for several weeks; he was ill for some time.

One of Robert's friends and his son were also on that trip, but Grandison was not with them; the young man was presumably at the boarding school from which Robert had received reports. If Grandison had been there, things might have turned out differently for Polly, her boys, and Rufus.

The fact that Polly's small family were some of the few people that went with Robert to Texas didn't stop him from exaggerating for the benefit of his relatives at home in Virginia. Along the trip, Robert posted two letters in the mail to his Uncle Joel:

> I am now one hundred miles on my route to Texas and have with me some families for that Country. It is truly pleasing to me to find that from the fine families already gone and that are preparing to

go to that Country that I shall be able in a short time to form a
Colony of such families as wou'd do credit to any part of the world
and that my long and unremitted exertions in obtaining the object
of my pursuit will afford the means of fortunes for thousands and
for myself all that I cou'd. [*sic*] ask for of the goods of this world.

The wealth and glory he had hoped for had not materialized for
Robert. But he clearly felt there was no reason to burden his family with
the truth: he was now a "Commander-in-chief" (of a nonexistent militia) leading "fine families" (seven people, five of whom he enslaved) after
"long and unremitted exertions" toward the "object of [his] pursuit." You
can almost hear the subtext: "Tell my dad that I did something with my
life and I'm as good as any of the other Leftwich kids." His final letter
from that trip is the last record we have of Robert writing Joel; there are
no remaining accounts of what Robert actually thought of Texas once he
arrived.

As far as I know, when Robert crossed with their small group over
the national border, it was the first time any of my relatives stepped foot
in the state. Polly, Lewis, John, James, and Rufus went with Robert
straight into the political hornet's nest of Haden Edwards's colony.

By the time they landed, Edwards had been in Texas almost six
months. After receiving his grant in August 1825, Edwards arrived to
find that his land was already filled with squatters—Anglo economic
migrants and fugitives who had been coming to Texas from across the
South for years—thus limiting his ability to profit from new immigrants.
Despite the fact that Mexican officials had explicitly stated that all previous settlements should be honored, Edwards set to work kicking people off the land. Over the next several months, the entire colony would
be in turmoil as the people who felt they had some claim to the land
battled with the new empresario. Leaders in Edwards's new colony were
beginning to hone tactics that would be employed more and more effectively in the lead up to the Texas Revolution and then, on a widespread
scale, in the years preceding the Civil War in the United States.

When Polly and the other enslaved people stepped foot on Texas soil, they would have been instantly free—had the Baron de Bastrop and others not been so successful the previous year in shaping the 1825 state colonization law. Still, in those months that she lived in Texas, freedom dangled closer than Polly might ever have imagined.

IN AN AREA OF MEXICO'S TERRITORY POPULATED BY SWINDLERS AND con men, Polly was unfortunate that Robert almost immediately befriended one of the most devious. He was named Martin Parmer, and his nickname was the "Ringtail Panther of Missouri." He was called that because once, during a fight, he held up his gun and yelled, "I'm the Ringtail Panther of Missouri!"

In a region populated by unsavory and idiosyncratic characters, Parmer stands out—historians often describe him with words like "eccentric." Parmer had fled to Texas from Missouri the previous year, where he had been accused of swindling money from the federal government, and ended up on what became Edwards's settlement. When his horses ran off, leaving him stranded, he lived in a hut on the property of Peter Ellis and Candace Bean.

When Polly arrived, Parmer had probably already moved out of that hut and into the house with Candace Bean. Her husband, Peter, was living in Mexico at the time; he'd lived there before as a young man and married another woman, but he left his first wife behind when he came to the United States. He became a soldier under Andrew Jackson and then a kind of mercenary for hire; he met and married Candace, though his first wife was still alive in Mexico. Eventually Peter and Candace made their way to Nacogdoches, Texas after Mexican independence. Then in 1825, he went back to Mexico City to get a land grant and also, subsequently, hooked up again with his first wife. Candace stayed behind on their land in Texas—and soon probably started a relationship of her own with Parmer.

That left Parmer's shack free. According to some family historians, Robert Leftwich and his household stayed there, though details of those days are sketchy at best. While there, Robert got a letter from the Baron de Bastrop, written near the end of May 1826. Bastrop told Robert that what the empresarios and their allies had long feared was becoming true. There was a new political threat to slaveholders' interests in Texas: an early copy of the state colonization law of 1825 had included a clause that "all the slaves who set foot on our soil would have been declared free." Bastrop had worked tirelessly to get that clause struck from the 1825 law, but now politicians wanted to add it to the state constitution. Bastrop said that, if he couldn't "succeed in removing it, or at least in modifying it, the colonies will be set back, or, to put it more accurately, they will be completely ruined." He goes on to call it "a mortal blow without anybody being able to stop it."

The language of life-or-death danger is important here: Bastrop wrote unironically as if slaveholders' lives were at stake if they could not settle in Texas. Along with Polly, Lewis, John, James, and Rufus, there were thousands of other enslaved people already living in Texas for whom this truly was a matter of life and death—not to mention the tens of thousands of people who would be trafficked into the state if Bastrop succeeded in his terms.

The mortal blow, of course, would not be felt by the enslavers, but the enslaved.

WITHIN THE FIRST MONTHS OF POLLY, HER BOYS, AND RUFUS ARRIVING in Texas, the new community they landed in was already on the edge of rebellion. The people in Haden Edwards's land grant had held an election in December 1825 for an alcalde—a Mexican official who was like a judge and mayor rolled into one. Edwards had not liked the candidate that the previous colonists put forth, and his son-in-law ran for the office and won. The original settlers accused Edwards of voter fraud. The political chief over the area, José Antonio Saucedo in San Antonio, sided with the anti-Edwards group. He overturned the results of the election in March 1826—the very month Polly arrived with Robert.

From March till about June 1826, there's very little information that can shed light on how Polly and her boys spent their days. If they were in a shack on the Beans' land, where Parmer was planting corn, it was probably a miserable place to live. Robert, meanwhile, was already getting ready to go. His health was once again struggling, and it seems he made plans to leave almost as soon as he arrived.

Court documents would later reveal that he and Martin Parmer struck a deal: he would "rent" out the services of Rufus for "ten dollars per month until Leftwich's return." Polly was left to "do such things as said Parmer might require of her as cook washerwoman." Robert also left behind his wagon, some oxen, and some farming tools. The deal implied, at least, that Robert thought he was going to return to Texas.

Those same documents cite Robert's ill health in 1826. No information is ever given that indicates the nature of what ailed him throughout his years of serving as an agent for the Texas Association, but it frequently interrupted his plans or travels. Perhaps he had been hoping that the climate in Texas would be an improvement, but it seems clear that living on the outer edges of civilization in a rough frontier community populated by thieves and scoundrels did not help his health.

The circumstances under which he left Polly, Lewis, John, James, and Rufus in Parmer's care are critically important, however—by signing that deal with Parmer, in the eyes of the law, they became indentured servants, presumably with a written contract that showed that their labor earned them a wage. Of course, they did not see a cent of that "salary," but doubtless Parmer and Robert planned to testify if need be that the money was being saved for them, or that they were compensated in some other way—ensuring that they could not be freed no matter the outcome of the debates in Saltillo.

Pseudo-indenturing the five enslaved people was both cruel and illegal. It was Robert's last act in Texas. He left at some point in June 1826.

IT WAS NOT THE END OF THE STORY FOR POLLY, LEWIS, JOHN, JAMES, and Rufus. In a pattern that would be repeated until Juneteenth almost four decades later, enslavers in power thwarted their freedom with lies and suppressed information.

Mere weeks after Robert "indentured" his slaves to Parmer, Stephen F. Austin got a pressing letter from Peter Ellis Bean in Mexico. In July 1826, Bean told Austin the news Bastrop had already written to Robert—that slavery was about to be abolished in Saltillo. Bean suggested that settlers take the people they enslaved to Mexican officials and "liberate" them through an act of "subterfuge"—as one historian put it—by "taking contracts from them to work for their former owners at stipulated wages until they had repaid their values." They would set the wage so high that the laborers working for their release could never actually attain it. As Bean wrote Austin, the slaves "will be the same to you as before and it will be no more notised [sic]."

"Indenturing" slaves was not a new idea, of course; it's not like Parmer and Robert were the first ones to think of it. But I am struck by the coincidence that Robert was scheming with Parmer—who was probably sleeping with Candace Bean—to indenture Polly and then, a few weeks later, Peter Ellis Bean wrote Austin a proposal for the same idea. Did Candace write her husband in Mexico, where he was reuniting with his first wife? Did someone else tell him about the deal Robert and Parmer had struck on his land back near Nacogdoches? Had they both independently heard about it from others? Or did Peter Ellis Bean just have the same idea around the same time his wife's lover came up with a clever way to defraud the government and extend slavery indefinitely?

I can't prove it, but it seems possible to me that the same insidious plan that Robert and Parmer hatched up inspired Peter Ellis Bean, and he rushed to tell Austin. That makes the circumstances of Polly, Lewis, John, James, and Rufus not just personally harsh. There would be wider repercussions of this act of subterfuge for other enslaved people in Texas who hovered on the cusp of freedom.

Austin thought it was a great idea. Through his connections in Saltillo, he even managed to convince politicians there to pass legislation saying that long-term contract workers were allowed to come and that their contracts would be honored in Texas.

With the slaves-as-indentured-servants scheme, Robert crossed a new legal line. Though the Memorial on behalf of the investors in Tennessee was deceptive in the fact that it did not actively disclose their plan to enslave people once they arrived in Texas, Mexican officials seemed to have been aware of the deceit, and to recognize it as part of a subtle political game. But as the government in Saltillo moved toward abolishing slavery, Robert and the other enslavers and empresarios twisted words in ways that would later become part of the fabric of Texans' political rhetoric. If they turned "slaves" into "indentured servants"—though everyone involved knew the difference was only semantic—then Black people could be legally oppressed indefinitely.

It recalls a twisting of words that happens even today. It occurred recently, when a state politician called victims of a mass shooting in Texas "illegal immigrants" even though at least some of them were legal residents, a calculated move to make their deaths less heart wrenching, to distance voters from mothers dying to protect their toddlers from a shooter with an assault weapon so those voters would not rise up in outrage.

In learning about this story, I realized how powerful specific terms have been and remain in setting the course of history. They lead to action, to acts of legislation, to policies that affect real people's lives.

WHETHER THEY KNEW IT OR NOT, POLLY, LEWIS, JOHN, JAMES, AND Rufus spent months in Texas while their freedom was hotly debated in the state capital. Following the letter from Bean and others, Austin arrived in Saltillo himself to lobby Mexican officials. They eventually secured a compromise that allowed for the slaves currently living in Texas to remain enslaved. But newspapers in the United States began reporting that slavery had already been abolished in Coahuila y Tejas—which created a public relations nightmare for the empresarios trying desperately to convince enslavers to move to their land grants.

Robert did not return to Texas to rescue Polly, her boys, and Rufus from the clutches of an unpredictable charlatan. Two months after Robert left the country, Parmer filed a suit of damages against Robert for destruction of part of Parmer's cornfield, which he said were incurred shortly after Robert had arrived in Texas, when one of Robert's oxen broke onto Parmer's property. Though it's impossible to know fully, I think because Robert had already left town, Parmer filed the suit to be able to legally keep Robert's possessions—including the people he enslaved. Together they had planned to swindle the government; after he left, Parmer planned to swindle Robert.

A few months later, Haden Edwards's campaign to kick out settlers who had been on his land for years finally exploded. The Mexican government revoked Edwards's land grant in October 1826. By December, he and several others, including Parmer, decided to secede from Mexico.

They called it the Fredonian Rebellion. They made flags. The rebellion itself consisted mostly of signing articles and making speeches about their new land they dubbed the "Fredonian Republic" in December 1826.

Their hot-air-fueled rebellion did not last long. When they learned in early 1827 that Mexican troops were on their way, the would-be Fredonians all fled across the border into the United States. Martin Parmer bolted from Texas, taking Polly, Lewis, John, James, and Rufus out of Mexico into the deep American South. Their brief brush with freedom was over.

This moment of extremism—the rupture from what social norms existed in the precarious community that settled on Haden Edwards's land before he arrived—seemed to burn out quickly. But though the Fredonian Republic was short-lived, it fomented Mexican fears that Anglo settlers were planning to rebel against the government. And it set the tone for Texians—the term Anglo Texans used for themselves in those years—about how that rebellion would take place. As one historian put it, the extremist calls of the Fredonian Rebellion and the words "Independence, Liberty, and Justice" they wrote on their flags "sparked the powder for later success."

The fiery Fredonian extremism was not extinguished but banked, ready to flare up in the coming Texas Revolution.

THE END OF THE STORY FOR ROBERT PROBABLY OCCURRED BACK IN KEN-tucky. There are no details about his death that I could find, but some family historians argue convincingly that he died before March 1828. That's the month when Parmer filed a bill of sale at a courthouse in Washington, Arkansas, claiming that Robert had not rented out his enslaved people but in fact sold them to Parmer. That Parmer felt free to file the court document almost certainly shows that the other witness to the deal whose word would have held up in court—Robert Leftwich— could no longer challenge him.

Polly, Lewis, John, James, and Rufus could not serve as witnesses in a court. Their bodies remained legally violable by a swindler, as well as the larger society in the South.

In 1830, Martin Parmer was in Vicksburg, Mississippi trying to sell Polly, her boys, and Rufus. In the kind of twist a nineteenth-century novelist might have manufactured, Grandison happened to be in town. How Grandison made the connection that Parmer had Polly, Lewis, John, James, and Rufus is unclear—perhaps he had been following Parmer, perhaps someone told him. I want to think Polly found a way to get word to him. But there will never be any way to know.

What is recorded history is that Grandison had Parmer arrested in Warren County, Mississippi. Through a deposition, Grandison proved that Parmer had swindled his father. Parmer lost the suit. He eventually went back to Texas, where he would be one of the signers of the Texas Declaration of Independence.

Presumably Polly, Lewis, John, James, and Rufus were returned to Grandison in August 1830. I wish I could say reuniting with Grandison was a happy ending for them. But after being buffeted by the gale force winds of Robert Leftwich and Martin Parmer, no one cared to write down what happened to them after 1830. At some point, Grandison ended up in Maury County, Tennessee, near Robert's brother, Jesse Leftwich, and his family. The next year, Sally Reese and her clan would sell the land Littleberry Leftwich left them and move to Bedford County, Tennessee—two counties to the east of Grandison Leftwich.

I have no way of knowing if Polly realized how close she and her children were to freedom, in those months when it was possible for enslaved people whose feet were on Texas soil to dream of being free. I am certain that her enslavers did everything they could to keep that knowledge from her. For the next few decades, the enslavers' goal of preserving the institution that allowed them to get rich was their guiding motivation. Defrauding the government by calling slaves indentured servants was one of many lies they concocted to win. As long as the ends justified the means, the act of lying never seemed to bother them much.

They continued the practice of keeping enslaved people in ignorance of their official freedom on multiple occasions, until June 19, 1865— when they could no longer control the story.

To the people in power, slavery was worth two secessions that would lead to two different wars: one with Mexico and later—using the lessons they learned during the Texas Revolution—a darker, bloodier one within the United States.

PART 3

PERRY REESE

(1818–1836)

All new States are infested, more or less, by a class of noisy, second rate men, who are always in favor of rash and extreme measures, but Texas was absolutely overrun by such men.

—SAMUEL HOUSTON

Unknown (Possibly Hugh) Reese

Slowman Reese
(Before 1750–After 1803)

Multiple siblings, most names
and dates uncertain

Sarah "Sally" Reese
(1765–1854)

10 children

James Joseph Reese
(1741–1839)
could be Slowman's nephew
or other relation

Drury Reese — **Martha Lewis**
(1774–1830)   M.   (1798–1876)

James T. Reese   **Perry Reese**   **Martha Reese**
(1816–1875)   (1818–1836)   (1823–1851)

CHAPTER 17

The first time I heard the word "genocide" in connection with the history of Texas was during research for my first book about refugees. I was interviewing a refugee advocate in Dallas who mentioned he'd been at the opening of the Dallas Holocaust Museum and learned about the genocide in Texas.

"What genocide in Texas?" I asked. At that point, I was deep into research of humanitarian crises around the world. I had many of the best scholarly works on genocide on my shelves in my office. I pulled out *Blood and Soil*, a thorough and devastating history of genocide in the history of the world, and there it was—Stephen F. Austin and the killing of the Karankawa people.

It floored me that I had never heard the story.

At the time, one of my children was taking Texas History in the fourth grade. That night at dinner, I asked her if she'd ever heard of the Karankawa people.

"Of course," she said. "My teacher told us all about them. He said Stephen F. Austin and his settlers killed them all. There are some of them still in Mexico, but almost all of them died. It was really sad."

She wrote a report that year about the Karankawa people, and I researched too—things I feel embarrassed I never knew.

The summaries from a number of sources were predominantly the

same. Five distinct groups with their own traditions and cultural attri-
butes who lived along the Gulf Coast made up the larger Karankawa
people: the Carancahuas (which the colonizers turned into "Karankawas"), Cocos, Cujanes, Coapites, and Copanos. They based the rhythm
of their lives on the seasons. They spent the winters near the bays off the
coast. The bays were rich fishing areas—a long thin island took the force
of the coastal waves, leaving the placid bays just behind the island filled
with fish. Their two most important fish species, which the Anglos would
later name "redfish" and "black drum," spawned during the late fall and
winter and into the spring. When their spawning seasons were over, the
Karankawa people moved toward the interior to hunt white-tailed deer
and sometimes bison or other large mammals.

The first recorded encounter with Europeans and the Karankawa
people were with the Spanish in 1528. More than a century later, in 1684
Frenchman Robert Sieur de La Salle's boat wrecked off the coast. The
Karankawa people gathered debris from the coast, as they always did.
The ocean washed up some blankets and other items that the Karankawa
people picked up for their use.

La Salle's soldiers accused them of stealing their property that was
on the shore, and in a response significantly outweighing the Karankawas' perceived sin, the French troops took and destroyed the Karankawas' canoes. The Karankawas' response to French aggression was the
first recorded skirmish between colonizers and Karankawa people. As a
witness reported a decade later, "Monsieur de La Salle would never have
had war" with the Karankawa people if upon arrival "he had not high-
handedly taken their canoes . . . nothing is easier than winning their
friendship."

The settlers wrote letters that described the Karankawas in ways
that emphasized their appearance as "savage" to their audience, rather
than practical: the Karankawa people walked through briar-filled un-
dergrowth with no shoes, leaving behind no footprints, which worked
well for hunting but which colonizers viewed as threatening. They smeared
their bodies with alligator grease to ward off mosquitos—an ingenious
solution for anyone who has ever faced a mosquito-infested Texas sum-

mer. They carried long bows as tall as they were, but as tales of the Karankawas' supposed great heights grew taller and taller, so the bows did as well.

When Austin came along in 1821, he was only the next in a long line of colonizers to covet the Karankawas' coastal territory. The Mexicans living in Texas, the Tejanos, passed along to Austin and his surveying expedition the now well-used characterization of the Karankawa people they had received from the Europeans before them. Austin's journals in 1821 repeat almost verbatim the stories about the Karankawa people that began with La Salle.

If my teacher taught me about the Karankawa people, I did not remember it. This is how my seventh-grade Texas history textbook described them:

> The Karankawas lived in families. In fact, in some ways the Karankawa family was similar to our own. However, the family members manufactured the tools necessary for their existence. They made pottery jars and bowls and wove baskets. Both the pottery and baskets were coated with tar for water-proofing. For hunting and war, they made bows, sometimes six feet long, from cedar.
>
> Although the Karankawas greeted the first white and black visitors with kindness, the tribes later became enemies of the newcomers. The tribes plundered the ships wrecked along the coast. Spanish, French, English, and other people came to respect and fear them.
>
> Like the Coahuiltecans, the Karankawas had almost disappeared by the time Texas became a part of the United States.

One of the things I teach students when we close read texts is to keep an eye on the verbs. Verbs in any sentence do so much heavy lifting, and you can often recognize something important by a verb phrase. If I were teaching those paragraphs in a classroom, I would begin with two phrases: "became enemies" and "had almost disappeared." As if the Karankawa people woke up one day and arbitrarily decided to hate the people who washed up on their shore, or as if they just evaporated into thin air. As if anything that followed were their choice.

In all of the books I have found about the Karankawa people, the stories are remarkably similar. One other seventh-grade textbook gave a little more insight: "European reports tell of the special treatment of children by the Karankawas. A Spanish explorer remarked that the Karankawas 'love their offspring the most of any in the world, and treat them with the greatest mildness.' Small children were carried around by either mother or father on specially made cradle boards. . . . Warfare with Europeans and other Indians eventually wiped out the remaining Karankawas."

The fact that the colonizers knew, and recorded how much Karankawa people treasured their children, makes what happened later that much more horrific. And always, the narratives end citing the extinction of the Karankawa people.

UNDERSTANDING WHAT HAPPENED TO THE KARANKAWA PEOPLE AND why—especially in the years from 1821 to 1826, as the earliest settlers in the Austin colony arrived—is critical to understanding the making and consequences of the myths of Texas. While Austin was in Mexico petitioning the government with Robert Leftwich, he was also writing letters to his earliest new colonists giving them directives. And part of the land he asked for—and eventually received—from the Mexican authorities was where the Karankawa people had lived for centuries.

On an individual level, I saw how Robert's view of himself as inviolable, but others as violable, made him act without ever considering the consequences for the other people who shared his home. On a larger cultural level, this concept became clear to me when I read the work of Kelly Frank Himmel, one of the first scholars to really examine the history of what happened to the Karankawa people after they met Stephen F. Austin. Himmel noticed a difference between Austin's stories of the Karankawa people and how he wrote and talked about other indigenous groups. Himmel calls it the "power of cultural constructions to channel behavior."

Austin had heard stories from other Europeans when he arrived that were cultural constructions—large-scale stories generally agreed upon by a group that became stereotypes or tropes or commonsensical viewpoints. He passed those views on to his colonists, which then determined the policies they enacted on an increasingly larger scale as the colony grew. The cultural stories became myths about the Karankawa people that are prevalent to this day.

The greatest myth Austin's colonists eventually told about the Karankawa people—a myth strong enough that it has survived intact for two centuries—is that they were extinct.

"The truth is, we are not extinct," Chiara Sunshine Beaumont told me. "Here I am."

CHAPTER 18

I met Beaumont at a coffee shop in central Austin called Genuine Joe. As it turns out, it's a favorite workplace we both share. In a city overrun by bougie chains, Genuine Joe retains its commitment to the kind of nineties eclectic garage-sale-chic décor that I always associate with coffee shops—ramshackle tables and chairs, assorted stools and leather sofas, paintings that are always slightly askew, a collection of plastic dinosaurs dotted throughout the space, a giant plastic *G* above the unusable fireplace. I spotted Beaumont as soon as I walked in and we made small talk while I ordered a black coffee and she got water, before sitting down at a large table with wooden slats. Beaumont wore her hair in two braids with colorful earrings of multicolored string around loops and a beaded choker necklace. We both pulled out our notebooks.

Beaumont is a mixed-media artist who posts pictures of many of her art pieces online. In researching for the interview, I found myself returning again and again to a sold 18" x 12" collage she crafted with photos and illustrations from textbooks. The emotional center of the piece is a photograph of Tosahwi, an influential Penateka Comanche leader, who also went by the name White Knife. The original photograph, taken in 1858 by W. S. Soule, was a cabinet card; Tosahwi wears what looks like a Union Army Hardee hat with a white star in the middle. In Beaumont's piece, there are other images and objects—a photo of cactuses laid on top of a 1960s-era textbook illustration of an indigenous man on horseback shooting a gun; an image of the sun breaking through clouds over a mountain; a beige scallop seashell. Over the collage, just below Tosahwi's pursed lips, Beaumont has layered the words: "EVERY-WHERE IS HAUNTED AND THERE IS NO WHERE ELSE TO GO." The letters are slightly askew, like an anonymous ransom note. Beneath it, in much smaller letters, Beaumont pasted a cutting from another textbook, a full sentence: "The Karankawas, very fierce and hostile Indians, who roamed along that part of the coast annoyed the Spaniards so much that the fort had to be moved twice."

Like her art, Beaumont's story is layered and complicated: subversive, hidden, and open in turns. She always knew that she was Karankawa; growing up, her mother told her they were the last ones because they had never heard of other family members. Their extended family lived in Corpus Christi and around South Texas, but Beaumont's mother moved to rural Virginia—not far from where I took the trip to trace Sally's family—and that's where Beaumont mostly grew up.

Beaumont's mother passed down the Karankawa traditions faithfully, as her mother had passed them on to her. Most important to Beaumont was their spirituality, which is closed practice. But many of the aspects of their culture were external. Their sport, grappling and wrestling, was something Beaumont and her siblings all learned to do. And her mother refused to let her cut her hair until she was fifteen, which was often the source of other people's questions about her life and past; Beaumont hated her long hair, but she understood her mother's reasonings and the importance of the cultural practice. Her mother instilled in her children early on a clear sense that they were respected and loved. On almost anything else besides her hair, if Beaumont could express her reasoning behind wanting to do something, her mother would allow it. She told her children she treated them with kindness and respect because they were "gifts straight from the Creator." It confounded her mother's co-workers that her mother referred to Beaumont and her siblings as "ma'am" and "sir," when they just called her "Mama."

For all of Beaumont's childhood, her family lived with the heavy

knowledge that they were the last remaining keepers of a beautiful culture that had been all but obliterated by colonists who came to Texas.
Beaumont grew up with an understanding of the myths that had been
told about the Karankawa people: First, that they were extinct, which
her very existence proved false. Second, that they were cannibals: "In
fact, it was the Spanish who crashed up on the shores who were cannibals." And third, that the fierce Karankawa warriors were seven feet tall:
"We varied in height like any other group of people." Before Europeans
arrived, Beaumont grew up learning, the ways of the Karankawa people
were peaceful and the land was shared peacefully, "as peacefully as you
could share with estranged family members from tribe to tribe." All of
that changed when the first Europeans arrived: "After years of turbu-
lence, a lot of us were killed; that was the intention of the colonizers, to
exterminate us because we were the defenders of the gulf." Groups made
it north to Oklahoma, south to Tamaulipas or Nuevo Leon, or they
stayed and assimilated with the Tejanos in the area—which is what
Beaumont's family did. To the eyes of the colonizers, they had disappeared, but they always knew who and where they were.

When Beaumont was a young adult, she and other Karankawa
began finding each other on the internet, eventually starting a Facebook
group of Karankawa Kadla—"kadla" meaning "calico," or the mixed
clans. They had an emotional first group call over Facebook Messenger,
all those squares with their faces all together on the screen. Since then,
they have organized in-person gatherings; Beaumont is part of the Five
Rivers Council of the Karankawa Kadla, which holds monthly meetings. One of the members of the council is Alexander Joseph Perez, who
is also known as Wol Ba'h Strong Wind. Perez is their language keeper;
his book *Karankawa Kadla—Mixed Tongue* came out in 2021. There are
others who have retained critical aspects of medicine or their spiritual
practices that they fit together like cultural puzzle pieces. Those whose
families passed along stories about the Karankawa traditions share the
same stories of a peaceful people with deep connections to the gulf land.
Many of them show that commitment now through environmental ac-
tivism, recently working together to stop an oil terminal expansion that

would cause the destruction of Karankawa marshland that contains ancestral artifacts.

They often gather for other reasons—sometimes just to see each other, or to hold reconnection reunions, or when someone dies. From the very first, Beaumont felt an instant connection with the other members of the Karankawa Kadla as they rebuild their extended family together. Like Beaumont, each of them thought they were the last ones.

"'Extinction,'" she says in a measured tone. "That is a big, heavy word. In my family, and in a lot of indigenous cultures, words are medicine, good or bad, and people don't think about that as much in Western culture. But knowing that they were incorrect in thinking we were extinct, that does give me a good bit of peace."

CHAPTER 19

S tephen F. Austin encountered Karankawa people on his very first trip to Texas in July 1821, mere weeks after Moses Austin's death in June, before he eventually traveled to Mexico and met Robert Leftwich and the other empresarios. To Austin, the land was laden with personal meaning—a chance to fulfill his dying father's last wishes. He wrote, "The country is the most beautiful & desirable to live in I ever saw." After surveying the area, he found the land where he wanted to start his colony, a section along the Gulf of Mexico coast from Matagorda Bay to Galveston Bay.

It was the land the Karankawa people had tended and protected for centuries.

The story as many Texas historians often tell it focuses on Austin's efforts over the next several years after spotting the land that first time. The arc of that narrative is clear: Austin worked hard lobbying, politicking, and networking in Mexico, while governing the recruits from his father's original land grant and fundraising to support his efforts. It seemed for a time he might not get the land at all, that "dark night of the soul" time period we expect our heroes—or antiheroes—to endure. That was when he knew Robert, when the camera angle of Texas history closely follows the efforts and disappointments of the Anglo empresarios in Mexico City, none more important than the "Father of Texas" himself. The climax of that narrative arc might be when he rode back into Texas in 1824, leaving the other empresarios behind, with the first land grant from the new Mexican government to an Anglo empresario and a profound sense of accomplishment. He had not only fulfilled his father's dying legacy; he'd gotten excellent coastal land that all but ensured the wealth of the future colony he would build.

Of the Karankawa people, he penned, they "may be called universal enemies to man. . . . They frequently feast on the bodies of their victims." The charge of cannibalism was one of the most potent colonizers could make against any indigenous group because it justified violence against them. If the Karankawa people were inclined to eat children, then the colonizers could justify killing them as an act of self-defense. It didn't matter that that charge was based on rumors that were greatly exaggerated, or, as Beaumont argues, based on the actions of the first Europeans who encountered the Karankawa people.

Soon the name "Karankawa" was not synonymous with peaceful fishers, potters, or hunters, nor did it connote people who cherished their children. To Austin's colonists, "Karankawa" became interchangeable with "child-killer."

The inherited colonizer story Austin received about the Tonkawa people—neighbors to the Karankawa clans—was very different. Austin wrote in his journal that they were "great beggars." Led by Austin, the settlers seem to have decided that the Tonkawa people were harmless rascals who had to be carefully watched to keep them from thievery and duplicitousness (an irony the colonists did not seem to notice). In their cultural construction, the Tonkawa people were not the colonists' equals; in the same way that American settlers always viewed people of color as needing their oversight, the Tonkawa were in need of their superior Anglo morality. The stories made them inferior but not a threat.

Of course, the Tonkawa people were also not on the land Austin wanted.

Rarely told in that story of Texas was Austin's plan for dealing with the Karankawa people who lived on the land he hoped to settle. He laid the plan out in eleven words, recorded in a diary entry from that very first trip: "There will be no way of subduing them but for extermination."

I AM RELUCTANT TO SHARE THE STORIES OF WHAT HAPPENED NEXT IN the horrifying details. There is a tendency we Westerners have to sensationalize stories—it is almost as if the recounting of violence allows us to distance ourselves from the actions. But at least in part, the answer to some of the constant, ongoing questions of our times—how we can justify allowing school shootings to continue, why it is not politically expedient to ban the assault weapons that are responsible for so many mass murders in Texas and around the country—has to do with how violence was understood, enacted, and recorded in those years. The story of what happened to the Karankawa people, and then how that story solidified into myth, reveals the instincts beneath many of the narratives in today's debates.

And, after years of interviewing persecuted and displaced people, I have learned that sometimes the first step available to those of us who care about past injustice is a relatively simple one: to actively remember what has been forgotten.

THE CLASHES BETWEEN THE TEXIANS AND THE KARANKAWA PEOPLE began almost immediately. We know about the interactions over the next few years between Austin's colonists—sometimes with Austin in command, other times under the authority of various militia leaders when he was traveling—because of letters to Austin and others, as well as oral reports passed on to their descendants.

The settlers kept Austin in the loop on news from the colony in the years when he traveled back and forth from the colony to Mexico to ensure his Spanish land grant was legal in the eyes of the new Mexican government, as well as to New Orleans for supplies and funds. One of the subjects they reported about was what the Texians called the

Karankawas' "depredations" that they responded to with their own "chastisements." The language was part of the story: they never said "We murdered Karankawa children." They said they chastised criminals or "savages" for acts of piracy or plundering. Their accounts usually began with how many Texians the Karankawas killed—as if the Karankawa attacks were unprovoked, rather than stating that settlers moved onto Karankawa-held territory and that the Karankawa people retaliated against the colonizers' acts of aggression.

As the tension between the colonists and Karankawa people escalated, Austin suggested that ten men from within the colony be hired "to act as rangers for the common defense." That phrase stuck—those ten men became the first Texas Rangers. It would eventually be an elite fighting force whose reputation became intertwined in Texas with the myth of men in white hats valiantly—and violently—defending their community.

The killings increased. In 1823, two settlers died at the hands of Karankawa warriors. One of the colonists said they rushed to see to the Karankawas' "chastisement with alacrity." He led a group of Texian men to the camp. There they scalped nineteen Karankawa people. In 1824, ninety men from the settlement tracked down some Karankawa people and killed twenty-three of them. In another incident that year, colonizers shot nine unarmed Karankawa people as they stepped out of their canoes.

One myth more than any other seems to have settled the Karankawas' fate at the hands of Austin's militia. A Texian told his grandson that in the earliest days of the colony, Karankawas raided an encampment of white colonizers on their land and carried off a little girl. There had been fighting and people had been killed; whether the settlers had provoked the attack by the Karankawa people was left out of the story. The remaining Texians followed the Karankawas and found them cooking and eating quartered meat over a fire.

They decided the meat was that of the taken little girl. As the old colonizer described it, the Karankawa people "were so completely absorbed in their diabolical and hellish orgie [sic] as to be oblivious to their surroundings and taken by surprise." The Texians killed everyone but one woman and two children. Later, a Karankawa woman showed up at another settlement asking for food. The settlers there followed her, murdering the mother and her children in cold blood.

Then, after years of escalating violence, the colonists almost made peace with the Karankawa people. On October 3, 1825, seven of Austin's settlers wrote him: "We give it as our opinion it is requisit [sic] to treat with them." The request was initiated from the Karankawa leaders, though no one recorded whether it was from the united Karankawa clans or a specific group. It seems to have been a new tactic: "They have never solicited peace until now." They communicated to the settlers that "they are tired of war and the conduct of them induces us to believe they are in earnest for they have encamped in our stock range and have disturbed nothing to our knowledge." Because of the distance at which these settlers lived from other colonizers, who were "not in their power to aid us," and because they were not sure they could defend themselves, Austin's settlers felt it would be appropriate for Austin to impose the following conditions for peace: that the settlers could "secure hostages," and that the Karankawa "not permit over three to cum [sic] to geather [sic] to one house."

But within weeks of receiving the letter asking for Austin to negotiate peace with the Karankawa leaders, that tentative peace was destroyed. In February 1826, two colonist families died in some sort of tension with Karankawa people. The reports to Austin did not give details about who instigated the incident or how. Instead, the Texians reported that a group of Karankawa people attacked two families, killing the two wives and some of the children.

The Texians' retribution was brutal and complete. A militia captain led a party of sixty colonizers and found dozens of Karankawa people disembarking from canoes on the banks of the Colorado River. No Texian was sure whether they were the same people who had attacked the two families, where they stood on the request for peace, or what their intentions were in the area.

The Karankawas could not have been part of a large marauding party. There were whole families in those canoes. Certainly, the Karankawa children—adored by their parents, held as closest to the Creator, cherished by the entire community—had done nothing to deserve what came next.

One of the men whom the militia captain sent to spy on the Karankawas was high above them, looking over the bank where they disembarked. The ground beneath him gave way. He fell and fired his gun. Hearing the shot, the men charged toward the sound, firing indiscriminately.

The militiamen slaughtered them all, including the women and children. Many of the Karankawa people tried to jump into the river to escape the gunfire. The colonizers shot them from the high ground above the river like fish in a barrel. A handful of Karankawa warriors escaped in one canoe. Austin's men tracked them down and murdered them too. The settlers later called that day the "Dressing Point Massacre"—for the "dressing down" the settlers gave to the Karankawas.

Eyewitnesses reported that the water of the Colorado River ran "literally red with blood."

THE YEARS OF ANGLO MIGRATION WERE ALL EXTREME, THE EDGE OF violence always unsheathed. But even within those chaotic, capricious years, the Dressing Point Massacre stands out. The historian of global genocide included the act in his comprehensive book, *Blood and Soil*, because it meets the definition of the term genocide—it was "total extirpation, utter destruction."

After the Dressing Point Massacre, it was not long before the Texians concluded that the Karankawa were extinct. One of the later settlers to the colony wrote that in the 1820s, "in the first settleing [sic] of Texas, the old settlers told us they were quite a large tribe of Indians, and knowing that they were always at war with the other tribes and whites, they were reduced to a very small band when I first knew them." By 1832, at a ceremony, one Texian led others in a toast to their success and praised the efforts of the "farmers of Texas" who "expelled the savage."

By 1836, Anglo historians reported that the Karankawa people had been reduced to twenty-five or thirty men. By 1858, the myth of the extermination of the Karankawa people by Texians was well established. In his slaughter of the people who defended the coastland that he wanted, Austin demonstrated the single-minded ambition that defined his dealings with Mexican authorities—he almost always got what he wanted.

Beaumont's ancestors, and the other living Karankawa people, moved away or slipped among the Tejanos. They learned Spanish and intermarried with Tejanos and other indigenous people. While the Texians may not have known about it, they kept the stories of their tribe alive for their children over two long centuries of family separation.

The Texians told a different story than the ones the Karankawa children learned. By the time I took Texas history, it had been covered up completely: I never learned that the Father of Texas sanctioned and committed genocide in order to start his colony. That is probably in part because, for a long time, no one controlled the story of Texas like Stephen F. Austin.

The Karankawa people and other indigenous groups who would share at least some of their fate—displaced from their homes and land, slaughtered by violence or disease—were not the only victims of the narratives the early Texians told. The power of cultural stories to direct the behavior of large groups of people held consequences for others, including some of my own family members.

Implicit in the stories they told in those years, in the myths that would eventually be polished up into the history of Texas, were important questions: In writing about the adventures and opportunities waiting for settlers they wanted to bring to Texas, what were the future leaders of Texas trying to sell? And what were they trying to hide?

CHAPTER 20

O n September 15, 1829, President Vicente Guerrero declared an end to slavery in Mexico. It was a major victory for the abolitionist movement there. The news, a cause for celebration throughout Mexico, was met with dismay by the American settlers and empresarios hoping to convince more enslavers to come to Texas. Guerrero eventually issued some exemptions, allowing slavery to continue in some areas of the country including Coahuila y Tejas, but the writing was already on the wall. It was clear public sentiment in Mexico was moving to totally abolish slavery throughout the country.

When the news hit San Antonio, authorities refused to publish the decree. Instead, they hid it from enslaved people who were for a time—until Guerrero's exemptions—legally freed.

It was a cycle that would play out over and over again in the years from 1821 to 1836, as those in power kept the news of freedom from those who were enslaved. The Mexican federal and state government often tried to repeal slavery in the region and then instituted some policy change or last-minute loophole that allowed it to remain in Texas, and Texian and Tejano leaders alike worked to suppress that information, as Robert Leftwich and Martin Parmer did with Rufus and Polly and Lewis and John and James. Later, after Texas was part of the United States, Confederates in power would do the same thing, preventing enslaved people from hearing about the Emancipation Proclamation for more than two years.

The instinct to control the narrative and clamp down on who hears a story has deep roots in Texas politics.

IN THE LATE 1820S, BEFORE SLAVERY WAS OUTLAWED, EMPRESARIOS HAD reason to feel like things had been going relatively well for the new Texian colonies. Austin had convinced Mexican officials to protect new Texians from foreign creditors. That was an excellent branding tool to entice newcomers to take a chance on the colonies; Texas already had a reputation as a haven for debtors and swindlers, but now US immigrants could legally get rid of their debt as soon as they crossed the border. This law benefited Austin as much as anyone else—the Father of Texas was up to his eyeballs in debt.

Those were dizzying years in Mexican politics. Soon after he outlawed slavery in 1829, Guerrero was ousted; he would be executed by 1831. Mexicans elected Anastasio Bustamante in 1830, and he moved the country toward centralism, once again taking away the power of the states. The idea that some things would be permissible in Coahuila y Tejas that were not permissible in the rest of the country concerned many Mexicans, and they were increasingly unhappy about what was happening under Texian influence.

The Fredonian Rebellion in 1826 hadn't helped. Neither did the repeated offers by the US government to buy Texas. Mexican officials worried that the influx of Anglos had already fundamentally changed the area. In 1830, the government sent Brigadier General Manuel de Mier y Terán to Texas to track what was happening. The Mier y Terán report showed the full extent of the cultural shifts made by Anglos in Texas—from the vantage point of the majority pro-abolition Mexicans, the report did not look good. Mier y Terán wrote up a set of in-depth recommendations for what to do next, including Article 11, which stated that they should stop all immigration by Americans immediately.

Based on most of Mier y Terán's recommendations, Bustamante in-

stituted sweeping border policies that were a massive blow to empresarios: an April 6, 1830 law limited immigration to Texas. Texians had
enjoyed a ten-year reprieve from taxes after moving to Texas, but the
new law ended that policy. The law encouraged Mexicans to move north
through a large financial package and land disbursements. And they
continued to crack down on new slaves coming to Texas, trying to stop
the rampant smuggling trade.

The goal of the law was for Mexicans to bring the colony to heel and
to sever connection to the United States. The deterrent worked for my
next relative to arrive in Texas. Robert's brother, Jesse Leftwich, did not
stay long when he arrived in April 1830. Robert had begun what would
seem like a trend among my relatives, and certainly many others, for the
next several decades—showing up in Texas and deciding it wasn't worth
it to stay.

WORRIED ABOUT THE RAMIFICATIONS OF MEXICO OUTLAWING SLAVERY
for his ability to retain colonists and bring in new ones, Austin got to
work, as he always did. He wrote letters to officials, trying to ensure that
the changes would not impact "colonies already established" but only
"contracts that have not been fulfilled." He consulted with others. He
despaired and cajoled and wheedled and pleaded.

He controlled the only press in the area at the time. He suppressed
the news about the April 6, 1830 law, publishing it only in January
1831—that pre-Juneteenth move. By the time he did finally allow the
news to be published in his colony, Austin had managed to finagle allies
into overturning some of the antislavery articles in the law. But the
goodwill and close relationships he had enjoyed with Mexican officials
was already frayed.

Austin continued to try to sell potential settlers on the idea of Texas
as a proslavery paradise, but his private letters showed he increasingly
doubted he could trust many of his Mexican allies. They were committed to ending slavery and seemed unwavering in that goal. Austin was
stuck in the empresarios' continual bind: convincing Mexican officials

that the settlers would not always enslave people, while wooing would-be settlers with the promise that Mexican officials would always allow slavery in Texas. It was an impossible line, of course.

In June 1830, Austin got sick of being stuck. He had an uncharacteristic change of policy. He decided—briefly—that slavery had no place in the Texas he envisioned. Austin wrote some letters trying to convince would-be settlers to stop relying on slavery—not because it was wrong, or because he had been convinced by his abolitionist friends in Mexico, but because he was afraid that a growing population of Black people would necessarily be a threat to white rule. Those letters are important because they reveal the cultural fears Austin both received and passed on.

A Virginia-born lawyer named Richard Ellis wrote Austin to ask what was really going on in Texas: "You know such is the sensitive feelings of the Slave holders on the subject, that the least agitation will deter them from emigration." It was the same question other empresarios and their representatives had been fielding from interested Anglo settlers: could they ensure that the enslavers could bring their slaves without fear of them being liberated?

Austin wrote back not with a guarantee but an argument about an overlooked threat to the colonial project: "I cannot believe that any reflecting man, either in Texas or out of it, can seriously wish that slavery should be entailed upon this country." He argues that, within a few generations at the current rate of population growth, Black people will outnumber white people in Texas.

In his next assumption, he relies on a narrative that will be the driving force behind much of the violence committed in Texas against Black men for the rest of the century and the next—that their very existence is a threat to white women: "suppose that you will be alive at the period above mentioned, that you have a long-cherished and beloved wife, a number of daughters, granddaughters, and great granddaughters" for whom "fears for their fate, a horrible fate" would keep the farmers up at night.

In Austin's writing, both rape and interracial relationships are equally "a horrible fate." It is this "tainted blood" trope that will be the driving force behind anti-immigration laws well into the first half of the twentieth century in the United States and the lynchings that would be the hallmark of the post–Civil War South, including Texas.

In my research on the founding of Texas, it did not take any digging at all to see these kinds of racist views. Austin wrote it all out very clearly. In fact, he couched his argument as logical: "If Texas is wisely and prudently managed"—by which he means in this case, if slavery isn't allowed in Texas—"it will be saved from the overwhelming ruin which mathematical demonstration declares must overtake the slave states; and the white population will find within the Mexican limits a refuge." He laid out a future Texas without slavery—not as an abolitionist refuge, but as a place for white enslavers to flee when he felt they would inevitably face reprisal by Black people.

I hear in his argument the kind of dystopian narrative that is so popular in films and books today. It makes me wonder if those kinds of stories—fugitives surviving the zombie apocalypse, a scrappy band of renegades defeating an invading army of aliens—have their roots in passed down, colonial fears. Austin's views were common at the time: the same fears prompted many of the Black slave codes in Virginia at the turn of the seventeenth century, the fears that continued to haunt slaveholders through the Haitian Revolution and other uprisings by oppressed Black people over the centuries.

Austin wrote in other letters that week that he thought slavery was a bad idea, hoping to convince would-be settlers that Texas could do without slaves. The person who seemed to have changed his mind back again was a Northern, non-enslaving farmer named Samuel Rhoads Fisher.

Fisher wrote that, because Texas was closer geographically to Southern states in the US, and because Southerners had "favorable feelings" toward Texas, it made more sense to recruit settlers from the Southern states than the North. But to entice them to become economic migrants to Texas, Austin had to make it worth their while—which could only happen by guaranteeing slavery. Fisher wished there were another way; if they could make money hand over fist as a "grain-growing State," Fisher would support it. He told Austin, "Like yourself I detest Slavery," but as practical men, they had to acknowledge there is not the same profit in wheat as there is in cotton.

Austin was persuaded by the economics of Fisher's argument, and once more changed his tack to recruit enslavers to come to Texas. His views matter so much because of the breadth and depth of his influence. As the major empresario bringing over colonists, his values became Texas policy for the fifteen years in which he was responsible for convincing many of the earliest settlers to come to the state. Austin's fears were one of the narrative threads at the heart of the Texas myths about who they viewed as a threat, who white Texans needed to subdue or defend themselves from.

But as the Southerners poured in and became Texians, Austin's sometimes more nuanced views—that many Mexican officials could still be allies, for example—became less and less widely held. Within a handful of years, the distinctions of early empresarios' positions would be collapsed into one overarching, fearmongering narrative like the one Austin wrote out in his letters to Ellis—that any non-white Texian was a threat to the tenuous power the newcomers held. The results of those cultural constructions were the slaughter of indigenous people on a massive scale, the further oppression of Black people, and two wars against Mexico in less than a decade.

THE APRIL 6, 1830 LAW BANNING ANGLO IMMIGRATION INTO TEXAS was, as it turned out, poorly timed for Mexico. Mexican officials tried to iron fist colonies steadily finding their own strength. The Mexican troops arriving to enforce the new law in Texas found themselves in hostile territory, even as the land still technically belonged to Mexico.

Austin's fears that the law would curb the arrival of settlers were unfounded—as Fisher predicted, settlers from the US South came in droves to make money. An increase in global cotton prices made the enslavers richer and their oppression of Black people more profitable than they could have imagined in the lean years following the Panic of 1819. By

1834, slave-harvested cotton wasn't only the leading export in the Texas economy, it *was* the Texas export economy—96 percent of it. Cotton prices went up every year in the early 1830s, culminating in a fifteen-year high by 1835. Of course, those prices reflect the legal, measurable financial gains; smuggling, especially in trafficked people from the Caribbean, remained a very lucrative shadow economy in Texas along the poorly regulated coast.

The ensuing population boom, as US settlers swarmed the territory, changed the power dynamics. Because most of those arrivals were not granted official documents through the recognized empresarios, they came illegally—like those settlers on the "Tennessee Road." The Anglo population more than doubled, from ten thousand settlers in 1830 to more than twenty thousand in 1834. Texians soon outnumbered Tejanos at a rate of almost six to one. And those new settlers did not share Stephen F. Austin's long-held loyalty to the Mexican government. As events heated up, Austin publicly preached peace but privately became increasingly frustrated with Mexican policies.

Tensions exploded between the Texians and Mexican forces in June 1832 at Fort Anahuac. After terse exchanges over escaped slaves from Louisiana—men that the Mexican troops declared were free, against the protests of the Texian enslavers—a colonel in the Mexican army arrested William Barret Travis, a hotheaded young lawyer who had recently arrived in the colony. The Mexican troops jailed him and another lawyer in a kiln at Fort Anahuac. Supporters reacted by kidnapping Mexican soldiers; Mexican troops retaliated further by imprisoning other Texians. The conflict escalated quickly.

On June 13, 1832, a group of Texians released a manifesto against the Mexican government. What became known as the Turtle Bayou Resolutions declared that Texians were still bound by the Constitution of 1824—meaning states had the right to control slavery. They were against Anastasio Bustamante, who the Texians viewed as a dictator and betrayer of their interests; they came out in support of General Santa Anna, who they thought would return to a Federalist government and give control back to the states. Nearby skirmishes in the weeks after the Turtle Bayou Resolutions escalated tensions and signaled that the Texians were increasingly ready to fight.

The embattled President Bustamante had little time to worry about the disgruntled Texians; he was already facing revolutionary eruptions in the central part of the country. The rebellion led by General Santa Anna directly attacked supporters of Bustamante in Mexico in 1832. Bustamante was ousted in December 1832.

IN OCTOBER OF 1832, FIFTY-FIVE TEXIAN DELEGATES MET IN THE MAIN settlement of Austin's colony, San Felipe de Austin, to debate what they should do next. They elected Stephen F. Austin as the convention's president, and made a few resolutions to request of the Mexican government, including a three-year extension to Texas as a tariff-free zone and a request to separate Texas from Coahuila as its own state. Tellingly, Tejano leaders in Texas were not present at the convention run entirely by mostly new Anglo Texians; despite Austin's good relations with many of the Tejano leaders, the split between the two groups' interests on slavery and other issues was becoming more pronounced.

Austin began to think that perhaps Texas should secede from Mexico. Like his thinking about slavery, this was a sharp deviation from his past written positions. But unlike that short-lived antislavery moment, Austin didn't change his mind about this one.

He only believed it more strongly after heading to Mexico in 1833. He traveled to the capital to convince officials—as he had many times before—to let Texas be the exception on slavery, this time as its own state separate from Coahuila. Government officials were uninterested. Frustrated, Austin wrote a letter in October 1833 to the ayuntamiento of San Antonio. He suggested the officials there form their own independent state government, which he knew to be against the wishes of the federal government.

The letter got into the wrong hands. Mexican officials arrested Austin in Saltillo on charges of sedition and treason. He was jailed in

Mexico City, where he remained in solitary confinement for several months. Eventually he was allowed to interact with other prisoners, and on Christmas Day 1834, he was released on bail but had to remain in the city.

He came back to Texas in September 1835. By then, his views on the government in Mexico had darkened profoundly.

IN NOVEMBER 1833, WHILE AUSTIN WAS IN JAIL, SANTA ANNA WAS ELECTED Mexican president by a popular majority. Though he opposed Busta- mante's Centralist government, Santa Anna was not the leader proslavery Texians had hoped he would be—he still intended to concentrate power in Mexico City. He was not inclined to continue allowing some regions to get away with things other regions couldn't. Stakeholders who still wanted control to be in the states—like Coahuila y Tejas, but also Zacatecas, Jalisco, and Tamaulipas—flashed revolts that Santa Anna's troops scur- ried to stomp out. The brief alignment the Texians had with Santa Anna when he opposed Bustamante did not last.

The Anglos in Texas were mostly the second or third generation born after the American Revolution; they had been weaned on stories of Paul Revere and the Boston Tea Party and George Washington on the Potomac. They knew exactly how their fathers had handled British roy- alists during civilian trials to root out spies. They had heard old men reminisce about routing the British in 1784 and again in 1815. They had better firearms than their fathers' muskets. They had come to Texas with high worries that the Mexican government would try to free the slaves that were essential to their profit. They had money and a way of life at stake. After Anahuac and Velasco, debates ignited across the colony— whether it was time to fight or whether they should stifle the trigger-happy hot heads among them.

When the Mexican troops—now under the rule of Santa Anna— finally took the Anglo conflicts seriously, what had seemed like isolated blazes scattered around the region blasted into the fire storm that would destroy any hope Mexico had of keeping Texas.

LEADERS IN TEXAS HAD DIVIDED FIRMLY ALONG THE PARTY LINES THAT
began around the time of the Anahuac Disturbances in 1832: the aptly
named Peace and War Parties. Though they were not organized political
parties and therefore kept no records, many historians think the Peace
Party more fully represented the majority of Texans. They were loud in
wanting the War Party to stop pushing the region toward war: "The
peace-party, as they style themselves, I believe are the strongest, and make
the most noise," William Barret Travis wrote on July 30, 1835. Travis,
whose arrest at Anahuac had caused much of the conflict, was a staunch
member of the War Party.

The raucous minority War Party took any opportunity to fan the
flames of resentment and conflict. In the summer of 1835, members of
the Peace Party began calling for a decision to be made by Texas leaders,
one they hoped would quash the calls for revolution. At a meeting in
August of that year, opponents of conflict suggested that Texians con-
vene a "consultation"—a word they hoped seemed less revolutionary
sounding than "convention"—to decide the matter. Without local government in a state occupied by Anglos but run by Mexicans, the consultation would have been perceived by skittish Mexican leaders as the
precursor to war, when instead Peace Party advocates hoped to bring the
war agitators under control. Many people assumed that Austin—who
had often counseled peace and diplomacy over conflict in his years as a
leader of Texas—would return firmly on the side of the Peace Party.

Austin had only been back in Texas for a few days after two years
imprisoned in Mexico when he gave a speech in Brazoria, Texas on
September 8, 1835. Excerpts of it were reprinted in newspapers all over
the United States. Austin reported on what was happening in Mexico
and remarked on the changes he found after returning to Texas: "I fully
hoped to have found Texas at peace and in tranquility. . . . Texas needs
peace, and a local government" since its "inhabitants are farmers, and
they need a calm and quiet life. But how can I, or anyone, remain indif-

ferent, when our rights, our all, appear to be in jeopardy? It is impossible." Instead, he declared, "The constitutional rights and the security and peace of Texas—they ought to be maintained; and jeopardized as they now are, they demand a general consultation of the people."

That night, Austin set the narrative that would dominate the coming Texas Revolution. He relied on the rhetoric of the American Revolutionary leaders—that the peace, rights, and security of the Texians were at risk from an oppressive dictator. No one mentioned slavery and that the major point of contention with the Mexican government was about local control precisely because the Texians refused to give up enslaving the laborers making them money in a booming cotton market.

The freedom they wanted was to enslave others. But naturally "give us the right to profit off the forced labor of others, or give us death!" did not have the same ring.

So they pulled out Patrick Henry's phrase from those early days of the American Revolution in Virginia. They tacked it on to letters and calls to arms. They wrote themselves a story in which they were oppressed freedom fighters seeking independence.

Weeks later, War Party agitator Travis—who often disagreed with Austin—wrote him a letter: "All eyes are turned towards you. . . . Texas can be wielded by you and *you alone*; and her destiny is now completely in your hands. I have every confidence that you will guide us safe through all our perils." Austin had stepped firmly across the political line from the Peace Party to the War Party.

Austin, that great influencer for Texas, created an effective branding campaign. Through letters, newspaper articles, and personal appeals to allies in the US government and supporters with funding, Texians urged their neighbors, relatives, and friends in the Southern United States to grab their guns and help the Texians fight off the Mexican leaders. It also became the foundation for Texas history—erasing slavery and the Texians as economic migrants and turning the fight for Texas independence into a question of liberty rather than profit.

Austin's shift would have real life implications for thousands of people: For the Texians who would go to war. For the Mexicans who would try to keep the Texians from stealing the land they once stole from Spain, who stole it from the indigenous people before them. For the global politicians, especially in France, Great Britain, and the United States, watching the squabbling in Texas with an eye toward taking the land for themselves. And for the volunteers who would be enticed by that bold rhetoric of freedom and the offer of land for anyone who joined Texas in the fight.

One of those volunteers was my next relative to come to Texas: eighteen-year-old Perry Reese, from Pine Flat, Alabama.

CHAPTER 21

Perry Reese was born in 1818 in Autauga County, Alabama. He was the second son of Drury Reese, who was probably Sally Reese's first cousin. Drury's branch of the Reese family moved to Georgia from one of the "burned" counties in Virginia, where records are all but impossible to untangle, which is why Sherry and I could never fully uncover whether he was Sally's first or third cousin. Drury met and married his wife in Georgia before they settled in Alabama. Always, they were on the search for land to farm—the perpetual push of generations of Reeses, along with so many other newcomers across the frontiers of the United States.

Drury bought a farm in 1824, when Perry was six, soon after his little sister was born. Maybe everything in their family seemed optimistic, with three kids and a farm to raise them on. Drury was a war veteran, a sergeant from the War of 1812. Presumably he told his children stories of the days when he rode with cavalry against the British: how the army was really just neighbors who banded together into loose militias, how they took their weapons to defend their homes in the name of freedom. Maybe those stories early in his life had something to do with Perry's choice later.

Drury died in 1831, when Perry was thirteen. A year later, his mother remarried and a year after that, she started having more children, one a year. It might have felt to Perry, with an older brother who was already on the path toward becoming a doctor and a mother focused on a new marriage and a houseful of babies, that he had to do something to get out of the house, to prove himself.

His father was gone, but the soldier's legacy lived on in Perry. There was glory to be had still, just not in Alabama.

IF PERRY'S HOUSEHOLD SUBSCRIBED TO THE CLOSEST NEWSPAPER, THE Selma *Free Press*, they read news every Saturday in the summer and fall of 1835 about what was happening in Texas. Or they heard about it when they went to town for supplies, while they gathered to help other farmers with their crops, or on off nights drinking with friends. Perry was not the only man from Autauga County, Alabama who proved to be susceptible to the excellent branding campaign of Stephen F. Austin and Sam Houston and other leaders of Texas as war ignited.

Like Virginia in its early days as a colony, Texas was land rich and cash poor. They offered bounty land grants to those who would serve in the military. For each three-month period of service, men could earn 320 acres, up to a maximum of 1,280 acres.

It was a chance to gain both military honor and their own farms. The story told to Perry—and dozens of men in Alabama and across the South—was a glorious one full of easy victories and immediate gains. It must have felt impossible for a young man in a precarious family situation to resist.

The leaders of the Texas Revolution wrote an early advertising campaign in their letters and articles. It was a narrative they carefully controlled, using the same principles that would dominate Hollywood less than a century later, that the Mad Men would use in the 1960s, that social media influencers would capitalize on two centuries later: the principle was that image matters as much—or more—than reality when trying to sell something.

The story, as it emerged every Saturday in the Selma *Free Press*, made war in Texas feel logical, inevitable, even exciting. On October 3—the day after the revolution officially started, though the news had not made it to Alabama yet—the newspaper described Texas "at the eve of revolution":

> The alarming progress of centralism through the rest of the Mexican republic—a threatened invasion by Santa Anna—a mediated sale of a large quantity of settled territory—the imposition of burthensome and unequal taxes on the commerce of the country, and the arrest of the Governor, are circumstances which have aroused the people of Texas to the defense of their rights, and to resist oppression. . . . Texas cannot submit to it; her only resource is in arms.

The story that the coming revolution was a culture clash between independent Texians who refused to kowtow to an oppressive government was already in place.

Perry must have read, or heard, the many, many times the newspaper mentioned that Texas was an easy place to get rich quick: "This colony, planted by the enterprise of a few individuals, has within a few years past sprang into an importance, as regards her products and population as to cause the eyes of the adventurous from all parts of the Union to be turned toward her borders, as a place where affluence could be soon obtained." Next to the stories about Texas were articles about the continued rise of the price of cotton.

The wealth was Perry's for the taking; the glory was too. If Perry left home, he might have the chance to brush shoulders with some of the most famous heroes of the day who were also going to Texas. The paper reported on Austin traveling back via New Orleans in September 1835 after being jailed in Mexico, on his way to make the speech in Brazoria that would tip Texas into war. Davy Crockett was headed to Texas too. The legendary woodsman—whose exploits in the backwoods of Tennessee had catapulted him into the public eye, including a political career he was ill-suited for—had just lost his bid to represent Tennessee in the

US Congress. Resentful at losing, he famously said, "You all may go to Hell, and I will go to Texas." In October 1835, the paper reported that his road not to hell but to Texas passed near Selma, Alabama.

Perry had no way of knowing that what his newspaper was reporting was different from the news about Texas around the country. Newspapers throughout Alabama began to print urgent requests for aid to Texas, organized in part by loosely affiliated groups in bigger cities who called themselves "friends of Texas." Like political PACs of the next century, the people funding these appeals had an economic stake in the argument; this was not about the pure spread of freedom but of increasing profit on their investment.

Not everyone agreed with the Texians' grandiose appeals. One editor at another paper criticized their rhetoric: "If they have kicked up this dust with Mexico, in order to advance their ambitious or avaricious designs . . . If our *brethren* have got sick of the government of Mexico, which was lately so mild and good, that they selected it as the most fitting one, under which to rear their children, then they have nothing to do but to *claw back* to their native country and be at peace."

But that editorial was not reprinted in Selma. There, the story about Texas was all glory and cotton—the new gold.

THE ARTICLES ABOUT THE WAR READ LIKE THRILLERS. NO STORY WAS more exciting than the one about the "Come and Take It" flag. In late September, the two sides squared off in Gonzales, Texas. The village of Gonzales was where the empresario Green DeWitt had lived with his family and the colonists he brought to Mexico. The Mexicans wanted a cannon they said they had loaned the colony. The Texians' defiant response became instant, printable legend.

The real story, left out of the papers, was more nuanced. DeWitt was a poor manager of the colony; he sunk all of his family's resources into the land grant experiment and it cost him enormously. He would die in almost complete poverty in May 1835, less than six months before Mexican troops came knocking at his door for the cannon.

But his wife, Sarah, had not kept her family together on the frontier for Mexican troops to take things away from them. A few years earlier, when it became apparent that her husband would not be able to fulfill his empresario contract, she applied for a grant in her own name "to protect herself and her family from poverty to which they are exposed by the misfortunes of her husband" and was one of only a few Texian women with land in her name.

Sarah DeWitt was still there when the Mexican lieutenant showed up with some troops in Gonzales. The lieutenant told them to hand the cannon over. The Anglos said no.

The *Selma Free Press* reported it breathlessly, leaving out the women: when word reached the Mexican commander at San Antonio, Domingo Ugartechea, that the Texians refused to give back the cannon, he ordered his troops "to march (75 miles) and take the gun by force. The Colonists assembled to oppose him. . . . The people rose in arms—and marched for the battle field [*sic*]. O, the heart ache [*sic*] of suspense. Before this time, in all human probability, the battle is won or lost—and we know not yet the result."

It was a hell of a cliffhanger.

The result was not reported immediately in the paper, but Perry must have heard it—everyone did who was paying attention to Texas. Though whether they heard the full version is more doubtful. None of the seventh-grade textbooks I have from the library tell the real story either.

Sarah DeWitt and her daughters, Naomi and Evaline, and their friend Cynthia Burns, designed, painted, and sewed a flag on Naomi's old wedding dress: A centered black star above a simple picture of a cannon on white fabric; beneath it, the slogan—"Come and Take It."

It was the first of many flags the Texians would fly during the revolution, their defiance unfaltering as their banners grew more ragged in the wind. Another read "Constitution of 1824," after Austin's assertion that the state of Texas was supposed to have a special dispensation under the old constitution.

The Texians raised the women's flag, and the Mexicans withdrew after a few shots were fired, leaving the cannon behind. The battle amounted to little more than smoke in the end.

The myth remained after the details were forgotten—the flag became an enduring symbol of Texian fortitude and defiance. Few remembered it had once been a wedding dress, or the role of the women who handcrafted that act of Texian defiance.

It made for breathtaking reportage. The newspapers described a war that was almost laughably easy. On October 31, the paper published the story that, with only one hundred men, "Texian forces under General Houston had taken the town of San Antonio . . . without resistance." The Mexican forces, as they were portrayed in the newspaper, were weak buffoons, their leaders distracted by "petty rivalries between petty generals."

Alongside those stories were articles, like the public circulars of the Delegates of the Texas Association, designed not just to report but persuade. One encouraged any men interested not to wait: "Greater inducements were never held out to settlers in any country, since the discovery of America." These were Virginia Trading Company tactics, employed by "friends of Texas" investors in Alabama, in an early form of a now-familiar sales pitch: Hurry now! This deal won't last! Our land is priced to sell! Get it before it's too late!

PERRY SIGNED UP, ALONG WITH SEVERAL OTHER MEN FROM THE AREA. They enlisted under Captain Isaac Ticknor and met up in Montgomery. Forty of them under Ticknor called themselves the "Alabama Grays." They were the fourth company to arrive from Alabama, following the Huntsville Company, the Red Rovers, and the Mobile Grays.

Volunteers poured in from all over the United States—predominantly the South, but from other areas of the country as well. There were the Kentucky Mustangs and the New Orleans Grays and a full battalion from Georgia under the leadership of James Fannin.

It remained highly illegal for citizens of one country to enlist in an internal revolution in a neighboring one. They went anyway.

Perry's company mustered into service in Texas on January 19, 1836, meaning they probably left Alabama right after Christmas. Maybe Perry spent it with his family, with his brother and sister, with his mom, her new husband, and the babies all under the age of four. Maybe they knew Perry was leaving. Maybe he ran away without telling them.

However he spent it, it was Perry's last Christmas.

When they arrived in Texas, they were scooped up to join the Georgia Battalion, sailing in to Copano—south of Goliad, where several Texian forces gathered—on January 24, 1836.

There, presumably, Perry trained. And waited.

HUNDREDS OF MILES AWAY, OTHER TEXIAN TROOPS WERE RUSHING TO action at an old Spanish mission outside of San Antonio. The Texian forces usually kept some supplies at the mission, but a battle a few weeks earlier had left the mission stripped of what they required.

On January 14, word got to Goliad, where Sam Houston had just arrived, that Texian forces desperately needed men and supplies near San Antonio.

General Santa Anna had arrived in Saltillo, the town where Robert Leftwich spent his final months in Mexico petitioning the state legislature and where Austin had been arrested after writing a seditious letter about the Mexican government. Santa Anna came with a mandate from the Mexican Congress that all foreigners who rebelled against the government were to be treated as terrorists and shot on sight—making him the legal force in this fight. And he brought six thousand experienced troops, many of whom had already put down other uprisings around the country.

They were not the laughable buffoons of the US newspapers, but hardened soldiers defending their homeland against rabble-rousing foreigners. Santa Anna marched with ire toward San Antonio. The Texians tried to shore up a church with very little supplies and dozens of untrained men. The War Party was there in force—William Barret Travis joined his friend, James Bowie, on February 3. And the celebrities showed up too—Davy Crockett had finally made it to Texas, ambling into town on February 8.

There, they waited as Santa Anna made his way across Southern Texas. The troops arrived in San Antonio on February 23.

They fired at one another. The Mexicans surrounded the old church. For a few days, the Texians held the mission.

There was an unexpected cold snap. Both armies suffered. A few of them died on each side.

Travis got a letter out to James Fannin, who was leading the Georgia Battalion among other volunteer militia companies. That's where Perry Reese waited, a foot soldier in Fannin's army. Fannin had spent two years at Westminster, which he tried to leverage into a position as a brigadier general when he came to Texas; most Texas historians agree that Fannin's ambition far exceeded his capabilities.

Fannin marched with reinforcements from Goliad toward the Alamo, bringing 320 men along with much-needed supplies—including four cannons—to the Texian men. It was about ninety miles to San Antonio. Then, inexplicably, Fannin turned back. Later, Fannin blamed his officers, and they blamed him. The men in the Alamo assumed Fannin was coming, but he never showed up.

The ragtag militia in the Alamo kept waiting. Eventually a few other reinforcements came, but it was too little, too late. The Mexican troops attacked on March 5 and then paused. Before sunrise the next day, they surprised the Texian army by attacking again.

It was a complete rout. The Texians fought hand to hand, taking many Mexicans with them, but they were outnumbered. Santa Anna ordered that all of the Texians who did not die in the battle be executed.

The almost two-week Battle of the Alamo ended in a slaughter. By sunrise on March 6, the battle was over. The two most famous survivors were a woman named Susanna Dickinson, who survived with her baby girl, and a man whom Travis enslaved named Joe.

Santa Anna let Dickinson go with some silver coins and instructions to tell the story to anyone she could.

Santa Anna wanted the other Texians to know they were coming, that Mexico had no patience for an illegal uprising led by enslavers trying to secede from the nation, and that they would follow Mexican law in executing any foreigners engaged in illegal sedition on the spot.

THE WAR WAS QUICKLY MOVING TOWARD PERRY, WHO WAITED IN GO-liad under Captain Ticknor and James Fannin. As they waited, the volunteer troops grew resentful: of Fannin's lack of leadership; of the Texian farmers, most of whom went back to their fields when it was time to plant and left the fighting of the Texas Revolution to the volunteers from the United States; of the stark difference between the easy battles they had been promised and the hardships they endured; and of their families for not writing and not sending money. By then, many had no shoes and few clothes. As one soldier wrote home, they lived off beef with no salt and little else.

In his military diary, a Mexican general called the Texian leaders "pirates." He wasn't far off. The word "pirate" now has a whimsical association, but in the 1830s, pirates were essentially terrorists. Fannin was a literal pirate, having trafficked more than one hundred enslaved people across the border—he was responsible for about a tenth of the human trafficking that occurred into Texas the year before the Texas Revolution.

As a smuggler, Fannin was excellent; as a military leader, he was as resentful as his troops. The Texian leaders had been so eager to bring in volunteers, they did not stipulate levels of military service or even marksman abilities. The militia could come and go as they pleased; if they didn't like something, they were not bound by the same military regulations. Fannin was angry at having to try to whip three hundred volunteers from across the United States into shape, especially when they did not have the same motivation of fighting for their own homeland that Mexican soldiers did.

Perry was probably not the youngest person to serve in the militia, but he certainly did not have any experience in this type of fighting. It is easy to imagine how frustrating this new life must have seemed to him, the glory of war tarnished by a cold winter and snappish comrades and waffling military leaders.

Following the Battle of the Alamo, when Fannin did not show up to provide aid to the embattled Anglos who died, his name was mud among Texians. A letter from Houston reached him four days after Santa Anna killed everyone who fought in the Alamo. Fannin was supposed to retreat with his troops to Victoria.

Instead, Fannin did what he had done before: he wavered.

OSTENSIBLY, IN MID-MARCH 1836, FANNIN WAS WAITING FOR HIS VOLUN- teer troops who were supposed to be helping nearby Texian families to escape Mexican soldiers. Instead, the Anglo volunteers burned Tejano ranches and shot eight Mexican soldiers sitting around a campfire. In retaliation, the Mexican army killed fifteen of Fannin's men.

A wise, or even a cunning, military leader would have gotten his troops out of there days before, especially if his untrained militia men had pissed off experienced soldiers who were headed their way. But Fannin just fortified the fort.

On March 18, the Mexican army arrived under General José de Urrea. The fighting began. The next morning, at the worst possible time, Fannin ordered a retreat on March 19 at 9:00 a.m.

He took no provisions for the troops or the oxen. The lack of water would become especially important—they couldn't fire cannons without water, much less hydrate beleaguered animals and men. A cart wheel broke. A cannon fell into the river. Fannin decided to stop and let the oxen graze for an hour.

They were sitting ducks. Three hundred Mexican troops under Urrea caught Fannin's men in a low valley. And then the Anglos' ammunition cart broke. With no other defenses around them, with no trees or hills to hide behind, the Texian militia formed a square.

Somewhere in that square—probably nowhere near the front—was young Perry Reese. We have no idea if he was wounded, what he thought, what he experienced in his first and last battle.

Others later wrote about the bravery of Fannin's men. As one soldier wrote, "Column upon column of the enemy" came at the huddled Anglos. "It was a sorry sight to see our small circle: it had become muddy with blood."

Like most of Fannin's men, Perry lived through that miserable night. He was alive the next morning when Fannin and his officers agreed—after watching fresh Mexican troops and artillery arrive—to surrender.

Urrea, who accepted their surrender, wanted to give the inexperienced US troops clemency. Santa Anna did not.

The volunteer Texians marched back to the fort at Goliad. They stayed there for a week, on the edge of starvation. Letters later show most of them assumed they would be held as prisoners of war and then released to go home. They were US citizens, after all. They were only here for the easy land and an adventure.

A week after they surrendered, on Santa Anna's orders, Mexican soldiers divided Fannin's men into three groups and marched them in three different directions, all under heavy guard. The largest group—the one with Perry and the other men from Alabama—moved toward the San Antonio River. The other two groups split up: one trudging toward Victoria, the other toward San Patricio. The critically wounded remained behind at the fort.

They filed almost a mile in each direction. In three different locations on three different roads, the Mexican troops halted their Texian prisoners. The guards who had led them drew back alongside the column of prisoners.

At all three sites, Mexican soldiers turned and fired on the unarmed prisoners.

If they did not die in the first round, the Mexican troops gutted them with bayonets. Or they shot them at close range. Back at the fort, Mexican soldiers murdered the remaining wounded—including Fannin.

Perry Reese died on Palm Sunday, March 27, 1836, at the age of eighteen. He was one of almost 450 men, mostly US citizens, who were slaughtered that day.

NEWS OF THE MASSACRE OF GOLIAD REACHED THE UNITED STATES weeks later in newspaper reports and letters. While the Alamo would be the battle picked up by Hollywood later during the insatiable appetite for Westerns, what happened at Goliad galvanized public opinion in the US against Santa Anna and Mexico during the Texas Revolution. The repercussions would be felt in US-Mexico relations for the next several decades.

I have no idea when Perry's mother, Martha, was informed of what happened at Goliad, and what she knew about how her boy had died. Word probably reached Pine Flat, Alabama three or four weeks after the massacre. A few months after that, in July 1836, the local newspaper printed the story of a survivor of the Red Rovers, most of whom died that day as well, a "gallant, tho' unfortunate little band." Would it have given Martha comfort to know that the small band of men repelled "charge after charge" of Mexican soldiers? Would Perry's siblings have told their own children that the men did not retreat from the creek where they stood because they did not want to leave their wounded behind? Did his actions seem courageous or selfish or hopelessly naive?

I will never know the effects of Perry's death and its impact on their family. Perry's mother, like others in the first half of the nineteenth century, lived a life that spanned several wars in the early American South. I found no record of how she felt about the violence that marked her life so tragically. Like so many women, her experiences vanished with her when she died.

PERRY REESE'S NAME DID NOT LIVE ON IN TEXAS HISTORY; HE WAS listed among the rolls of Fannin's men, but only as a foot soldier. His relationship with my own line of the family was too distant for his story to have been passed down to us even if we had known more about Sally's cousin.

But in a way, Perry and the other men killed at Goliad that day became a critical part of the myth of Texas, both within Texas and in the United States. Less than a month later, on April 21, 1836, General Sam Houston met Santa Anna in battle at San Jacinto. With a bird's-eye view, you could have watched the newspapers carrying the news across the United States: first in New Orleans, then in Jackson and Natchez, Mississippi, then in Nashville, Tennessee, and Richmond, Virginia, and Lancaster, Pennsylvania, and New York, New York.

Within weeks, the narrative was already set: How Houston led the Texian Army to victory in less than an hour. How they defeated the general who would go down in Texas and US history as an evil dictator, Antonio López de Santa Anna. How Santa Anna would never return to power in Mexico after being marched in shame to meet the US president Andrew Jackson.

How the Texian troops chanted "Remember the Alamo!" and "Remember Goliad!" and "Travis! Crockett! Fannin!" How the memory of rousing defeats and newly minted heroes spurred Texas on to victory.

CHAPTER 22

In the years I spent researching the history of Texas, I could not stop thinking about these two mass killings—the Dressing Point Massacre in 1821 and the Goliad Massacre in 1836. I could not shake my sense that these two moments, and the differences between how they were remembered, marked something critical about the making of the myth of Texas and our own discussions about violence today.

On the surface, the two acts of violence fit into the moments of extremism I am examining throughout our history and have a great deal in common: killers shot large, unarmed groups of people point-blank. Both sets of shooters justified the acts as retaliation after a series of small but escalating conflicts. Austin's colonists and Mexican Army officials intended the slaughters to be spectacularly cruel as a way to send a message to others.

Yet of these two profoundly horrifying moments in Texas history, only one became a rallying cry. News of what happened at Goliad spread throughout the United States. News of what happened at Dressing Point was largely erased from Texas and US history, passed down only by the Karankawa families when they fled or assimilated instead of "disappearing" like they were expected to, or by the handful of scholars diligent enough to record the act of violence decades later.

The difference between how these two massacres were remembered or forgotten in Texas history for dozens of years shows as much about power and the act of remembering as it does the violence itself.

Perry Reese was a victim of a story—the low-risk, high-reward war he had been implicitly sold was a lie. The reality was the massacre.

The Karankawa people were also victims of a story. The cultural construction of them as scary, seven-foot-tall cannibalistic warriors had nothing to do with the peaceful defenders of the land who loved their children above all else, and it led to the slaughter of those precious children—closest to the Creator—at the hands of frontiersmen who had been taught by a myth to see savages and not people.

In the history of Texas and the United States, how many acts of violence on either small or large scales can we point to and say: This is the result of a myth that turned out to be a lie, but which had real life-or-death consequences for its victims?

CHAPTER 23

O f all of the periods of extremism I am chronicling, few share the
rhetorical fire of our own time like the nine years, eleven months,
and seventeen days in which Texas was its own country. That feisty defiance would never really go away in Texas. After defeating Santa Anna,
Texas declared independence from Mexico. The Constitution of the Republic of Texas was ratified in September 1836. Many aspects of Texas
Independence were modeled on the rhetoric and tactics of the Revolutionary War. The constitution was no exception.

But in Section 9 of the General Provisions, there was one feature of
the constitution that would make it unique in the history of the world:
it remains the only constitution of any independent country that secures
slavery as an indisputable right of its citizens, and ensures that slavery
cannot be outlawed.

The section begins, "All persons of color" who were "slaves for life"
before coming to Texas "shall remain in the like state of servitude." Slaves
cannot be freed by Congress, which will not "have power to emancipate
slaves" nor can any enslaver "be allowed to emancipate his or her slave or
slaves, without the consent of Congress." This forceful constitution would
be a sticking point for Texas in international relations from the beginning. Many of the Texians assumed that they would join the United
States fairly quickly. Sam Houston, the commander in chief who had led

Texian troops to victory against Santa Anna, became the first president, and he actively advocated for Texas to become a US state.

Austin wanted that too, though he did not have long to change policies in the new republic. The Father of Texas died of pneumonia in December 1836, four months after the constitution was approved.

But the United States, with its precarious balance of slaveholding and non-slaveholding states, was not interested in adding a vehemently proslavery territory to its country. Despite repeated appeals by Texian ambassadors, and the fact that the vast majority of the Texian citizens were from the US originally, it would be almost a decade before the political path would be cleared for Texas to become one of the United States.

Texians had also assumed they could easily start a new country based on the wealth they had experienced in 1835, when the cotton industry was booming. But Southern cotton-growers in the US already had an existing supply chain pipeline to England, and they were wary of this new nation encroaching on their market. British importers remained disinclined to disrupt their established relationships. And writing slavery so blatantly into their constitution had immediate ramifications on the market in England. Abolition had become the fashionable political position in Europe, and cotton that was not slave-farmed—or at least, that was more discreet about being slave-farmed than the Texians were being—was much more palatable to Europeans.

No one, at any point in those years, would have called Texians discreet.

An economic downturn in 1837 and complicated international relations devastated the cotton economy in Texas. Still, immigrants kept coming. They came the same way that economic migrants and displaced people around the world today often embark on long treks across borders, planning routes based on rumors and the mirage of a happier life to come.

The population in Texas exploded during the years of the Republic. An 1836 report to US president Andrew Jackson recorded a Texas population of almost fifty-three thousand people, including estimations of indigenous groups, of which a tenth were enslaved. Over the next ten years, the country more than doubled. By 1847, official records show 141,714 people living in Texas, though this figure no longer included an estimation of indigenous people. Almost forty thousand enslaved people ended up in Texas during the years the republic was a slaveholders' sanctuary.

Those years were marked by profound fears and tensions as the fledgling country tried to figure out its place in the international community, to protect itself from being snatched up by the colonizing powerhouses around them, or to prevent itself from imploding because of infighting.

As far as I know, none of my relatives came to the Republic of Texas during the nine years it was a backwoods, muddy, thorny young country.

THE TENSION BETWEEN THE EDUCATED AND THE UNEDUCATED THAT had marked the early days of the United States was rampant in the Republic of Texas; educated leaders who advocated for nuance and reason found themselves overwhelmed by hotheaded newcomers with no sense of the history of the state who would stop at nothing to make a buck.

For some time after Austin's death, while Sam Houston was the republic's first president, there was still some measure of complexity in Anglo-Texas policies toward Tejanos and indigenous groups. Houston tempered the hot-blooded Texians who wanted revenge against Santa Anna by helping to negotiate for the Mexican general's release and then eventually normalizing relations with Mexico; he and Austin had both held good relationships with many of the Tejanos who stayed in Texas. Houston hoped to annex Texas to the United States, and he developed financial plans for getting the new country out of debt. He remained a slaveholder during his years of leadership in Texas.

Houston had lived with Cherokee people as a young man and viewed himself as an ambassador of the Cherokee people afterward. Throughout his time of leadership in Texas, he mostly communicated well with, and advocated on behalf of, many indigenous groups. He negotiated peace treaties with them and intended to provide a place for indigenous people in the vast land of Texas. He hoped to establish peaceful relations between the Anglos, Tejanos, and indigenous people, despite the fact that many Texians viewed all indigenous people as a threat. Tensions heated up, however, when in 1838, a group of Cherokee people combined forces with several Tejano leaders to begin a rebellion they hoped might drive the Texians away. Because of Houston's known sympathies for the Cherokee people, Texian leaders sometimes directly disobeyed his more measured orders. By the end of his constitution-mandated two-year term limit, a group of agitators were already pushing for more brutal treatment of the Cherokee people and other indigenous groups.

When Houston passed the reigns of leadership to his vice president, the firebrand Mirabeau Lamar, his political allies must have reasoned—how much harm could one man do in two years?

Lamar immediately reversed Houston's policy toward indigenous groups. In the two years that he was the republic's second president, the scale of the atrocities he committed and the funds he spent were outrageous. Relying on the early tactics of Stephen F. Austin's colony, Lamar enlisted the Texas Rangers in 1838 to ruthlessly persecute indigenous people who, until Lamar's election, had been told that they would have a safe place in the new country. Even accounting for the blatant racism of his time, Lamar's language about indigenous people was extreme—he called it an "exterminating war" on "tigers and hyenas" who were the "wild cannibals of the woods." The ill-considered war was not only genocidal, it cost the indebted nation millions of dollars it did not have—but Lamar was not known for his subtlety or his pragmatic strategic vision. He hoped to push the border of Texas west, all the way to the Pacific coast. By the time his term was up and Houston was reelected, Texas was drowning in debt.

The Texas Rangers benefited from Lamar's presidency, though; their reputation for cruelty and mercilessness only grew.

Internally, Texas was a mess, but externally, they remained excellent at branding the country to would-be immigrants: They asserted that cotton diplomacy—the idea that international markets would care more about cotton than slaveholding politics—would work to get the country out of its deep debts (it would not). They said they did not need either peace with indigenous people or the United States (they definitely would). They offered a refuge for poor, misunderstood enslavers (which Texas would remain for decades). They swore their republic would become, in a few years flat, a vast cotton empire (it never would, not on the scale they anticipated).

Texians ended up politically isolated because of their slavery policies, in debt and threatened because of their disastrous indigenous wars, and populated with newcomers who were often deeply disappointed that the hyped-up marketing oversold the reality of the mucky handful of villages that made up this new frontier country.

OUTSIDE OF THE TEXAS REPUBLIC, OTHER NATIONS SENSED BOTH OP-portunities and threats waiting in Texas—none more so than the United States. They were worried about a Mexican invasion on their southern border to retake Texas land—a well-founded fear, since statehood brought renewed conflict with Mexico when Texas finally did become a state. They fretted that England would take it over, also a well-founded fear since England was definitely trying. They feared the toxic political mess Texas had become, that its economic implosion would only hurt the US economy.

Mexico was equally concerned the US would get a foothold in the region; they were also anxious about overextending themselves again in trying to get vengeance on their former colony. They worried France or England would worm their way into Texas.

England's fears were less sharp, since it did not share a border with Texas, but they thought that the opportunities they saw in Texas—to perhaps control a cotton market or have a region outside of US control—might be too good to be true. Several politicians in England were firmly convinced that they could persuade the new country to abandon its slaveholding ideals; clearly, only people who had never been to Texas thought they could change the Texians' minds about their deepest held views.

While international countries intrigued and politicked around who would control the fledgling country, the population continued to explode.

After taking over the presidency for a second term in December 1841, Houston worked hard to convince the US that Texas was worth annexing to what they often called the "mother country," and Texians that it was worth joining the United States. It was not always an easy proposition on either side. Lamar, no longer president but still an influential figure in Texas, was one of the biggest proponents of Texas nationalism.

But even Lamar eventually changed his mind, based on his fear that staying independent would cost Texas the right to own slaves. He worried about growing British influence in Texas, especially that of abolitionists. In a November 1845 letter, Lamar wrote that he sought "for my country a shelter from the grasp of British cupidity beneath the only flag under which her institutions could be saved."

Joining the United States was a complicated proposition that took years; the US Senate initially rejected it in April 1844. James K. Polk ran for president in the United States on the platform of expanding the country through adding in Oregon and Texas territories.

Finally, in February 1845, the US Senate barely passed the legislation allowing the embattled, fiery, slaveholding republic to become the twenty-eighth state. Texas officially joined the country in December 1845.

Less than six months later, the United States declared war on Mexico, invading in 1846.

THE BRIEF, FIERCE WAR WITH MEXICO THAT EXTENDED FROM APRIL 1846 to February 1848 added more than five hundred thousand miles to the growing United States. In the Treaty of Guadalupe Hidalgo, Mexico gave up more than half of its land, which became parts of New Mexico, Arizona, Utah, Nevada, and Colorado. The treaty stipulated that Mexican citizens who lived on the surrendered territory were supposed to be able to choose whether they preferred US or Mexican citizenship; since citizenship in the United States was only allowed for white people at the time, they were commonly said to have become "white by treaty." They were also supposed to be able to keep their land, even if they chose to go back to Mexico. The reality was that many of them lost access to land either during the war or in the years following it. One newspaper editorial called the United States "the hungry condor of the North" that "feasted upon Upper California, Texas, New Mexico."

President James K. Polk and other leaders saw the expansion of the United States as the country's God-given right; 1845 was the year when the idea of Manifest Destiny entered the American vernacular and became a key concept in domestic and foreign policy. In less than two years, the war killed about forty thousand soldiers—twenty-five thousand from Mexico, fifteen thousand from the United States. Many of the military leaders in the US who would eventually fight in the Civil War, including Ulysses S. Grant and Robert E. Lee, gained battle experience along the border. And during those battles, the Texas Rangers earned the nickname "los diablos Tejanos" because of their relentless ferocity against Mexican citizens.

Many families who trace their ancestry to the days before the US-Mexico War, and who would forever have to explain to Anglos where exactly they were "from," passed down the phrase: "We did not cross the border; the border crossed us."

PART 4

SAM HOUSTON REESE

(1859–1899)

On the western side of the United States . . . [the vigilance committee follows] that sometime dissolute principle of political ethics, the right of the governed at all times to instant and arbitrary control of the government. The right thus claimed was not to be exercised except in cases of emergency, in cases where such interference should be deemed necessary, but it was always existent. . . . The vigilance committee will itself break the law, but it does not allow others to do so.

—HUBERT HOWE BANCROFT,
"POPULAR TRIBUNALS," 1887

[The feud members'] ideas about what it meant to be a Texan went a long way toward defining the term in the popular culture and the popular imagination for years to come. Their intention was to protect family honor. However, they believed that the right and proper way to do so was to become one of the most dishonorable kinds of human beings, a murderer.

—BILL STEIN, QUOTED IN
NO HOPE FOR HEAVEN,
NO FEAR OF HELL

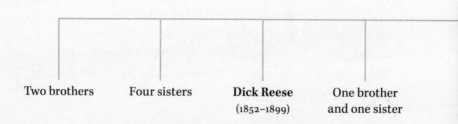

Sarah "Sally" Reese
(1765–1854)

Nine older siblings

Two brothers   Four sisters   **Dick Reese**   One brother
(1852–1899)   and one sister

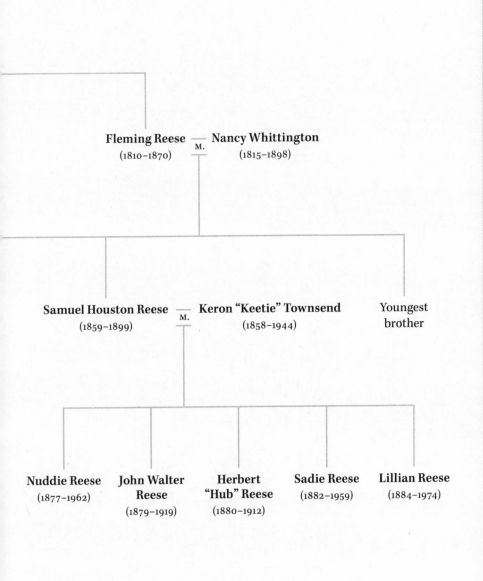

Fleming Reese
(1810–1870)

M.

Nancy Whittington
(1815–1898)

Samuel Houston Reese
(1859–1899)

M.

Keron "Keetie" Townsend
(1858–1944)

Youngest
brother

Nuddie Reese
(1877–1962)

John Walter
Reese
(1879–1919)

Herbert
"Hub" Reese
(1880–1912)

Sadie Reese
(1882–1959)

Lillian Reese
(1884–1974)

CHAPTER 24

Growing up in Texas, I remember hearing—among other things—that the Civil War was about "states' rights." It was one of those phrases that stuck with me, that sounded like critical thinking because it pushed back against a narrative interpretation that the South was born from a racist past. I did not fully understand until I was a young adult that the right that Southern states fought so vehemently to defend was, simply, the right to own slaves.

Put another way, it was the right to determine their own economic systems, which—for the states that became part of the Confederacy—meant being able to profit off slave labor. The marketing campaign that had successfully sold the narrative about the Texas Revolution a generation before laid the groundwork for the persuasive arguments in the 1850s as the South moved closer and closer to dividing the once United States. Leading up to the Civil War, the extreme language escalated for years; the playbook for that fiery rhetoric was written in Texas before and during the Texas Revolution. As Texas went in the 1830s, so did the rest of the South thirty years later.

Beginning in 1860, Southern states began seceding over their perception that President Abraham Lincoln planned to abolish slavery. Lincoln publicly insisted that he supported states' rights to own slaves if it kept those states in the union, and that his goals were to keep slavery from spreading to Western territories and prevent other states from leaving the nation. Despite those statements, Southern leaders painted Lincoln like the Texians had Santa Anna—a centralist dictator trying to oppress freedom-loving people.

Eleven states seceded. Their fear-based reaction caused the very action they had been worried about. Had they stayed in the nation, it seems unclear that Lincoln would actually have abolished slavery.

Texas was the seventh state to pull out on February 1, 1861, following South Carolina in December 1860, and then Mississippi, Florida, Alabama, Georgia, and Louisiana in January 1861. Lincoln successfully rallied to keep the border enslaving states—Delaware, Missouri, Kentucky, and Maryland—from leaving the nation. But by June 30, 1861, Virginia, Arkansas, Tennessee, and North Carolina were also part of the Confederacy.

For a very long time, the Civil War did not come close to Texas. The first major battle—the First Battle of Bull Run—was fought on July 21, 1861 near Manassas Junction, Virginia, where a combined total of 4,700 Union and Confederate soldiers died. The battles came thick and fast after that: hundreds died in eight skirmishes; 17,398 people died at the Battle of Fort Donelson in February 1862; 23,741 died at the Battle of Shiloh in April 1862. In 1862, the casualties remained staggeringly high in battles at Seven Pines, Gaines' Mill, Bull Run, Antietam, Perryville, and Fredericksburg.

The Battle of Stones River, in which 23,515 soldiers died, was roaring when Lincoln issued the "Emancipation Proclamation" on January 1, 1863.

On New Year's Day in 1863, hundreds of thousands of people in the eleven Confederate states were suddenly freed. The limitations of the proclamation were many—Lincoln was still trying to thread a complicated political needle and keep the border states in the country. But when he declared that "all persons held as slaves" in those states "are, and henceforward shall be free," it was the first time since the founding of the country that slavery was outlawed at a federal level.

Lincoln pulled a Bustamante and gave exceptions to abolition, allowing some states to keep enslaving people. Also, any Southern areas of the Confederacy that were already under Northern control got to keep slaves. Contrarily, Lincoln's exceptions meant that only in states that illegally seceded were slaves legally freed—including Texas.

The great power of the document was in its promise—if the Union won, slavery would be abolished. Word spread quickly in the Southern states, especially among Black communities who literally fought for their own freedom. By the end of the war, two hundred thousand Black soldiers would join the Union's cause.

In Texas, the news certainly reached the enslavers that the people they held in bondage had already been freed. But they used the same tactic that Texian and Tejano officials perfected when Mexico was trying to outlaw slavery—they did everything they could to keep that information among themselves. Rumors ran through the Black community like water, but enslavers controlled their movements, so they limited the knowledge as best they could. Like the San Antonio governor after the Mexican law freeing slaves in 1829, and like Austin controlling the newspaper after the immigration law in 1830, so Texas enslavers did not advertise the Emancipation Proclamation to the people they oppressed.

They knew then what generations of politicians after them would also come to grasp: keeping people in ignorance is a way to retain power.

TEXAS SAW RELATIVELY LITTLE ACTION, AND ONLY WELL INTO THE Civil War. Tens of thousands of soldiers died on land battles in Tennessee, Virginia, Maryland, and Kentucky leading up to the Emancipation Proclamation. On September 24, 1862, Union steamers and schooners began an offensive against the Confederate shore battery at Sabine Pass; the next day, the town surrendered, providing Union access to the interior of the state. A week later, on October 4, 1862, the port of Galveston fell to the Union Navy. However, within the next year, the Confederates regained control of Galveston and Sabine Pass. Union troops abandoned their posts at camps and forts throughout the state.

The short-lived Union blockade in the Gulf of Mexico affected Texans' trade—"Texians" became "Texans" around 1850. The cotton industry in Texas suffered when international markets boycotted Confederate cotton. It took some time, but Texas cotton-growers found a workaround, sending their cotton south to Mexican ports to export, where they were paid in Mexican gold rather than the soon-to-be worthless Confederate currency. The economic devastation that the postwar South would face was not as bad in Texas. In fact, many Texans profited enormously off the war.

In contrast, most Texans saw nothing of the destruction that pockmarked the rest of the Confederacy. In 1864, Lincoln and General Ulysses S. Grant began a campaign, which many historians chart as the move from a "limited war" to a "total war," to hasten the end by allowing civilians to bear the consequences of war. The campaign destroyed the homes and livelihoods of ordinary citizens. Virginians called the Union's assault in 1864 on the Shenandoah Valley "the Burning." In Atlanta, Sherman promised to "make Georgia howl" to crush the spirit of the Confederacy; his horrific March to the Sea marked a turning point in the war and was memorialized in *Gone with the Wind*.

As the war raged on, Texas became a Confederacy haven. As Union soldiers moved through other Southern states, enslavers forcibly relocated enslaved people to keep them from being freed or from escaping to join the Union army, often bringing them to Texas. By some estimates, 150,000 still-enslaved people arrived in Texas only *after* the 1863 Emancipation Proclamation.

The last battle of the Civil War was in Texas. On April 9, 1865, Robert E. Lee surrendered to Grant at Appomattox Courthouse in Virginia. Even though Confederate troops in Texas knew the war had officially ended, they kept fighting. At Palmito Ranch near Brownsville, two hundred and fifty men of the 62nd US Colored Infantry Regiment fought alongside other Union soldiers against Confederate troops who refused to acknowledge defeat.

The Confederates won the last battle in Texas, but soon after it was over, they surrendered completely.

On June 19, 1865, federal troops arrived back in Galveston to take over the state. That's where they gave the official proclamation announcing the end of slavery. Enslavers could no longer prevent Black people from hearing that they were free. The end of slavery was still technically ad hoc and state by state until it became federal law later with the adoption of the Thirteenth Amendment in December 1865.

But beginning with that first "Juneteenth," slavery in Texas was essentially abolished.

THIS IS ANOTHER POINT IN THE NARRATIVE IN WHICH MORE SIMPLIS-tic versions of history focus on the happy ending rather than a more complicated story. June 19, 1865 represents not just the end of slavery in Texas, a turning point after which enslaved Texans would never again have news of their freedom kept from them. Juneteenth marked the end of one way those in power used to retain control for more than three decades: a complete suppression of information.

But it was also the beginning of a new era in which those who held power would develop and hone new strategies and narratives to preserve their political domination. The Union troops coming through Galveston ushered in the beginning of a period that would last forty years, until the Democrats—then the more conservative party—were able to finally wrangle control of the state.

The debates that erupted in Texas and the United States after Juneteenth and the end of the Civil War have never gone away, including who should have access to voting, education, and affordable homes; who has the right to citizenship; who has the right to bend or break the law in the service to larger ideas of justice; among many other topics we wrestle over. In many ways, though we celebrate that Juneteenth closed one chapter in Texas political history, we're still living in the era that began that day.

As Juneteenth was a turning point in Texas history, I also want to mark a turning point in this book. When I first started reading about this time period in Texas and found how deeply it resonated with my lived experiences in the last few years here, I worried: Have we really learned nothing in the last century and a half?

But as I began to fit this narrative together, thanks in part to the courageous and thoughtful historians and writers and community members and ancestors who have been doing this work for more decades than I have, their work deepened my hope.

The hope for me comes from the moral courage of the people who refused to back away from the truth of what was happening in their own communities, who stood up to neighbors and friends and relatives and demanded an end to terrorizing fear and unjust power-grabbing politics. I have so much hope because those people who lived in the places they both loved and criticized were strong and brave in the face of grave danger and personal loss.

But to glean that hope, we have to first know the story of what they lived through, to understand the moral codes that drive the behavior of people in violent times, and mourn what happened in those years in Texas.

THE END OF THE CIVIL WAR FOUND MANY PRO-CONFEDERACY TEXANS itching for a fight, with plenty of money and no incentive to give up a lifestyle that benefited them enormously. The fear that Black people would rise up against white people in power—the same fear passed down in each generation since the earliest days of the Virginia colony—gripped leaders in Texas. After Juneteenth, almost from one day to the next, they had gone from enslavers to fellow citizens with freed people they still viewed as inferior.

Reconstruction happened in three phases. The first was Wartime Reconstruction, which aimed, among other things, to shorten the war and move toward reconciliation in a nation that was actively slaughtering each other. It lasted until 1865: when President Lincoln was assassinated in April, Andrew Johnson became president in May, and the Thirteenth Amendment abolished slavery in the United States in December.

President Johnson ushered in the second phase, Presidential Recon-struction, but still, it did not change things drastically for Black people in the South, including Texas. Under Presidential Reconstruction, the former enslavers returned to the idea used by Peter Ellis Bean and others in Texas when they called slaves "indentured servants"—they just gave oppression and persecution another name. In 1866, the Texas legislature followed in the footsteps of Mississippi, South Carolina, and other Southern states in trying to circumvent federal laws that gave rights to recently freed Black people in a series of "Black Codes."

Under the Black Codes, any Black people who did not have a job had to have a white guardian who forced them to work without pay; if they quit that job, they could face imprisonment. They could be fined for violating curfews, for carrying firearms, or making insulting gestures in public. They could not perform any of the duties of civil life: serve on juries, testify as witnesses against white people, or vote. For a time, it seemed like the lawlessness of the Texas Revolutionary days would re-turn to Texas, that slavery would stay under another name. But nothing was certain.

The third stage, Congressional Reconstruction, only exacerbated the chaos in Texas. At the national level, Reconstruction sounded glorious—the Reconstruction Act of 1867 provided a path back into the Union for Confederate states and the Fourteenth Amendment declared for the first time that Black men could be citizens, with all the rights citizens were entitled to, and that any state that tried to limit the citizens' right to vote would be punished. The Fifteenth Amendment in 1870 made it even more explicit: no one could disenfranchise anyone based on their race, skin color, or "previous condition of servitude." The Black Codes in Texas became illegal.

However, whether that legality was enforceable was another ques-tion. Anyone who had fought for the Confederacy—which, in many Southern states, was almost all white men—was disqualified from elected offices. Since many county law enforcement positions were elected, that meant that officers faced down men who had recently been their enemies in war. Men in trouble with the law simply fled the county for a while to keep from being imprisoned or prosecuted. Or they stayed and counted on a justice system made up of sympathetic peers who had no interest in serving real justice. Or they stayed and fought and fought and fought.

In 1870, a former Union general named Edmund J. Davis became the governor of Texas and one of his first priorities was to institute a state police force. The Texas State Police both curbed and contributed to the violence in the state; in their first month of existence, they arrested 239 people accused of murder or attempted murder, and enforced the Congressional Reconstruction policies designed to protect Black people. They also committed murder themselves.

By 1870, Texas was by far the most violent state in the turbulent nation. In that one year alone, Texas had 250 percent more murders than the closest contending state. Contrary to popular depictions in later Westerns, Texans were not allowed to openly carry weapons—at least, they weren't supposed to. The Texas legislature passed a strict gun law in April 1871 that stated it was illegal to carry "any pistol, dirk, dagger, slung-shot, sword-cane, spear, brass-knuckles, bowie-knife, or any other kind of knife" unless that person had "reasonable grounds for fearing an unlawful attack on his person" or was serving "as a militiaman in actual service, or as a peace officer or policeman." This meant that political power in a community also correlated with firepower—whoever was elected to office could fill the law enforcement positions with their handpicked allies, thus arming their side in disputes that frequently turned deadly.

From the 1860s to the 1890s, what one historian called "the law of private vengeance" dominated several parts of Texas through long-lasting feuds. These were more than just occasional conflicts in a community; the feuds reached far, affecting entire families or communities. The feuds revealed critical aspects about the beliefs and values of some people in the state at the time. And they transformed narratives and cultural instincts that would be passed down later in the myths of Texas.

Historians at the time and later often compared the feuds that marked the Reconstruction era in Texas and throughout the South to clan battles centuries earlier in the United Kingdom, where many of the feudalists' ancestors came from—including my own family in Texas.

Counties became like small kingdoms, in which elected officials who held power could arm their own militias and manage policies in ways that benefited them—profit off land deals, strengthen political alliances, and seek revenge against their enemies so that their family members and allies prospered.

Newspapers across the United States could not get enough of the stories of feuds in Texas. At the height of the yellow journalism time period near the end of the nineteenth century, sensational stories about feuds helped create a national myth about Texas. Those articles would become the basis for many of the later tropes of cowboys in films and movies: the long-held grudge match over minor slights, shoot-outs at saloons, brave or foolhardy heroes willing to die because they would never back down from a fight.

The articles were often factually incorrect, but the truth was secondary to the myth they were helping to write about Texans as gunslingers who shot first and asked questions later.

IN GRADUATE SCHOOL, I HAD RESEARCHED AND TAUGHT NINETEENTH-century literature, so I thought I knew what to expect when I began looking into the Reconstruction era. In fact, I did not think I would spend much time in this half of the century; I did not know then about my family's connection to the feuds, and I was more focused on the empresario- and Republic-building eras in Texas.

I had just begun to dig into this research when the January 6 attack on the US Capitol happened; I read books and articles about Reconstruction fights while watching almost nonsensical shouting matches at my local school board meetings during the controversial days of masking during the pandemic in Texas. It felt in those days—often, it still feels—as if something dangerous and volatile were boiling to the surface.

I cannot tell you how many sentences I underlined in books about feuds that stopped feeling academic to me because they sounded so much like the time period I found myself living in. I started reading them almost like societal self-help books, identifying underlying issues I'd never thought of but suddenly seemed obvious. Much of what I read felt as if it could be lifted wholesale out of the past and spoken by a pundit on the news today. I learned that a strong motivator in the organized vigilantism of the Reconstruction era—one that I think is also a strong one today—is aggrieved morality. Then or now, these aren't "crazy" times of upheaval caused by "ignorant" people—these are tumultuous times of clashing, competing moral systems. One historian said the people involved in the Reconstruction-era feuds were not "rebellious and unrestrained": "Strictly speaking, such people are not lawless—they are just operating under an earlier, more primitive code."

In the late nineteenth century, the depths of that complexity was lost in newspaper stories that had a sensationalist tone about mass shootings and serial murder: "What can you expect?" the article writers seem to be asking. "These are Texans, after all, and everyone knows they'll kill any man who looks at them wrong." It's the same thing that happens today when outside journalists helicopter into Texas, look for someone with the thickest accent they can find who says exactly what they expect to hear, and then leave to report on what "locals" really value. Those of us who live here know to expect it, but it can still be galling.

Underneath the stereotypical representations, we see the complex truth of what is happening here. This is especially true when it comes to an increase in violence in Texas. Of the ten deadliest mass shootings in the recent history of the United States, five of them have happened in Texas.

When I originally wrote that sentence, it read "four of them." The shooting at a mall in Allen, Texas on May 5, 2023 was the fifth. I worry that by the time this book goes to print, that figure will again be obsolete.

As I honed my research and found that my family had been in one of those feuds, I saw eerie parallels between what happened in Colorado County from 1871 to 1911 and the rise in vigilantism in Texas—and around the US—that began in the 2010s.

I am not the only one to notice. During our first interview, I asked the historian James Kearney—whose story I will tell more of later—whether he saw parallels between that time and where we are now. His reply was immediate: "Absolutely. Are you kidding me? You have all these 'un-Reconstructed' Confederates and they set out to dismantle all the Reconstruction programs one by one; it took them forty years to do it. They won the second Civil War. It's all a legacy of slavery, that certain human beings can control others."

And then a sentence I can't stop thinking about: "Slavery has disappeared, but the attitudes are still there. It's not a parallel, it's a continuation. It's just a new manifestation of the same old attitudes."

IF WE ARE STILL GRAPPLING WITH A POST-JUNETEENTH WORLD IN Texas, then we are right to take the rising storm of violence today seriously. The extremist language and accompanying violence are the same now as they were during the years when feuds racked Texas.

Those feuds were not just feuds; they were waterspouts to the Civil War's hurricane. And like those destructive storms, that kind of divisive, one-side-take-all violence can be very hard to control. One historian of Texas feuds wrote that the habit of using violence outside the law was "catching"—once you begin assaulting or killing others, it becomes difficult to pull back from the extreme edges: "Vigilantes, mobsters, and feudists are all alike in their inability to stop of their own accord. Once men take the law into their own custody, they seem unable to lay it down. . . . Only a higher authority or mutual extermination can stop the proceedings." It can be stopped, but it is very difficult, he said: "A feud has no brakes." As the extremism that led to the Civil War razed a region, so the extremism of a feud razed their communities.

In no place was that fact more evident than in Colorado County, Texas, where Sally Reese's grandchildren lived.

CHAPTER 25

The first of Sally Reese's children to make it to Texas was her youngest child, Fleming Reese, who came in 1849. Like the rest of her children—including his oldest brother, my ancestor, William—Fleming had been born in Bedford County, Virginia. By 1836, when he was twenty-six, Fleming had joined the family in Tennessee with Sally and most of the clan. He did not stay long in Tennessee.

By 1838, he was in Montgomery, Alabama, marrying Nancy Jane Whittington. Nancy and Fleming had six children in Alabama before finally arriving in Texas in 1849. They had five more kids in Texas, including Samuel Houston Reese, born in Austin County in 1859, the tenth of eleven children.

Sally ended up with more than seventy grandchildren. It seems unlikely that she ever made the long trek to Texas, or that these Reeses returned to Tennessee for a visit. In all likelihood, when Fleming left, they never saw each other again.

Around the time my direct ancestors were settling in Arkansas in the small village chronicled in *Corinth and Its Kinfolk*, the two oldest sons of Fleming Reese became Confederate soldiers in Texas. All eleven of the children—including the two soldiers—would lead long lives, well into the twentieth century, except Sam and his older brother, Dick

Reese. Living in post–Civil War Texas turned out to be more dangerous than living through war.

A few months after the last battle of the Civil War was fought in Texas and federal troops moved into the state to aid with the transition in May 1865, the Reese family moved to Colorado County, Texas. That's where they were when Fleming died five years later, in 1870. An entry from a 1916 history book that mentions the Reeses says that after the family's move, "There they spent the remainder of their lives—earnest, intelligent, industrious and God-fearing folk who lived up to the measure of their opportunities and who merited and received the respect and good will of their fellow men." There was no mention of the simmering, unresolved tensions left in Texas at the end of the Confederacy, the battleground that Colorado County became, or that many of the Reeses—along with many of the other "God-fearing folk"—were less earnest and industrious and more ambitious, vindictive, and willing to stop at nothing to stay in power.

Following decades of seemingly endless opportunities to be a soldier—the US Revolution, the War of 1812, the Texas Revolution, the Mexican-American War, and then the Civil War—the Reconstruction era should have ushered in a time of relative peace in the area. Instead, it left a generation of men around the ages of Dick and Sam Reese too young to be soldiers but deeply influenced by the battle stories of their fathers, brothers, cousins, and community members.

They were primed for the viciousness that would come. Eventually, the escalating violence in the county would devolve into the longest running feud in Texas history. Of all of the feuds that marked those years when Texas was the murder capital of the country, this was among the deadliest. Despite the fact that historians often call it "the Reese-Townsend feud," the Reeses were affected by but not really involved in the feud for at least twenty years.

The Reeses would have the last word, though. They may not have started it, but Sally Reese's descendants were there till the bitter end.

CHAPTER 26

There is one man who knows more than anyone living about the feud in Colorado County. James Kearney—who told me in our first interview that the Reconstruction-era views remain intact today—is a historian who teaches at the University of Texas. When I emailed Kearney, who wrote the definitive book *No Hope for Heaven, No Fear of Hell*, on this feud, I had no idea he had grown up in Colorado County, and that he and his wife still live on land that had been in his family since their original land grant in the 1830s. Nor did I know about his conversations with a man named John Goeppinger.

Without Kearney, the story of this feud would probably be very different. For almost a century, the newspaper depictions from the nineteenth century set the tone historians and popular writers took up later when describing the feud, a tone echoed from mid-twentieth-century Westerns on TV and film and pulp fiction. You can almost hear them dropping their *g*'s to talk about the gun-slingin', cattle-wranglin', whiskey-drinkin' Texans shootin' and carousin' in Colorado County.

For a post–World War II nation rocked by the horror of the Holocaust and the loss of American lives, those trope-heavy Westerns—whether books or comics or movies—did important psychological work. They were a way to make sense of an otherwise topsy-turvy world. A nation grieving soldiers in battle found comfort in the black-and-white tales of good and evil and courage in the face of injustice. As one historian of Texas feuds defined the idea, "There will be times when we need a man who will die before he will run."

Those myths were solidified in Colorado County in the years when Kearney was a child when the local piano teacher (and Sally Reese's great-granddaughter), Lillian Reese, wrote a book about her family's involvement. Kearney calls her "Miss Lillie" when he talks about her. Miss Lillie's narrative is simple and straightforward and very, very clear—her father, Sam Houston Reese, is the hero of her story and his enemies were the villains, and everything he did was right. It's not that everyone in the county believed Lillie's version of the story, of course, but it remained one of the only histories written about the feud for a long time.

That myth shifted for James Kearney through a series of conversations he had in the early 1970s; Kearney's coming of age correlated with the changing narratives in Texas and the US as the simplistic hierarchical stories of his childhood in the 1950s and 1960s grew into the complicated narratives of the Civil Rights era and Vietnam War years. In the early 1970s, Kearney had just returned from a year serving on the frontlines of the Vietnam War as a battle medic. He had seen firsthand the horrendous physical and psychological cost to war.

When he came home, a friend named John Goeppinger—whom everyone called "Goep" (pronounced "Gup")—wanted to tell him some stories of what happened during the feud. Goep was like an uncle to Kearney. Goep was now an old man, but he had been young during the feud—a Reese man who witnessed almost everything.

Kearney went into the interviews with some of the same attitudes of his childhood watching Westerns, of a boy hearing some cowboy tall tales. But Goep did not tell him feel-good folksy stories. He confessed dark secrets that changed everything Kearney knew about his hometown.

I know what Kearney's views were in his interviews with Goep because I heard the recordings. It took a little bit of time for Kearney to trust me with them; I am one of only four people who have listened to them in almost fifty years. I heard Kearney's young voice asking naive questions, and heard Goep's harrowing, otherworldly laugh. James Kearney is still protective of his beloved town. It is also precisely because he loves his hometown, his home state, and his country that he has committed his life to telling the story of what really happened.

The stories of the Reese-Townsend feud had their hold on the community for a long, long time. I wove these three sources together—Lillie's book, Goep's confessions, and Kearney's scholarly work—to first lay down the myth and then the truth about the Reeses' role in the feud in Colorado County. In doing so, I found hope in the moral courage of James Kearney and others who have uncovered their community's complicated past, and learned what I needed to begin this work for my own beloved hometown in Texas.

CHAPTER 27

Lillian Reese's book was a family chronicle like *Corinth and Its Kinfolk* but feud-style. *Flaming Feuds of Colorado County* was published in 1962 by a small Texas publication company. The front cover of the book gives the author as John Walter Reese and the editor as Lillian Estelle Reese, but Walter died in 1919. The story in the book was controlled entirely by Lillie, the last surviving member of the close-knit Reese family, who vetted, compiled, edited, and finally published a narrative that was her final act of the feud.

She was not quiet about her views even before the book came out. Kearney remembers how, every year on the anniversary of her father's death, Miss Lillie hung her father's bloody clothes on the clothesline outside of her house—her own personal memorial ceremony.

In a "Publisher's Foreword," the unnamed editors at the press acknowledge the slanted tone of the book ("The reader, we hope, will appreciate the nice sense of tolerating the protagonist's right to his opinion and a broad, generous willingness to let bygones be"). But they point out the morality at the heart of the feud: "A sort of code of ethics, unwritten but rigidly understood by both actors and spectators in the tenuous ground rules." Ultimately, the foreword argues that things in Colorado County weren't really as bad as the book might make them seem to be: "Life in the modern city is not as tranquil as it was in Colorado County in the '80s and '90s. Criminal acts were at a minimum and, come to think of it, divorce, narcotic and psychiatric problems were very rare. . . . The feud-fever rarely attained epidemic proportions." It was the early 1960s version of the rhetorical and political move that has become so prevalent in Texan and American culture: a nostalgic look at a romanticized past. Even when that past included open acts of warfare on the streets, the publishers argue, it was better than "life in the modern city."

That was certainly Lillie's view—that life when she was a child in the 1890s was simple and wonderful. Everyone knew their place in a society that followed strict hierarchical lines. In *Flaming Feuds*, Black people are portrayed with the same tropes they had been previous to the Civil War in the South, as they would be later in propaganda films like *Birth of a Nation*: Black people were either "good," meaning grateful and happy to serve white people at all times; or "bad," meaning they were threats that white people had to respond to immediately with violent acts that restored the social order.

There is not a lot of complexity in Lillie's book. Her brothers, Walter and Hub, are rascals with hearts of gold; her mother, Keetie, a saint; and their Townsend cousins evil incarnate. It is not so much the story of the feud as the story of how the Reese family was wronged during the feud.

Lillie's spin on the homicidal rampages in Colorado County makes her sweet family stories even more horrifying—a little girl's music box tinkling merrily at a blood-drenched murder scene.

LILLIE'S STORY BEGINS IN THE EARLY 1870S, WITH THE INCITING INCI-dent of a feud between the two original families: the Staffords and the Townsends. Lillie's mother was a Townsend. The Stafford and Townsend clans had both been in Colorado County for decades and were well respected—the Staffords were rich ranchers and Townsend family members helped capture Santa Anna at San Jacinto. In 1867, one of the Townsends was accused of being a horse thief and was killed by a posse of men. Those men went to trial in 1871, where Bob Stafford served as a surprise witness on behalf of the defense. Because of Bob Stafford, the men who murdered the horse-thieving Townsend got off. The Townsends came after Bob and the other Staffords to avenge that horse-thieving Townsend in a shootout that left both sides wounded. After that, the feud would continue on and off for decades.

The specifics of the feud can be frankly dizzying; some iterations of the story feel like the Texas history version of listening to middle schoolers explain how a fight in the lunchroom started, with more detail than any outside observer could ever want about who said what and who gave the side eye to whom. But understanding the key players in broad strokes makes the story clearer, especially since almost everyone in the story is related, and half of the people the Reeses hated were their close cousins, nephews, or nieces.

The racial makeup of Colorado County also matters to the story. Even when the feud was between two powerful white families, the violence in Colorado County was always about race and political power. The verdant land along the Colorado River had brought enslavers to the area in astounding numbers, especially after Texas joined the United States in 1845. A few of those enslavers became very rich. In the years leading up to the Civil War, there were almost as many Black people in Colorado County as white people. By 1860, 306 white families enslaved 3,559 people in the county, and fourteen of those families held huge fortunes of at least one hundred thousand dollars each—more than $3.5 million in today's currency.

Bob Stafford was not one of those men in 1860, but he was paying attention. Over the next few decades, he would become a self-made cattle tycoon in a time period racked with economic recession by navigating the tumultuous Reconstruction-era years well. The Staffords—Bob, his three brothers, his son, and their employees or other relatives who were loyal Stafford men—were deeply racist and had a reputation for ferocious brutality.

After the Civil War ended, once-powerful former enslavers worried they would be in the political minority. Colorado County also had many white people who were of German or Czech descent or who did not enslave people. That meant that, in terms of population, the former enslavers' fear might have been true, especially if the non-enslaving white people joined forces with the Black voting bloc. And that bloc was sizable: By 1870, 44 percent of the population of Colorado County—8,326 people—were Black and possessed the newly acquired right to vote.

But the economic disparity remained profound—the average white family owned $2,331 in combined real estate and other properties, worth about $51,158 today. The average Black family owned only $14–$15 worth of property, worth only $330 today. Five years after slavery was abolished, white people owned 645 percent more than Black families in the county. The acute poverty of the people who had, less than a decade before, been enslaved affects this story significantly because, while Black voters had the strength of numbers, they were in every other way outgunned and out-empowered by the white population.

However, white people in power still felt they were threatened by a large, now-free Black population and remained anxious to "contain" that perceived threat, often resorting to widescale violence at the slightest provocation.

The Townsends, though, sought to alleviate this apparent threat through political persuasion. They realized fairly early on that it was easier and more profitable to entice or manipulate the Black population to vote in ways they wanted. They listened to and worked with Black voters, which on the surface might appear to be admirable from a modern vantage point. But the history of the county shows their motivation was almost entirely about benefiting the Townsend political machine. Townsend kin and their handpicked candidates dominated elected positions in the county and profited enormously. Black people in those years in Colorado County chose the lesser of two evils in aligning with the Townsends; they were used as political pawns, but at least they could negotiate some benefits to their community.

Not all of the Townsends were willing to lay aside their racism to attain political power. The youngest sister of the original feuding Townsend clan was Keron "Keetie" Townsend. She was thirteen in 1871 when the feud began with her family on one side and Bob Stafford and his men on the other.

For a long time, her involvement with the feud was nominal. Keetie married Sam Houston Reese when she was eighteen and he was seventeen. For ten years, while they had five children—Nuddie, Walter, Hub, Sadie, and Lillie—Sam made his living as a farmer. Then, in 1886, he was elected constable in a small town in Colorado County. It was the beginning of a profitable, meaningful career for Sam in law enforcement, and for Keetie as a high-profile wife in the community. Within a few years, they would take Bob's place in the feud that would rack the county for decades. Keetie, and then their youngest daughter, Lillie, would be the keeper of the family's stories of that feud.

FROM THE 1870S TO THE 1890S—AT WHICH POINT BARBED WIRE PUT AN end to the open range and effectively ended enormous cattle drives—the Staffords stayed on top of the cattle industry out of sheer cussed meanness. Stafford men fought with a variety of people, none more than the Townsends, but not only them; the fights were usually contained to small skirmishes. There were few things Bob Stafford couldn't buy or bully his way past. If someone bought land on what he considered his territory, even if he was grazing cattle on public lands legally available for purchase from the government by homesteaders, he had no qualms about running them off—through force if necessary, relying on his relatives or cattlemen to do the job. Bob himself rarely got his hands dirty.

Bob was the most successful of the Stafford brothers, employing many of his family members in his multiple businesses: ranching, meatpacking, banking, and real estate. He had plans to be the most powerful man in the county. He wanted to be more than rich; he wanted to be cultivated. He built an opera house that would put his name on the map as a cultured leader of the community.

As the balance of power in the county shifted and the Townsends efficiently built a political dynasty through the Black vote, Bob Stafford became more and more enraged. It didn't help that those were the waning days of the great cattle industry in Texas: in fact, they were all waning days. The glorious years immortalized in countless movies and books lasted only about twenty years or so, not even a generation, not long enough for cross-country cattle drives to become a way of life. Bob and the vengeful Stafford men found themselves thwarted in their efforts to make money and seize land the way they had in the past, just as they watched their enemies profit off political power.

By 1890, when the second phase of the feud exploded, there were really only three things that stood in Bob's way: the barbed wire fences that blocked his ability to take any land he wanted; his drunk son, Warren; and the Black voting bloc of Colorado County controlled by the Townsend political machine.

CHAPTER 28

Accoring to Lillie's book, the soft-spoken, music-loving, right-living Reeses were victims of a feud they happened to get caught up in on one hot evening in July 1890. The town of Columbus gathered to celebrate laying the cornerstone for a new courthouse. Bob Stafford had built his opera house by then, along with a bank and a big, beautiful house in town. Those buildings lay in his corner of town.

The courthouse was Townsend territory. Keetie's first cousin, J. Light Townsend, had been the elected sheriff for a decade; he lived with his family above the city jail. One of Light's nephews, Marcus Townsend, was a lawyer with powerful business connections; he was the brains behind the Townsend political machine. From the beginning, Lillie writes derogatorily about the Townsends. Light was only elected, Lillie states, because Black people "could be bought with money or fear . . . and Mr. Townsend and his friends controlled the negro vote of Colorado County. Of course, the Stafford faction fought Townsend at each election, but being avowed enemies to the negro race, never succeeded in defeating him." Lillie frames the fact that the Staffords and Reeses remained committedly racist as a sign of their integrity.

Light's other nephew, Larkin Hope, had just been elected city marshal. In that role, he deputized his brother Marion. Lillie calls Larkin "a killer and a gunman" who "posed as a friend of the Staffords" but was really a traitor all along.

These four men—Light and Marcus Townsend, Larkin and Marion Hope—are the villains of Lillie's story, and Marcus Townsend especially is the mastermind.

As Lillie tells it, for ten years, the Staffords' pressure on Sheriff Light Townsend increased until he was afraid to be alone. But when Bob Stafford came to Larkin the marshal—who Bob thought was a friend—and asked a favor, it seemed to the Townsend side that the time had come to strike against the Staffords. Bob's son, Warren Stafford, was a well-known killer himself in the county; he committed brutal acts, some under his father's orders, some under his own volition.

According to Lillie, before the courthouse cornerstone festivities began that day in July 1890, Bob pulled Larkin aside: "You know my son Warren will be in town and will get drunk as usual. I want you to take him home. Don't lock him up. . . . It would hurt his mother to have this happen. I don't care what you charge. I'll pay the price gladly."

Lillie said that Larkin took this information back to the Townsend faction and they schemed together.

On July 7, when the community gathered to celebrate, Sheriff Light Townsend was at home with a real or fabricated illness, keeping him out of the fray. As Bob predicted, Warren Stafford got drunk. Rather than secreting him home like Bob had asked, Marshal Larkin Hope and Deputy Marion Hope paraded Warren past the Staffords' large home, where Lillie says his mother saw "her son's degradation and mistreatment." Then the Hope brothers went to the saloon down the street.

They did not have to wait long. In Lillie's telling, Bob was reasonable. He came to confront the Hope brothers with his own brother, John. They were unarmed. Bob asked, "Larkin, why didn't you do as you promised me? I don't think I've been treated right."

Then Hope cursed them out and, without provocation according to Lillie, "Larkin shot Bob and almost simultaneously, Marion shot John, who was not even showing anger."

In Lillie's account, Bob Stafford died as a kind, thoughtful leader in the community betrayed by malicious enemies, and John Stafford was shot for being in the wrong place at the wrong time supporting his brother.

REWIND AND WIDEN THE LENS, THIS TIME TO INCLUDE THE ACCOUNTS of historians and several eyewitnesses in the local paper: Bob came into the saloon calling the Hope brothers "a goddamn set of worthless curs" and then stood in Larkin's face, threatening him and cussing him out, growing increasingly irate. Larkin's wife tried to get Larkin to leave but he refused; Bob's brother John tried to get Bob to leave, and he also refused.

And then Bob delivered awful last words to Larkin, accusing him succinctly of courting the Black vote and possibly sleeping with Black women.

Larkin shot him point-blank.

John Stafford was watching his brother die when Marion shot him.

FOCUS IN ON JOHN AS LILLIE'S STORY CONVERGES WITH EYEWITNESS AC-counts again: John Stafford survived Deputy Marion's first shots. John's wife was nearby. He begged the Hope brothers to let him live to say goodbye to her; he knew he was dying already.

Larkin walked up to him and said, "Take your medicine like a man, you son of a bitch." And then he shot John in the face, killing him.

Marion Hope fled to his Uncle Light's house, where the sheriff was at home, apparently still sick. Larkin Hope stayed at the scene of the crime. Both Hope brothers were charged with first-degree murder.

LILLIE'S STORY IS OBVIOUSLY BIASED, BUT EVEN THE MOST OBJECTIVE accounts certainly make it seem like the Townsends had a well-laid plan in place. Why else would a city marshal and a deputy antagonize and then publicly murder the richest, most powerful man in town on the afternoon of one of the city's busiest days?

Marcus Townsend—the Hopes' cousin and lawyer, and Lillie's vil-lainous schemer—successfully represented the brothers in the murder trial. Within two years, both Larkin and Marion had been exonerated of a murder that numerous witnesses saw committed firsthand in broad daylight. Light Townsend ran for reelection as sheriff in November 1890 and won, carried to victory by the Townsends' connections again.

In 1890, Light appointed his niece's husband as his chief deputy. If Light intended to find someone who was neutral and who might help ease the tension in the county, it seemed like a good choice—the deputy was not only married to a Townsend, he was the son of Bob Stafford's close friend, and he was well respected by everyone in their fractured, contentious community.

And that's how Sam Houston Reese came into the story.

ONE OF THE TWISTS OF HISTORY THAT I WOULD NOT WRITE IF I WERE a novelist because it would not be believable is this: Sheriff Light Townsend probably feigned illness to be absent on the day Bob Stafford was murdered in 1890. And then, four years later, and only days after he had been elected to his fifth consecutive term as county sheriff, Light Townsend was done in by a bad can of oysters.

Sam Reese, who was his chief deputy, was voted in as interim sher-iff in 1894. In those years, Sam and Keetie profited enormously off the insider knowledge they gained in the sheriff's office. At first, Keetie didn't want him to be sheriff, but as Lillie described him, Sam "was from the old school and was his own man," and soon Keetie and Sam both liked the position of power and influence they attained in the community.

In 1896, Sam Houston Reese ran for reelection as sheriff. Despite tight competition from two other men, Reese won—in large part because of Marcus Townsend's support. Over the next two years, however, Sam and Keetie increasingly chafed against the expectations the Townsends obviously had that their cousin and her husband would toe the family line. Anyone who knew Sam Reese could have told Marcus Townsend he would not sit quietly in anyone's pocket.

Exactly where and when the Reeses' relationship with the Townsends frayed is up for debate. But Sam's independence, and his sense of what it meant to be a Reese who was beholden to no one, played a big part.

IN SAM'S SECOND TERM AS SHERIFF, THE TWO MAIN VILLAINS OF LIL-lie's story became Marcus Townsend and Larkin Hope; she portrayed them as one-dimensional villains tripping over themselves to harm Sam Reese and his family—the coyotes to Sam's clever roadrunner.

The Sam Houston Reese of *Flaming Feuds of Colorado County* was too smart to be fooled by the antics of wily criminals, wranglers, and smugglers trying to pull one over on him. He was quiet in his anger and quick with his gun, but affectionate and loving with his children. Lillie framed even his blatant racism as reasonable discernment: a Black man who covered up for a friend who had broken the law "did not fool" Reese and his comrade, "for they were Southerners and knew this species well."

In 1898, after four years as sheriff, Sam's great enemy—and Lillie's buffoon—Larkin Hope decided to run against him.

Lillie does not portray this part of the story: Sam knew that, because of Larkin's relationships within the community and the Townsends' influence, Larkin would garner a much higher percentage of the Black vote. Larkin was less a threat to Sam's life and more of a threat to the job that gave the Reeses wealth and status in the community.

Larkin was shot and killed before the election could take place, on August 3, 1898.

In describing the shooting, Lillie makes it seem as if Larkin's bad past caught up with him: "Reports were to the effect that as Hope walked down the main thoroughfare on the sidewalk of Milam Street, a man stepped out from a narrow space between two buildings and emptied two loads of buckshot into him. It was about nine o'clock at night and no one saw the person who committed the deed."

She wants to be clear that her father had nothing to do with it; her father "had gone out to the colored part of town at the time, having been called to stop a disturbance." And she portrays Hope as almost demonic:

"Although Hope was an infidel, it is said that he kept saying, 'I'm look-ing into hell,' until death stilled his utterances." By her account, Larkin Hope's killer was "A young man by the name of Jim Coleman," who was subsequently "arrested and put in jail by Sheriff Reese. He was indicted but later acquitted."

The killing of Larkin Hope would set off a chain of explosive events leading to altercations and gunfights that would terrorize the county for years to come and cause the deaths of many of Lillie's relatives. But be-fore I return to what happened in Colorado County over the next de-cade, there are two more narrators I have to include in this multi-voiced story. And we have to go through the killing of Larkin Hope again, this time not through the rosy lens of Lillie's family myth but with the truth.

One narrator is the historian James Kearney, the son of Colorado County who wrote the definitive scholarly book about his community. And the other is John "Goep" Goeppinger, who told his story to Kearney almost ten years after Lillie published her book, just a few years before he and Lillie both died. Perhaps Goep even read Lillie's book; perhaps that's why he finally decided to tell the truth and make Lillie's lies in *Flaming Feuds of Colorado County* clear.

When he was young, Goep had been close friends with the Reese boys, Walter and Hub, and a longtime Reese man. He was at the Reeses' table—with Lillie—the night when the family planned for Jim Cole-man to shoot Larkin Hope. It was one of dozens of secrets Goep almost took to his grave.

Almost.

CHAPTER 29

James Kearney's unique mix of college professor and rancher was apparent the first time we met—his "Harry Ransom Center" baseball cap, from the University of Texas's premier archival library and museum, was worn from years in the sun. He had sporty sunglasses perched on the brim. His moisture-wicking long-sleeved shirt and pocketed vest were the uniform of a working rancher. His hands are more callused than most scholars. His voice has the cadence of a professor—he delivers well-paced answers with enunciated words, clearly accustomed to speaking at a pace for undergrads to take notes while he talks—and still proudly holds traces of a lilting Texas accent.

As a young man growing up in Columbus in the 1950s and 1960s, Kearney had been curious about the feud. People might no longer have plotted murder against each other during his childhood, but they still spat at each other when they passed their enemies in the street.

His mother was an English teacher who moved to the area in the 1930s from DeLeon, closer to West Texas in Comanche County. Kearney's father's family had lived for generations on their ranch outside of Columbus, but from his mother, Kearney gained an outsider's awareness that something was very wrong in Colorado County.

When Mrs. Kearney first heard as a young teacher about the feud, she asked her students to go home and interview their family members to write a report on what happened. The next morning, she was called to the principal's office and told, "If you ever bring that up again, you'll be fired immediately." She didn't bring it up in class again, but she taught her son to ask good questions.

No one in Colorado County forgot. They just didn't speak about the feud.

IN 1972, KEARNEY HAD JUST RETURNED HOME TO COLUMBUS FROM THE Vietnam War. He went to the war in a unique role: he was a conscientious objector who served on the frontlines as a combat medic. The tension put him in a complicated moral position. He thought war was horrific, and yet he refused to turn away from the aftermath of the war he objected to. The courage to face the hard truths without turning away would become a hallmark of Kearney's life and scholarship.

His first action as a medic was a mass casualty event mostly affecting children. With only eight weeks of training, he had to triage young victims of a brutal attack. He had seconds with each child to evaluate their chance at life or death, separating out the little ones he thought could survive from those who he thought were beyond saving.

In my interviews with people who have seen real trauma—the kind that causes their minds to dissociate—something changes in their eyes when they talk about it. In telling me about that triage moment in Vietnam, it was as if Kearney retreated inside of himself so he could describe what happened. He protected himself from the feel of babies' hands grasping his, the battlefield stink of smoke and charred hair, the memory of being an impossibly young man weighing the lives of children with no real idea of what he was doing.

He came back from the war with memories that fractured the minds of other men, an ironclad sense of right and wrong, and an excellent reel-to-reel recorder. He started studying history at the University of Texas. One weekend Kearney came home to Columbus and his dad said, "You know Goep? He wants to talk to you about the feud."

Kearney's dad joined that day, so that it felt less like an interview and more like a conversation between old friends about the past. Kearney asked a few questions, but mostly, Goep wanted to talk. Kearney had no idea that Goep intended their conversations to be his confessional.

IN OUR FIRST INTERVIEWS AND EMAILS, KEARNEY WOULD ONLY DE-scribe for me the contents of those recordings. In Kearney's words, Goep showed up and said, "'I'm the last one, and I want to confess.'" Regarding the Reeses' role in killing Larkin Hope, as Kearney put it, "Everybody suspected they were behind it, but [Goep] was there in the meeting and he told me. They were going to lose the election to Larkin Hope. . . . They'd gotten comfortable and gotten rich, and there was only one thing to do. Goep said, 'Let's kill the son of a bitch!' And they did. They got this sociopath to kill him."

That sociopath was Jim Coleman, whom Lillie described as the man who "stepped out from a narrow space between two buildings and emp-tied two loads of buckshot" into Larkin Hope.

Kearney told me historians had been trying to get their hands on his recordings for decades. It is now priceless documentation of a time that has increasing interest to scholars. It took some time for Kearney to let me hear Goep's interviews for myself: he feels protective of Goep's grandchildren, who are Kearney's friends still; he only included a small portion of the recordings for his own book about the feud. I understood Kearney's dilemma—telling the truth about your family or community can be freeing if it's done with respect and love. Telling the truth to hurt and expose others causes divisions that only increase tension.

There was also a small element of protectiveness I think Kearney felt toward me; he reminds me in many ways of my college professor father, and I'm about the age of his kids. I assured him I've become desensitized after years of conducting my own interviews with people who have been persecuted or tortured; I've had to listen to truly awful things in order to record the stories I usually write about. Kearney finally agreed to let me hear the recording on the condition that I would only tell what impacts this story.

When we met next, he handed me a flash drive with the name "Goep" scrawled on the side with Sharpie. I listened to the recording the day after Kearney gave it to me, on a long flight so I could hear it in one sitting. I knew within minutes of pressing 'play' that I had been wrong when I said I would be fine.

Kearney's interview with Goep is one of the most horrifying things I have ever listened to.

IT IS NOT ONLY THE CONTENT OF GOEP'S STORIES THAT IS SO SHOCKING; it's his voice and tone. For the entire interview, Goep sounds like a grandfatherly storyteller. He has an extraordinary recall of details and an ear for punchlines cultivated by telling tales around the campfire or a round of drinks at the saloon. You could picture him entertaining the children at bedtime with his "yarns."

If Goep had sounded like a serial killer in a movie—if his voice were flat and remorseless, Hannibal Lecter stretching out "Clarice"—perhaps it would have been easier to listen to. But even as he made those awful stories sound like jokes, I could hear the hint of uncertainty in his voice, the way speaking with a humorous cadence was his attempt to come to grips with what they did, to give him some distance. I could hear how the stories haunted him all those years later.

Kearney was worried I might not understand Goep's Gullah-like accent, but that's another reason the tape affected me so much, because the older members of my husband's Cajun family talk almost exactly like Goep. I understood almost every word as Goep confessed to the atrocities he witnessed and performed during the lawless years in which the Reese family and the Townsend family engaged in open warfare with each other. Many of the instances he described had little to do with the feud; Goep's testimony made it clear that, over a century later, the descendants of one of the first seventy-eight men to face Lynch's law in Bedford County, Virginia instigated countless lynchings against people of color in Colorado County, Texas.

Goep's stories revealed that the narratives put forth by the Reese side were lies. They make the tone of Lillie's book audacious rather than folksy.

In the recording, college-aged Kearney asked questions in a voice almost painfully young and earnest. But Goep almost always addressed Jim's father, Charlie Kearney: "You remember, Charlie? How it was?"

How it was that time they shot a man for his bottle of liquor? Or shot a man for walking on the wrong side of the street? Or shot a man because someone wanted his cattle?

How it was to tar and feather a man before he was lynched?

How it was to do exactly what your elders asked of you, no matter how appalling the task?

Goep's stories were in no particular order, especially toward the end of the interview. Every question Kearney asked—about the age of the cattle on long drives, about the clothes the cowboys wore, about the racial makeup of the county—Goep turned toward confession of another deed that obviously weighed on him. The vast majority of the murders he described were probably not covered by the media or prosecuted by the law—not when the officers of the law were the ones ordering the hits. It is probably not possible to place many of his stories in time or space or identify the people he is talking about.

There is one incident that Goep seemed to view as a turning point in his own life, an encounter with two men "what made me so damn mean." These men worked for Bob Stafford. One "was the meanest son of a bitch in the world."

Goep was going up to Osage, now a ghost town in Colorado County, for a camp meeting. In those days, Goep took his grandfather to join "all these old farmers" to "sing and pray for about a week." They gathered people all over the county at the shaded grove of one of the big ranches that was beautiful and parklike.

While they were camping out and "just singin' and prayin' all night and all day," the two Stafford men saw a Black man with a few cattle. They decided they wanted the cattle, so: "They took 'em. They went up there and stole them cattle and killed that ole" Black man, hanging him and putting his body across the road. When it was time for the people around the area to come to Sunday morning worship, Goep said, "you couldn't pass in the road" because there was a body hanging there.

Then Goep cackled, this unworldly laugh.

He tried to turn the conversation light again, naming with Charlie some of the families who always used to go out to the camp meeting at Osage. It was a real country celebration, Charlie told his son: "Singin', eatin', and dancin'. Fellows'd go up there to court the gals."

Goep added, "That's where you done your courtin' then."

Young Kearney replied, "And then they'd come home and kill everybody to death."

Goep agreed. "That was the great old days."

CHAPTER 30

Goep's story of Larkin Hope's death was much more thorough than Lillie's. They had a meeting over Sunday night dinner with all the Reese kids—Nuddie, Walter, Hub, Sadie, and Lillie—and some friends, including Goep and Jim Coleman. Goep admitted it was his idea for Coleman to kill Larkin. After dinner, Hub asked Goep to saddle Hub's horse, who had a unique gait—Goep called him "a single-footin' horse." When the horse was ready, Coleman came out of the house and "Hub handed him . . . I believe it was a ten-gauge shotgun." Goep opened the gate and wished Coleman luck. He saw Coleman turn west, toward the alley near Goldsmith's Saloon.

Coleman tied up the horse and went to wait for Larkin Hope between the buildings with his shotgun.

Walter went to town, where he sent a Black man named Tom Schein who worked for the Reeses to Larkin's house with a message that the Reeses wanted to talk to him at the saloon over beer. Larkin's wife begged him not to go—the stories always seem full of women begging men not to do the things that they do anyway—but Larkin ignored her. He walked toward the saloon.

Goep said, "Just as he passed, ole Jim put that buckshot to him, then ole man Larkin empties his gun six times."

Goep was sitting on a nearby bridge with a young woman ("I wanted to love her a little") when he heard the shots fired. The young woman asked what was happening, but Goep said it was nothing. A few minutes later, Goep heard the horse's distinctive single-footing gait.

Coleman passed close to the couple and the horse jumped. Coleman grabbed his shotgun. Goep's voice rang out, "Look out there, Jim, this is me. Don't shoot me!"

Coleman kept riding, across the bridge, over to the Burtschell farm where the family, who were friends of the Reeses, already planned to give him an alibi. When law enforcement went over to arrest Coleman, the farmer's wife swore he had been there the last two or three weeks for planting.

Coleman was accused of murder but later acquitted. The Reeses vehemently denied any involvement in Larkin's murder. Public opinion was divided. Decades later, Lillie would write her book featuring Sam Houston Reese as the perfect father, trying to convince her community of his innocence in Larkin's murder to the very end.

While all along, as Goep later confessed, the Reeses were guilty.

THE GOAL OF KILLING LARKIN WAS TO REMOVE HIM AS A CANDIDATE SO Sam would be elected sheriff in 1898. By then, Marcus Townsend no longer supported the Reeses and wanted them out of office. The Townsend political machine found another candidate: Marcus Townsend's brother-in-law, William Burford, ran against Sam Reese. Burford beat Reese by about five hundred votes. In the end, killing Hope didn't keep Sam in power. He was only sheriff for four years total.

Sam Houston Reese did not accept losing to Burford well. The day after the election, he quit rather than finishing out his term. The county eventually asked someone from a neighboring town to serve as interim sheriff, but it was difficult. According to Kearney, "Reese never turned over the keys [to the jail] and a rumor spread that he had thrown them into the river. Further, he allegedly destroyed many of the records of the sheriff's office."

The fact that the Townsends controlled the sheriff's office meant that the men who were deputized—and therefore legally allowed to openly carry arms in Columbus—were Townsend men. Even though Sam's family had murdered their political opponent, the Townsends still handily won that round against the Reeses.

Two more villains entered Lillie's book after that election: the first was the new sheriff, William Burford, who she almost always describes as a raging drunk; from every other description, he was a sober, thoughtful, overly methodical man who got in way over his head. The other was Burford's new deputy—Will Clements.

Clements was Keetie's nephew, the Reese kids' first cousin; Will Clements's brother had basically been adopted by the Reeses. They viewed Clements joining their enemy as a deputy as a major slap in the face. Now one of their nephews lived in the Reeses' home and the other was firmly on the other side of the conflict as Marcus Townsend's man.

The Reeses had other allies; their side legally got their guns back through the city marshal, who was a friend. That man deputized both Sam and Sam's oldest son-in-law, Joe Lessing, a dentist. Joe Lessing was also Larkin and Marion Hope's younger half brother, now married to Nuddie Reese. The battle lines seem to make little sense—Lessing joined the side of the family who murdered his brother, while his wife Nuddie plotted to harm her cousins.

I tell you of these connections not so that you will remember all of these names, but to show the scope and interwoven nature of the feud among families. If I had read about the feud while living through another era, I might have found those divisions unbelievable. But like most Americans who are living in this polarized time, I can sadly picture it now more clearly.

It was a mini Civil War, a family-wide acrimonious divorce, in which everyone was armed and angry all the time.

SAM HOUSTON REESE WAS A MAN OF ROUTINE. AFTER LEAVING THE sheriff's office in a huff, he returned to farming with occasional stints as a deputy when he was called up to help. He left the house in town every morning to ride three miles to their family farm and rode back in the late afternoon. In the early evening, Sam and his sons, Walter and Hub, would often join other men loyal to them at Brunson Saloon before heading home for the evening. There were several sharp encounters between the Reese boys and their cousin Will Clements especially. But for weeks, a tense truce reigned.

On March 16, 1899, Sam Reese rode to town in the early evening like he always did. Marcus Townsend and other allies were in a nearby drugstore. The new deputy, Will Clements, was harassing a friend of the Reeses when Sam rode up, tied up his horse, and tried to give the man his pistol. Then Clements threatened Sam.

Sam drew his gun. Clements drew his. Townsend men came out of the drugstore and Reese men poured out of Brunson Saloon. Shooting erupted. A farmer who was driving in a wagon to town with his pregnant wife and two of his eight children was killed in the crossfire. A six-year-old playing nearby took a bullet to his left hip.

Sam Houston Reese was shot in the forehead, blinding him with his own blood. A second bullet to his neck killed him instantly. The bullet to the neck was a .38; Clements had been firing a .45 Colt revolver. The Reeses, at least, assumed the killing shot had been fired by Marcus Townsend. As Goep put it, "Ole Marc Townsend was a crack shot with a .38 pistol. He made one shot and broke Sam Reese's neck out of that grocery store. He put his gun in his pocket and walked on home. Left the rest of 'em up there to be arrested."

The Reeses and their allies did not think it was a coincidence that so many Townsend men happened to be in the drugstore at the exact time of day when Sam normally came to town. They accused the Townsends of orchestrating a plot to kill Sam.

Walter, who had been waiting for his father in the saloon, held a cloth to Sam's neck to try to stop the blood flow. Keetie and Lillie rushed up the street from their house when they heard the shots. As Lillie writes, "Mrs. Reese had reached the scene of this foul murder and her grief was terrible to behold for she idolized her husband, as did his five children. . . . To his five young children or any later descendants,

Sam Reese left a heritage of honesty, bravery, fearlessness, integrity, honor, and love for his wife, his children and the true heritage of the Christian faith."

He also left a propensity for violence. Sam Reese's death threw kerosene on the fire of the Colorado County feud. As the rhetoric and violence escalated, it encroached on the community—the vast majority of whom were not involved in this tit-for-tat, vengeful retribution.

THE WEEK AFTER SAM HOUSTON REESE WAS KILLED, TELEGRAMS WENT out around the state. The Reeses wired their cousins and uncles, Sally's grandsons and great-grandsons, to come from nearby Lavaca County. Slowman's descendants arrived en masse, armed and ready for battle.

A local district judge wired the governor to send in fifteen to twenty Texas Rangers as reinforcements since the feud was between rival officers of the law. The Rangers' stories were well established by then, seventy years after they first started by patrolling Austin's colony, fifty years after they became los diablos Tejanos, through their aggressive acts of border-patrolling and thief-tracking. As with so many law enforcement officers in those violent days in Texas, the line between keeper of peace and instigator of violence was often in the eye of the beholder—or the mouth of the person who lived to tell the tale. Rangers were sometimes called in to cities or communities that required outside arbitrators to return to order, like Colorado County.

Captain Bill McDonald, who had a reputation for being tough in the face of conflict, arrived first and alone. McDonald met with the Townsends and then the Reeses, with, Kearney reports, "the Reese faction being the more recalcitrant and difficult." Eventually McDonald called for a few more men, and the Rangers effectively instituted emergency law enforcement in the county.

There were still some incidents. Will Clements reported shots fired at his house on March 28, 1899. Later, Goep implied that he and Hub "got slippin' around" and that he got in legal trouble for shooting at Clements. Clements and another deputy followed Goep when he left town;

Goep made it as far as Houston when they caught up with him, but he slipped their grasp and boarded a ship bound out of the port toward South Africa, where he spent two years during the Boer Wars. He eventually came back to Columbus, but we lose Goep as a witness for what happened next.

IT SEEMED, FOR A FEW WEEKS, THAT THE FEUD MIGHT DIE DOWN AS IT had in 1871 and again in 1890. But, after a biased and embattled trial, the Reeses' friend, Jim Coleman, who had point-blank killed Larkin Hope, was freed on April 30, 1899, returning back to Colorado County. He went to Alleyton, a neighboring town to Columbus, where several of the Reese family members were still hanging around, six weeks after Sam Houston Reese had been killed.

Reese family members continued to arrive. On May 16, several more came to town. On May 17, Sam's brother Dick arrived by train. Townsend spies reported that he was meeting with Coleman in Alleyton. Sheriff Burford deputized more Townsend men, placing them around town, especially along the bridge from Alleyton, where they thought Coleman would arrive.

In Alleyton, Dick Reese borrowed the buggy of the Burtschell family, the ones who had given an alibi to Coleman after shooting Larkin Hope. Dick made ready to head to town, getting in the wagon only after the sun set a little after 7:00 p.m. that evening.

One of Dick Reese's arms was paralyzed, and he could not ride a horse and shoot at the same time; presumably that is why he was in a much noisier wagon. The disability that kept him from riding also kept him from driving the Burtschells' team into town.

So they hired—or coerced—a driver for the wagon, a Black man named Dick Gant.

A little before 9:00 p.m. on May 17, Dick Gant drove Dick Reese toward Columbus. They used the only route—the bridge over the Colorado River. Two Townsend men waited for them there.

THE RECORDS FOR DICK GANT'S LIFE ARE SPARSE. HE WAS PART OF A
large family that lived near Alleyton. He married a woman named Lou
Bostick on June 19, 1880, and there are tax assessment records that list
"Richard Gant" or "Dick Gant" from 1879 to 1894 near Alleyton. The
records are missing for the year 1883 and the years 1885–1891. In the first
four years, Dick is mentioned every year with three of four other names:
Boston, Fayette, Primus, and—in 1879—Peter. In 1884 there is both a
Primus and a Peter.

Because Boston is mentioned first every time, I assume he is either
their father or oldest brother, though that might not be a correct assumption. In 1879, the Gant clan have between them one carriage, two
horses or mules, and four hogs, for a total value of fifty dollars.

They never have hogs again. Every year, they switch the numbers
around—one year, Primus has the horse or mule, then Fayette, then
Dick. It seems intentional, that the Gant family is sharing the taxes. But
perhaps it is not. They add one cow in 1881 and one more cow in 1884. In
1892, Fayette has $1,500 worth of "Goods, Wares, and Merchandise."
There is no indication what those goods, wares, or merchandise were. From
1892 to 1894, there are more people mentioned: John. Jesse. Boston Jr.

In 1893 and 1894, the record keeper wrote: "Dick + Wife." No other
man has "+ Wife" listed next to his name. I don't know what it means. I
want to think it means Lou, or Dick, insisted she also earned money and
should be listed on the tax records. I want to think it means Dick wanted
her name on the census, the one official record Black people had in the
1890s, even if the tax collector refused to write "Lou" and wrote "Wife."
I want to think Dick loved her. That might not be the correct assumption to make either.

After those census records end in 1894, the only mentions of his name
are in the newspapers, where for a few brief days, Dick Gant's name appears
across the nation. Without knowing anything else, I feel confident that his
family would rather his name have been left out of this moment in history.

TWO WITNESSES LATER TOLD LAW ENFORCEMENT AND REPORTERS THAT, around 9:00 p.m., the buggy crossed the bridge. The Townsend men halted the buggy and said they wanted to search it. The two groups exchanged words.

Then, the shooting began. One of the Townsend men fired buckshot; the other fired a pistol. Dick Gant tried to jump off the buggy to escape into the night. They shot him while he ran. He died instantly. The horses, scared by the gunshots, ran toward Alleyton with the buggy still attached. Searchers scoured the land around the horses' home farm. Finally, they found the buggy and secured the skittish horses.

The body of Dick Reese was inside, with three gunshot wounds—both buckshot and pistol bullet. He had a pistol with him, still there on the floor of the buggy. It had never fired.

About thirty minutes after the shooting, the Townsends found a Reese spy hiding outside of the jail. It was Nuddie—Sam and Keetie's oldest daughter, and Joe Lessing the dentist's wife—dressed in men's clothes with a charcoal-blackened face. Sheriff Burford or one of the deputies arrested her. She was released the following morning.

By the time the searchers located the buggy with Dick Reese's body, both the Townsend men had already turned themselves in at the jail.

Keetie's rage over the next several years was cataclysmic—one of the Townsend men who turned himself in for shooting her brother-in-law, Dick Reese, was her own brother.

Three days after the killing of Dick Gant and Dick Reese, the *Houston Post* reported on how the constant fear affected ordinary citizens of Columbus: "The business of the town is demoralized on account of the feud between the factions and the citizens of the town earnestly hope that steps will be taken by the governor or the Rangers to effectually end it."

It would be some time before the people of Columbus would get the peace they so desperately longed for. Even then, that peace was only available for some.

CHAPTER 31

In January 1900, the trial of the Townsend men who murdered Dick Gant and Dick Reese was set to take place away from Colorado County because of the bad blood between the two groups there. The trial was being held in Bastrop County, and the train ride there was nerve-racking—brothers and sisters, nieces and nephews and cousins on opposite sides of the feud packed the same train cars.

All of the trials were a sham and everyone knew it: in the trial of Jim Coleman for the death of Larkin Hope, and the trial of Will Clements, Marion Hope, and Mark Townsend for the death of Sam Houston Reese, either charges had been dismissed quickly, or the culprits served laughably short jail sentences for minor infractions.

It was not just that the white men who were being tried had family members and allies in all aspects of the county government, ensuring that they could not truly receive an impartial trial—though that was true. It was the conundrum that the non-feuding community faced—to publicly name anyone a murderer was to face swift repercussions from their gun-wielding family and allies. No individual wanted to put their neck on the line by serving as a witness, lawyer, judge, or jury to convict those killers. In all of the feud, no one was ever convicted of the many murders—most of which took place in daylight, often in the middle of town—despite multiple witnesses and ample proof.

The Reese and Townsend men came to Bastrop County armed to the teeth; they knew the trial would end without justice, and they were determined to be judge, jury, and executioners for the other side. The Texas Rangers came to Bastrop heavily armed too, equally determined to forcibly keep the peace. The Colorado County Feud was now making national headlines. It was excellent branding for the Rangers; they did not have to prove they were tough if the reputation for toughness preceded them and deescalated situations. And the myth of the Rangers was why so many of them had taken the job in the first place—the power and prestige of being part of the elite law enforcement team was heady.

On the first day of the trial, January 15, 1899, there were seventy-seven witnesses listed for the defense and fifty-six for the prosecution. The overwhelmed lawyers asked for and were granted a continuance. The court was dismissed at 4:30 p.m.

Rangers had kept the courtroom free of arms, but now two sides at war with one another spilled out into the streets.

Will Clements, the Reese boys' hated cousin, walked down the street with the son of Sheriff Will Burford and the son of the late Sheriff Light Townsend—straight into an ambush.

Many of the Reese men had not gone to the trial, including Sam's and Keetie's oldest son, Walter. They were stationed in a saloon and nearby hotel rooms, armed with handguns, rifles, and shotguns, ready to kill.

The Reeses aimed for Will Clements, but he hid behind young Arthur Burford, who took a bullet to the brain and died instantly. Clements was hit in the lung—but he lived.

The Texas Rangers, hearing shots, shut the courthouse immediately, keeping the Townsend men inside. One Texas Ranger entered the saloon where Walter and the other Reese men had taken up position. With several guns aimed at the Ranger, Walter informed him that if he wanted to live, he would leave. He did. The Ranger returned with backup and, after some intense negotiations, successfully arrested Walter Reese. As in every other case, that murder trial for the death of Arthur Burford was delayed and prolonged and eventually dismissed in 1904. The Rangers would only stay in Columbus until March 1900.

NEWSPAPERS AROUND THE COUNTRY PICKED UP THE STORY OF THE shootout in Bastrop: "The tragedy is another chapter in the worst feud ever known in Texas," one newspaper claimed. In statements that were not accurate but were nonetheless repeated around the country, several papers claimed: "The origin of the Townsend-Reese feud was an unbranded vagrant steer. Lawsuits have eaten up thousands of dollars on the question of ownership and more than 200 men have lost their lives in various affrays in connection with it during the last twenty years."

There were certainly thousands of dollars spent on legal fees for the time the murderers spent in court or in lawsuits with one another. And the original bad blood between the Townsends and Staffords that began the feud could have had to do with their role in the cattle industry, long before their conflict spilled over into bloodshed in 1871. But there was not one "vagrant steer" that hundreds of enraged Texans were fighting over. Yet that story was repeated in newspapers in California, Washington, Utah, Montana, Ohio, Missouri, New Mexico, Iowa, Louisiana, Virginia, and New York, among many other places.

What was happening in Colorado County had to do with conditions of lawlessness, corruption of the justice system, a culture of vigilantism, and a community with easy access to guns governed by a code that made vengeance a moral imperative. But that's not what was in the news; stereotypes took over the national coverage. In reducing them to simple people who didn't know better than to shoot at each other over a steer, those articles distanced the readers from what was happening. And they covered up the truth—that the same conditions anywhere could lead to the same kind of behavior.

The conditions might have been unique to Texas at the turn of the century, but the human behavior is universal—something we forget to our detriment.

LARGER TEXAS POLITICS DID WHAT THE REESES HAD NOT BEEN ABLE TO and crumbled the Townsends' nearly immutable hold in Colorado County. In 1891, the Texas legislature passed its first Jim Crow laws. By the turn of the century, as the second phase of the feud was taking off, the policy of "separate but equal" (though never truly equal) became the norm in public settings.

In the early 1900s, after more than four decades of trying, white people in Colorado County finally found a way to legally disenfranchise Black voters. The conservative Democratic Party in Colorado County held a meeting in June 1902 at Stafford Opera House. They planned what they blatantly called the "White Man's Primary" for the following month, a pre-voting election to determine how the white population would vote. Those who participated committed to falling in line behind the winner of the White Man's Primary and consolidating the power of the white vote.

It worked. Black people were effectively disenfranchised, and white people took complete control of the county. The violent extremism of those feud years ended, as T. S. Eliot wrote a couple decades later in "The Hollow Men," "not with a bang but a whimper."

There were other acts of violence between the Reeses and the Townsends, including a train shootout in July 1900 that left Walter Reese badly injured. The Reeses had little to show for the extraordinary violence they had enacted on the region. They were now deeply in debt, chiefly from medical and legal expenses.

In 1902, Will Burford lost the election for sheriff. The Townsend political monopoly was effectively over. A type of peace came to white people in Columbus. Many of the players in the feud—including many of the Reeses—moved on to other cities, coming home only occasionally. The trials for the murders came and went with no convictions. The ill-will from the feud continued, but there were no overt acts of violence in public between the Reeses and the Townsends for the next four years.

In July 1906, the last shootout of the public feud began with a lit cigarette at a skating rink. The Stafford Opera House had turned its upper floor into a place to skate. Hub Reese was back in town; when he skated past the bleachers, Marion Hope—the brother of Larkin Hope the deputy on the Townsend side and Joe Lessing the dentist on the Reese side—stuck his burning cigarette in Hub's face. The fight turned out into the street, with everyone running for backup. The final shootout of the feud was among deeply entangled family relations—all brothers and first cousins fighting one another, and almost all of them descended on their mothers' sides from the Townsend clan. The one person killed was a Townsend cousin who was involved in the feud only on the day he died—a twenty-four-year-old father whose young wife had just had a baby girl. The men involved in the shootout were inevitably arrested and also inevitably released with no punishment.

That shootout was a fitting end to the public part of the feud—profound violence among serial murderers all related to one another, with the only person killed being the most innocent, and the murderer allowed to go free.

AFTER 1906, THE SHOOTOUTS BETWEEN THE REESES AND THE TOWNSENDS that had so often gripped the community were over. However, the peace the white community finally achieved was not for everyone; there would be no peace for the communities of color in Colorado County. Losing the only political leverage they had had left them open to the blatant racist attacks that Goep confesses to in his recordings. Lynchings against people of color would continue unabated through the next several decades. The extremism was not over for those communities—it was concentrated against them.

One of the largest crowds in Texas to attend a lynching happened a few decades later in the middle of Columbus, and it reveals what the culture was like in that town. In 1935, a young white woman died by drowning in a local creek. Law enforcement officers concluded—without proof—a few days later that her death was murder and that two Black teens—fifteen-year-old Ernest Collins and sixteen-year-old Benny Mitchell—

who had been picking pecans nearby had committed the crime. While the young men were on their way to the trial, cars filled with armed white men stopped the sheriff on a bridge, demanding that the young men be released to be lynched. A crowd of over seven hundred watched as Collins and Mitchell were hung from the sprawling live oak in the center of town. With no judge, jury, or evidence, their possible innocence didn't matter.

By the light of headlights, someone took a picture of the lynching. The photo, published later by Colorado County historian Bill Stein, is eerie and ghostlike. The background is black and the tree with the bodies of the heartbreakingly young boys—lit by the headlights—is white and gray. In white letters, someone wrote, "Colorado Co protects 'womanhood.'"

Once again, driven by the same fears that had been in the country since the earliest days of the Virginia colony, based on the received narrative that urgent times allowed men in power to act outside of the law, two young men were hanged because a community believed the story that they were a threat because of the color of their skin. Time and again, the murderers who instigated lynchings and other acts of injustice remained unpunished because of widely shared views among people in power about what was acceptable outside of a legal framework—what moral codes ran deeper than the laws on the books.

The Townsends had been self-serving, but they had provided at least some layer of political protection for the Black voters while they were in power. After their reign ended, there would be no peace for the people of color in Colorado County for decades.

CHAPTER 32

Over the next several years, most of the men involved in the feud died violent deaths—some at the hands of each other and others in unrelated ways.

In 1907, it seems likely that Marcus Townsend hired Marion Hope and some other men to kill Jim Coleman, the sociopathic friend of the Reeses; by then, Townsend was living in San Antonio. Coleman—who had an addiction to drugs and alcohol and a personal vendetta against Townsend—followed Marcus Townsend to San Antonio. According to Kearney, Coleman's murder by six bullet wounds in May 1907 was Marcus Townsend's preemptive strike to keep Coleman from killing him. In 1915, Marcus Townsend died of edema of the brain—one of the few members of the feud not to die by another's hand.

In 1911, Marion Hope died in what seemed to be an accident on a horse. The community speculated that it had been a murder made to look like an accident, but no one could prove it. Only later, when Goep recorded his interview with Kearney, did Goep allude to it: "Marion Hope went out in the pasture there to see about some cattle and he never come back. Nobody knows what happened."

And then he laughed, that eerie cackle: "Pretty terrible, wasn't it?"

Later, without the reel-to-reel, Goep provided the full story to Kearney, who told me what had happened: "He killed Marion Hope. He confessed it. My wife was there, and we were sitting in the back seat of his car. He liked to sit in the front seat; he told us the whole story. He told us he didn't want to tell anyone. He didn't want it out."

Goep—possibly working with Hub or others—made it look as if the horse fell on Marion and broke his neck. That is what the coroner's report concluded; the sheriff sent the body a few counties over to a neutral coroner who knew nothing about the feud. The coroner's report—which Kearney has—also mentioned an "unexpected welp" on the back of his neck. But the official ruling was an accident.

The next to last page in Lillie's book also describes an old railroad man hearing the story about Marion Hope's death as a result of falling off a horse, and "the old man laughed, leaned back in his seat and calmly remarked, 'A damn fine horse.'"

John Goeppinger was that "damn fine horse," performing the last final, terrible act of the feud in vengeance for the death of Jim Coleman and so many other murders—a Reese man to the end.

IN 1911, THE SAME YEAR THAT MARION HOPE WAS MURDERED, WILL Clements was killed by someone unconnected to the feud. Two of the Reese cousins on Sam's side—Flem Reese and Stafford Reese—came to the trial the next year to serve as witnesses against Will Clements's character. By 1912, those Reeses were living in Beeville, Texas, where my mother's family would move, and their children went to school with my mother's relatives.

In 1912, Hub Reese died when he accidentally discharged his gun at home. In 1919, Walter Reese died in a car wreck in El Paso, leaving behind a new wife and a little daughter named after his brother—Lola Herberta. Keetie lived a long life, saving every newspaper clipping and scrap of memory from the feud. She died in 1944 in Columbus and passed those scrapbooks along to her youngest daughter, Lillie, who also took up Keetie's tradition of hanging Sam Houston Reese's bloody clothes outside as an act of remembrance every year on the anniversary of his death.

Their fourth child, Sadie, died in 1959. Then Nuddie Reese Lessing died in 1962, the same year that Lillie published *The Flaming Feuds of Colorado County*—which would be the last word of the Reeses on their side of the story.

When Goep asked to interview with James Kearney and his reel-to-reel in 1972, he and Lillie were the only ones left alive who had witnessed the Reeses' acts of terrorism. Lillie's memories, however biased, were available to anyone who could read the book. Goep's memories stayed safely hidden with James Kearney for a long time. Goep died not long after recording his confessions, on October 1, 1972.

Journalist Ann Jones once wrote, "War is not over when it's over." That will always be true. Even when the war is contained to the county seat of a seemingly unimportant county in the middle of central Texas, held in the memory of the last remaining foot soldier who outlived everyone else—war remains.

FOR JAMES KEARNEY, SERVING IN THE VIETNAM WAR CHANGED HIS PERspective on growing up in Colorado County. Before, the feud had felt like something terrible but also fascinating, his own TV Western come to life. But then he spent a year treating the gruesome casualties of a senseless war. "I've seen a lot of bloodshed," he told me. "Even with that experience, I'm shocked at Goep's story, and the sort of casualness of it all."

He believes Goep "must have a conscience somewhere" because he requested that unorthodox confessional in which Kearney served as the unwitting, unprepared priest who could offer no absolution and no peace other than to receive the story and then contain its contents for several years. When he finally started to document and verify Goep's story, Kearney joined forces with others who grew up in Colorado County in telling the truth of their community.

In the 1990s, the Colorado County library archivist Bill Stein—a descendant of the Stafford family on his mother's side—began cataloging and researching the true facts of the feud. He kept immaculate records, publishing a chronological history of Colorado County beginning in 1821 in the *Nesbitt Memorial Library Journal*. He named his series "Consider the Lily: The Ungilded History of Colorado County." As Kearney told me, Stein "wanted to lay bare the shameful racial relations" in the county's past. Stein's series only made it up to 1883 before he died in 2008.

Another man, James Smallwood, entered into the picture. Smallwood was a well-known Texas historian; the foundation underwriting Stein's work hired him to come to Colorado County after Stein's death to help organize and write up Stein's extensive research. Smallwood had witnessed a lynching when he was a little boy and it changed his life; he was obsessed with the origins of what he called "private justice." He worked on the feud's history for a few years before he also died, in 2013.

That left only James Kearney to tell the story. When he published *No Hope for Heaven, No Fear of Hell* in 2016, Kearney relied on the research of Stein and Smallwood and many of their insights about the feud; in fact, Kearney shared the writing credit with both men. In the back of the book, he published some quotes from the transcript of his interview with Goep—revealing the truth of several murders in print for the first time in more than a century.

In weaving all of those voices together—along with the dozens or hundreds of witnesses who fearlessly talked to reporters or the police or told their neighbors, the historians and librarians and scholars who came later, the teachers and community members who refused to be silenced—Kearney collected their community story.

The voices form a haunting Greek chorus from a Texas county, moving the action forward toward the inevitable end.

Since the interview with Goep when he was a history undergrad, through his long career as a historian, Kearney has been haunted by a singular question: What happened in Colorado County to make it so violent when the neighboring counties were not? It is part of a larger question he wrestled with after his time in Vietnam. As he put it, "Humans are capable of the most awesome achievements in literature or history, but we're also the most awful creatures. We all have in us the potential for good or for evil; it's latent in all of us. This was a situation that obviously elicited the worst things in those people. What tips the scale? What drives somebody to move from awesome to awful?"

Kearney draws that phrase from a line in Sophocles's 441 BC play, *Antigone*, which Kearney translates as "Much is awesome, but nothing more awesome/awful than man." It's the tension inherent in the double translation, the dualism in humanity's capacity for awesomeness and awfulness—often in the same person or community—that grips Kearney all these years later.

The chorus of people who tell the stories in Kearney's community memoir, which is also an act of impeccable scholarship, do not provide the answers. I do not have them either. We can only serve to witness the fact that it occurred. And that, if it happened in Colorado County, Texas, it can happen anywhere.

Many of the conditions in Colorado County so easily ignored by the newspaper reports about the shootout after the trial in March 1900— which made it sound like a bunch of hick Texans were killing each other over a "vagrant steer"—exist in Texas today. The questions of who will hold political power, who can limit the right to vote, who gets to control the story, remain the same. There are crucial differences between then and now, certainly, but I am not alone in seeing the rise of a culture of vigilantism and a vengeance-based moral code. And of course, the violence is exacerbated by easy access to guns.

I think of Kearney's question constantly: How can the Texas I love be so wonderful and so frightening at the same time?

The hope I found in researching the history of the Colorado County feud was not in my family members who killed so many people. It is not even in much of the community, where racism continued to breed violence at an astonishing rate after the feud ended. The hope I find was in the work of Bill Stein and James Kearney and so many others who pushed past the myth of the gun-slingin' cowboys of Colorado County to call murder by its name. To record the truth of what happened. To provide a record of the past so future generations would not forget. To rise up in the face of widespread family and community pressure for the descendants of those who had benefited from a political system that kept them in power to say nothing.

To take a stand.

I only hope I can find the same kind of courage in telling the story of my own hometown.

PART 5

J. C. REESE

(1881–1930)

West Texas is the most American section of America. . . . The present census will show that there are 2,000,000 people in what is called West Texas. Over 95 per cent of these are native white people.

—PORTER A. WHALEY, GENERAL MANAGER OF THE
WEST TEXAS CHAMBER OF COMMERCE, MARCH 3, 1920

A lot of people don't consider Abilene a part of the national story. . . . Our national history is connected with who we are as a city, who we are as a country, as a regional area. Those things are connected. Sometimes, when we look at history, we can view it as a mythical ideal far away from us, a long time ago, when really those things happened in our own backyards, and it's important to document that history.

—JEREMIAH TAYLOR, ASSISTANT CURATOR,
CURTIS HOUSE CULTURAL CENTER, 2022

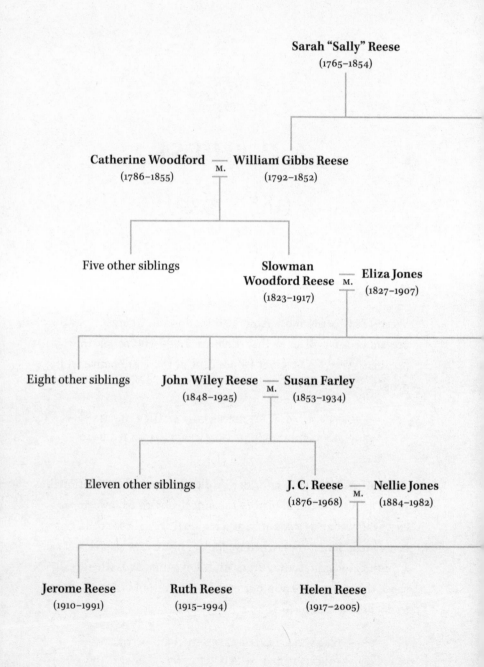

Sarah "Sally" Reese
(1765–1854)

Catherine Woodford — M. — William Gibbs Reese
(1786–1855)   (1792–1852)

Five other siblings   Slowman
                        Woodford Reese — M. — Eliza Jones
                           (1823–1917)   (1827–1907)

Eight other siblings   John Wiley Reese — M. — Susan Farley
                                (1848–1925)   (1853–1934)

Eleven other siblings   J. C. Reese — M. — Nellie Jones
                                  (1876–1968)   (1884–1982)

Jerome Reese   Ruth Reese   Helen Reese
(1910–1991)   (1915–1994)   (1917–2005)

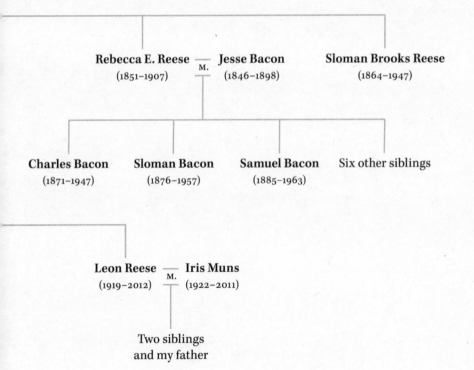

Nine younger siblings

Rebecca E. Reese — Jesse Bacon   Sloman Brooks Reese
(1851–1907)   M.   (1846–1898)   (1864–1947)

Charles Bacon   Sloman Bacon   Samuel Bacon   Six other siblings
(1871–1947)   (1876–1957)   (1885–1963)

Leon Reese — Iris Muns
(1919–2012) M. (1922–2011)

Two siblings
and my father

CHAPTER 33

I was miserable when we moved to Abilene, Texas when I was a fifth grader. I had been unhappy in Memphis too. I spent most of my formative years in San Antonio, in the house surrounded by live oaks. I had loved that home and hometown the way children do—as if it were not a house or a city but my whole world.

Though even at the time I knew it wasn't the case, I am sure I acted as if my parents had set out to personally torture me by moving us again. We left San Antonio for Memphis for my dad's job, and then, when his dream job came open in his hometown, moved to Abilene a year later. It meant that I went to four different schools in four years: third grade in San Antonio, fourth in Memphis, fifth at an elementary school in Abilene, and sixth at middle school.

Moving had only increased my bookishness. My parents already had to cajole me out of the worlds I created in my mind, and a new place had me seeking escape in those fantasies with increasing regularity.

In the fifth grade, I was all elbows and knees. It's an age of uneven development, and I was not the kind of girl who noticed when cute boys got haircuts or whether they glanced in my direction. While other girls flipped through magazines and learned to curl their bangs, I was thinking of the Renaissance cloak I wanted my mom to sew for me—one I had the sense to only wear at home—but that I loved because of the feel of it on my shoulders, brushing my wrists, as I stalked around my backyard pretending to be on a quest.

On the first day at my new school, I felt a lump of fear during recess—the only person I knew was my boy cousin in another class, and he wasn't outside and was unlikely to give me social cover even if he were. I wandered off alone and ended up on the edge of the field furthest from the school by the chain link fence, hating everything and everyone around me, my own awkward self most of all. But then I scuffed the grass and saw a lizard scuttle away. I squatted down and noticed that, beneath the sunbaked stalks of grass, there was a world where beetles and lizards and ants acted out their own dramas. I studied them, comforting myself as I always did by entering another place. My mind was so full of the questions I was framing about how dune-colored lizards here differed from the garden snakes I had played with in my Memphis backyard that I didn't hear two girls running up.

They were somewhat breathless when they arrived, as if they had hurried to welcome me. I was pleased, a bit surprised. Hopeful.

They introduced themselves and asked my name. Then they asked, "What are you doing out here by yourself?" They meant, I am sure, "Why didn't you stick around to meet us and say hi?" It was a gentle nudge that they would have welcomed me, that they would still welcome me.

But I was thinking about lizards. So I answered the question literally. "I'm studying the topography. It's so different here."

At that, my fate was sealed. Within weeks, I had gotten the nickname I would carry through the end of high school, "Dictionary Breath." Eventually, I leaned into it—if I was going to be made fun of for being nerdy, I might as well be the nerdiest nerd I could be. I made good grades and read stacks of books and tried to convince myself on Friday nights when I knew everyone else was at a slumber party that I was happier alone with my dog.

The girls who came out to be friends with me that day were, even after that exchange, kind to me. And it was not all loneliness. I made some friends, many of them the children of my dad's and grandparents' friends. Abilene families tend to stay for generations; it was no surprise to anyone we had moved back. But I never felt like I really belonged in the larger Abilene, Texas that dominated my childhood.

I had moments of almost belonging. The summer after my junior year when I figured out how to style my curly hair and deepened my friendship with three smart girls from my church youth group and tuned in to country music when I was driving my own car around town and belted out songs by Shania Twain and Reba McEntire and Trisha Yearwood, I felt—maybe for the first time—like a real Texas girl. But mostly, I lived in a state of constant alienation from the town and state around me.

There was another Abilene, however, a smaller, more intimate one, that I belonged in no matter how much other kids at school viewed what I liked and did. I belonged to it because I was born into it. It was my birthright. I did not realize until years later, when the fantasy memories I had built up were challenged by the truth, how much that second Abilene meant to me.

The second Abilene was a section of town my grandparents, who had lived there the vast majority of their lives, always called "the Hill." It was not—as far as I could tell, with my apparent childhood interest in topography—much of a hill in the middle of our flat, flat terrain. That older Abilene extended back three generations and shimmered in the late summer heat with other people's memories.

The stories were from my great-grandparents, my grandparents, my aunts and uncles, my parents, my cousins, or family friends—fragments of old stories, anecdotes, photos, half-overheard ideas, collaged over the places we went on any day: school, the grocery store, church, my father's office, a friend's house. We could walk or drive in the car and as we turned a corner, I would be in that Abilene.

That past was endlessly fascinating to me. Every story I heard felt like another small line tethering me to the place. I cocooned myself in that shared past when I was sad or felt alone or needed comfort. Without those memories connecting me to the earth, in those isolated years in Abilene, some days I felt like I might float away into the limitless West Texas sky.

THE STORIES CENTERED AROUND ONE OF THREE CHRISTIAN UNIVER-
sities—an unusual number of schools of higher learning for such a small
town. And they began around my great-grandfather J. C. Reese, who, I
was told, arrived in Abilene at some point in the 1920s when my grandfather was a toddler.

J. C. was kind and considerate, a gentleman of few words who nonetheless held the respect of everyone who knew him. He was a "land
man"—he negotiated with landowners for mineral rights, opening the
door for oil companies to drill for oil or gas. He had to research titles to
properties—which in West Texas were mostly ranches—to know who
the legal owners were and where the property lines sat. He was an independent contractor, purchasing the mineral rights and then selling them
at a profit to oil companies. He could have profited enormously off the
rights, especially in the Great Depression, but he did not; in those lean
economic years, he worked with ranchers on terms that gave them the
advantage so they did not have to lose their land or homes. Later, when
my father was growing up in Abilene, people would stop the Reeses at
church or at restaurants in town and tell them how much they owed my
great-grandfather: "If it weren't for J. C. Reese," my father remembered
them saying, "where would we be?"

While they were not rich, J. C. set his family up well. Each of his
four children were college educated and three had at least a master's degree, a huge feat at the time, especially for women. The work he was
proudest of was being on the Board of Trustees for Abilene Christian
College. It started as a small private school, elementary through junior
college and then senior college, in 1906. Someone would always say, "It
was Abilene Christian College back then" when they told a story about
the past—which meant the school had achieved something, it had taken
on a larger importance by becoming a university years later. In my mind,
the years when it was ACC were more interesting. The school was always associated with the Christian denomination of the Churches of
Christ; the other two universities in Abilene were Baptist and Methodist.

This was another favorite family tale: Within two decades, ACC outgrew the handful of buildings where the school was housed and they began looking for a new site. Charles Bacon, J. C.'s cousin, whom the family called Charlie, was a pillar of the Abilene community. He was the president of the Abilene Chamber of Commerce, and the Alexander Building, the first skyscraper of sorts—all seven stories of it—held the offices of Bacon Securities.

One day, as family lore framed it, J. C. was visiting his cousin in the office and Charlie told J. C. that he had found the land for the university's next site; Charlie took him to the window and pointed to the new land out to the northeast. It was the old Hashknife Ranch, close to both the creek and the railroad and a little more than two miles northeast of downtown. There was the slight rise to the land that gave it the nickname "the Hill."

J. C. went out to walk around the land immediately and liked it. He came back and told the rest of the ACC Board. They voted and agreed; they fundraised and achieved their goals. As a land man, when he surveyed the land for the school, he also secured a plot for his family just down the street from the new university. Within a few years, construction began—mere weeks before the stock market crash in October 1929. J. C. and the other members of the board shepherded the school through turbulent economic times—that's when J. C. saved so many people's land—and the university eventually thrived. When the magisterial administration building was finished, J. C.'s name and his role, Vice President of the Board of Trustees, was etched with the rest of the board's to the right of elegant rising stairs.

To the left, words were carved deeply along the edge of the building: "Ye shall know the truth, and the truth shall make you free."

SOMETIMES AS A CHILD, ON WALKS AROUND THE CAMPUS, I WOULD TRACE my great-grandfather's name in stone to the right of the stairs, an irrevocable link to that communal past. It was a tangible reminder that I belonged to this smaller, beloved neighborhood on the northeast side of town when I felt out of place in the larger Abilene. I could, at any point, place someone else's memory into my mind's eye like a viewfinder—another way to escape. In that world of other people's memories, I always had a place.

Here was the house my great-grandparents built in the 1920s, the first house on the Hill. Across the street, three houses my family members lived in later—a tight row of homes owned by Reeses on the same street.

Here was my father's first office in the building bearing my great-grandfather's name. Here were the paths where women who once used the term "co-ed" walked slowly in pearls, cardigans, and tweed skirts for dates with young men in football sweaters holding arms full of books.

Here was the stadium where my grandfather, a long-time amateur sports announcer, got to broadcast the US Women's Olympic track try-outs in 1960 in Abilene, where Wilma Rudolph blazed past her competition before going on to win three gold medals at the Rome Olympics; where my sister, brother, and I pretended to race when we were young.

Neatly manicured lawns leading up to well-swept porches. Old-fashioned bikes left scattered by the curb and the echo of children in trees. Thick wooden doors that never needed to be locked. Flowered aprons tied neatly over Sunday dresses. Ties straightened and tucked into buttoned suit coats before digging into Sunday roast. Radios that filled the house with big band and jazz and news announcers' solemn voices while women washed dishes. Books that smelled like dry paper and honeyed binding glue, an aroma that mixed pleasantly with an after-dinner pipe but never a glass of whiskey—the right-living people who lived in the Abilene of my collective memories were all teetotalers.

I stayed in Abilene for college half because of those collective memories, a shared past I wanted to be a part of. The almost-free tuition was also an incentive, but I escaped without much of the baggage that haunted many of my relatives, most of which I would only fully understand later. I will probably always be a people-pleasing oldest child, swayed by a desire to put a positive spin on anything. Even accounting for that, I loved my years at that university.

I left the broader Abilene of my childhood—the place where I never belonged—as soon as I could. In staying at ACU, I did not feel that I had really stayed. Everything that was miserable to me about the first Abilene was gone, or diminished, in the second one. I made new friends, I emerged wholly myself and connected to my past. I also retained my ties to the smaller, more tight-knit Abilene where my family memories bound me to the Hill. I returned often. I loved it with my whole heart. I love it still.

I did not love it unquestioningly. My father, who spent his entire childhood in Abilene, had had an immense rebellion within the Churches of Christ doctrine by the time I was born, embracing a larger worldview than his parents' and certainly larger than his grandparents'. By the time I came along, my parents had reversed their thinking about many of the theological beliefs that had been bedrock in my family for generations, like what women's role was in the church, and whether instrumental music was allowed, among other controversial Church of Christ topics. I didn't realize until I was older that it was unusual in our circles for me to freely say I was a feminist even as a child.

As the daughter of two theology professors, the history of the Churches of Christ was a common dinner-table topic, as were Nietzsche and Buddhism and any number of complex topics. My parents were not one-issue or even one-party voters; I could articulate by high school why Churches of Christ were not Evangelical despite being what I now call "Evangelical-adjacent"—we had much of the same music and movies and other cultural markers, but my parents never subscribed unthinkingly to anything close to the political views of the Moral Majority.

Much of this has to do with the fact that Churches of Christ have a habit of being skeptical and intellectually rigorous; the denomination still practices what is called "congregational autonomy," meaning each congregation makes its own decisions led by teams of leaders called elders. The lack of a hierarchy made the Church of Christ universities, of which ACU remains one of the bigger ones, especially influential. Without denominations making decisions for the larger network of churches, the loosely connected universities became the hub of theological thought.

The congregational autonomy means Churches of Christ ran the gamut politically and theologically: When I was young, my grandparents' churches used "thee" and "thou" to pray. A friend grew up in a congregation where having a gym at church meant you were going to hell. That congregational autonomy also meant a strong propensity for splitting churches over doctrinal disagreements; the way Chiara Sunshine Beaumont described the five original Karankawa clans as "estranged family members" was exactly the relationship among many of the other Churches of Christ in the region. The church I grew up in is considered wildly progressive in some circles today because we added instruments to our church worship when I was young and because women are equal members. Sometimes outsiders who do not understand our gradations of complex views seem to think my attending a Christian university was an act of brainwashing or indoctrination. Instead, my years learning in a sincere, thoughtful community at ACU fostered in me two of my highest values today: compassion and critical thinking.

It can still feel to me, all these years later, like something of a betrayal for me to turn those skills onto that place, to look back on Abilene with a critical eye in a public way. I want to leave it wrapped in tissue paper in a box at the top of a high shelf, protected from anyone's gaze.

But if that historical Abilene is my birthright, if that university is— as I still vehemently believe—an institution where many people have always worked to overcome its complicated origins, then I can and must bring my questions and doubts to examine the legacies of one of the places I love the most. This was the truth my parents taught me early on about faith, about worldview, about existence and my place in the world— questions are never something to be afraid of. They are always a way to the truth. And, as my great-grandfather and other leaders believed enough to have inscribed on the side of the administration building—the truth will set you free.

There was much more to the story that I did not fully understand until growing up. Abilene was not only the collective idyllic past I wove in my mind to cover over my childhood feeling of being out of place. There was a more insidious legacy that caused tangible, real-world trauma to generations of people and changed the trajectory of many, many families, mostly for the worse.

Everything this branch of my family did in the years of moving to and establishing themselves in Abilene and rooting our family for generations in Texas—unlike the other branches of the family, with the empresarios or feuding murderers—was absolutely legal, completely aboveboard, and socially correct. However, the question I bring: Does that make those actions right? Because the consequences of my family's move to Abilene would be felt for generations when my land man great-grandfather helped set the boundaries of the city, determining who had the right to live where.

Even as he helped create a space where my family, and thousands of others who looked like us, would thrive in that bright city on a hill.

CHAPTER 34

In 1881, as Texas and Pacific Railroad extended its tracks from Fort Worth to El Paso, the company planted a town in the middle of arid West Texas. It was an unlikely place for a city. There were no lush river valleys and rolling hills, like in Colorado County; no access to the temperate coastal land that had drawn so many cotton growers to Austin's colony a few decades earlier. The town was founded to meet the company's needs: the railroad needed reliable frontier communities along its route. The company tried to market the dusty collection of houses to would-be settlers by promoting it in Texas newspapers as the "garden spot of the state"—a description that made me snort when I read it.

Still, the campaign—including front page ads in the Fort Worth newspaper—must have paid off: at least three hundred people lived there in the 1880s. Leaders in the small town wanted to be the next stop for the major economic generator in the region: cattle. They named the town after the legendary end point of the cattle drives over the last fifteen years, hoping that Abilene, Texas would someday be as successful as Abilene, Kansas. There was some debate in newspapers and marketing materials; the railroad didn't care which small towns thrived as long as some prospered along their route, and for a while, it seemed like the nearby towns of Buffalo Gap or Baird would be bigger. But eventually, the economic development in Abilene was more organized and more effective and it became the regional hub.

Though not exactly the desert, the lack of reliable sources of water had deterred settlement in the region before the railroad came through. The colonizing nations who fought for centuries for more clement sections of the enormous state never wanted much to do with West Texas. Jumanos, and then Comanche and Apache groups, lived in the area for several centuries.

By 1881, Abilene did not have much to attract newcomers besides the railroad and the dream of cattle drives to come. That dream lasted exactly two years: a massive drought in 1883 showed the limitations of the newly settled frontier town. The creeks that crisscrossed the town dried up quickly in droughts, only to flood—sometimes catastrophically—when it rained too much.

The 1883 drought stoked an already ongoing tension in the region brought on by barbed wire fencing. As it had destroyed Bob Stafford's cattle drives in the 1880s, along with most of the cowboy culture, the invention of barbed wire made it impossible for cattle to be driven large distances. By creating a cheap, secure way to keep some cattle inside and others outside of property boundaries, large ranches effectively closed off the open range where cowboys had moved herds in huge drives to the handful of towns where they could be processed, and then the resulting meat and other cattle products could be shipped around the country by train. Abilene had set itself up to be that kind of processing town in the middle of expansive ranches with excellent access to the train line, but barbed wire meant the cattle drives would never come in the large numbers city leaders needed for that industry to be economically stable. Almost immediately, the city's name would become an ironic reminder of a dream never actualized.

It seemed like Abilene would be like any number of small towns dotting the railroad lines, a collection of houses with a store, a saloon, and a post office and not much else. But something happened in that small town, a determination to thrive despite the limitations of their beginnings.

WITHIN THREE YEARS OF THE FOUNDING OF THE CITY, AN ABILENE NEWS-
paperman wrote a pamphlet laying out the unique qualities of a community they hoped to cultivate out in the middle of nowhere West Texas.
In the "Trade Guide and City Directory," William Gibbs, the publisher
of the *Magnetic Quill*, wrote that there were three pillars of economic and
social stability that would make Abilene prosper: businesses, churches,
and schools.

Growing up, we called Abilene the "Buckle of the Bible Belt," but I
had no idea that the exorbitant number of churches and Christian universities in my hometown was not happenstance but the result of a
planned marketing campaign. From almost the beginning, Abilene was
branded as a hub of right-living, a separate place away from the bustle
and danger of bigger cities. The town became dry in 1903.

In the 1910s, the Abilene chapter of the chamber of commerce formed
and spent the next several decades trying to grow the city based in large
part on their reputation for morality. They even developed a booster organization called the West Texas Immigration Association—trying to
increase "immigration" to the city. Their pitch, through newspapers and
pamphlets across the country, relied on Gibbs's pillars to describe Abilene
as a unique city. With the forming of two Christian universities—what
would become Hardin-Simmons University in 1891 and Abilene Christian College in 1906—the city was well on its way; later it would lose the
bid for Texas Tech to our neighbor to the north, Lubbock, but gain a
Methodist university as well: McMurry, which was founded in 1923.

And though they did not fix the water issues completely, in building
a lake and redistributing water at the turn of the century, the community
in Abilene made the barren region habitable. The dry air was an especially good draw for people with health issues, like my great-grandfather.
In the history of the city, though, very few came because of the topography or the weather. The selling point was always the people; the goal
was always isolation from the plurality of cities in a culture of Christian
purity.

One leader in town called the community "straitlaced," meaning it as a high compliment.

NO ONE ALIVE REMEMBERS J. C.'S EXACT DIAGNOSIS, BUT IT SEEMED TO have involved his lungs. J. C.'s health was never great, and as a young man, he left Corinth, Arkansas—the town at the center of *Corinth and Its Kinfolk*—to visit a distant relative's sanitorium in Roswell, New Mexico. There he met Nellie Jones, daughter of the owner and J. C.'s third cousin, who was loud to his quiet, boisterous to his stoic, quirky to his hypochondriacal. They married in 1909.

By 1910, they had moved to Quanah, Texas, where my great-uncle Jerome was born. They moved back to New Mexico at some point before the next child was born. There is a five-year gap after Jerome and the next three kids they had in six years: Ruth in 1915, Helen in 1917, and Leon in 1919.

Leon was my grandfather. By the time he was born in 1919, the family had moved back to Texas, living in Mineral Wells for a handful of years. J. C. Reese had already begun his association with ACC. My grandfather would never know a time when Abilene Christian College was not the moral and cultural center of the Reese family.

Nellie and J. C. were an unlikely couple. He was much shorter than she was; she was what the family always called "big-boned." I knew her as a little girl. She died when I was five, and I remember holding her hand in the hospital. I called her Grandmother.

Grandmother had spent her childhood years living in a dugout in New Mexico—the kind of cave-like homes dug into the ground that were common among poor white settlers on the frontiers. She did not like to sleep above ground, which meant that all of their houses had basements where she slept, even when—in Abilene—it required dynamite to excavate enough of the bedrock to dig a basement. The grandchildren found those basements eerie, except my dad's oldest brother, Randy, who spent the night sometimes with his grandparents. J. C. went to bed by seven p.m., and then Grandmother would let Randy stay up for hours listening to the "Big Daddy" radio show at midnight on Saturdays. For Randy, it was one of the first experiences listening to a Black radio announcer or jazz music; he credits his grandmother for helping to change his perceived perspective about race through that small act. He also loved it because it was a secret hour just for the two of them; he felt like he was getting away with something because they were staying up late together.

Grandmother never fit the mold of an Abilene housewife. Her antics were family legend. She talked and lived her life at full volume. When her husband spoke, quietly and confidently, she would hold back her opinion respectfully. Otherwise, she "held forth," as the family put it—expressing her opinion even on theological matters, even to men and women at church, even if no other women around her did. She always said she played the piano "like a man." She also drove "like a man"—her grandsons remember her gunning the engine of her boat-sized sedan as she drove their grandfather around town. Grandmother ate raw onions like apples, perhaps because of an article she had read or some other health advice she had gotten; the origins of her habit are gone, but the memories of her breath remain among her grandchildren and great-grandchildren.

I loved those stories and others when I was young. The stories about Grandmother explained to me in a way I could not put into words as a child that there was a disconnect built into the right-living narratives of our family's roots in Abilene. Around the time I was reading *Corinth and Its Kinfolk* and obsessing about our family being from Wales, I intuited that the cleaned-up stories I was hearing had been rigidly cropped, that things were not as straitlaced as they might have seemed. I wanted to know what else, besides a delightfully irascible great-grandmother, remained in the cuttings left out of the frame.

FOR SEVERAL YEARS, J. C. REESE TRAVELED BACK AND FORTH BETWEEN Abilene and Mineral Wells for ACC events, like the yearly Lectureship series based on tent revival meetings where preachers gathered to teach

ACC students, faculty, staff, and throngs of visitors to the college. It was the closest thing the Churches of Christ in the region had to an official gathering, and J. C. Reese—whose family had been Church of Christ since my great-grandfather's great-grandparents joined the "Campbell Reformation" sometime before 1847—was right in the thick of it. The ACC newspaper, *The Optimist*, reported his attendance in long lists of out-of-town Church of Christ men who came for the conference for a few days.

A photo from the time period shows J. C. Reese at a board meeting, one of twenty-four men all wearing three-piece suits. Some are smiling, others look serious. J. C. has his chin tucked down a bit, the corners of his mouth folded into a slight smile as if he were sharing a secret with the photographer. He is not the most gregarious in the group, but the smile lines are deep, the expression warm, someone likelier to twinkle than grin.

In 1922, my great-grandparents bought a small house on Russell Street that would hold my grandfather's earliest memories. J. C. Reese needed to establish his business in Abilene as an independent land man in the region. Word of mouth was especially helpful in his business, and J. C. was well positioned because of his connections. Not only did he move to town with an instant network because of his work on the ACC Board, he quickly got involved at one of the Churches of Christ. He had family connections as well.

The Bacon boys were J. C.'s first cousins; their mother had been a Reese. Charlie Bacon was not on the ACC Board, but he had his finger in almost every other pie in Abilene, including years of being involved with the Abilene Chamber of Commerce. Charlie was five years older than J. C., but J. C. and Sloman Bacon were the same age, only two months apart—what we called when I was growing up "twin cousins." Sloman and J. C. had both lived in Mineral Wells and moved to Abilene within months of each other; Sloman's boss in Mineral Wells owned a thriving grocery store chain based out of Abilene. The youngest Bacon brother, Samuel, was nine years younger than both Sloman and J. C. Reese and was a manager at the local candy factory.

When he moved to Abilene, J. C. was lucky to be instantly connected with many of the city's leaders as he grew his own business; it wasn't long before he knew many of the white Christian men in the area, all eager to grow the city in the way they envisioned.

WHEN MY GREAT-GRANDPARENTS PURCHASED A HOUSE IN ABILENE IN late 1922, it was one of the most violent years in its history. That violence did not come from the outlaws who had roamed the frontiers during the fence wars, or the criminals in the big cities the marketing campaigns always promised Abilenians could escape.

The violence came from the hands of the white civic leaders of the city, the kinds of people my great-grandfather was getting to know as he grew his consulting business. My great-grandparents arrived in Abilene at the height of Ku Klux Klan activity in the city as well as the rest of the state. Secret state records show that the Abilene leader, whom they called the "Exalted Cyclops," was a preacher with considerable local influence. Without seeing the roster for the rest of the Klan in the three years that it dominated civic life in Abilene—a document which, if it exists, I have not found—it is only possible to guess which other leaders were in the secret organization. But several indicators, including the size of a crowd that had come out to march with their hoods on the year before, demonstrate that it was a significant number of men.

To be clear, I do not think my great-grandfather was in the Klan. I imagine, based on everything I have heard from others and know about him, that he would have actively hated their tactics. I think my great-grandfather was possibly in the minority in disagreeing with their violent ways, at least for the handful of years before public opinion turned against the Klan. But I also think that he—like almost everyone else in Abilene at the time—would have agreed with at least some of the basic tenets of white supremacy. I think that because of how mainstream those viewpoints were—they were commonly held, everyday ideas.

Decades later in Abilene, I grew up at a time when many people in power might have held racist ideas but they were coded or somehow hidden, tucked beneath the surface of polite society. In my research, it shocked me how *un*-shocking it seemed for racism to be baldly printed in newspapers and editorials, in letters and stories. In trying to understand my families' and communities' opinions on race in the past, I did not need to do much real digging. The views were blatant and clear, openly stated and apparently often widely accepted.

On January 1, 1922, a small piece titled "Statistics" appeared in the local newspaper, the *Abilene Daily Reporter*, and revealed the values at the time. Based on the 1920 census information, the piece showed there were 10,274 people living in the city, almost exactly half of whom were men. There were 2,360 families. The article breaks down the population by race: there were "two Indians and 410 negroes," a reduction of almost two hundred Black people from the previous 1910 census, the article reports, which counted 602. There were "only 132 foreign-born whites in Abilene," with an itemization of their countries of origin: fifty-two people from Mexico, the rest from European countries, with the most—fourteen—from England. The origin of each individual immigrant betrays the obsession at this highly xenophobic time with racialized purity. A few years later, Hiram W. Evans as leader of the Ku Klux Klan in Dallas, would call it the "great mass of Americans of the old pioneer stock" who were primarily "Nordic Americans."

The newspaper announced a figure that would be touted in advertisements, chamber of commerce speeches, and newspaper articles throughout the decade: "Abilene has 9,720 native white inhabitants, or 94.6 percent—which is considerably higher than any city of over 10,000 population in Texas."

There was a direct correlation between the fact that the city proudly pronounced itself to be 95 percent white, and what occurred in Abilene in the early 1920s. The number of members the KKK had for a few short years makes it clear that a large portion of the white civic leaders in my hometown probably kept their hooded robes in a secret place at home. A deluge of widespread political extremism flooded Abilene and the rest of Texas in the 1920s.

CHAPTER 35

Texas Tech University in Lubbock has a special collection with an inventory of Ku Klux Klan records in Texas from 1921 to 1925. Those documents provide some clues about who was in the KKK throughout Texas. Most of the records are from Amarillo, the panhandle city to the north of Abilene and Lubbock. The records reveal the scope of the outreach and careful bookkeeping of the Klan at the time. One sheet dated "6-15-25" gives hand-typed financial records. Each member's address is logged to the right in an organized column; some names are crossed through or have a check mark through them. Some members have their occupation or storefront listed: they include butchers, grocers, carpenters, firemen, shoe repairmen, an ice cream man.

Detailed records like the one of Amarillo are not especially common; many historical facts about the KKK might never be known, or are based on educated guesses. In Dallas around the same time, an estimated one in three eligible white men—who were not Jewish or Catholic, for example—were in the Klan. In the earliest days, they recruited leaders in the community, focusing on white collar men, before moving into the ranks of the working class; one historian called it "a pyramid scheme" because Klan members would get a rising percentage of the dues depending on how high they moved up in the ranks.

The Amarillo records list each Klavern in Texas, recorded in order of their numbers, starting with the first one in Houston and ending with number 318 in Woodville. And next to the number and town are two columns of names: the "E. C." and the "Kli." Those stand for "Exalted Cyclops" (the local leader) and the "Kligrapp" (the secretary). Those records give me the only two names I have for Klan members in Abilene. In 1925, those records list the Exalted Cyclops as Rev. L. N. Stucky [*sic*] and the Kligrapp as R. M. Barnes.

Those names give the tiniest insight into what was happening in Abilene in the years right after my great-grandparents moved to town, a tear in the papered over version of the past.

OFFICIALLY, THE REVIVED VERSION OF THE KLAN IN TEXAS—HOUSTON, No. 1—was established in October 1920. Over the next few years, the Klan would have a profound, feverish grip on the state. By targeting civic leaders—preachers and bankers, teachers and newspaper editors, businessmen and elected officials—the Klan rebranded its messages as the response of reasonable men to the fears that haunted the white public, the same fears arrayed in the slave codes of Virginia and passed down through generations over the centuries. According to witnesses in Dallas, the KKK talked significantly less about race than they did the social order—they recruited to keep those in power still in power. Publicly, they would show up to community events like revival tent meetings or chamber of commerce meetings with checks or donations. They attempted to be seen as pillars of the community.

For a time, the money they threw behind their cause seemed to work. The Ku Klux Klan became increasingly influential in the state of Texas. By the early 1920s, Klan members claimed that they dominated city and county politics in several areas of the region. Texas—founded as the only country to enthusiastically write slavery into their constitution—seemed bound to become a KKK-held state.

By January 1921, almost exactly a year before the "Statistics" piece about the town being 95 percent white, the *Abilene Daily Reporter* was beginning to cover the Klan's influence. The archived documents in

Amarillo show that the newspaper editors there were part of the KKK; without a list of Abilene members, it is impossible to verify who specifically supported the Klan, but the Abilene paper was often openly sympathetic. When covering a Klan parade in Dallas in March 1921, the Abilene paper repeats that the editors at the *Dallas Morning News* thought the parade was a "'slander on Dallas,'" but the Abilene editors are not so sure: "Any secret organization which usurps the prerogatives of constituted law is a nuisance, but it remains to be shown whether the Ku Klux Klan can properly be classified in that category." Klan leaders presumably recognized they needed to demonstrate the strength and popularity of the group in Abilene to make it clear that their group was not a vicious few, but a majority of white men in town.

In fact, the Ku Klux Klan's goodwill branding campaign was to make themselves look like any other civic organization. The Kiwanis Club, Lions Club, Abilene Woman's Club, and other community-minded groups were a critical part of the social fabric by the 1920s in Abilene, as they were nationally. Scholars call it "fraternalism," the lodge-style orders and associations that provided a shared identity, a sense of social standing. Pro–Ku Klux Klan articles often invoked that fraternal language—like those mainstream clubs, they insisted the goal of the KKK was only to make their communities better. One article in the Abilene newspaper defined a Klansman as someone "whose function is to spirit away undesirables."

In August 1921, a singular article appeared on a Wednesday in the *Abilene Daily Reporter*, a "List of Those Who Signed Petition for Employing Whites." The *Reporter* said it "received the following with the request that it be published"—an occurrence that would become more frequent in the following months as the editors received what they framed as anonymous letters and notifications about Klan news. The article is an open letter addressed "To All Employers of Laborers in the City of Abilene, Texas." Their request is short:

We, the undersigned citizens of the city of Abilene, Texas, petition you and each of you to employ white men upon all public or private work going on or to be hereafter begun in this city where such la-

borers can be had in preference to Mexican laborers. We call your
attention to the fact that this is a white man's country. We also call
your attention to the further fact that at this time there are a great
number of white laborers with families to support who are citizens
of this city and who are idle because the Mexicans have been employed as laborers because they can afford to work at prices white
men cannot afford to work for.

The article then lists 190 men and companies who sign the request
to only hire white men. Several of the men are in the Abilene Chamber
of Commerce; toward the end of the list was the name of one of J. C.
Reese's first cousins. Beyond the overt racism that is clearly widely socially acceptable at the time, the list implies a subtext: hire white people
or face being boycotted.

I am not saying that the people who signed the list in any way admitted to being a part of the Ku Klux Klan. To me, the overt language
corresponds with the directness of racist views at the time. This does not
seem to have been an especially controversial open letter; it was printed
below the fold on page three, between an ad for rash ointment and a list
of who attended the Kiwanis Club meeting that week.

On November 16, the newspaper announced the result of a community-
wide campaign to raise money for the Salvation Army, led by Chairman
R. W. Haynie—whose name had been close to the top of the "List of
Those Who Signed Petition For Employing Whites" a few months earlier. Haynie only has one quote in the short article: "'A noticeable feature
of the appeal in Abilene,' states Mr. Haynie, 'was the bringing to light
of a Ku Klux Klan in Abilene which gave $100 to the cause,'" a gift
Haynie later called "spectacular." One hundred dollars was the equivalent of $1,658 in today's currency; the entire fundraiser brought in over
five thousand dollars—close to one hundred thousand dollars today. The
paper reported that Haynie found a hundred-dollar bill with a note
signed by the KKK on his desk. Later, it was widely referred to as a public announcement: The KKK was in Abilene. They had money. They
planned to use it.

A week later, the newspaper editors reported they received a mysterious call informing them that the Ku Klux Klan would parade through "the principal business streets of the city at eight o'clock Thursday (Thanksgiving) evening." The paper reported the Klan had already sent a letter to the mayor and city council assuring them that there would be no "acts of lawlessness or disturbance," that their goal was "to assist in keeping and assisting in the enforcement of the Laws of our country." The paper speculated that thousands would come to see the "white-robed Klansmen" in the "first parade of its kind in West Texas," and that "interest . . . is expected to be at a fever pitch."

The Friday morning after Thanksgiving 1921, the editors ran an effusive write-up of the Ku Klux Klan parade from the night before on the front page of the paper: "Silently, through a stillness broken only occasionally . . . a column of members of the Ku Klux Klan estimated to number about 225 glided through long lanes of watching people lining the principal business streets of Abilene Thursday night." The crowd was enormous, perhaps the biggest that had ever assembled in Abilene. The parade began at the corner of North Fourth Street and proceeded along the main downtown street, Pine, eventually ending five blocks later, at Chestnut. At 8:00 p.m., all the lights in town went out.

"The close-packed crowd surged forward" when the "silent hooded figures" appeared. Through pitch-black streets, the parade began with "Old Glory"—the US flag. Behind it was the "flaming cross of the Invisible Empire," the "three prongs of the cross were points of sputtering fire of a rose color" that cast a "rosy glow over the marchers and the assembled thousands, presenting an eerie setting which awed most of the spectators into silence but which brought forth scattering salvos of applause." The men kept coming and coming, their line broken only by other flaming crosses held up at regular intervals, a "gliding, noiseless column of marching figures" lit by "an unearthly glow."

At 9:00 p.m., the lights went back on. The white robes were hidden away. Families left the spectacle to return to homes that still held the fragrance of Thanksgiving dinners to tuck children into bed. Though the article does not mention the racial makeup of the crowd, it was almost certainly only white people who felt safe enough to be out on those streets that night. The paper reports that the parade "passed off without an untoward incident of any kind, so far as known."

But everything in Abilene changed that night. Now everyone in the city and entire West Texas region knew: the Ku Klux Klan was public, active, and ready.

Within weeks, a few weeks before the article was published in the new year about the town being 95 percent white, the newspaper announced that *The Birth of a Nation*—the movie that had launched the second iteration of the Klan across the nation—would show at the Queen Theatre in Abilene on December 23 and 24, 1921.

THE TOWN WAS ALREADY WELL VERSED IN THE MOVIE'S MESSAGE. IN THEIR write-up of the movie, the editors of the Abilene paper no longer dithered on their support of the KKK: they reported it set "forth the clansmen in their true light . . . a band of heroes instead of outlaws." The movie was an adaptation of a book and then a play called *The Clansman*; the play had already been produced in Abilene three times.

I had seen snippets of it before, but I decided I needed to watch all three hours and fifteen minutes of *Birth of a Nation* one day. What I found so disturbing about the film was its tone of cool rationality and persuasive storyline. I was not prepared for how it would affect me. I found myself having to turn it off to walk away. It ended up taking me the better part of a day to finish.

It is one of the most offensive things I have ever seen. As Roger Ebert famously said, "'The Birth of a Nation' is not a bad film because it argues for evil . . . it is a great film that argues for evil. To understand how it does so is to learn a great deal about film, and even something about evil." It is offensive precisely because it presents deeply racist ideas as if they are historical realities. The movie relies on familiar turning points from the preceding century—the Civil War, the death of Lincoln, the enactment of Reconstruction policies—to provide a factual backbone. They change the facts, skew the storyline only slightly at first.

For the first hour at least, I could see how a contemporary audience would be nodding along: yes, that did happen; yes, there were reasonable people on both sides; yes, the human loss was incalculable; yes, the Civil War was a massive tragedy that cratered our once connected country. Yes, yes, yes.

The movie pulls masterfully at its audience's heartstrings. I teach narrative writers that one of the best ways to write a sad scene is to pair it with something funny or playful or calm—a lull that allows the audience to catch their breath. The filmmaker D. W. Griffith does this over and over again: A senator's daughter goofs around with her brothers before they leave for war so they walk away laughing before she falls apart when they are out of eyesight; it is, inevitably, the last time she will see them. A brother mourning the loss of two brothers and a little sister poignantly watches children at play—two white kids are playing chase with four Black children, and, to hide, they tuck themselves under a white sheet. When the Black children find them, the white children scream and run after them. The man not only chuckles, he is struck by inspiration—the idea for the white-robed figures. The start of the KKK is presented as innocent, born of humor in the midst of grief.

In the film, slavery is presented as a happy time for "faithful souls" with unchanging loyalties to their master—a masterpiece of the Lost-Cause narrative. The character of the white master is literally playing with two puppies and a kitten when he is introduced. The "faithful souls" remain in their roles even once slavery ends. Before the war, everyone in the film is portrayed as content. After the war, the once-proud white people are deeply impoverished, and the world is in chaos.

The source of that chaos in the film is leering Black men who want to have sex with white women, and the "radicals" who push the country too far. The villains in the movie are biracial, showing what happens, the filmmakers argue, when people of different races "mix." President Abraham Lincoln is presented as a sympathetic, persuadable ally caught up in tensions he did not create, whose death becomes an opportunity the radicals exploit. It gives the filmmakers a chance to connect with a possibly skeptical audience—see, we're not unreasonable, we liked Lincoln too; he's not really to blame, it's those radicals.

The goal of these radicals, according to the movie, is always inter-marriage. Black representatives in Congress immediately pass a bill allowing mixed-race marriage, while Black representatives—many of them white actors in badly applied blackface—sneer at the white women now relegated to the balconies. In the worldview presented in the movie, when the government has become a hotbed of usurpers with a sexual agenda that threatens "traditional" marriage, the only reasonable response is vigilantism outside of the law. The movie's takeaways are simple: good men must take matters into their own hands when the government proves untrustworthy.

As with Stephen F. Austin in the 1830s, the enslavers before the Civil War, and white civic leaders afterward, the movie argues for vigilantism as "a mere instinct of self-preservation."

In the film, the instigators of societal chaos were Black people and advocates of post–Civil War Reconstruction and anyone else "radical" who was a threat to post-enslaving white society, including Jews and Catholics and immigrants. Those "radicals" were the source of societal upheaval; all that was required to return to the happy time without chaos was for those cultural threats to be eradicated. In the South, including in Texas, the interpretation of history and the moral code the film presented were wildly convincing.

THE ARGUMENTS AND THE TACTICS ARE EERILY SIMILAR BETWEEN THE 1910s to 1920s and the 2010s to 2020s. Once, when I interviewed a refugee resettlement official and asked him how we had gotten to the point in the late 2010s where victims of terror and persecution were being portrayed across the nation as the very terrorists they were fleeing, his answer was simple: a lack of knowledge about history. Because refugee resettlement was no longer controversial after the Refugee Act of 1980 passed unanimously in the Senate, there was no longer the need to educate the US public about it. An entire generation grew up knowing very little about what it meant to be a refugee, without having lived through World War II or even the Vietnam War or sharing memories of Holocaust survivors and the United States leading the world in a promise that genocide would never happen again. Without knowing the truth, people were easily swayed by arguments that sounded factual but were based on false ideas about what it really means to be a refugee.

The Birth of a Nation was a successful and remarkably similar misinformation campaign, and it changed the political spectrum on national, regional, and local levels the same way anti-refugee memes and social media campaigns and conspiracy groups and all kinds of other misinformation have affected politics around the world over the last decade or longer. The truth was disguised by an electric narrative of a threat to society that needed to be eradicated. That narrative erased the truth—real people made vulnerable by massive displacement or injustice outside of their control just wanted to have a chance to live, to be safe, and to be free.

It is not just former refugees, of course, who are figured as caricatures and then made out to be societal "threats" in Texas or other areas where these kinds of widescale debates are raging. You could substitute almost any group whose bodies and lives are triggering the same kinds of cultural fears that have prompted reactive legislation or public storytelling since the earliest days of the Virginia colony. The "threats" shift every few generations; but the formula for the stories, and the tactics for how to remove those threats, featured in *Birth of a Nation* remain remarkably the same.

IN 1922, THE HUB OF THE NATIONAL KU KLUX KLAN SHIFTED TO TEXAS when Dallas dentist Hiram Evans took over national leadership. Evans advocated for a cultured, well-mannered Klan that focused on family outreach and educational reforms as a way to achieve a homogenous society. He hoped to move away from the Klan's thuggish reputation. The tension between the public-facing side of the Klan and the private vigilantism—always couched as helping the local police—would remain a feature of the revised KKK.

The police chief in Abilene had no interest in the local Klan's help. Chief John J. Clinton had been in his role for more than thirty-seven years. He was incredibly well respected and liked in Abilene, enough so that he was also the fire chief. Clinton was Catholic, which meant he would never have been accepted by the Klan. A staunch enemy of the Klan, he had no tolerance for masked amateurs trying to play sheriff.

Despite his opposition, vigilantism picked up in Abilene in 1922. A Black porter was whipped by a group of men with a stiff wire bat. Another man was run out of town. A Catholic priest in nearby Slaton was tarred and feathered. There were rumors and unspoken attacks. It was not just Abilene—almost daily, the paper ran news stories from across Texas of whippings, floggings, kidnappings, lynchings, murders. The torrent of Klan-led violence seemed out of control, even as the leaders continued to swear it was someone else, other groups of white men, not the supposed well-behaved members of their secret white supremacist organization.

Chief Clinton, who held the respect of the small Black community as well as most of the people in town, tried to keep the violence at bay, but the newspaper began to describe what was happening in town as a "crime wave." Sometimes the editors seemed to blame the Klan, other times they printed articles about prohibition, or out of control youths—especially "flappers"—as the source of moral degeneration in the community.

April 1922 was a dramatic month in the county. On Monday, April 17, a grand jury was convened to indict instigators of the recent violence. Taylor County District Judge W. R. Ely told the jury that they were going to investigate the "unlawful whippings." The Ku Klux Klan had denied responsibility, and Ely took them at their word, but he was "opposed to any organization that proposes to take the law in its own hands. The constitution and statutes of the state must be supreme."

The next day, a representative of the national Ku Klux Klan gave two speeches to large audiences at the S. S. S. Motor Company building. He was introduced by R. W. Haynie—the chairman of the Salvation Army fundraising campaign who, the previous November, had "happened" to find a hundred-dollar bill on his desk with a note, right before the Thanksgiving Day Klan parade. At the speeches in April, Haynie admitted that he was a part of the KKK. Then the two of them gave an overview of what they said the Klan stood for—a secret organization that did not participate in whippings or other forms of violence but that did care about upholding the tenets of "supremacy of the white race, free public schools, and the purity of womanhood." The KKK representative cautioned that the audience should not trust the media because it was "controlled by Jews and Catholics." These papers were underreporting the Klan's strength, he said; it was growing at a rate of "2,500 per day" from the "men of character, prudence and poise," not "law-breakers, thugs, and those on the outer fringe of society." In Fort Worth, for example, he said there were six thousand members: "judges, county officials, mayor, ex-mayors, bankers, members of the Chamber of Commerce and every preacher except one."

It was a fine rhetorical line they tried to walk: almost every white man in the neighboring big city was in the Klan, including most civil and religious leaders—and sure, violence might be on the rise, which called for vigilantes to support the police, but any "unlawful whippings" were not caused by the *particular* vigilantes in the Klan.

Then, a week after the national Klan representative recruited in Abilene, the news turned away from the crime wave and the rising tension to a profound natural disaster—Abilene was deluged with rain.

ABILENE'S FLOODING PROBLEM HAD BEEN PARTIALLY SOLVED BY THE construction of lakes and dams designed to hold water for the city to use and to keep it from flooding the creeks. But even with the system that had taken years to build, the rains in April of 1922 were a powerful force. There had already been rains in the weeks before. With flat topography like Abilene has, once the ground is saturated, there is no place for the water to go but up.

On Wednesday, April 26, 1922, the water in Lake Abilene had reached a forty-foot depth, which the mayor estimated would last for three to four years without any additional rainfall. And still it kept coming—sixteen additional feet within a few hours. The creeks were "running at a rapid rate," and Elm Creek in Abilene, at one point, went from a few feet across to half a mile wide. The railroad lines were under water. Families were stranded. Crops and homes were lost in a handful of hours.

The dam on the lake held, which was good news for the city, but it brought home the fact that the location of homes in the growing city really mattered.

Business leaders and real estate agents and land surveyors paid attention. Land near creeks meant flood damage. High ground saved homes. Within the next few weeks, the waters receded. I have lived through other rainy times in Abilene like that spring in 1922 must have been, so I can imagine the sudden flush of wildflowers, the parched landscape swathed in gorgeous greens. It is a heady time, in a dry land, after the rains are gone and before the sun scorches the vegetation back to dust.

With the rains receding, the Ku Klux Klan flourished like the land around them. The more members they had, the more money they made and the more power they wielded.

Then suddenly, the respected police chief got sick. On May 31, after almost four decades on the job, Chief Clinton died.

One of the things Chief Clinton had been known for was attending every funeral in town, no matter who had died. Sometimes it was only the police chief and the funeral home attendants and the minister. At his own funeral, held at Sacred Heart Catholic Church, thousands of people came to celebrate his long tenure in Abilene. Two truckloads of flowers "completely hid the grave." The small Black community came out in force.

That summer, as Clinton's successor, R. E. Burch, took over the position of police chief, the growing Klan flexed its muscles. Despite the loud public relations campaign in Abilene that the KKK was only a service organization, violence ramped up again. Judge Ely convened another grand jury in August to try to ascertain who was behind the acts of vigilantism.

Just days before that grand jury finished its work, the Ku Klux Klan struck.

CHAPTER 36

On Friday, September 3, 1922, a Black man named Grover C. Everett checked into the Joe Davis Hotel on Ash Street. A veteran of World War I, he had just turned thirty-eight and was in town for work. He was supporting a family in Sulphur Springs, Texas.

The hotel was part of the area of town designated for Black people to live. It was only a few blocks from Pine Street, the hub of Abilene's business district and the site of the Ku Klux Klan parade less than a year before. There were certainly people who knew how often Everett came to town, where he worked, or what he did, but those details were not deemed important enough to have made it into official records. He seemed to have been known in the community; one person had known him for eleven years. Later, witnesses would use words like "hardworking" and "harmless" to describe him—as if there were gradations of guilt for murder victims, as if some targets of the Klan were more deserving of receiving horrific attacks outside of the law than others.

All of the witnesses agreed that Everett retired early that Saturday night. He passed through the lobby around 8:00 or 8:30, went upstairs to the room where he was boarding: Room 3.

The hotel owner, Joe Davis, was there in the lobby when Everett came through. And he was there some time later when three masked men came in the lobby and then went into the dining room. Davis told the district attorney later, "One of them knocked on the counter. . . . And I went behind the counter." The men were dressed in white coats with eyeholes, Davis said; their entire faces were covered. One of them asked Davis for a match: "That's all I heard them say at any time."

They wanted a match to light a search lamp one of them carried. The men started to go upstairs, stopped, and talked to each other. Davis testified that he could not hear them—though they had only been feet away. It is impossible to know whether the words were audible, but Davis knew how to survive as one of only a few dozen Black men in Abilene. He had witnessed firsthand what the Klansmen did, and they knew where to find him.

As the Klansmen went upstairs, Davis started up behind them, followed by two other Black men. The masked men in robes told them, "You boys, get back there; we don't need you." Davis and the other men went back down the stairs. Davis heard knocking on a door: "Sounded like somebody was kicking with their foot. Then I heard the pistol. I didn't hear anybody say anything. There was one shot."

The masked men came back downstairs without speaking and went outside. The pistol was found later in a tub across the hall from Everett's room.

E. D. Lewis, the barber who ran the shop at the Davis Hotel, testified he saw the white men leave out the door and get into a car, where the driver was also robed. There were three other cars with white men who left at the same time; some were wearing robes, but not all. According to Lewis, there were between eleven and fourteen white men who waited outside that night, though only three went upstairs. With their faces masked, no one could identify them. But then, no one tried.

The Black men who witnessed the crime and bravely allowed their names to be included in the court and newspaper records gave only enough of a testimony to make it clear that the murderers were in the Ku Klux Klan. Any other identifying factors—voices or the color of pants or shoes or the make and model of cars—none of those details were recorded, if the witnesses shared them at all.

Everett was shot once through his right breast. When the district attorney asked Joe Davis point-blank, "Who killed him?" Davis took his life in his hands to tell the truth: "The men in robes."

The district attorney then said to Davis, "You know that's a lie; you know those men didn't kill that negro."

At that, the newspaper reported, "Davis dropped his head."

THE GRAND JURY THAT JUDGE ELY HAD CONVENED IN AUGUST HAD BEEN on recess for two weeks, but they were ordered to reconvene on the Monday following the killing. Ely gave them a long speech, punctuated by a statement from the district attorney who accused Joe Davis of lying. Both were reprinted at length in the newspaper.

Ely was obviously testy: "It is a bad blot on your town when men go out and wantonly kill in that way." Ely was no bastion of equality; he was less concerned with the murderers' white supremacy than them acting outside of the law: "Of course, he was just a negro, but under our system of government all men have an equal right in the courtroom."

The court called on anyone who knew anything to come forward. Ely already despaired of justice being served: "I will be frank with you and say that I do not believe that you will find who did this killing. The district attorney and officers have made a thorough investigation and they have been unable to establish the identity of the slayer."

Still, Ely called for a grand jury investigation. As he predicted—or as his fatalism predetermined—on September 21, 1922, just ten days after Everett was killed, the grand jury made their report. They agreed that masked men killed Everett. They called it a "deplorable tragedy" but after a "thorough investigation and impartial deliberation," they decided no further determination could be made. Ely dismissed the men of the grand jury.

Two years later, Judge W. R. Ely would be recommended for the board for the new Methodist school, McMurry College. Also on that board was the new reverend at St. Paul Methodist Church: Rev. L. N. Stuckey, who the records in Amarillo revealed decades later to be the Exalted Cyclops of the Ku Klux Klan.

THERE WAS A MAJOR SHAKE-UP IN THE KU KLUX KLAN IN ABILENE AFTER
the murder of Everett. Despite the fact that the killers were never identified, there were at least eleven to fourteen white men who knew exactly
who pulled that trigger. The national KKK leader who had been in
Abilene in April 1922 gave insight into who those men might have been
when he gave an overview of the members of the Klan in Fort Worth:
"Judges, county officials, mayor, ex-mayors, bankers, members of the
Chamber of Commerce."

And a line that has run through my mind every day since I've read
it: "Every preacher except one."

My family's legacy of Protestant faith is rooted in those years in
Abilene. It was always the thing Abilene was known for, all my life and
for generations before me—how many churches there were in town, how
Christian the city was.

Every preacher. Except one.

Abilene was not unusual in having a preacher as the Klan leader; the
statewide records from Amarillo listing every Klan leader are riddled
with reverends. I have no idea who the leader was before Stuckey. All I
know is that, at some point after he moved to Abilene in November
1922—two months after the lynching of Grover C. Everett—L. N. Stuckey
stepped into that role.

Were those same leaders in Abilene in the Klan? Judges. District
attorneys. County attorneys. Special police investigators. County officials. Bankers. Members of the chamber of commerce.

Every preacher. Except one.

What would it take for the Christians in Abilene to stand up to
the influence of the Klan? Especially in the Churches of Christ, with
a long tradition of saying we were—in the word I heard throughout my
childhood—"countercultural"? The answer came that autumn, less than
two months after the grand jury found no one guilty of killing a veteran
in cold blood for the crime of being Black.

It happened at a revival meeting in November 1922: ten members of the Ku Klux Klan walked down the aisle at the end. Everyone there knew what it meant to walk down the aisle like that—it was an altar call, the move of those who wanted to confess. To repent. The crowd was "silent and awe-stricken" as they watched the preacher, waiting breathlessly for his response as ten robed men came toward him.

The preacher was Jesse Sewell—president of Abilene Christian College, where my great-grandfather was on the board.

CHAPTER 37

The university president and theological leader referred to as "Brother Sewell" was known throughout the region as an evangelist with a good ear for sermons. According to the student paper *The Optimist*, that Sunday in November 1922, the last day of the revival meeting, Brother Sewell "preached the straight unvarnished gospel." They measured his gift as a speaker by the number of people who responded to him: "Fifty persons were added to the congregation. Thirty-four of those were by baptism, about fifteen by restoration and others who have just moved into this vicinity placed their membership with the local congregation." "Restoration" meant they were restored back to the "true faith" after leaving, or "falling away" from the church (in those days, that often meant converting back to the Churches of Christ from having been Baptist or Methodist). Many of them would have been restored during those nightly altar calls at the end of the revival meeting.

The college editors recounted paragraph after paragraph of Sewell's sermon that night: "God loves his children, every one of them, whether rich or poor, great or small, weak or strong." Knowing that changed everything: "We cannot serve two masters. . . . The question is, what are we as sons and daughters of God going to do with our lives? What will govern, control, restrain us?"

It couldn't be money and power, said Sewell, because humans who were "servants of mammon," made a bargain with the devil: "What is a man profited if he shall gain the whole world and lose his own soul, or what shall a man give in exchange for his soul?" Instead, Sewell preached, a person should "repent of his sins, fall out with sin and fall in love with Jesus Christ. Then when man has made the good confession, he shall be baptized." After baptism, they would become beloved children of God: "He is interested in you. He knows every child of his and all about each one."

Even in the racial hierarchies of the segregated churches at the time, Grover C. Everett counted in Sewell's theology as a beloved child of God. The God Sewell preached would know all about Everett—how he lived. What he did. What he loved. What he feared. How he died.

As Sewell finished his rousing sermon, those ten men in white robes came in through the east entrance and walked down the middle aisle. The audience watched. Had they come to confess? The men fanned out in front of Sewell. One of the men handed Sewell an envelope.

PRESIDENT SEWELL TORE IT OPEN.

The ten men turned to face the audience. One of them held a United States flag. Sewell read the letter while the Klansmen eyed the crowd through slits in their hoods. The newspaper later reprinted it verbatim:

Dear Sir—the personnel of the Knights of the Ku Klux Klan consists of true American citizens whose love for the country, for Christianity, and for the sacred homes has led them to organize into one great Klan whose members are striving to preserve and protect the true American ideals, established by our forefathers. They believe in a clean religion, a clean government and clean morals and proper education. The members of Abilene Ku Klux Klan Number 139 believe that the meeting which you are just closing has been of great benefit to our community and beg you to accept the enclosed $25 as an expression of our thanks for your efforts for good. Our organization is non-partisan, non-sectarian and non-political and is striving to render the best service possible in a time when real men are needed. Continue your good work and may your future reward be great.

   Yours for America always,

   Abilene, Ku Klux Klan No. 139, Realm of Texas

It was not a confession. It was not repentance for killing a beloved child of God less than eight weeks previously. It was praise for Sewell and the Churches of Christ, of their "efforts for good." Sewell publicly thanked the Klan members, and they left.

Sewell pocketed the money. Enclosed was twenty-five dollars for the school, but according to a local historian, there was also twenty-five dollars for Sewell; the total was close to one thousand dollars in contemporary currency.

The question might have echoed through the auditorium long after the crowd left that night: "What shall a man give in exchange for his soul?"

SEWELL LATER MADE IT CLEAR THAT HE FELT HE WAS NAVIGATING A complicated political line. The very quality that made Churches of Christ less likely to be caught in political fervor also made it harder to raise money for the growing school—there was no denominational hierarchy that could give a large capital fund; the school was at capacity and would need a new location soon. They had to ask individuals and churches one at a time for the money they needed. When the Klan presented him a check, Sewell was probably thinking not just about the twenty-five dollars, but about not alienating influential men in town who might also give to the school.

Sewell was not the only preacher receiving a check from the Klan that night. A similar scene was happening at the Baptist service where a close friend of the original Imperial Wizard, William Joseph Simmons, was preaching. Like Sewell, the Baptists took the check and went on. It was all part of the Klan's public relations campaign with local church leaders. Politically, especially in terms of the growth of the school, it might have been prudent of Sewell to demur on his views on the Klan, no matter how much it revealed about his theological hypocrisy that night.

But it was distasteful to many. Public opinion was already souring against the KKK. For some, their concern was the public act of taking money from the Klan; for others, it was the disruption of church and the political displays, the marching in costume with the flag. It was all too much. Jesse Sewell resigned the following year.

I have known that story most of my life. It was part of the history I received. In the 1990s and early 2000s, when I was the daughter of professors and then a student at the school, there was a strong turn toward examining the racialized past among faculty and staff at ACU. That's when this story came to light, or was told again to a new generation; at least that's when I first heard about it.

In telling what happened after Sewell pocketed the money, the much broader scope of what happened next, I am doing exactly as I was taught and uncovering the truth of the past.

It was not just twenty-five dollars. Tens of thousands of dollars and hundreds of acres of land, an entire new section of the city, my great-grandparents' home, the collective memory I had of generations of stories of how we thrived, the idyllic past of my beloved family—all of it was steeped in white supremacy.

CHAPTER 38

After President Sewell resigned in early 1924, power at the school rested squarely on the shoulders of the eleven board members who lived in Abilene. They appointed another man with the delightful name Batsell Baxter to be president. Of the local board members, there were three that a local historian called the "movers and shakers." One of them was J. C. Reese. He worked closely with Baxter to see Sewell's vision of a new site for their growing college come to fruition.

The local historian called Baxter's presidency "an era of good feeling" when enrollment skyrocketed. As the school continued to balloon, they needed more space: Multiple classes were held simultaneously in the auditorium or in dorm living rooms; the dormitories were crowded long past the point of comfort. By 1926, they began looking for a site big enough to build a new campus.

In the first few years of living in Abilene, my great-grandfather settled well into the community. He became an elder at Northside Church of Christ. He went from working out of his home to having an office in the business district. That office was right around the corner from Charlie Bacon's office. Charlie was also the president of the Abilene Chamber of Commerce by then and knew everyone of influence in town. Charlie lived with his family in a lovely two-story brick home mere blocks from his downtown office.

His next-door neighbor was also a person of influence in the town, the pastor of St. Paul Methodist Church—L. N. Stuckey, the Exalted Cyclops of the Ku Klux Klan.

By the mid-1920s, the Ku Klux Klan was less publicly visible. There were no more public parades or rosy-glowed displays of burning crosses in the business district, no money being conveniently found on desks or masked men marching into church services with letters. After the grand jury convened and no murderers were found in 1922, there were no more recorded lynchings in town. That particular era of violent extremism ended in Abilene relatively quickly by Texas standards after Everett's death; Goep would tell stories of the active Klan in Colorado County that continued for years, and other places across Texas would continue to see violence obviously associated with the KKK for a long time.

Though it differed in various locations, across Texas, openly public support of the Klan—men giving speeches as official representatives of the KKK or running for office on the Klan ticket—also faded in the mid-1920s. By 1927, Texas governor Dan Moody declared "the Klan in Texas is dead." It was not dead, of course, but its widespread influence was diminished.

In Abilene, the Exalted Cyclops moved away with his family to another posting in the Methodist church. I have no idea whether he remained in the Klan, if someone else took his place as leader in Abilene, or if in leaving, he pulled the plug on organized Klan activity in the city.

It is tempting to view the time when the Ku Klux Klan held the city of Abilene in its grip as one short, violent chapter, unconnected to the next chapter in my family's life and the capital campaign of the new campus of Abilene Christian College. But throughout Abilene, those "judges, county officials, mayor, ex-mayors, bankers, members of the Chamber of Commerce" and preachers mostly stayed in place.

As it did across the state, the KKK deluged Abilene for a few short years with hatred in a period of extremism that had no precedent in the city that was less than fifty years old. And then it dissipated. It must have felt like it was gone. Instead, the flood of racism seeped beneath the surface, became the groundwater that sustained the city.

When I say we have to look closely at how times of extremism end, this is what I mean: The consequences of those years in Abilene would be felt for decades, long after the murder of Grover C. Everett was forgotten by most people who lived in the city. The Klan might be diminished, but the views endured.

Whether they were publicly stated or privately held, printed in newspapers or spoken from pulpits, the hierarchical views—about whose lives were valued more, who had the right to enact violence without repercussion from the law, who could hold power over another person—remained firmly in place.

BY 1926, ABILENE CHRISTIAN COLLEGE HAD RAISED HALF OF THE $150,000 they estimated they needed to build a new campus from the ground up. They needed help. The chamber of commerce under Charlie Bacon's leadership decided to assist in raising the rest.

On a cool November evening in 1926, many of the men I suspect had been members of the Abilene Klavern a few years before—because they signed the petition in 1921, because of the church they attended or their close connections—met up again to attend a banquet at ACC. As the college paper reported, "Nearly 100 men, citizens of Abilene and members of practically every church in the city joined Thursday in outlining plans to raise the remaining $75,000 of the $150,000 building fund for the college." In attendance were judges, county officials, mayor, ex-mayors, bankers, members of the chamber of commerce, and preachers. The building fund drive was led by the mayor, who told the assembled leaders that all of Abilene was connected, and what was good for some people in the city was good for all of them. As the mayor put it, "The only investment worthwhile is that in human life. It is the only one that will endure."

And it would endure. They raised the money. They began to search for the right location for the new campus.

The summer of 1927 was when that scene took place—the one that meant so much to me as a kid listening to family lore—of J. C. Reese standing in Charlie Bacon's fifth-floor office. As a local historian wrote it, "Bacon rose from his chair and said to Reese, 'Come over here to the window.' He pointed to a wide strip of rolling land northeast of the city, and said, 'That is a wonderful place for Abilene Christian College.'"

I never noticed the rest of the story; it was more than two leaders dreaming of creating a city set apart on a hill. They were pragmatic men. The fact that the land was on a slight rise would make a major difference during floods. In April 1922, when the creeks overflowed the banks and the dam almost broke, Abilenians had seen what happened to anyone in the flood plain. They wanted to be sure to find a site that would not flood. This was not a secret; it was just not a connection I made when I was young.

By September 1927, the school had secured the land. Abilene Heights, the neighborhood on the Hill surrounding Abilene Christian College, began construction in 1928. The first building to be built was a prominent home—the first house on the Hill: "The promotion of Abilene Heights, the subdivision that opened up under the direction of A. C. C., has been one of Brother Reese's greatest dreams. He [has] given up his present home for the benefit of the school he loves so well."

With that house, J. C. Reese established my family's place on the Hill. Of all the pivotal moves in my family's history, this one—which might have seemed relatively small at the time—would potentially change my relationship with Texas more than any other. J. C. and Nellie formed the kind of clannish home base the Leftwiches had in Bedford, Virginia; the Joneses and Reeses had later in Corinth, Arkansas; or the Fleming Reese family had in Colorado and Lavaca Counties, Texas. I had the same small-town upbringing as generations of my family. When I picture the word "Texas," despite many more years living in Central or South Texas, it will always be West Texas to me—mesquite trees twisting in a biting winter wind beneath a glorious, unfettered sunset.

In his quiet way, with a series of bureaucratic moves, J. C. Reese was one of a handful of men who changed the trajectory of generations of families, his own first. Ancestral pivots do not have to be dramatic to be profound.

When my great-grandfather helped survey and map the land, his name appeared on at least two different maps I found. One is almost frameable; it is a beautiful blue color, and it shows the plots of land that would become houses in the years to come.

The other map looks more like a sketch. It is attached to the deed between the city of Abilene and the board of trustees. In that deed are a few restrictive clauses. They regulate things like how corner lots are allotted, what outbuildings can be built, where terraces may go in relation to the frontages of the home.

Between Clause III, "Corporation's Judgment Conclusive," and Clause V, "Easements," is one two-sentence restriction:

OWNERSHIP BY ANY OTHER
THAN WHITE RACE PROHIBITED.

IV.

None of the lots shown on said map shall be conveyed, leased, or given to, and no building erected thereon shall be used, owned or occupied by any person not of the white race. This prohibition, however, is not intended to include the occupancy by a person not of the white race while employed on the premises by any one of the several owners or occupants of said lots.

My great-grandfather the land man was one of Abilene's redliners. And the boundaries he drew around the land high enough to keep dry during floods would have cultural and economic repercussions for generations of Abilenians who were "of the white race"—including me.

CHAPTER 39

Redlining" is the word that has come to stand in for any sort of exclusionary clause or policy limiting where people could live based on race. Racially restrictive covenants began to appear in the late nineteenth century and became common by the early twentieth century. In the government-initiated New Deal programs of the 1930s, federal officials ranked various neighborhoods in cities along a risk scale denoting how desirable they would be on the market. The "riskier" neighborhoods were predominantly the ones where people of color had historically lived, or were near industrial sites or in flood plains. Those areas were coded red, and those neighborhoods came to be called redlined. Leaders during the Civil Rights movement would speak out against the practice of redlining neighborhoods, and housing discrimination was eventually outlawed with the passage of the Fair Housing Act of 1968.

In the United States, the true cost of redlining can be difficult to quantify, but one of the measures often used is looking at evident gaps in relative wealth among racial groups. In 2022, the US Department of the Treasury reported that white households owned their own homes at a rate of 75 percent. In comparison, only 45 percent of Black households, 48 percent of Hispanic households, and 57 percent of what the Treasury identifies as "non-Hispanic households of any other race" own homes.

White households held on average $145,000 to $175,000 more housing equity wealth than equivalent Black or Hispanic households.

On a national scale, decades of redlining cost people of color hundreds of thousands of dollars in economic security—a devastating generational deficit.

IN A DOCUMENTARY CALLED *A LEGACY UNEARTHED*, FILMMAKER ALISHA Janette Taylor captures the stories that reveal the consequences of restrictive policies on the Black community of Abilene. The Abilene Heights covenants were not the only clauses affecting where people of color could live; a proposed city ordinance in 1916 showed that they were legally only allowed to live in eight or nine streets north and south of the T&P Railroad on the eastern side of the city. Those restrictions prevented Black homeowners from gaining the kind of housing equity that allowed them to move their families into the middle class. They were redlined into parts of town that were loud—because of the railroad that cut through their neighborhoods—and low-lying.

In *A Legacy Unearthed*, Reverend Andrew Penns, founder of the Curtis House Cultural Center in Abilene, recounts that some of those neighborhoods gave Black people pride of ownership in their own homes. But it was always a tenuous pride. White developers neglected to mention to some of the newcomers that they were building houses in a floodplain. Only a few years after construction on my great-grandparents' house and the new campus had begun, on September 7, 1932, for the first time in Abilene history, three creeks—Big Elm, Little Elm, and Catclaw creeks—overflowed and met in what the newspaper called "one sprawling lake."

Those were already the lean years of the Great Depression, when J. C. Reese worked so tirelessly to save the ranches of so many white families. Just down the creek from his house, however, the enormous flood drove many Black Abilenians from their homes. It happened again and again, every few years, in 1938, 1945, 1957, and 1962, among many others. Floods wiped out their cars, photos, furniture, belongings. So much of what they had worked for was ruined in a few hours or a few days, every few years, in the only part of town they were legally allowed to live.

Effie Brewster, the first Black county tax appraiser in Abilene, was married to Robert L. Brewster, the first Black principal to serve in an integrated school in Abilene after desegregation ended. In the documentary, she talks about the pressures the older Black generation raising children in Abilene faced: "If you made it, it was great, and if you didn't make it, and you were Black, you tried . . ." Her voice cracks and she is too overcome with emotion to speak.

Her stepdaughter, Robin Brewster, says learning history helps younger generations understand who they are: "Our ancestors didn't come here by accident. Learn where we come from and what's going on that can impact you today that impacted us back then. There's some good and also some bad."

Rev. Penns, whose life work has been to make a difference in Abilene, works tirelessly to gather the proud history of Black Abilenians at Curtis House Cultural Center for his hometown. He founded the center because, as he put it, "I know the history, I grew up with this history and I am part of this history. . . . This history exists." Acknowledging will not always feel easy, he knows; "sometimes it's hurtful" but it is imperative "to tell it as it should be, and tell it correctly."

I WAS AN ADULT BEFORE I REALIZED THE SYSTEMS WERE PERFECTLY designed over decades for me and others who look like me, even on the small scale of my beloved hometown. After redlining was officially outlawed in 1968, the costs continued. The Treasury Department's housing equity numbers are conservative: some estimates give the average income in white homes as ten times that of the average income in Black households, mostly because of redlining and other restrictive laws that gave white families the best land, the best education, the best resources—the best of everything.

I cannot help wondering how the history of my city would have been different had J. C. Reese and the ACC Board of Trustees and other

Christian leaders truly lived out the faith that President Sewell preached that night in 1922, right before ten members of the Ku Klux Klan walked down the aisle. "God loves his children, every one of them, whether rich or poor, great or small, weak or strong," Sewell said. "We cannot serve two masters, he has said. The question is, what are we as sons and daughters of God going to do with our lives?"

What if they had decided that night that, instead of pocketing the money from the Klan, that they would live out that faith literally? That they would open the land around their new school to everyone? That they would do the very thing they heard preached that night and every Sunday morning—that they would treat all of God's children as equals?

They did not. So we cannot know. In Abilene, the redlining racism was politer, more palatable than the violence of the Ku Klux Klan years—but it was the result of that extreme time period nonetheless. Those views remained, present in everything. But it felt so much better for white people to cover over the hierarchy with a light layer of civility, to keep the focus on tea parties and board meetings and college pranks in that lovely neighborhood on a hill. We thrived there, on sprawling lawns under shade trees watered by the deeply sunk racism that funded the school and nourished our dreams.

My father and his brothers noticed. Growing up in the years of desegregation, they slowly learned to pay attention to the sewer-stink of racism. One of the other stories my father told me when I was young about J. C. Reese happened at a basketball game. My father's younger brother, Jim, was playing against the Black school in town in the years just before segregation ended. A Black athlete was fouled out of bounds and fell into the stands, landing on my small, genteel great-grandfather, who leaped up and uttered a racial expletive to get the player off him. My uncle remembers my grandfather dressing down my great-grandfather very publicly for what he said. As Uncle Jim told me, that moment is "frozen in my memory." Later that night, as an apology, J. C. bought the Black basketball player's family hamburgers.

That moment stands out to both my dad and my uncle because it was one of the few times they ever heard anyone yell their racist thoughts out

loud so publicly. And it was one of the only times they heard my grandfather yell at his father so angrily.

My father told me that story when I was young, with deep regret for
my great-grandfather's views. It was around the time I also learned about
Nellie's ancestor who enslaved the family and sold them for a lesser price
in order to keep the enslaved family together to fund the clan's move into
Arkansas when they left Tennessee. Those family stories were part of the
books my dad would write later about the history of our church tradition, books that do not mince words but speak honest truths about the
good, the complicated, and the awful sides of the Churches of Christ.

My parents passed those critical thinking skills on to me from an
early age, teaching me to see who was centered in a story, who was left
out, who held power, who stood to gain the most from any political action. They were certainly not the only members of their families ques-
tioning their received narratives—in our family interviews, my dad's
brothers and cousin told story after story of truly beginning to understand their family's views on race and learning to make different choices.
It was the process of several years.

In those discussions, everyone was quick to point out that our family did not do this work faultlessly, because none of us are perfect. But
when my grandparents knew better, they also did better; their opinions
were malleable, shaped by what they learned, and they continued to
transform even in the last years of their lives. In writing this story, I am
in no way the first person to say these things. I am joining the generational work of my family over decades to uproot racism and retain the
heartfelt love for others that is a crucial part of our legacy.

I also learned how to do this critical investigation of my received
views from the very university my great-grandfather helped found in
that redlined neighborhood. The people leading the charge on calling
out its racist past are coming from within ACU and the larger Abilene
community. It was McMurry students and professors—the university
where the Ku Klux Klan Exalted Cyclops was once on the board—who
uncovered the lynching of Grover C. Everett. They worked with others
in Abilene and with the Equal Justice Initiative to commemorate Ever-

ett's death in a 2019 ceremony in Abilene covered by the local news. White and Black faculty, staff, students, and former students at all three universities, and civic and religious community leaders from the city, are making films, writing books, hosting conferences, having conversations, and building bridges as they face the truth of the past and learn from it.

There's a tension when I write about this in today's terms, however. I both want to identify that this work is being done within the community, and that some of the strongest resistance to this work also comes from within the community. One Black preacher—whose name I am withholding at his request because of the ongoing nature of his work—told me, "People have come and gone that gave their all to make a meaningful difference, but their efforts have been short lived" as they have succumbed "to the ancestral gravitational pull of those who set up a racist arrangement in the founding of the city of Abilene."

It is relatively easy, from the vantage point of the present, to identify what people in the past should or should not have done. As I pointed out in the story of Slowman Reese and his preacher, David Rice, at the church that enslaved people in Virginia in the eighteenth century, I'm uncomfortable looking back and dismissing people's views as just being "of their time," when there were contemporary peers around them who woke up to the reality of the injustice in their daily lives. That one Fort Worth preacher who refused to join the Klan might have been the David Rice of his day.

But the point of telling this story is also not for me to judge my great-grandfather and his colleagues and friends by the values of today. That's a cheap, unhelpful condemnation. My goal is to identify the foundation of our received views from generations past so we can make decisions in the present that will inform the future.

The community in Abilene I interviewed and learned from is doing that work now. And that is the task that is personally in front of me. In the story of the basketball game that my dad and uncle remember, I see a series of ancestral pivots: my great-grandfather yelling a racist epithet he later felt contrite about; my grandfather lambasting him in public for saying it; my father and uncles passing the story down as a cautionary tale to show that racism has always been in the family and that there is more work to do. Each pivot was a major shift from the generation before.

I'm making my own kind of shift in this book. When my father read an early draft, he wrote me an endnote in which he identified what he called a "pathology" passed down from his own family alongside the Reese myths he'd already told me about: that it was almost impossible for him, growing up, to talk about hard things. And he wrote something that took my breath away: "You are a strong woman. You are working, even in the writing of this book, to stop the pathologies passed down to you, even as I have tried to halt the racism passed down to me."

He identified for me the ancestral pivot I am trying to make. Even when it hurts, because I love my hometown with my whole heart; even when it's hard, because it feels disloyal to identify racism that benefited people I love: I want to say the hard truths. Not because I want to point an accusatory finger at the past; my ancestors' decisions have come and gone, and all I can do is record the effects on them and on others.

But because I want to point that finger at myself: what choices am I making now? I have the ability, in the present and every day, to make decisions that affect my children and my community and the people around me. I can uncover the views in my own mind, the ones I have received and the ones I am always forming. I can change what I say, what I do, and what I'm passing down. That is the kind of ancestor I want to be: one who finds the moral courage to get all the way to the foundations of the stories that have shaped me, and then to change the narratives I tell to the next generations.

CHAPTER 40

One winter's day when I was visiting family in Abilene, I slipped away to see the house J. C. Reese built, that first house on the Hill. Though no one in my family has lived there in decades, I had been to the house several times; when I was growing up, a high school friend lived there. We snuck cigarettes once my junior year behind the back of the house, leaning against the wall above the dugout basement my great-grandmother required to sleep.

The land is built into the rising hill, and up the slope from it now is a dormitory parking lot. I parked my car, grabbed a notebook, and went to the edge of the curb. I stood shivering above the house my great-grandparents built that overlooked the creek.

The back of the house faces downtown. The sun was setting, grey clouds folded softly like a knitted blanket across the pink-orange light. I had never realized that my great-grandfather constructed a house looking toward the Alexander Building, as if he could see into the very window where he'd stood with Charlie Bacon and dreamed of this land. I wondered if it meant anything.

Unearthing the complexities of this story about my great-grandparents connected with the other research I had done about my family in a way I couldn't quite put my finger on for months. When I first started thinking about the Slave Codes of 1705 and what those acts of legislation revealed about the fears of the people in power in Virginia, I could sense the shape of an underlying belief statement about human rights on which those codes depended. I could feel it beneath Stephen F. Austin's letters arguing against slavery in Texas because he wanted to limit the population of Black people in the state. It was there in the constitution of the Texas Republic and the Jim Crow laws and in innumerable acts of legislation and manifestos and letters and philosophical treatises. I kept digging for months, trying to uncover that core belief that felt unquestionable to the people in power.

The belief was about more than just self-centeredness, though it was that too, of course. Asking "How does this benefit me?" was the central question of many of my ancestors in their quest for new places to thrive. When I pushed past the petulant grievances of Robert Leftwich toward the belief he held—one that was both personal and collective—that some people's lives and bodies were inviolable, and others could be violated, I could tell I was getting closer to this bedrock value.

And it was more than the greed that motivated many of my ancestors, that uncomfortable formulation that allowed centuries of enslavers to effectively turn their backs on a system they knew was oppressive so they could profit. Greed was part of the makeup of this belief—somehow this belief justified that greed even though many of the people in power subscribed to a Christian faith that preached specifically against greed of any sort. But it wasn't only greed; that is bald and straightforward, and this belief was subtler, buried beneath it all.

The belief, I could tell, was connected to the kind of reactive fear that justified committing heinous acts of violence against anyone perceived as a threat. The fear that ruled Colorado County—the fear they felt, the fear they caused—was a crucial part of the formulation I could sense.

But in Abilene in the 1920s, that fear overflowed for a few years, and then sank beneath the surface again. It spewed forth other times, of course. However, in this right-living, God-fearing town, that kind of violence was not publicly condoned for decades like it had been in Columbus, and like it was in other places in Texas—including, I would learn, in the county where my mother's family landed. Fear was part of this belief, but it was not all of it.

For months, I had pulled out several sentences to try to understand that underlying belief statement, but none of them quite fit: that we the people in power thought we were the only ones who deserved life, liberty, and the pursuit of happiness.

That we believed we were better than others.

That we didn't recognize the rights of others.

That we viewed other people as less than human.

Those ideas, though broad, were often true, but they were not fully arriving at the depths of the belief that I felt resonating beneath these stories as I held them. There was something about *The Optimist* coverage of the gospel meeting with the Ku Klux Klan that put it together for me. It was the juxtaposition of two columns printed on the same page with conflicting, hypocritical views: in one story, Jesse Sewell preached about an inclusive God who loved every single child, and in the next, he took a check to fund the school from men whose group had killed one of those beloved children. When I read those stories back to back, I began to understand what the belief was.

I played with the words for weeks. The statement finally locked into place for me as I stood at the curb of the dormitory parking lot above the first house on the Hill, watching the sun slip beneath the horizon as the creek flowed south where, a mile downstream, generations of Black families endured floods that my family largely avoided.

The unquestioned bedrock belief was that our right to flourish was God-given, and higher than anyone else's rights—including the right to exist.

THE NEXT DAY, AS I DROVE HOME TO AUSTIN, I RAN MY TONGUE OVER my newly formed sentence, with its inherent differences between "us" and "them": Our happiness, our pleasure, and our comfort were always the higher value in a hierarchy that benefited those of us in power. The power we held was providential, manifested, God-given. If threatened, we were allowed to do whatever it took to protect our right not just to survive, or to live, but to *flourish*. That right to flourish mattered more than any other rights any other group or individual possessed. It mattered more than their lives. More than their children's lives. More than their community's continued existence.

The belief that our right to flourish was God-given, and higher than anyone else's rights—including the right to exist—has always been there, in every generation as far back as I could trace my family roots.

I was headed back to write the hardest section of this book, the one I could barely face because my mother's grief about what happened in her family will always affect me viscerally, even if her wounds have been scars for most of my life. Something about that uncovered belief statement gave me insight into a question I have wrestled with almost my entire life: why my mother's mother and my mother's grandmother did what they did.

Why they covered over and perpetuated the deep abuse they knew firsthand. Why they never protected the daughters of the family. Why they knowingly allowed my mother to endure what they had too.

Driving home from Abilene with this new sentence in my mind, I understood those questions in a fresh way. Those women also believed—unhesitatingly, as they'd been taught for generations—that it was especially the men in their lives who had the God-given right not just to survive, but to flourish. They believed a woman's role was not to challenge that right, but to enable it.

For many of the men on my mother's side of the family, that God-given right meant taking and doing whatever the hell they wanted.

PART 6

FRANK PROBST

(1905–1990)

The story of the Rangers is the story of Texas, and of the American West: majestic in its sweep, unmatched in its violence, luminous in its glory, and monumental in its deceptions.

—DOUG J. SWANSON, *CULT OF GLORY*

I imagine one of the reasons people cling to their hates so stubbornly is because they sense, once hate is gone, they will be forced to deal with pain.

—JAMES BALDWIN, *NOTES OF A NATIVE SON*

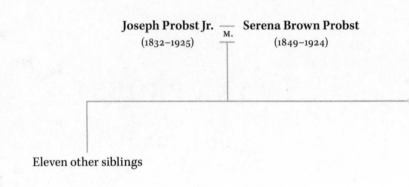

Joseph Probst Jr. — M. — Serena Brown Probst
(1832–1925)   (1849–1924)

Eleven other siblings

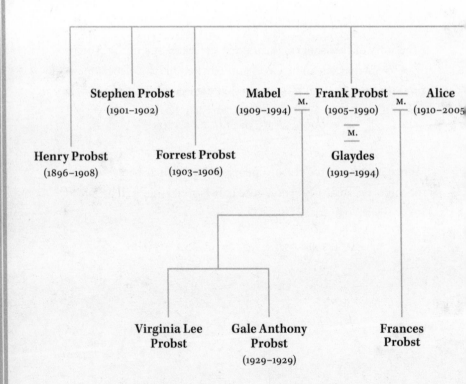

Henry Probst
(1896–1908)

Stephen Probst
(1901–1902)

Forrest Probst
(1903–1906)

Mabel — M. — Frank Probst — M. — Alice
(1909–1994)   (1905–1990)   (1910–2005

M.

Glaydes
(1919–1994)

Virginia Lee
Probst

Gale Anthony
Probst
(1929–1929)

Frances
Probst

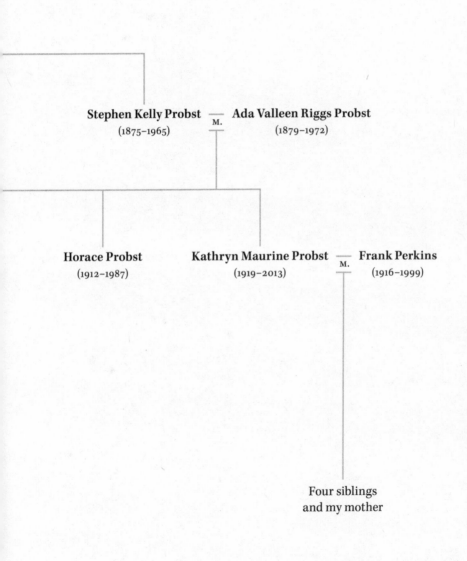

Stephen Kelly Probst — Ada Valleen Riggs Probst
(1875–1965)   M.   (1879–1972)

Horace Probst   Kathryn Maurine Probst — Frank Perkins
(1912–1987)   (1919–2013)   M.   (1916–1999)

Four siblings
and my mother

CHAPTER 41

Perhaps no Texas myth holds more power inside or outside of the state than that of the Texas Rangers. The Rangers were the subject of sensationalized, popular stories representing the state since as early as 1856. There have been dozens of examples of shows or books that rely on their outsized reputation, ranging from the radio show "Riding with the Texas Rangers" in the 1930s; to the *Lone Ranger* radio and TV shows in the 1930s, 1940s, and 1950s; the *Lonesome Dove* series by Larry McMurtry and *Texas* by James Michener in the 1980s; the *Walker, Texas Ranger* series in the early 1990s; and of course the Texas Rangers baseball team. When my classmates asked me, as a new fourth grader in Memphis, Tennessee, if I knew any Texas Rangers, they were probably thinking of baseball. Without my horse tied up outside the school like they seemed to expect, it was the one very Texas-y thing I had going for me—my great-uncle Frank Probst had been a Ranger, and I could tell them about the visits we'd made to Uncle Frank and his third wife, Glaydes, on his ranch not far from Brownwood, Texas.

On the few occasions when we stopped at their house on road trips, the dry heat off the sprawling land around their mobile home was harsh, and our minivan made a cloud of dust as we pulled up. On their porch, Frank and Glaydes usually sat on rocking chairs; when we pulled

302 WE WERE ILLEGAL

up, Frank stood, glaring against the sun, to see who it was. They always held rifles in their laps at the ready.

The visits were short, a few hours at most. My mother did not let her children spend the night with any members of her mother's family. Frank was the oldest brother of my mother's mother, my Nanny. But we stopped for lunch sometimes on road trips to and from San Antonio. My memories of that house are brief impressions—sweet tea in a pitcher, thick glasses dripping with condensation in the heat, pages of a photo album we flipped through on a dark wood coffee table. I remember Frank's nose—the prominent bulbous Probst nose Nanny hated, the one I worried as a kid I'd inherit—and Frank's shiny belt buckle holding up his jeans under a protruding belly.

My other memory of Uncle Frank is at Nanny's house; he was there once when my family belted out a cappella church songs around Nanny's faded red Formica table. We sang from a Church of Christ hymnal—upbeat quartets beloved in rural churches across the South, with songs like "A Beautiful Life" and "Count Your Many Blessings." My mom's family could sing for hours together in mostly impeccable four-part harmony. Uncle Frank didn't sing, but he was there in the background, watching and listening.

During Perkins family gatherings, that side of the family avoided hard topics but loved a good story, the more outlandish the better. So I knew—from Nanny, or maybe from another relative—about the time Uncle Frank escorted a movie star on a tour through the Valley as a highway patrolman, or the time he saved a cat from a telephone pole with a contraption he made out of a plastic trash can. Most of Nanny's best yarns were not true, including her much-loved fable that we were descended from a "Cherokee Princess," though I didn't know that at the time.

I told some of those stories in the fourth grade to my new classmates, trying to impress them. It was the first time I had thought of Texas as a place that other people told stories about. One journalist called the Texas Ranger myth "the stoic, square-jawed manifestation of all that is honorable or exceptional about our state," and, while I didn't have the words at the time, that's what I felt when I talked about my great-uncle the

Texas Ranger. There was a pride in being part of a tradition larger than myself, a sense that I too could be stoic and cool under pressure, even if that pressure was just trying to make friends at a new school.

Uncle Frank died three years after I talked about him at a Memphis elementary school, when I was twelve; by then, we were living in Texas again. I never asked him to tell me any stories about being a Texas Ranger. It was just always a fact I knew about him.

When I asked my mom and her relatives about the family myths, one I had never known before was that my mother's mother's poor family kept alive the myth that they had once had wealth and standing in society. Because of that myth, they felt they still retained their superiority to the other poor people around them. The loss of that once real or fabricated cultural respect grated on them. That meant that when my great-uncle Frank got a job as a Texas Ranger, he became an immediate family hero. It was not just that he earned more money in a year than they might see in a decade, it's that he brought the Probsts up several pegs in their small-town society. Frank's job made him, in many ways, the savior of the family.

That family myth of Frank as the hero was never mine. In fact, though this is not how my mom framed the story for me, it is what I saw for myself and now firmly believe—the heroes of that family were not Frank Probst or the other violent men. They were the women, too often made victims of the men, who found within themselves the strength, integrity, and resilience to change our family story.

NO STORY IN THIS BOOK WAS EASIER TO UNCOVER THAN THIS ONE. ONE day early on in my research for this book, I typed "Frank Probst" and "Texas Ranger" into the Google search bar. The third story down on the list was about Frank's involvement with a shooting in Bee County, Texas. It's the first time I had ever heard it.

This never made it into the family lore. I was surprised to find through my research that some of the more outsized family yarns about Uncle Frank, like his movie-star and cat-saving escapades, were true:

The movie star he escorted around the Valley was Ginger Rogers. The saving the cat contraption was a local color story in the *Beeville Bee-Picayune*. In our family stories, Nanny made Uncle Frank Probst out to be—in one of the highest compliments that side of the family paid anyone—a "real character."

It's typical that I never heard the darker sides of his past from anyone except Mom, who didn't know half of them herself, including this story. Nanny's commitment to the sunny side of life was often aggravating for her kids; it was also sometimes the only thing that protected them. Nanny saw the good in everyone the way only a survivor and enabler could; it's no surprise that Nanny's stories about Uncle Frank were more zany than horrific. But I knew, even from the earliest years before I found out the details, that there was a shadowed past on their side of the family. Mom had never heard of the trial that took place six years before she was born, but Nanny must have known—she was an adult by then, married for five years, mother of a three-year-old son herself.

There's a larger scholarly and pop cultural move right now, two hundred years after the Texas Rangers' beginning in Austin's colony, to reveal what lies beneath their storied myth. What I know about my family's history gives me insight into one Ranger, at least, whose actions were anything but heroic. Frank was a complex man, a provider who could be kind, but whose values and sense of right and wrong, of justice and compassion, came from a childhood home that was toxic and dark; my mother calls it evil. Understanding his past and where he came from gives me insight into the decisions he made leading up to a criminal trial that took place in 1946.

I believe that my great-uncle Frank C. L. Probst—Texas Ranger, friend to the most notorious sheriff in Bee County history, and probable accomplice to murder—lied under oath to free a serial killer.

CHAPTER 42

Frank Probst was the grandson of an economic migrant who arrived in the country without documents in order to seek a better way of life—what is now often referred to pejoratively as an "illegal immigrant." His grandfather and my great-great-grandfather Joseph Probst arrived in the early 1850s as a stowaway on a ship from Bavaria—later part of Germany—to the Port of New York. A distant cousin recorded a family story passed down through generations that eighteen-year-old Joseph came as the vanguard of the large family. According to that family story, Joseph's mother had been a wealthy only daughter with a sizable dowry and royal connections. Joseph's father managed to lose the entire fortune in a few years through a combination of gambling, horse trading, and unprofitable business ventures.

A few months after he got to the US, Joseph wrote to his family to join him. By the time the family arrived in October 1854—legally, through paid passages from Bavaria to New York rather than stowing away—the Probsts had lost almost all their possessions. They had one money belt and the clothes on their backs. The recorded family story says their belongings were "lost at sea," but the way the line is framed in the story, it seems more like "lost by their father gambling while at sea." However it was lost, they were destitute upon arrival.

By 1855, the family made their way to Wisconsin. By the end of the

Civil War, Joseph moved first to Georgia and then Alabama, where he became a millwright. He married Serena Brown; they had twelve children over twenty-two years. Their seventh child, born in 1875, was Stephen Kelly Probst, my great-grandfather. His family called him Kelly.

By the time Kelly arrived, Joseph Probst had come a long way financially from a penniless undocumented migrant. In part because Kelly and his siblings had been raised by a Black caretaker—which was to them a sign that they had achieved a class status lost by later generations—the Probsts passed along a sense that they were "better" than the people around them. They taught their children never to forget it.

On December 20, 1894, Kelly married Ada Valleen Riggs. The Riggs and Probst families would remain particularly close. Ada's older brother had already married one of Kelly's younger sisters earlier that year; a few years later, one of Ada's sisters would marry one of Kelly's brothers. The children had several double cousins. But despite their families' close connections, according to my aunt, Ada and Kelly did not have their parents' permission to get married. They eloped when he was nineteen and she was fifteen. Maybe it was just young love—knowing they were married for more than seventy years, that seems plausible. It's certainly how the community framed it later in their anniversary celebrations.

Or: Kelly's predilection for young girls had already begun.

WHEN I READ WILLIAM FAULKNER'S *AS I LAY DYING* AS A JUNIOR IN HIGH school, I told my English teacher that it sounded just like my mom's family. There was a Southern Gothic feel to our family's shared memories of Kelly and Ada. My teacher only believed my story about Kelly's toes after my mother confirmed it for her at a high school parents' night.

Kelly worked at the family's mill as a teenager. One day, he stood too close to some dangerous machinery—possibly a big saw—and lost four of his toes. The other workers picked up the toes, supported Kelly out of the mill, and delivered Kelly and toes to his mother. She propped his foot up on one of the kitchen chairs, pulled out a needle, thread, and a jug of kerosene, gave him a stick to bite, and sewed the toes back on.

He went back to work. A week later, his mother said his foot smelled. He took his boot off; he had gangrene. She cut his toes off. She soaked them in kerosene. And then she sewed them back on. For the rest of his life, Kelly had toes Nanny called "catawampus."

It is one of the few stories that my mother can confirm is not a tall tale because she saw the toes when she was thirteen, when Kelly was an old, bedridden man and my mother helped Nanny care for him.

KELLY MOVED WITH HIS TEENAGED BRIDE TO TEXAS EITHER AT THE end of 1895 or early 1896. Ada was sixteen when their first son, Henry, was born in a workers' camp. In the next few years, Ada would birth five sons, including Frank. When I asked my mother, her sister, and their cousin about Frank in the 1940s, they all began by talking about Ada and her many baby boys, and what Frank learned in those early years.

By the time Ada's first son, Henry, was nine, she'd had three more sons: Stephen, who died before he was two; Forrest, who died soon after he turned two, and Frank, who lived. Both little Stephen and Forrest died of diseases that would later be preventable, diphtheria and dysentery. No one is alive who remembers which one died of which disease.

And then came the accident that broke Ada: on April 11, 1908, Henry was twelve when he joined his dad and uncles in their back pasture to go hunting. Frank was two and a half at the time. As my mom and aunt remember Nanny telling the story, Henry had premonitions that something bad would happen in that pasture. One of Henry's uncles handed him a shotgun and said it was not loaded. It was loaded. Henry blew his head off in that back pasture nine days after his twelfth birthday.

After Henry died, according to Aunt Stephanie, Ada pulled away from young Frank completely: "She wouldn't have anything to do with Uncle Frank. She figured it was just a matter of time before he died too. He grew up without a mother's love."

In 1912, four years after Henry died, Ada and Kelly had another little boy, Horace. And then on October 14, 1919, when Ada was forty, her only little girl was born: Maurine, my Nanny. Ada never missed a chance to tell her precious little girl that she was ugly like her brothers, with her Probst nose and her features Ada called "homely." Ada told her over and over and over again that no one would ever love her. Nanny internalized her mother's message that she was unlovable and turned it into a life determined to provide love to others; that love was messy and chaotic and often needy, but she gave a home to the misfits and the quirky creatures of the world, a profound act of rebellion to prove an abusive mother wrong.

Uncle Horace was seven when Nanny was born. According to the family, Horace was unloved and mostly ignored, neither the most despised nor the most admired child.

Uncle Frank was fourteen when Nanny was born. He left high school not long after that, quitting after his second year to go to work. Kelly worked as a truck driver in 1920, and within a few years, Uncle Frank joined his father in the auto industry. As my mother put it, Frank was "not loved but he was revered." As it would turn out, that combination was to be both toxic and dangerous.

From Ada, the children received no affection and deep rancor. From Kelly, the three living Probst kids learned two different things: Nanny learned that women had no option but to do whatever men wanted. It was a lesson her father, and possibly her uncles and older male cousins, taught her over and over again.

From their father, Frank and Horace learned that young white men could take or do just about anything they wanted.

CHAPTER 43

On July 4, 1926, when Nanny was seven, Frank married his first wife, Mabel. Within a year, their daughter, Virginia Lee, was born. Nanny was closer in age to her baby niece than her older brother; she would remain close to Virginia Lee for the rest of their lives. Over two years later, in 1929, Gale Anthony Probst was born and lived for one day—another baby Probst boy lost in infancy.

Frank became a Highway Patrolman by 1930 and by 1935, his work took him to Three Rivers, Texas. It's unclear whether he was stationed there and then his parents followed, or whether he came after them. His marriage with Mabel was disintegrating in those years, though none of the relatives I talked to know exactly how and why the marriage fell apart. Frank's younger daughter thinks he probably deserted Mabel after their baby boy died, "just left her up in Grayson County to tough it out alone. Being a father wasn't his thing."

By 1940, Frank had married Alice Freasier. His daughter from his first marriage, Virginia Lee, lived on and off with Frank's parents in those years. In Three Rivers, Kelly and Ada opened the Dixie Camp Café and a small compound of interconnected businesses on three lots of land that would eventually include a laundry service, a mechanic's shop, a hostel-like camping ground called a tourist's court, and other service-oriented ventures. Sometime in those years, Kelly fell from a roof and broke his back; he spent the rest of his life on crutches, his mobility already impaired by the foot with the catawampus toes. His granddaughters all remember that Ada did most of the work.

They barely broke even from those businesses. Nanny, in her late teens at that point, was attending high school and working at home with her parents. The Probsts owned a home worth only about eight hundred dollars ($15,200 in today's currency), despite the fact that Ada and Nanny, at least, worked every day, around the clock, all year long. In 1939, according to the 1940 US Census, the family earned about $360 for fifty-two weeks of work—the equivalent of $6,840 today. Kelly passed down those stories of being raised by a Black caretaker, of the wealth his family once had, but those stories did nothing to stave off their extreme poverty.

Many of the family stories about Frank Probst in those years are heartwarming or funny. He bought an old biplane that had crashed in a nearby field; he fixed it up and taught himself to fly. He caught his sister wearing pants after high school at a time when that was still risqué for a young woman. Nanny complained with a laugh that it had been hard to have a highway patrolman brother at the age when she wanted to spend time with "her beaus."

Though in truth, there were few beaus: the message that she was unlovable was ingrained in her at a visceral level by then. She was engaged for some time to a man named Jimmy, whom she really loved. When Nanny found out he had cheated on her, she broke off their engagement.

She was frustrated and angry when she met Frank Perkins, the son of the town drunk, who was well on his way to taking his father's place. Frank Perkins told Nanny the first time they talked that he would marry her. She gave a sharp retort. Six weeks later, they were married in front of a justice of the peace in January 1941. She always said she wondered how in the world he talked her into marriage less than two months after they met.

Nanny did not go to college. She lived at home and worked for her parents and then she got married. All the relatives I interviewed told me the same thing: Nanny married my grandfather to escape her home. By then, Virginia Lee had moved in full time with her grandparents.

This is the question that still haunts Uncle Frank's other, younger daughter who was born years after Virginia Lee: Did their father know what happened in the home of Kelly and Ada? And if he knew, did he just not care enough to stop it?

WHAT UNCLE FRANK CARED ABOUT WAS BEING RESPECTED. HE WAS THE earner in the family, with his salaried job as a deputy sheriff for Live Oak County; Alice worked for the county too, as a tax operator. By the time Virginia Lee was twelve, Uncle Frank and his new wife were living on the back of his parents' business property in a stone house Uncle Frank built himself. The census collector valued the house at six thousand dollars (about $114,000 in today's currency); his home was worth what his parents could earn in about sixteen years of work. He earned two thousand dollars a year and Alice earned nine hundred dollars; their combined income was less than $55,000 today, but it was staggering in comparison with his parents'.

In 1936, Uncle Frank's name began to appear in the local paper, the *Beeville Bee-Picayune*. Published every Thursday in the nearby town, it chronicled the weekly happenings in Bee County and Live Oak County. For a few years, the articles that mentioned Deputy Probst were routine: information about traffic stops, how he held an arrested man at the county jail, the time he assisted when a farmer died of a heart attack in the fields.

On February 27, 1941, the paper featured the story of Uncle Frank killing a man as a law enforcement officer in the area. Alice was in the car with Frank when he stopped to help a car stalled outside of Three Rivers. When the two men in the car saw that Frank was an officer, one of the men grabbed a rifle and took off. Frank followed him but turned back quickly. The other man was waiting for him, gun drawn.

The two men were escaped convicts named Bill Garrett and Bracken H. Huddleston. They were serving ninety-nine-year sentences at Retrieve

Prison Farm, more than 150 miles away. It was a notoriously cruel plantation turned prison that inmates nicknamed "Burning Hell." Escape was almost impossible. Nonetheless, Garrett and Huddleston had pulled it off.

They had stolen one car to get to San Antonio, the largest city to the north, and abandoned it there. They were making a getaway in their second stolen car when it stalled outside of Three Rivers. They had already robbed three stores in the nearby city of Hondo. They still had their prison uniforms on beneath their snatched clothes.

Garrett was the one who ran from Frank; he was caught hours later in a railroad culvert more than ten miles away by officers from San Antonio. When Frank gave up chase, he turned back to find Huddleston waiting for him with a pointed .22. The article called Uncle Frank "a fast man on the draw and a deadly pistol shot." He told his younger daughter later that he "reached up and tipped the light on top of his police car into the man's eyes, getting the drop on him when he flinched." With one shot, he killed Huddleston.

It merited only a thin mention on page ten. The tone of the article (blasé, sparse, matter of fact) and its location within the paper (sandwiched between articles about pioneer relics given to a nearby museum and news that the Red Cross Chapter had named a new chairman) made it seem that what happened on the road when Frank shot Huddleston was an everyday occurrence. The paper framed the fact of Alice watching the shooting occur with the same informative tone used for recording who was at which social events, like baby showers and afternoon teas: "The officer's wife was with him at the time."

This was, as far as we know, the first time Uncle Frank killed a man. Six months after the shooting, the *Bee-Picayune* reported that Frank, his wife, and then-fourteen-year-old Virginia Lee were moving from Three Rivers to Beeville, southwest of San Antonio, and about halfway between Three Rivers and Corpus Christi. It was about thirty miles away from his parents' compound of poorly performing businesses. For Frank Probst, grandson of a stowaway migrant, it was a major achievement.

That small town was also where some of Sally Reese's great-grandchildren, Flem Reese and Stafford Reese, already lived. Their children would go to school with several of the Probst cousins, relatives of Kelly and Ada who moved down with the clan.

Alice as "Mrs. Frank Probst" would be mentioned several more times in the society pages of the paper over the next few years. But that marriage was already deteriorating too. As Frank moved up in law enforcement, he became bolder about his womanizing habits. By then, he'd already met Glaydes, a waitress at the local café where the law enforcement often ate. By the early 1940s, as Uncle Frank's other daughter put it, Glaydes had already "set her cap" toward Frank.

FRANK'S SECOND DAUGHTER, FRANCES, THINKS HER MOTHER, ALICE, GOT pregnant in order to save their marriage. She is also fairly certain Uncle Frank was not thrilled to be a father again: "If I had been a boy, it might have been different." Frances was born in 1942.

Later that year, at the age of sixteen—young like her grandmother and mother—Uncle Frank's oldest, Virginia Lee, got married in Corpus Christi. Her husband, who was eighteen, went off to war immediately, which probably explains their haste. Perhaps she also wanted to get out of her grandparents' house, like Nanny had.

On July 1, 1943, Frank Probst was appointed police chief of Beeville, solidifying his move up in respectable society. There was an opening because the former chief of police had enlisted to serve in World War II. It was a question all men of a certain age had to entertain—why they stayed behind when many of their peers enlisted or were drafted. Frances was a baby at the time, but he told her years later that he was not drafted because his job was considered essential, though other law enforcement officers from around the area enlisted voluntarily, including Frank's predecessor. He probably had a better idea than many men what war actually entailed.

I am uninterested in questions of whether Uncle Frank should have enlisted or not. It is difficult for me—as the daughter of a father who was anti-draft during the Vietnam War, and as a journalist who often writes about victims of persecution and violence—to want to shame anyone for not signing up voluntarily for war.

But the fraught conversations around the war, and the role of men of eligible service age, are the background of some of the violence in Bee County in those years. The conversation became more pressing the summer Frank became Beeville police chief, when the US Navy turned the local airport into a naval air training center called Chase Field. As Frank would later tell Frances about those war years, criminal activity spiked with the influx of sailors drinking, fighting, and looking for other ways to let off steam in the community. Keeping the once-peaceful town safe became, almost overnight, a much more fulsome task.

There was probably also a public relations element to the way Frank and other police officers framed the uptick in violence in those years. While newspapers billed local men on the frontlines around the world as "heroes," law enforcement officers who stayed behind wanted to send the message that peace officers were desperately needed on the home front. No one was better at making that argument to the community than the man who was the county deputy sheriff when Frank took over as the Beeville chief of police.

That deputy sheriff's name was Vail Ennis.

ENNIS HAD ALREADY BEEN INVOLVED WITH THE PREVIOUS POLICE CHIEF in an indictment for murder. While arresting a man for intoxication, the officers said that the man's son attacked them. Ennis killed the son with one shot. That incident launched Ennis's double reputation in the community: some valued his quick efficiency on the job; others worried his response was disproportionately vicious. In his first murder trial, the grand jury took two and a half minutes to find Ennis and the former police chief innocent.

When Uncle Frank took over as police chief, he continued the practice of partnering with the sheriff's office. He and Ennis worked together on a stolen narcotics case. They busted up a gambling ring. They issued warnings about double parking. They worked with the FBI to recover a safe filled with food stamps. They organized a fishing expedition with other town leaders. They didn't just work together; they were friends.

By 1944, the son of one of the poorest families in town had become a respected person in the community. The Probst family was also highlighted in the paper's social pages—who came to whose house for lunch, whose relatives came for extended trips, what was happening at their Dixie Camp Café. In May 1944, Frank was nominated to be a member of the Kiwanis Club, the local service club for men that was frequented by bankers and business leaders and local politicians.

In November 1944, Uncle Frank's friend was elected sheriff in Bee County. In December, the newspaper covered Kelly and Ada's fiftieth wedding anniversary—as if they were somebody, as if the Probst family had finally arrived.

CHAPTER 44

In the close-knit Beeville community, Ennis's past was well known. In 1903, before he moved to Beeville to work on the oil field, Robert Vail Ennis was living near Nacogdoches, Texas—a few miles from the land where, seventy-seven years earlier, Polly and her boys lived in Martin Parmer's house after Robert Leftwich abandoned them in Texas. Ennis made it to South Texas and then out of the oil fields and into law enforcement. His mentor was a renowned Texas Ranger, Alfred Allee.

Along with his older brother, Ennis had already earned a name in the community for his propensity for fighting. Stories of his fistfights and his meanness were legendary. Within a few months, it became clear that people were right to be concerned about his reputation. No sheriff in recent memory in Bee County had killed anyone. Within seven months of taking office, Ennis killed four men. And he was just getting started.

BEE COUNTY, SO CLOSE TO THE SOUTHWEST BORDER OF TEXAS, HAD A long history of racial divisions that had been exacerbated in the last thirty years. Despite the fact that most Hispanic people in the region had been US citizens for multiple generations—they were the ones who had not crossed the border, the border had crossed them—during the highly racialized 1910s, 1920s, and 1930s, their patriotism was repeatedly questioned at a local and national level. As xenophobia and isolation became mainstream views that controlled foreign policy, the accompanying racism took hold in Bee County, as it did in the rest of the state and nation.

Many of the white male leaders of the community joined the Ku Klux Klan in the early 1920s. The elections from 1922 to 1932 in Bee County were deeply polarized. At first, the Klan got a foothold in the area. But like it had in Abilene and much of the rest of the state, as the community increasingly got tired of the Klan's violence and spoke out more and more against the blatant racism of the early 1920s, the KKK's influence faded.

By the 1930s, some of the sharpest public tensions had eased between the white and Hispanic communities. But there were still clear divisions between redlined neighborhoods where people of color lived and those where white people bought homes. And, as was true across Texas, the fact that the Ku Klux Klan became less and less popular certainly did not mean racism went away.

Ennis's tenure as sheriff brought those racial divisions to the forefront of the county again, especially with the shooting of Jon Earle Leslie in January 1945.

The local paper covered Leslie's death in a measured way. Leslie had been legally discharged from the Navy but had been harassed by shore patrolmen from nearby Chase Field for appearing out of uniform despite his dismissal paperwork. The patrolmen called Ennis and asked him to pick Leslie up again after seeing him later in the day out of uniform.

Leslie, who had just married a local woman from Beeville, had done nothing other than being a Black man on the street to warrant his arrest by the local sheriff. Ennis locked him up in the local jail. Ennis was taking him to the courthouse to file charges of vagrancy against him when, Ennis stated, Leslie "tried to get my gun."

There were no other witnesses to contradict Ennis's statement. Ennis shot the unarmed man three times in the chest.

In late February 1945, a few weeks after he shot Leslie, the newspaper

covered a report made by Sheriff Ennis and my Uncle Frank. He and
Ennis reported on crime and violence statistics for the Kiwanis Club's
"Tuesday luncheon program." There had been 129 arrests in January and
February alone, a number that "surprised the Kiwanians," since the pop-
ulation of Beeville was only about seven thousand at that point.

But Sheriff Ennis argued that things were much more violent than
anyone knew. Many of the men who "posed as innocent vagrants" were
instead escaped convicts and dangerous characters who, "with many
years hanging over their heads," were "ready to take any advantage of an
officer to gain their freedom after they had been apprehended." After
raising the men's fear, as chief of police, Uncle Frank showed them the
tear gas guns that "were used to break up mobs." They then walked over
to the jail together which was "spotlessly clean," to show off the thirty-
six medals the sheriff had won at pistol shooting events. Over a polite
luncheon on a Tuesday, Ennis and Uncle Frank made a case to community leaders for why they would be using weapons intended for the battlefield as part of their routine duties.

Five months later, they would bring those weapons along on what
should have been a routine stop in a child custody dispute case.

ON APRIL 30, 1945, UNCLE FRANK LEFT HIS ROLE AS BEEVILLE CHIEF OF
police and officially became a Texas Ranger. For the poverty-stricken
Probst family to have a son who was an elite fighting officer—it was a
remarkable feat. Uncle Frank still worked closely with Ennis. He took a
position under Alfred Allee, Ennis's mentor, as a Rangers criminal investigator.

During those months, Ennis got involved in a feud between two
separated parents, Geronimo and Jesusa Rodriguez. They were bitterly
fighting over custody of their young children, Geronimo Jr., who was
four, and Angelita, who was two. Geronimo lived with the rest of the
extended Rodriguez family on land leased from a rancher outside of
town; Geronimo's father, Felix, was the patriarch of the family, and he
and his wife lived in a house on the land they farmed, with Geronimo

and his sisters and some other family members. Behind them in a smaller shack out back lived Felix's brothers, Domingo and Antonio.

Geronimo had his kids on weekends. He was supposed to take them on Fridays out to the ranch and then bring them back to Jesusa on Sundays. There were no phones at the ranch at the time. When Jesusa did not receive the children one Sunday in early July 1945, she had no way of getting word about what was going on with the kids except for driving out to her ex-husband's home. According to what the family said later, the children had been sick, and the doctor told Geronimo to keep them at home. No one knows whether he told Jesusa and she disagreed with his decision, or she never got word about why the kids didn't make it home for several days.

Either way, Jesusa complained to Sheriff Ennis. He stopped Geronimo's uncle, Domingo, on the streets of Beeville and told him to send Geronimo to the courthouse to "straighten up the matter of the children." His heavy-handed approach angered Domingo, who told a fellow farmer, "I don't like the sheriff." Apparently, either Domingo did not send his nephew to the courthouse to figure out the custody, or Geronimo decided not to go—and that it would be fine to keep the kids with him while they recovered.

Jesusa went back to Ennis, who drove out to the ranch himself on Saturday, July 7, 1945.

I FOUND THE DETAILS OF THIS STORY IN THE THOROUGH COVERAGE OF the later trial by the *Beeville Bee-Picayune* and other local papers, but I wanted to hear from the Rodriguez family members themselves. I spent weeks researching the family, trying to see where they had ended up. It turns out the siblings at the center of the dispute, Geronimo Jr. and Angelita, now in their eighties, are still living in Bee County.

Eight decades later, Angelita still finds it too hard to talk about that day. But Geronimo Jr. was willing, and we talked on the phone for a long time. He gave me a sense for how this story was passed down to his family.

ACCORDING TO THE WITNESS TESTIMONIES OF GERONIMO'S SISTERS, Victoria and Trina Rodriguez, Ennis came to their house three times that Saturday. The first time was that morning around 9:30 a.m. That summer was an especially good harvest for several South Texas crops, like watermelon, broom corn, tomatoes, and cotton. The Rodriguez family followed the rhythm of farmers in the community and worked in the early morning before the brutal heat of the day.

Trina was there the first time Ennis came to the house. She told the sheriff everyone was out in the fields except her father. Felix was running errands in Beeville.

The second time Ennis stopped by, around 12:30 p.m., Victoria was back from the fields and eating lunch. He had brought the children's mother, Jesusa. The patriarch, Felix, had also returned from town, so he handled the conversation with Ennis this time. Because Geronimo was still in the fields, and Ennis did not have a court order with him, Felix sent Ennis and Jesusa away. He told them that Geronimo would deliver the kids to their mother later that day.

Neither Trina nor Victoria heard any threats of violence against Sheriff Ennis from their father or anyone else in the family, either at lunch or at any other time.

Geronimo came back from working the fields around 4:00 p.m. that afternoon. His father had been taking a midafternoon nap, leaning against the ice box to keep cool in the sweltering heat. His uncles, Antonio and Domingo, were behind the big house in the shed, sharpening some hoes that had gotten dull. Shortly after Geronimo walked inside the house, two cars pulled to the edge of the scrubby grass-covered field between the red house and the road.

The first was a metallic-green Hudson, the flashy car Ennis drove around town. Inside of that car, Ennis drove Jesusa and her sister-in-law.

In the second car was Uncle Frank. He was driving a civilian, Joe Watson, whom Ennis had deputized in town less than an hour before.

None of the records mention where the deputy sheriff was, whether there were any other officers nearby, or why Ennis had to deputize a civilian. Nothing about the day was urgent; the children were in absolutely no danger. But Ennis and Uncle Frank did not wait for backup.

Geronimo Jr. and Angelita—the subjects of the custody battle—were inside the home the entire time. Their older cousin, Teresa, was also there; she was about fourteen.

When the officers pulled up, Victoria went to the window and told her father, "Here comes the law." At her words, Felix got up, walked from where he'd been napping in the kitchen in the back, and moved into the large living room in the front of the house.

While her father was heading unarmed to the front door, before he had greeted anyone, Victoria later testified: "I heard the first shot . . . fired from the outside." Trina was right behind them, coming from the kitchen into the living room. She agreed the first shot came from outside of the house. The Rodriguezes' story never varied. They said the officers did not return fire—they initiated it.

One of the main questions of the later trial was whether the Rodriguezes pulled their weapons against the officers, and where those guns were located. There were two guns in their house: a shotgun kept at the front of the house by the door, which would be a disputed part of the competing narratives later; and a rifle in the back, which all of the Rodriguezes testified no one in their family used. Even under cross-examination, Victoria was adamant that the rifle, which she had seen in its place in the back of the house at noon that day when she came back to freshen up and change her clothes after working in the fields, remained in its place. The rifle could not have been used against Ennis or Uncle Frank or the brand-new civilian deputy, Joe Watson, because no one in the family had had time to get it before the shooting began. And Victoria swore Felix did not use the shotgun. As Victoria put it succinctly, even when Felix was fired upon, "My father did not touch the gun we had in the house."

Ennis, however, used multiple weapons. He began with a machine gun. He shot up the house and the neighboring buildings, including the water tower and the shack in the back where Antonio and Domingo lived. After the first machine gun burst, Felix yelled out the front door not to shoot. He shouted that there were children in the room. Victoria followed her father to the open door, where she saw Sheriff Ennis pointing a gun toward them.

Outside, Watson said one of the Rodriguez women came to the door and asked the officers to stop shooting. He said Sheriff Ennis demanded the children come outside.

Ennis began shooting the machine gun again. Victoria said, "I saw Mr. Ennis shoot my father. I carried my father to the dining room. He was wounded and had blood on his side and it got on me." Minutes later, Felix died in his oldest daughter's arms. He was sixty-two.

While Victoria focused on her father, Ennis and Uncle Frank continued their assaults on the family home.

Uncle Frank shot tear gas—presumably from the gun he had shown those Kiwanians a few months earlier—into the screen door of the home. Tear gas, for a child custody battle. Shot into a home where children cowered in fear. Children who were close in age to his own toddler daughter, Frances.

Geronimo Jr. remembers that his cousin, Teresa, was tasked with taking his sister and himself out the back door, away from the gunfire. When he told this part of the story, Geronimo Jr. switched to the third person, as if he were dissociating from what happened to him: "Either my aunt or my grandma told Teresa to take the kids." Teresa carried Angelita and Geronimo Jr. walked beside them, around the left side of the house, the opposite direction from where Vail Ennis was shooting. They walked toward the fence line and their cousin put them over the fence. He saw his mother then, and they ran toward her. She had the car door open for them.

He thinks he remembers his mother's sister yelling to the sheriff, "Just kill them! Kill them!" But he was so young, he is unsure whether that is a memory or a story that he heard later.

A few minutes later, Watson said that Sheriff Ennis pulled out a pistol and went into the house to search for the family's shotgun. When he found it, he took it outside, broke it on the back steps, and then took it back inside and placed it on the table.

According to Victoria's testimony, that is the only point at which anyone touched the shotgun. It was broken by Ennis and never used.

THE ASSAULT BY THE TWO OFFICERS CONTINUED INSIDE THE HOUSE. Ennis attacked Geronimo with his blackjack. Victoria and Trina tried to stop the officers from killing their brother and the other family members as well as their father. Victoria testified that Ennis hit her on the head with a closed fist and then kicked her in the stomach after she fell. Trina's face was "bathed in blood."

Outside, the civilian deputy Watson could not see what was happening, but he said there was "a lot of noise and screaming from women" after Ennis and Uncle Frank went into the house.

Bruised and covered in her father's blood, Victoria ran outside toward the highway, where she tried to hail a passing pickup truck. Her family members still fought with the officers inside the home. The truck didn't stop. Victoria turned back toward the house.

That was when she saw the unarmed bodies of her uncles, Domingo and Antonio, lying in the dust of the yard beside the house.

It would be critical to the prosecution's case that Victoria found her uncles already dead while the officers were still inside. When they heard the first shots fired, Antonio and Domingo had run from the small shack, where they had been sharpening the hoes to use in the field, toward the big house, only to be mowed down by Ennis's machine gun.

Victoria ran back inside the house, where she heard my Uncle Frank say to Vail Ennis, "Come on, you have done enough."

Uncle Frank pulled the sheriff off Geronimo. Inside the house, Felix was dead; outside of the house, his brothers Antonio and Domingo were dead. Geronimo, Victoria, and Trina were bruised and bloody. The other family members were deeply traumatized.

That's when I think Uncle Frank and Vail Ennis got to work covering up their crimes.

I CANNOT KNOW FOR SURE THAT UNCLE FRANK PLANTED EVIDENCE AFTER the murders. But a neighbor later wrote that the reason Ennis brought Uncle Frank along was because Ennis knew he would need a witness to help get him off: "It was his intention to kill Felix, as he had killed people in at least two other situations when his will was resisted." If that was the case, then Uncle Frank did exactly what Ennis brought him there to do.

It must be clear by now that I think the witness testimony of Victoria and Trina is much more trustworthy than Uncle Frank's, which he provided a few months later on the stand. Part of the reason I think they're telling the truth is because Victoria and Trina had nothing to gain by testifying: having watched their father and uncles brutally murdered by a sheriff wielding assault weapons, they must have felt afraid of the repercussions they would face by speaking out against Vail Ennis. I understand why the witnesses to the feud killings at the turn of the century in Colorado County, and the lynching in Abilene in the 1920s, would not want to testify for fear the murderers would come after them. Victoria and Trina had every reason to also be afraid. And yet they spoke out anyway, calmly and cogently, on a number of occasions, including in a packed courtroom. That is why their clear testimonies are that much more compelling to me.

And the other part of the reason I think Victoria and Trina are telling the truth is simple: Frank's daughter Frances thinks he probably lied on the stand to get Ennis off. She especially finds it plausible he created an alibi for Ennis: "Protecting a fellow friend and lawman would be the type of man he was." And she thinks Alfred Allee—Ennis's mentor and Frank's boss—probably had a hand in "making a story for the public."

Covering up the crime to protect his employee, Uncle Frank, and protégé, Vail Ennis, would have been completely in character for Allee. As one writer about the history of the Texas Rangers put it, "Allee showed fierce loyalty to the men who worked for him." Allee was himself a complicated Ranger who, over a long and storied career, would be accused of lying on the stand himself. He was also involved in multiple acts of excessive viciousness against people he was investigating or arresting. One case would make it all the way to the Supreme Court, where the justices determined that Allee arrested striking workers in South Texas "in a violent and brutal fashion." Though he would often deny it, Allee was charged many times over the years with racism. As one of his victims described Allee's attitude, "Something made Allee hate Mexicans."

In Frances's view, in killing the Rodriguez men and attacking the women in their house, Vail Ennis went too far for Uncle Frank. She hears in Frank's statement to Ennis that day—"Come on, you have done enough"—a measure of disgust. She thinks "any friendship they had was dissolved in that house." But Frances, who was a toddler then, between the ages of Geronimo Jr. and Angelita, cannot be sure. As she put it later, "What happened in that house is a mystery and the truth held only by those now dead."

If the Rodriguez women are right, then Frank and Ennis must have cleaned up the crime scene and coordinated their story. If they planted evidence, then they put three shotgun shells into the pocket of Felix Rodriguez inside and one 30-30 Winchester rifle shell into Domingo's pocket outside.

It was not a particularly good cover up; the prosecution was piecing together a slam-dunk case against Ennis. They would build upon several hours of testimony by Victoria and Trina Rodriguez, with the other witnesses for the prosecution corroborating their story. Expert witnesses would testify to the location of bullet hole patterns in the house, the grounds, and the nearby water tank. All of them would point to Vail Ennis firing on unarmed civilians and children with military-grade weapons and murdering three men in cold blood.

Ennis was the only one charged. The case against him seemed crystal clear. Uncle Frank was not only *not* charged with murder or assault—he became what the press called "unquestioningly the defense's star witness."

CHAPTER 45

Following Ennis's murders of Felix, Domingo, and Antonio, there was an immediate uproar in the community in Bee County, Texas. More than a thousand people attended the Rodriguez brothers' funeral a few days later, the biggest in the town's history. After charges were filed against Ennis, a grand jury determined he would face a trial, and then that the trial had to be moved to nearby Victoria County because the alleged murderer had already been tried in the court of public opinion in Bee County.

While they waited for the trial to start, life continued almost normally. Some youths set fire to an old house and Uncle Frank was called to the scene. Alice Probst was elected secretary-treasurer of the Beeville National Farm Association. The paper reported she attended a "lovely surprise party for Louise Martin."

On January 16, 1946, Ennis announced his intention to run again for sheriff of Bee County. He told the press he had received "numerous letters and telegrams from servicemen and others encouraging him in his efforts to maintain law and order in Bee County." The news ran on the same day the local paper began coverage of Ennis's trial in Victoria County.

THE TRIALS FOR THE RODRIGUEZ BROTHERS' MURDERS WERE SCHEDULED separately; Felix's was first in January 1946. It was covered with breathless attention by several local newspapers. The prosecution made it clear during jury selection that they were seeking the death penalty, which heightened the tension of the witnesses' testimony.

The prosecution could not have been more thorough. Members of the Rodriguez family hired a special prosecutor from San Antonio to assist the state's case be as meticulous and methodical as possible. The first of the prosecution's six witnesses was Felix's daughter, Victoria Rodriguez. She spoke earnestly for four hours and fifty minutes on the first night of the trial. The court reporter for the *Victoria Advocate* noted her clothes (all black from her lace shawl to her stockings), her age (forty-one), and her marital status (single). Her sister Trina followed her the next morning on the stand. Despite the fact that both Victoria and Trina spoke English well enough to give investigators information without a translator on the day of the shooting, in their court testimonies they spoke in Spanish and used interpreters so there could be no confusion about what happened. The *Advocate* reported that Trina was twenty-five and also unmarried but did not give the color of her stockings.

At one point, the prosecutor asked Trina, "Who shot your father?" Trina's response was simple and clear: "Vail Ennis."

The prosecutor questioned the sisters to the point of exhaustion. The other prosecution witnesses included the husband of the woman who owned the Rodriguezes' farm, their neighbors, expert witnesses who testified about the layout of the house, and Allee, who carefully laid out the location of the bullet holes in the nearby water tank and the home, entering photographs as evidence to show the many "bullet scars" on the property.

By the time the prosecution rested, they must have felt like they had done everything possible to convict the violent killer who was the Bee County sheriff.

AROUND 4:30 P.M. ON THE SECOND DAY OF THE TRIAL, THE FIRST WITNESS to take the stand for the defense was Uncle Frank. He stated for the courtroom that he was a criminal investigator for the Texas Rangers, which gave his testimony a veneer of credibility.

Frank's testimony directly countered Victoria's and Trina's in several key points. Frank testified that he calmly walked to the door to explain the court order to Felix, and that Felix responded, "'No, no, señor,'" and closed and latched the screen door. Frank said that while he spoke with Felix, he saw a shotgun and a 30-30 rifle "leaning against the open wooden door inside the house." He then backed up and fired "a tear gas projectile" into the house. (No one seemed concerned about the fact that Uncle Frank fired tear gas into a home containing children; that part of his testimony was never interrogated as far as I could tell.) He walked around the edge of the house to reload, when he stated under oath that he saw "another gun barrel protrude from the opened screen door" and that Felix stepped out of the house and "raised a gun."

Critically, it was at this point that Frank testified that Ennis opened fire with the Reising .45 submachine gun. If Frank's testimony were accurate, the two guns—the rifle and shotgun—that investigators found in the Rodriguez home would already be in use at the front of the house. Frank stated that he returned to his car to put the tear gas gun away and retrieve his rifle. As he moved around the house, he stated that he heard a "second burst from a machine gun." He looked beneath the house which, like many of the houses in the area, was raised to protect it from flooding. He said he saw Domingo on the ground, leveling a rifle, and Antonio lying beside him. Then, as he moved around the house, Frank testified that he saw the bodies of the two men and "later found a rifle underneath them, Domingo's finger still in the trigger guard, the hammer back and a loaded shell in the chamber."

No one ever asked him how Domingo got the rifle from the front of the house, which was under machine gun fire, then took it to the back in order to lie on the ground and shoot at the officers.

This is where the testimony really derails: Uncle Frank testified that next, he went inside the house, where he witnessed "Geronimo Rodriguez kick a woman in the stomach." He then stated that Ennis "came in and jerked a shotgun out of a woman's hand and took it outside and broke it." He "denied seeing the sheriff kick a woman, or of using a blackjack on one of the women."

All of the physical harm that came to the sisters, Frank said, was caused by Geronimo.

The interrogation by the prosecution was intense. Uncle Frank swore that the only shot that he fired was with the tear gas gun, and that he heard rather than saw Ennis shoot with the machine gun. When it was over, Ennis's lawyer placed into evidence the statement made by Uncle Frank that he did not plant any evidence.

THERE WERE OTHER WITNESSES AFTER THAT. ONE WAS JOE WATSON, THE deputized civilian. Then the Beeville undertaker testified that he found "three shotgun shells in Felix Rodriguez's pants pockets and one 30-30 rifle shell in the pocket of Domingo." Apparently, the sworn statement by Uncle Frank that he absolutely did not plant evidence was not vehement enough, because Frank was called back to the stand later that day to identify the guns and shells he swore again were used by the Rodriguez brothers and found on their bodies later.

The arguments between the defense and the prosecution attorneys grew heated at times, and the judge called for a recess to give them time to cool off.

Frank's testimony must have seemed contrived to at least some of the listeners. It certainly did to the newspaper editor from Beeville, Camp Ezell. He would spend the next several years dogging the law enforcement in Bee County to keep them accountable, and we know most of the facts of the next several, violent years in the county in the area because of his diligence. Eventually, Ennis would be stopped only because of a concerted effort by several citizens, including Ezell.

But it would not be at this trial. After deliberating for only an hour and thirty-five minutes, the jury returned on the fourth day of the trial with a verdict: Vail Ennis was found not guilty.

THAT TRIAL WOULD FOREVER ALTER FRANK PROBST'S LIFE, AND SUBSE-quently, the life of little Frances Probst.

For the Rodriguez family, the trial only confirmed what they probably already knew—there would be no justice for the deaths of their family members. And the testimony of two Hispanic women, even when they spoke the truth, even when they hired a special prosecutor, even when it seemed obvious the other side lied, would never counter the testimony of white men—not when all of the people in power were white men who knew each other. The Rodriguezes had to watch their family members' murderer be lauded as a hero for decades, long after he died, when they knew firsthand the truth of what he had done.

However, not much changed for Vail Ennis. The trials for the deaths of Antonio and Domingo were supposed to occur after Felix's, but with the first jury's verdict, those trials were over before they started. Ennis was acquitted in Domingo's murder. Antonio's trial was dismissed.

CHAPTER 46

Rather than damaging his reputation, the trial for the murder of Felix Rodriguez seemed to have solidified for many voters Vail Ennis's role as defender of the county. He ran for sheriff again in 1946 and won, despite a petition to oust him led by several concerned citizens. For the next few years, Ennis's star would only rise in Bee County, Texas. He even made the national news during his second term as sheriff.

On November 10, 1947, Ennis arrested two counterfeiters at a gas station in Pettus, Texas. He was alone. He handcuffed the men inside of the gas station, then went outside to make a call for backup. One of the men fired on Ennis, who was shot four times.

Ennis returned fire. He got off twelve shots, six at each of the prisoners. Then he told the station manager, "You'd better get me to a doctor quick. I'm dyin'."

The Old West–style shootout, and the number of men Ennis had already killed, gave the story a life of its own. Before doctors knew whether Ennis would live or die, a short Associated Press article got picked up by newspapers in Texas, then around the country. A few days later, it became clear Ennis was going to live. The newspapers reported on it again, the inexplicably miraculous recovery only adding to Ennis's mythical reputation.

That's when *Time* magazine got involved.

ON NOVEMBER 24, 1947, *TIME* PUBLISHED A SHORT, TWELVE-PARAGRAPH article about Vail Ennis. The article was accompanied by a picture of Ennis, his left arm leaning against a wall, his right arm behind a hip holster holding a gun. He is wearing boots with slacks, a cowboy hat, and a tie that is too short—he looks like a man unaccustomed to dressing up. The hat shadows his eyes. He is not smiling.

The article's colloquial tone could have been lifted straight from a Hollywood Western set—not the way Texans talk, but how someone who had never stepped foot in Texas would assume we talk. Ennis was a "Rip-Tale Roarer" who "keeps evildoers under lock & key." The article begins with two quotes by Ennis: "I am hellbent to keep Beeville cleaned up so a lady can go up the street day or night" and "I never take but one shot." The writer asserts that the first statement is true, "Day or night a lady could sashay unmenaced up Beeville's streets." The second statement, however, reveals the "roughness" of Beeville, where Ennis had already killed seven people with his ".44 Colt revolver and his .45 sub-machine gun—not all, however, with one shot."

Some of the basic facts of Ennis's life in the article are true, but the language is so over the top, they sound made up: "Ennis high-tailed it for the oilfields when he was 16 . . . he was a heller who would try to whup the pants off anybody he met."

When it comes to describing Ennis's murders, the language is downright offensive. *Time* turned the killing of Jon Earle Leslie—the harassed discharged Navy man Ennis shot when he was unarmed—into a story of how Ennis "blasted the life out of a big Negro he had brought into the jail office for disturbing the peace." The massacre at the Rodriguez house became a shootout at the OK Corral: "Old Felix had a shotgun in the house; whether or not he pointed it at Sheriff Ennis is still in dispute. Anyway, the sheriff let go with his submachine gun. Felix tottered backward, died in his daughter Victoria's arms. Geronimo's uncles, Domingo and Antonio, came running from the back of the house. Ennis wheeled on the porch, fired another burst. They fell dead too. Economical Ennis had fired only five shots—two for Felix, two for Dom and one for Tony."

"Economical Ennis" fired significantly more than five shots, as forensics investigators proved and the newspapers reported. And the *Time* reporter shortened the victims' names to Italian American nicknames: Dom and Tony. But the truth would have interfered with the image the writer so clearly wanted to portray. In that short *Time* piece, Ennis became a checkered antihero, out on the still-wild frontier of Texas, not afraid to stand up to bad guys so women could "sashay unmenaced" in town. For doing that, Ennis was still in the hospital, "hothouse blooms banked all around his big room," where he lay "gravely wounded, his intestines riddled, a hip and arm ripped by bullets."

The sheriff of Bee County survived that shooting. He had already killed seven men in cold blood, and his recovery solidified his mythical reputation. He was not just allowed to continue his reign as sheriff; he was nationally lauded as a hero.

CHAPTER 47

By then, things had already begun to unravel for Uncle Frank. On June 27, 1946—five months after his testimony got his friend off for murder and more than a year before Ennis's getting shot would make *Time* magazine—the *Beeville Bee-Picayune* included a small note: "Ranger Frank Probst left last week for Austin to report for duty to his commanding officer in the Ranger force, having been transferred to the Austin district." There was a brief overview of Uncle Frank's tenure as chief of police, and then: "Mrs. Probst will join her husband later, but for the present will remain in Beeville."

Several readers probably knew the truth by then—Uncle Frank had been sent away, presumably by his boss, Allee, to get him away from Glaydes, and probably from the heat of the trial. The newspaper announcement came soon after Frances's fourth birthday. She and Alice went with Frank to Austin for a while, until Alice realized Glaydes was still on the scene. Alice eventually divorced Frank and he married Glaydes not long after it was finalized.

No one is quite sure why the relationship with Glaydes was the one that stuck for Frank; perhaps she turned a blind eye to his womanizing but it continued. Perhaps they each found their deceptive, scheming match in the other. Perhaps they genuinely fell in love and it lasted for the rest of their lives.

Nanny always told Frances the reason Glaydes married Frank was that she had something on him, that she knew some information he did not want anyone to find out. The timing of their leaving Beeville for Austin together makes it seem likely that, if she did blackmail him into the relationship, it was because of something that happened with the trial. But there is no way to know the truth for sure.

Uncle Frank never spoke about the trial. The first time that I talked to Frances on the phone, she told me within five minutes, "I think that when Dad got on the stand, he did not tell the truth. He had a way of sort of shaking his head. I remember him mumbling once, 'I only heard one shot.' That was all. He absolutely would not talk about it."

Nanny never spoke of the trial either. My mother learned about it through my research. She saw the fallout of their relationship in Nanny's rancor toward Frank's third wife. Nanny and Glaydes were the same age almost to the day, both fourteen years younger than Frank. It must have grated on Nanny to have watched Frank leave her friend, Alice, to take up with Glaydes. Nanny remained loyal to Alice, Virginia Lee, and Frances for the rest of her life.

Loyal, but within the patriarchal framework that she understood to be the way of the world—namely, that the role of women was to serve the men in their lives. If Nanny questioned that system, she would have had to pull out the abuse that was so woven into the fabric of her life. And to tug on it might have pulled out a grief and a rage so strong, it could unravel her entire existence.

AFTER FRANK LEFT ALICE TO LIVE WITH GLAYDES IN AUSTIN, THE BILLS didn't go away. Alice had a tiny daughter and a life her husband no longer wanted that she now had to finance, in a city where everyone knew her husband had left her for a waitress at the café. In September 1946 she wrote a small advertisement trying to sell their house: "Must be seen to be appreciated." She leaned on her husband's family.

It made sense that little Frances would spend so much time with Frank's family over at the Dixie Camp Café while Alice worked. Frances practically lived there some weeks; when her dad was back in town, she got to see him some there too.

Nanny's oldest child, Frank Jr.—named after my grandfather, also Frank—wasn't much younger than Frances; the following year Nanny added Stephanie to the mix. They lived in nearby Pleasanton, in the house where my mom would climb the palatial live oak trees in a few years, but they came back to Three Rivers almost every weekend. The "camp" part of the Dixie Camp Café were small cabins in the back and Nanny always stayed there with her kids and helped out around the place. On many weekends, possibly on weekdays when the kids were young, and during the summer once they started at school, Frances could count on having other cousins around. But there was no question that, for a long time, she was her grandfather's favorite.

Frances was five or six when she said to Little Frank, in Nanny's hearing, that "Grandpa had a secret and he might share it with them." Nanny told Frances not to talk dirty. Frances never told her father or her mother what happened on those nights when Ada tucked her into the rollaway bed in Kelly's room and then went to sleep in another room. But surely, Frank knew.

EVENTUALLY, KELLY LEFT FRANCES ALONE. ONE NIGHT SHE SPENT THE night at their house, and they started making up the bed for her in her grandmother's room instead of her grandfather's. Ada told Frances that she and Nanny had talked it over: "You can't sleep in that room. We're not allowing that to happen anymore."

To this day, Frances has no idea what changed their mind; she thought Ada and Nanny had a change of heart somehow, years after the abuse against her started. I suspect she got older and there were younger cousins around and that Kelly's enablers realized he was no longer interested in Frances. She remembers feeling grateful even as a little girl that, because they slept in the cabins out back, Nanny's kids were protected.

They were not protected; Frances just thought they were. It helped her, I think, to imagine she was the only one. My mother was three or four when it started for her and five when her mother found out. She remembers a screaming match between Nanny and Kelly. Everyone ended up crying.

For years, my mother would carry guilt for making her mother cry, for disturbing the peace of the family. She was baptized at age seven in hopes of cleansing herself from someone else's sin. The greatest guilt she carried was because she got back into her grandfather's lap after the first time, even though she knew what would happen. She just wanted someone to hold her.

Like many victims of childhood sexual abuse, it would take years of therapy for her to understand that none of it was her fault.

IT'S THE QUESTION I KEEP COMING BACK TO: HOW COULD MY NANNY, A loving woman who herself endured abuse, allow that abuse to be done to her daughter and other children I know she cared about so deeply? I have wrestled with the answer to that most of my life. It's probably due to the patriarchal culture and beliefs she was bound by; it's probably also due to the fact that she herself was a victim. I know about trauma and its impact on your brain, about victimization and how it changes your thinking. I know the psychological terms, but I still cannot fathom Nanny's actions, much less Frank's.

In part, that's because my mother refused to let that happen to me. In part, that is because something in my mind will not allow me to face these truths.

I am a journalist and a researcher. I am very good at facts and details. I take scrupulous, meticulous notes in my interviews and research. My memory is pretty reliable.

My mother has told me the story of what happened to her countless times in my life; she told me in age-appropriate ways when I was young. She told me again whenever I asked as I grew older, giving me enough information to help me understand without burdening me too much. She was committed to not having secrets, to bringing the light of clarity to the deepest, darkest corners of her family's past.

And yet, to this day, I can barely remember any of the details she has told me. I remember if I look at the pages where I wrote it down, but afterward, it erases itself from my mind. It's as if a fog descends when I think about my mom being abused as a toddler by her grandfather with her mother's full knowledge. She has a hard time remembering much of it too. The other day, she texted, "I'll have to ask my sister what Grandfather called his penis. He had a special word he always made us say." She did not remember to find out the word. I do not want to know.

THESE STORIES—OF FRANK LYING TO COVER UP THE MURDER OF THREE innocent farmers for a friend, of Frank allowing his father to sexually abuse his daughter and others—might seem as if they are unconnected. But to Frances, those public and private actions by her father are inextricably linked. In 1945 and 1946, her father made two pivotal choices from a position of power and prestige. He might not have abused his daughter himself. And he might not have pulled the trigger that killed Felix, Antonio, and Domingo.

But to use the language my mother and Frances do, Frank's sin—his area of greatest culpability—was that he did nothing to stop the enormous evil he stood beside. That is the trauma that never quite heals.

When I looked at the history of the Reese family in Texas, with our well-manicured lawns in our redlined area of town, I finally discovered the sentence I had been trying to uncover for months, that bedrock belief I sensed beneath so many of my ancestors' actions: our right to flourish was God-given, and higher than anyone else's rights—including the right to exist.

With this story, I realized there was a necessary correlation to that belief, an expansion of that underlying worldview that could explain not only Frank's actions but also Nanny's and so many others'.

Some people's rights were not worth fighting for.

If Frank could have changed his fundamental core belief, if he had thought unquestioningly that the Rodriguezes' rights were worth risking his professional reputation and friendship with Ennis for, the outcome of July 7, 1945 would have been very different. He would have been a Texas Ranger who stopped an out-of-control sheriff from using a machine gun at a child-custody battle. Ennis's reign of terror might have ended after the first murder he committed as sheriff a few months previously, and his next victims—beginning with Felix, Domingo, and Antonio Rodriguez—might have lived long lives. But even if Frank had not stopped Ennis before he left that afternoon, Frank could have changed this story at any point—when he saw Ennis pull a machine gun on an unarmed man. When Frank himself used tear gas at a farmhouse. When he saw children fleeing a house where their family was under military-grade fire. After, when he probably planted evidence in the pockets of dead men. After, when he stood on the stand and swore under oath that a traumatized brother kicked his own sisters and that Vail Ennis was innocent of the assaults and murders he knew very well Ennis committed.

And if Frank had changed that core belief, he would have thought Frances was worth fighting for. He would have been a father who—like my own mother did—refused to continue a cycle of profound abuse, who did not allow his little girl to endure what his own sister had. If Frank had made that kind of dramatic ancestral pivot, how different this story would have been: maybe nothing would ever have happened to Fran, and to Kelly's other victims—including my mother.

I can't spend much time contemplating Frank changing his beliefs and seeing the Rodriguezes and Frances and others as people whose rights and lives were worth fighting for. That potential future that was possible in the mid-1940s would have changed so many lives so drastically, it is impossible for me to imagine it without buckling under the grief of what might have been.

CHAPTER 48

It was the Beeville community, and not Frank Probst, who ended the violent reign of Vail Ennis. James McCollom, a son of Beeville, wrote an excellent book called *The Last Sheriff in Texas* about how that end came about. I read *The Last Sheriff in Texas* early on in my research, as I was still unearthing the stories that would end up in this book. McCollom's description of the time period before the Vail Ennis years, and how the two times connected, helped me shape the idea of these periods of extremism that rise up in communities, in states, and in nations.

The phrase that resonated most with me was one McCollom wrote about Beeville and that I quote in my introduction, that there was an "emotional stench as if something in the town had died." I felt the grief and toxicity of that statement. It was in a paragraph in which McCollom was reporting that the political turmoil during Ennis's years as sheriff seemed unprecedented to some in Bee County. But those kinds of divisions had happened before—a generation earlier, when the Ku Klux Klan had ruled the county. As McCollom wrote:

> During the worst of the KKK period, men who had been friends all their lives walked on opposite sides of the street to avoid speaking. Some men slept with pistols under their pillows. The town was

overcome with a rigid righteousness, an Old Testament distrust that tore the New Testament from its moorings and produced an awful political odor, an emotional stench as if something in the town had died. When the KKK period ended, no one spoke of it again.

THE DEATH OF THE MYTH OF A PLACE, THE BEAUTIFUL SPIRIT THAT makes a hometown cherished and unique, is a very difficult thing. Under Ennis, the community wrestled with the questions that had been prevalent since the beginning of Anglo colonization in Texas: Was violence, vigilantism, and lawlessness acceptable in service to "keeping the peace" and maintaining a social order that benefited those in power? Did the ends justify the means? For some of those who flourished under Ennis's regime, the answer seemed to be yes. They could use the formulation that *Time* magazine had used—women walking safely down the street—to answer the question of whether the violence was necessary.

For that formulation to work, the victims of Ennis's crimes had to remain dehumanized. If they were human, then their right to also walk down the street, to also live their lives unmolested by Ennis's violence, would destroy the pro-Ennis crowd's argument. It meant pushing back on the idea that the right of some people to flourish was God-given and more important than any rights anyone else may have—including the right to live while the sheriff held power.

What was different about the storm of the Vail Ennis years as opposed to the KKK years in Bee County, at least as McCollom describes them, was that the community had lived through this kind of extremism before, and within recent memory. The first time, it ended in buried silence: "No one spoke of it again."

But this time, they didn't let that happen. It certainly took some time—too long, many would argue. When Ennis murdered his eighth victim in 1952, the community came together to insist that everyone in Bee County had the right to thrive. And that the people whose rights had been ignored in the past were now worth fighting for.

ON SUNDAY, FEBRUARY 10, 1952, ENNIS WAS CALLED TO NEARBY TYNAN, Texas. As the *Beeville Bee-Picayune* wrote, Ennis received a report that "a Latin-American man was cutting screens, tearing down clothes lines" and acting drunk. That man was named Federico Gutiérrez; he was twenty-eight years old, a husband and father of three.

Ennis admitted that he "hit him over the head with a chain and put him in the back seat of the car." While in the car heading back to the holding cell in Beeville, Gutiérrez tried to open the window. Ennis hit him with the chain again. Then Ennis said that Gutiérrez grabbed him "around the neck and started choking him," so Ennis shot him twice and killed him.

Again, Ennis was alone when he killed a man; no witnesses could corroborate or dispute his story.

Ennis announced the following Thursday that he planned to run for reelection as Bee County sheriff for his fifth term. That same day, an ad paid for by Beeville lawyer Johnny Barnhart, a political opponent of Ennis's, ran in the paper.

It was a picture of Gutiérrez's widow, Ramona, and their three children. The ad was addressed to Ennis personally. It asks a series of questions.

> "Mr. Ennis, do you know who we are? We are the children of the man you killed last week, Federico Gutiérrez. This is our mother with us.
>
> "Mr. Ennis, had our daddy been to the horse races in Skidmore and been doped by someone?
>
> "Mr. Ennis, was our daddy mentally sick?"

The ad continues with questions addressed to Sheriff Ennis: "Was it really necessary for you to kill and take our daddy away from us?" It framed Ennis's killing of Gutiérrez as police brutality in the face of mental illness, asking if he could have used other means of restraining the man instead of "beating him on the head with a chain." And then, the awful sentences concluding the ad:

"Mr. Ennis, our daddy loved us and we loved him. . . . Are we to starve or go on relief because you killed our daddy?

"Mr. Ennis, was killing our daddy really necessary?"

As one scholar put it, "Although Federico Gutiérrez was Ennis's *direct* victim, he was not his only victim." In putting faces to the idea of these victims—Gutiérrez's wife, Ramona, and their children—the ad made the larger Bee County reckon with the cost of Ennis's violence. It made the community realize, as that scholar wrote, that "Gutiérrez's survivors would live thereafter haunted by the anger and humiliation from knowing that a lawman had casually killed their loved one, earned the approval or indifference of most Anglos, and gotten away with it."

IN ALL OF THE STORIES I FOUND OF HOW TIMES OF EXTREMISM ABATED within communities, none were as powerful as the Bee County effort to take down Vail Ennis. On July 23, 1952, a group of people opposed to Ennis's reelection—mostly led by the Hispanic community—organized a rally at the Fair Grounds Park, in a big venue that held about two thousand people. In their wildest dreams, organizers hoped they'd get five hundred people willing to organize to get out the vote against Ennis; they worried the venue would make their efforts seem small. They planned almost the entire program in Spanish, assuming they would predominantly draw Hispanic voters.

Instead, the venue was packed. More than two thousand people came out—an enormous turnout in a county with a total population of slightly more than eighteen thousand. One witness later described the crowd: "When I got there and looked around there were 40 or 50 percent Anglo people there. Never in the history of Bee County had anything like that been done, when it was motivated by Hispanics. They'd just stay away, and go vote. But this time they were there, in force."

Speakers referenced the fact that they knew they took their life in their hands by announcing their opposition to Ennis so publicly. A thread of fear laced through the crowd who were out in the open at the large venue. They could see and be seen. They were all publicly announcing to their community, whether they were on the stage or not, that they were done with innocent people being senselessly killed in Bee County, that they would band together and fight for the rights of everyone.

Vail Ennis pulled onto the park ground in his distinctive green Hudson. One witness said that Ennis parked on the baseball field "behind the pitcher's mound," and another that Ennis "had the machine gun in his lap." After a while, Ennis left. The speakers continued on, in Spanish and English.

The headline the next morning in the *Beeville Bee-Picayune* read "Political Rally Last Night Was Largest in Quarter of Century." Old-timers knew it was the largest in exactly twenty-eight years, since the Ku Klux Klan had been taken out of political power in the county through an election led by the Citizens Party. As they had decades before, the community in Bee County gathered together to make a change—to rid the town of that "emotional stench" of violence and toxicity and hatred.

THEY SUCCESSFULLY GOT OUT THE VOTE THAT FALL. IN NOVEMBER 1952, Ennis lost in what the paper called the "highest vote cast in any race in Bee County."

He would never serve as sheriff again. In six years in power, he had killed more men than any sheriff in Texas history.

True justice was not served; Ennis was never convicted of any of his crimes. This was not, after all, a Western in which the bad guy dies or is taken away. He died at the age of sixty-nine in nearby Corpus Christi in 1972.

The narratives that had been crafted over two hundred years of Texas branding campaigns provided the ideal cover for a conscience-less killer like Ennis. As they had for the robed men who killed Grover C. Everett and got away with it. As they had for Jim Coleman and the Reese boys plotting outright murder to keep Sam Houston Reese the sheriff, for Goep breaking a man's neck and making it look like he fell off a horse. As they had for Austin's colonists who committed genocide against the Karankawa people. As they had for the enslaving colonizers who illegally rose up and overpowered the Mexican government. As they had for the thousands or millions of other people who got away with literal murder and then went down in history as heroes instead of villains.

It was certainly not the end of racially motivated killings—in the area, in Texas, or in the United States. Or of the views that people could get away with legally dubious acts of brutality in urgent times, that the ends would justify the violent means.

But something changed in Bee County when the community banded together like that. It ended that particular period of savage bloodshed. And it changed the conversation in the county—for generations.

IN 2003, FIFTY-ONE YEARS AFTER THE COMMUNITY IN BEE COUNTY ousted Ennis, a series of letters to the editor in the *Beeville Bee-Picayune* publicly shed some light on how Ennis's actions affected the Rodriguez family. It had been almost six decades since Ennis and Frank Probst deployed weapons of war against a house full of children and killed Felix, Domingo, and Antonio Rodriguez. The paper had published some information about a talk a local lawyer was giving about Ennis. In response, Lucy Garcia, a goddaughter of one of the Rodriguez sisters, wrote a short, impassioned note. It is titled "Former Sheriff Not a Hero." She describes the shootings in stark terms: how the sheriff committed "gruesome killings" because Geronimo was late returning the kids since they "were working in the fields." Her godmother "never forgot" losing her father, Felix, and her uncles "in such a horrible manner." The writer hoped her godmother may "rest in peace and may the Lord have forgiven Mr. Ennis for when he was not a hero, but a murderer."

A few months later, Felix's granddaughter, Beatrice Solis Garcia,

WE WERE ILLEGAL

wrote her own letter. She was young at the time when Ennis murdered her grandfather, and her sister, Teresa, was at the scene; she is Geronimo Jr. and Angelita's cousin. Garcia tells what happened, how Ennis set the machine gun up in front of the house and "began shooting from one end of the house to the other." That was when Teresa took Geronimo Jr. and Angelita out to the car.

After Uncle Frank filled the house with tear gas, Teresa ran to get help, but there was nothing anyone could do. Garcia and others joined them outside the house waiting: "To this day I can still see the Galloway ambulance loading the dead bodies, and another taking the injured that Ennis had beaten with his gun."

Years later, Garcia was at a hospital when she overheard two people talking about another time Ennis almost killed someone; that man was saved because his wife got in front of him and yelled and Ennis wouldn't kill a woman. Garcia started crying. She told the men: "He was the man that killed my grandfather."

She ended the letter to the editor by framing a hypocrisy that might be one of the primary questions about the legend of Vail Ennis, but also other mythical Texas heroes: "I don't understand how a so-called 'hero' can kill innocent people and get away with it."

Though the grief is still evident in every line all these years later, Garcia wrote her own response and challenged the public perception of Ennis. It is clear Garcia dealt with the repercussions of that one afternoon of violence by my great-uncle and his sociopathic friend for the rest of her life. It is also clear that she retained the courage to speak out even when it was hard. Like Geronimo Rodriguez Jr. in our interview, and the larger Rodriguez family in their stories to their children and grandchildren and great-grandchildren about what happened that day.

Like the public testimonies of Victoria and Trina Rodriguez. Ramona Gutiérrez and her children. The courageous speakers at the July 1952 rally. Frank's daughter, Frances. My mother and her siblings.

They were direct and indirect victims of the violence and abuse in Bee and Live Oak Counties perpetrated or covered up by my family. And they refused to keep silent.

They refused to accept that the rights of some to flourish were higher than the rights of others to live. They refused to buy into the idea that the rights of some were violable while the rights of others were inviolable. They refused to believe that the rights of some were not worth fighting for; they believed instead that the rights of all were equal in every way. They refused to forget, or to let the memories fade.

And that's how they changed the story.

CONCLUSION

Here, in time,
we seek moments of transcendence
that can remind us of
who we are capable of being.

—PÁDRAIG Ó TUAMA,
BEING HERE

On a cool rainy afternoon in May, one of my children sat down to play the piano. I was in my favorite chair by a window I'd opened to let in the soft breeze while I finished revisions on this book. It was an increasingly rare day in our house in which no one had any plans. The pizza was ordered, the movie picked out. My husband was puttering with his plants, two of the children were playing a game, and I was finishing some paragraphs before our family evening, when the music began.

A few minutes in, I was struck, as I so often am now that my children are older, at how much they've grown. The years of plunking out "Twinkle, Twinkle, Little Star" had turned into this—a confident kid weaving together melodies on the keys. It took my breath away.

I thought: a time I have loved is coming to an end.

I had felt urgency in writing this book before, but in an outward, public-facing way. I felt, as I gained a bird's-eye view of centuries' worth of history, that I was learning about connections I wanted to share with others: from the "chastisement" of the Karankawa people at the Colorado River in the 1820s to a murderous manifesto shared before the mass shooting of people of color in El Paso in the 2020s. From the twisty language of Robert Leftwich and other leaders of Texas about enslaved people to prevent them from becoming free, to the twisty language of politicians today about immigrants' bodies and journeys to this country. From the profound polarization of the Texas Republic years and the feuding years and the Ku Klux Klan years to the profound polarization we see today. I felt an urgency in our own extreme time to understand how we got to this place in our state and in our country.

But as my child began to play that afternoon, I felt a different kind of urgency. It was inward, intimate, only for our family. What I am learning in the process of writing this book might be personally meaningful to me, but it is not for me—it's for the generations to come. Jonathan and I are figuring out, in the handful of years we have left when they are young, how to root our children in a complex, turbulent world so they can grow up sturdy and strong and unquestioningly themselves. I understood that day in a new way why I pushed to get all the way to the depths of these beliefs that have shaped our family. I wanted to understand and then change our family narrative—while there is still time left to do that work.

A FEW WEEKS LATER, I HAD A LONG TALK WITH MY MOM. WE'D BOTH been traveling, though I was finally home when she answered my video call from the other side of the world. Her hair was pulled back in a simple ponytail and our wry grins on the phone were identical. With our images next to one another like that, our resemblance is so clear.

After fully retiring as a professor that spring, Mom was spending several months in Rwanda working for a college preparatory program providing high school students with skills to study in universities abroad. Every time we talked on the phone, she was interrupted by the young staff and faculty in the program knocking on her door to ask if she wanted to walk to the classrooms or if she was ready for dinner. It's what

I think it will be like someday to chat with my kids in college, only it's my retired mother.

We made small talk for a while—catching up on how the kids were doing at camps, hearing about her classes and students. I wanted to ask her what advice she had as I finish revisions on this book, not for the writing itself but for me—for the things I was learning about myself, for the worries I have about how to teach these things to my children, for the grief I felt as time changes for our family. Suddenly it felt like I shouldn't burden her with my worries.

But even over video chat and half a world away, she could read me well. "Hey, I don't think you called to hear about cafeteria food. What's going on?"

And it all spilled out, the fears and the grief and the questions I felt about writing these stories. I talked for a long time. She waited patiently till I was done.

"Sweetheart, I know you're tired, and the process of writing this book has been really difficult. But really, these aren't new questions; you might be thinking about them in a new way, but it's something almost every parent faces at some point. In fact, I thought the other day while my students have been telling me stories here in Rwanda how glad I am that you're writing this book."

She continued, "Jess, we can never learn how to live in the present and look toward the future without knowing the past. We can't deny it. It happened. One of the things we learned in the 1960s during the Civil Rights movement is that too often we ignore what has been and think the crisis of the present is the only crisis. But somewhere, deeply rooted in our collective subconscious, are the truths of the past. If you can't look critically at your own family and your own life, you can't really move forward."

"But how do I do that without damaging my children by telling them these hard stories about our family? What if all they take away is the bad and they can't see the good?" I had not realized, until I spoke it out loud to my mother, that that was the fear I had about telling these stories.

"Honey, more damage comes from covering up than has ever come from soberly facing reality." She looked off for a minute, gathering her thoughts. "I'm the granddaughter of a pedophile, but that's not *who* I am—not at all. I am all the choices I've made to be a loving mother and grandmother and teacher and friend. I'm not defined by my grandfather's actions, but knowing about that past in my family helped you children know who I am, why I react the way I do, the scars that I'll carry all my life, why I'm so passionate about all of you being healthy. I don't feel guilty about the things that my grandfather did, but I also can't act like those things didn't happen to me. Sometimes it *would* feel better to ignore them, honestly—it's painful. It might feel easier to erase it, to shove it down. But recognizing the damage is the only way we can heal, or forgive, or move forward and see the world differently."

Then she told me the story of a new friend she had made in Kigali, a young man named Jacques who drove her when she was in the city. One day, Jacques took my mother to a genocide memorial. He told her about how his mother and grandmother were killed by their neighbors, how sometimes the only way he can deal with his difficult memories is to drive and drive and not stop. He said that during the genocide, his neighbors were brainwashed, that they felt they did not have opportunities in front of them; because they heard over and over again that the Tutsis were "cockroaches" and "snakes," they began to see the Tutsis as less than human. The way he described it to my mother, to kill his family felt to those neighbors like righteousness, like their deaths were justified.

"We're all guilty of that first step, of othering," my mom continued, "anytime we turn people into a category we see as different—whether they're immigrants or women, Black or brown people, Republicans or Democrats, trans kids or LGBTQ families. If we don't see people as worthy of care, attention, and love, they become disposable. And that's a really dangerous place to be." She leaned in a little toward the camera. "You have fears about telling your kids these stories or writing this book, but I'm more afraid of what happens if people who *can* tell these stories *don't* do that work. There's a lot at stake right now. People say all the time, we've never had a more divided country. Please, we lived through a Civil War; we've been very divided always. But being here in Rwanda has made me really question: Where will these great divisions in the United States and in Texas lead us?"

"I agree. It's scary."

She smiled at me. "We start by telling the story. The same way I told you about my grandfather and my family. I've noticed this about a lot of Rwandans—they talk openly about how the country got to the point it did. They're not ignoring it, they're keeping the story alive, so this doesn't happen ever again. There's forgiveness, but there's also honesty in how they've moved forward. It requires confession and repentance, service to the community and a commitment to not repeating the past. It's the opposite of the kinds of private justice you found in the history of lynchings in the family—it's out-in-the-open community justice."

She told me about learning about the Gacaca system in Rwanda. In the aftermath of the genocide, national and international courts prosecuted the leaders responsible for the Rwandan genocide. It took years, and the prisons were overflowing, and still there were thousands of accused people waiting for trial. She didn't remember all of the details, so later I looked them up: In 2005, the country returned to a traditional court system where locally elected judges heard the cases of the people who did not plan the genocide but participated in every other way. For seven years, until 2012, more than 1.2 million cases were heard in twelve thousand community-based courts throughout Rwanda. According to the UN, "The courts gave lower sentences if the person was repentant and sought reconciliation with the community," and they provided "a means for victims to learn the truth about the death of their family members and relatives. They also gave perpetrators the opportunity to confess their crimes, show remorse and ask for forgiveness in front of their community."

My mom finished, "Of course it wasn't a perfect system, and I don't want to act like everything is always idyllic over here. Americans love to go to another continent and have some sort of spiritual epiphany from the people they encounter, and that's not at all what I'm describing. It's

real life here too. But when I brought up the Gacaca trials and the idea
of restorative justice the other day in class, I thought of your book. It
probably won't be Gacaca trials in Texas; I don't know what it will look
like. But communal healing begins when we acknowledge what happened and try to prevent it from happening again.

"It's the question so many of us parents have wrestled with over the
years: How can we build good, healthy lives on top of the ashes of the
past?" She leaned in a bit. "I don't want you to be discouraged, Jess. Just
because it's hard doesn't mean it's not worth doing."

I CRADLED THE PHONE FOR A WHILE AFTER WE HUNG UP. EVENTUALLY
I got up, grabbed my notebook and pencil, and went outside to my back
porch, thinking about what my mom had said while I looked at the live
oak tree in our backyard. The live oaks that have grounded me all of my
life are a symbol for both of us of our love for this place.

This tree had been an acorn or a seedling when Robert Leftwich got
a grant for this land in 1825. Since I was a little kid, I have always found
it improbable that an acorn the size of the top of my thumb, one I could
easily crush with my heel, could turn into this—a sprawling tree with
gnarled branches reaching toward the sky, providing much-needed
shade for almost two centuries in Texas.

For an acorn to put down roots and thrive, it needs good, deep soil.
I had learned something about soil on that research trip to Virginia. I
took a sip of my water, felt it slip coolly down my throat as sweat beaded
beneath my knees, and flipped back through my notebook to reread my
notes from that trip.

ON OUR LAST DAY IN BEDFORD COUNTY, VIRGINIA, SHERRY FINCHUM
and I went together to tour Poplar Forest, Thomas Jefferson's retreat
home near where the Leftwiches and Reeses had lived before my family
eventually made it to Texas. The historic home is now nestled in the
middle of a suburban neighborhood. Unlike some of the other colonial

sites in Virginia, the juxtaposition of current and past is intrusive; where stately women in gowns might once have meandered, now tourists in athleisure wear watch sprinklers on a nearby golf course.

Sherry and I stayed with the tour group for a while, learning about the first octagonal house in North America and how Jefferson's own sons were apprentices to their uncle, a woodworker Jefferson still enslaved. The innovative nature of the architecture, which Jefferson took an exacting hand in, was one of the hallmarks of the tour. The guide really wanted us to notice the oddly shaped rooms all leading to a central dining room; the beds built into the middle of the bedrooms; the triple-sash windows that opened up to let a breeze in or allow Jefferson to walk out onto the porch; the octagonal bricks that were Jefferson's dream and an artisanal nightmare.

But after we toured the house, I found myself most fascinated by a feature of the restoration project that was outside. Sherry and I slipped away from the tour through the front door and down the expansive outside stairs. A circular driveway surrounded a small green field, before widening toward the poplars that gave the retreat its name.

At the apex of the driveway, directly across from the front door, is a window set in the middle of the tan and gold stones that are part of the renovated drive. It is odd and incongruent with the careful renovations in the rest of the house, a touch of permanent modernity. The window is like a skylight—designed to show the foundation of the road below.

When archaeologists began the process of renovating the home, they realized the centuries old drive would be too easily damaged by modern cars. They didn't want to just destroy it, however. They thought maybe future generations would develop techniques that might make restoration possible. They wanted to preserve what had been but construct something practical they could use every day on top.

So they built a window all the way down as a way to see what was underneath it all. And then they covered the original carriage drive with rubber matting and cement, protecting and conserving it. On top of all of that, they created a new driveway, one that is both aesthetically pleasing and usable for the many visitors coming to Poplar Forest.

In my notebook, I had written: *The past is preserved and always visible. But it is not the center of the building's restoration. Instead, that window is a constant reminder that the past laid the groundwork, but that changes were always possible in the present and future.*

I looked up from my notes to watch the wind play in the live oak tree on my back porch, as it has for centuries, as it hopefully will for centuries to come. Through storms and droughts and lush green springs, this tree grows. Roots burrow deep in healthy soil to provide an abiding foundation. Rainwater seeps down through the ground to sustain it. Through all the changes on this land, this live oak remains, stalwart and unbending, shelter and haven and shade.

ACKNOWLEDGMENTS

I could not do any of this without my agent, Mackenzie Brady Watson, who is part therapist, part editor, and part cheerleader, but always one of my very favorite friends; MBW, I'm lucky beyond words to have you in my corner. Aemilia Phillips co-agented this proposal while Mackenzie was on maternity leave, and I'm grateful for Aemilia's insight and enthusiasm from concept to the final draft (which she also read because she's amazing). The entire Stuart Krichevsky Literary Agency works beautifully together, and I have benefited from their collaboration in innumerable ways—thank you.

It is every writer's dream to get to work with a brilliant editor like Emily Wunderlich, who structures my half-formed ideas and shapes my writing so beautifully that the process of editing becomes a kind of shared alchemy between us; Em, I'm a better writer and person after two books with you. Nidhi Pugalia and Paloma Ruiz were immensely helpful in various stages of this book-writing process; Paloma in particular read as a fellow Texan who understood what I was hoping to achieve in this book and gave me excellent critiques and insights (I owe you a margarita next time you're in Texas!). The whole team at Viking is stellar; thank you to Marinda Valenti, Alicia Cooper, Bridget Gilleran, Mary

Stone, Magdalena Deniz, Kristina Fazzalaro, Raven Ross, Daniel Lagin, Jason Ramirez, and Jared Bartman.

Thank you to Christie Hinrichs and the entire team at Authors Unbound, who take care of a thousand tiny details effortlessly and connect me with some of the most amazing communities in the country at speaking events, where I am always the person who benefits the most. I'm so grateful for all of you.

Sherry Finchum is an ideal research partner; not only did we make it through a truly staggering amount of research in the week we spent together at the Bedford County archives, we had a blast doing it—I'm so glad to now count you as family. I could not have written the Sally Reese story without the work of Sherry and Shannon Reese, both of whom were so generous with their time and resources and ideas early on in this process, as well as Susan Allmond Redmond, Sherrie Boone, and George Leftwich. During our research in Bedford County, Karen Rowlett, deputy clerk; and everyone at the Bedford County Courthouse; and Jen Thomson, genealogical librarian and education director; and the rest of the staff at the Bedford Museum and Genealogical Library were especially helpful. I appreciate Dan Thorp, Peter Wallenstein, and Donna Davis Donald for insightful interviews while we were in Virginia.

Susan Chandler, the director of the Nesbitt Memorial Library in Colorado County, was supportive in so many ways, including connecting me to James C. Kearney. My conversations with him transformed the trajectory of this book and I could not be more grateful; Jim, thank you for your generosity in sharing your scholarship and your story but also for your extraordinary work in the world, which inspired me so much in writing this book.

In Bee County, Robbie Guerrero Jr., Geronimo Rodriguez, and the rest of the Rodriguez family were so gracious to trust me with their story; it means the world to me to have been able to play even a small part in setting the record straight after all these years about what happened that day.

I am deeply grateful to the community in Abilene, without whom I would not be who I am today. Thank you especially to Dr. Jerry Taylor,

Dr. Doug Foster, Tryce Prince, and Jason Fikes for our conversations and for the work you do in Abilene and throughout the world. And to Alisha Janette Taylor, for sharing her exceptional documentary with me; I cannot wait to follow your phenomenal career to come.

In the years in which I've been writing this book, I have worked out these ideas through conversations with more people than I can name, so I will say broadly that I appreciate anyone who let me pigeonhole them into talking about this book. Jennifer Wilks met me for lunch early in the process and helped me shape my representational inquiries. Olga Herrera is the kind of friend who not only answers my out-of-the-blue terminology questions, but also graciously queries her smart friends (thank you to Cristina Salinas, Veronica Martinez-Matsuda, and Jennifer Najera). In June 2022, I attended the inaugural Sewanee Veranda conference, where we talked about "the South," and I cannot imagine a more formative experience for shaping the ideas that became the cornerstone of this book; I'm especially grateful to Amanda Bullock, Justin Taylor, Lokelani Alabanza, Andrea Abrams, Ryan Chapman, Tiana Clark, W. Ralph Eubanks, Karen Proctor, Stephen Prothero, Jamie Quatro, and Meera Subramian, as well as the faculty and my students I got to work with for a summer at the Sewanee School of Letters, for many rich conversations. The first time I spoke publicly about this book was at AWP in Seattle, Washington, on a panel organized by Helen Benedict—one of my favorite writers and thinkers, as well as a good friend—with Rone Shavers, Stephen O'Connor, and Christina Yu; the thoughtfulness and depth of our conversation right before I began a round of revisions was transformative. I also loved my week working feverishly at the glorious lake house of Shelley and David Park.

From the minute I joined the faculty at the Maslow Family Graduate Program in Creative Writing at Wilkes University, it felt like coming home. To teach in a program with writers of exceptional talent that centers the work of people who often face obstacles to publication was a professional dream I wasn't sure I'd be able to attain, until I found Wilkes. Thank you to David Hicks for his outstanding leadership and friendship; I'm deeply grateful to the entire Wilkes Creative Writing community, especially Mike Lennon, Robin McCrary, Nisha Sharma, Rachel Weaver, Patti Naumann, Dawn Leas, and Gregory Fletcher, who got his own endnote because he's that wonderful. I'd love to name all of my fantastic students, but it would take pages; working with all of you is one of the great joys of my life. And of course, to my beloved Christine Renee Miller, who, within minutes, I felt I'd known all my life—I cannot wait for our shenanigans and shared projects to come.

I'm grateful for writing friends like Roxanna Asgarian, Megan Kimble, Carrie McKean, Jenna Krajeski, Deborah Jian Lee, Lisa Ann Cockrel, D. L. Mayfield, Stina Kielsmeier-Cook, Wajiha Rizvi, and Kelley Nikondeha, as well as the exceptional group that gathers once a month in Austin to talk about the writing life that welcomed me so warmly. Thank you to Amy Peterson for always being ready with wisdom, snark, or whiskey, depending on what I need. Thank you to Naina Kumar, who was already one of my best friends before she became an outstanding romance writer; I cannot wait to see you take the world by storm. I could not have written this book without Amy Sullivan, who is a gift of a friend; our weekly talks kept me going during the dark days of the Covid lockdown, and when I felt most hopeless about this book, it was you who got me through. And to Christiana Peterson, who was my first writing friend and will always be my best, for everything always.

When I needed early readers, I turned to my incredible community: thank you to Rick, Esha, Terra, Don, Brad, Holly, Whitney, Charles, Chez, Ashley, Jordan, D'Lanna, and John, among others, for being willing to read a rough draft of this book, for the support you give us always, and for being the kinds of friends I can trust so much. Thank you especially to Katie and Shanta for a wonderful, wide-ranging conversation and invaluable feedback. Joy was not my childhood friend growing up, which perpetually amazes me—I'm so glad, all those years after we both left Abilene, to have found you; thank you for the innumerable ways you've helped me think about my relationship with Texas and with the world around me. I'm so grateful for the friendship, encouragement, and support of "Mu Naw," "Amena," "Hasna," (and Hasna's whole family, who are my family too), as well as Ali, Mark, Jenny, Erika, Kim, Lindsay, Megan, Ashley, Lauren, Rachel, Sam, Sarah, Casey, Christie, and Claire, among so many others. Kameryn, you are top-shelf always. Constance, you challenge and bless me immensely. Chez and Ashley, I love how you make me see things in new ways. Ann, Amy, and Holly, you bring me lifelong joy. Caren, you tether me to the world in ways I can never explain; I can't imagine who I'd be without you.

I am deeply grateful to my family. My in-laws, Randy and Karen, are so dear to me, as are my sisters- and brothers-in-law, nieces and nephews, cousins and aunts and uncles and other family members—I love you all. My uncles, Randy and Jim, and their late cousin, Dwayne, joined me for interviews to share their memories; Randy and Jim read an early draft of part 5 and their thoughtful attentiveness made it better. I'm lucky that my cousin Derran is one of my best friends and one of the sharpest thinkers and kindest people I know; the whole time I was writing, I couldn't wait to share these stories with you. My aunt Stephanie told me stories I had never heard before and opened the door to a rich history of our family I had never explored, for which I'm deeply grateful. Our cousin Frances was candid and perceptive and worked with me through multiple interviews and several drafts to shape this story and understand the truth of our family; Fran, connecting with you was one of the greatest joys of this writing process.

My dad, Jack, taught me to love history and to care about the world around me; Dad, as you know, my goal in this book has been both to honor and continue your lifelong work, and I hope I've done that justice. My sister, Jocelyn, and my brother, Jay, helped me answer a thousand complicated questions about this book but also about the kind of people we want to be in the world; having siblings and in-laws (love you, Mark and Mary Kate) who are some of your best friends is a tremendous gift. And my mom, Jeanene, got the last word in this book because she's the person I turn to when I'm most vulnerable, who roots me and shows me how to live a full, meaningful life; Mom, thank you so much for letting me share just a tiny fraction of the wisdom and love you give me every day with others. And thank you for teaching me to love live oaks.

To Jonathan, who wrestled through every word of this book with me and who always helps me build bridges instead of burn them: I love you more every day. And to our children: this book is a love letter for you. Even when things sometimes feel overwhelming, I hope these stories show you that our family's roots are deep, and give you strength, insight, and hope to face the future. The world is already a better place because you're in it. I love you with all my heart.

NOTES

vii **About the difficulties:** Annette Gordon-Reed, *On Juneteenth* (New York: Liveright, 2021), 141.

INTRODUCTION

2 **One of my best:** I'm so grateful to Veronica for allowing me to share her story here. For more information about the bill that was passed under the Ronald Reagan administration, see "1986: Immigration Reform and Control Act of 1986," from A Latinx Resource Guide: Civil Rights Cases and Events in the United States, Research Guides at Library of Congress, https://guides.loc.gov/latinx-civil -rights/irca.

3 **Anzaldúa, through her writing:** Gloria Anzaldúa, *Borderlands/La Frontera: The New Mestiza* (San Francisco: Aunt Lute Books, 1999), 28–29.

7 **One day soon after:** Kying is a pseudonym.

9 **As I thumbed through those textbooks:** Sneha Dey, "1836 Project Promotes Sanitized Version of Texas History, Experts Say," *The Texas Tribune*, September 26, 2022, https://www.texastribune.org/2022/09/26/texas-1836-project-pamphlet/.

9 **One textbook stated:** Larry Willoughby, *Texas, Our Texas*, Teacher's Edition, Part 1 (Austin, Texas: Holt, Rinehart and Winston, 1987), 181–82.

9 **Another featured a pullout section:** Adrian N. Anderson et al., *Texas & Texans* (Dallas: Glencoe/McGraw-Hill, 1987), 226–27.

10 **The Texas myths began like gossip:** This idea was formed especially from listening to Kelsey McKinney with guest Liv Albert, *Normal Gossip*, podcast audio, season 4, episode 4, April 25, 2023.

11 **In a line that:** W. E. B. Du Bois, *Black Reconstruction: An Essay Toward a History of the Part which Black Folk Played in the Attempt to Reconstruct Democracy in America, 1860–1880* (New York: Atheneum, 1977), 700.

13 **Defining one of these time periods:** James P. McCollom, *Last Sheriff in Texas: A True Tale of Violence and the Vote* (New York: Counterpoint, 2018), 213.

PART 1: SALLY REESE (1765–1854)

19 **Virginia is the mother:** Singer and actor Woodward Maurice "Tex" Ritter—father of John Ritter—repeated variations on this joke in a number of appearances over the years, including an August 11, 1970 taping of "The Dick Cavett Show."

CHAPTER 1

25 **As Uncle Sloman framed the story:** Sloman Brooks Reese, *Corinth and Its Kinfolk*, unpublished manuscript, 1931, published online by David Kelley, 2022, http://o.pcahs.org/pcaolr/places01/corint01.htm.
26 **After stopping somewhere:** Howard County Heritage Club, ed., *Howard County, Arkansas: 1873–1988* (Dallas: Taylor Publishing Company, 1988), 380. The quotes in the next few paragraphs are from this book and *Corinth and Its Kinfolk*.

CHAPTER 2

31 **The first president:** Sam Houston was born March 2, 1793 in Rockbridge County, Virginia; Stephen F. Austin was born November 3, 1793 in Wythe County, Virginia; Davy Crockett's father, John, was born in the 1750s in Virginia; James Fannin's mother's family was from Virginia; Fannin's parents were not married and his mother's family, the Walkers, probably predominantly raised him after her death.

CHAPTER 3

32 **When it was officially:** Kajal Thakker read an early draft of this chapter, and I'm grateful for her feedback and insights. Details about the Revolutionary War and its political and sociohistorical context in part 6 come predominantly from Michael A. McDonnell, *The Politics of War: Race, Class, and Conflict in Revolutionary Virginia* (Chapel Hill: University of North Carolina Press, 2007); John E. Selby, *A Chronology of Virginia and the War of Independence, 1763–1783* (Charlottesville: University Press of Virginia, 1973) and Selby, *The Revolution in Virginia, 1775–1783* (Williamsburg: The Colonial Williamsburg Foundation, 1988); E. M. Sanchez-Saavedra, *A Guide to Virginia Military Organizations in the American Revolution, 1774–1787* (Richmond: Virginia State Library, 1978); Robert L. Scribner and Brent Tarter, eds., *Revolutionary Virginia, the Road to Independence: A Documentary Record*, vols. 3–6 (Charlottesville: University Press of Virginia, 1977, 1978, 1979, and 1981); and Thomas E. Buckley, *Church and State in Revolutionary Virginia, 1776–1787* (Charlottesville: University Press of Virginia, 1977), among other sources.
33 **Sometime before 1750:** Several counties in Virginia are called "burned counties"

because their courthouse records burned, some in the Civil War, some in other fires. Records about Slowman's ancestral line go through one of those, Dinwiddie County. Sherry's and my best guess is that Slowman was born sometime in the 1730s or 1740s and was one of at least ten children of a man named Hugh Reese; he might also have been Hugh's brother or nephew or the illegitimate son of Hugh's sister or one of Hugh's oldest daughters. There may also be some Reese connection we know nothing about. The knot of Slowman's origins might never be untangled, but for the purposes of this story—including part 3 about Perry Reese—I have assumed that Slowman is Hugh's son and that the descendants of his direct family members, including Perry, went to Alabama while his own family went to Tennessee.

34 **The word "capitalism":** Carl N. Degler, *Out of Our Past: The Forces that Shaped Modern America* (New York: Harper, 1983), 2.

35 **It was a relatively:** "John Rolfe," Jamestown Rediscovery, Historic Jamestowne, https://historicjamestowne.org/history/pocahontas/john-rolfe/.

35 **The land they arrived on:** For further reading about Tsenacomoco (or Tsenacommacah) and the colonial invasion of Virginia, see MariJo Moore, ed., *Eating Fire, Tasting Blood: An Anthology of the American Indian Holocaust* (New York: Thunder's Mouth Press, 2006); Brent Tarter, "The English Invasion of Tsenacomoco," *Virginians and Their Histories* (Charlottesville: University of Virginia Press, 2020), 17–38; Daniel K. Richter, *Trade, Land, Power: The Struggle for Eastern North America* (Philadelphia: University of Pennsylvania Press, 2013); Benjamin Woolley, *Savage Kingdom: The True Story of Jamestown, 1607, and the Settlement of America* (New York: Harper Collins, 2007); Burke A. Hendrix, *Ownership, Authority, and Self-Determination* (University Park: Pennsylvania State University Press, 2008); and Sean P. Harvey, *Native Tongues: Colonialism and Race from Encounter to the Reservation* (Cambridge: Harvard University Press, 2015).

36 **Immigrant indentured servants:** Warren M. Billings, "The Law of Servants and Slaves in Seventeenth-Century Virginia," *The Virginia Magazine of History and Biography* 99, no. 1 (Richmond: Virginia Historical Society, 1991): 45–62.

CHAPTER 4

38 **Though we know:** "Petition of Peaks of Otter Presbyterian Church, 1774," *The Virginia Magazine of History and Biography* 12, no. 1 (Richmond: Virginia Historical Society, 1904): 419.

38 **And second, Slowman:** "Slowman Reese vs. Wm. Moon," Chancery Case 1787–013, Bedford County Courthouse, Bedford, Virginia.

38 **Without being able to know:** *Born in Slavery: Slave Narratives from the Federal Writers' Project, 1936–1938*, Manuscript Division, Library of Congress, https://www.loc.gov/item/mesn170/.

38 **Thomas Jefferson once wrote:** "Feculum" is a word that has mostly gone out of fashion, but it means the fecal matter of insects, a starchy substance obtained from

plants, or a foul muddy mess; in this context, Jefferson is calling slave overseers the dregs, or the waste products, of society. "Thomas Jefferson to William Wirt, 5 August 1815," Founders Online, National Archives, https://founders.archives.gov /documents/Jefferson/03-08-02-0523. Original source: *The Papers of Thomas Jefferson*, Retirement Series, vol. 8, *1 October 1814 to 31 August 1815*, ed. J. Jefferson Looney (Princeton: Princeton University Press, 2011), 641–46.

39 **In 1700, there were:** Statistics in this paragraph are from Kathryn L. MacKay, "Statistics on Slavery: Population of the Original Thirteen Colonies," https://faculty .weber.edu/kmackay/statistics_on_slavery.htm.

39 **Several Virginia laws:** Gloria J. Browne-Marshall, *Race, Law, and American Society: 1607 to Present* (New York: Routledge, 2013), 4, 251–53.

39 **In early Virginia's society:** I am especially indebted to Rebecca Onion and Jamelle Bouie, *The History of American Slavery*, Slate podcast, episodes 1–9, 2015. See also Nikole Hannah-Jones, *The 1619 Project: A New Origin Story* (New York: One World, 2021); Ira Berlin, *Many Thousands Gone: The First Two Centuries of Slavery in North America* (Cambridge: Harvard University Press, 1998); Gerald Horne, *The Counter-Revolution of 1776: Slave Resistance and the Origins of the United States of America* (New York: New York University Press, 2014); John Craig Hammond and Matthew Mason, eds., *Contesting Slavery: The Politics of Bondage and Freedom in the New American Nation* (Charlottesville: University of Virginia Press, 2011); Hammond, *Slavery, Freedom, and Expansion in the Early American West* (Charlottesville: University of Virginia Press, 2007); Don E. Fehrenbacher and Ward McAfee, eds., *The Slaveholding Republic: An Account of the United States Government's Relations to Slavery* (Oxford: Oxford University Press, 2001); and Lacy K. Ford, *Deliver Us from Evil: The Slavery Question in the Old South* (Oxford: Oxford University Press, 2009).

40 **Enslavement as a life:** In 1640, three indentured servants ran away from their master; when they were caught in Maryland, they all received thirty lashes. But the two white men were sentenced to an additional four years of servitude; the Black man, John Punch, was sentenced to serve his master for life—the first recorded instance of lifelong enslavement in Virginia. See A. Leon Higginbotham Jr., "Virginia Led the Way in Legal Oppression," *The Washington Post*, May 21, 1978, https://www.washingtonpost.com/archive/opinions/1978/05/21/virginia-led -the-way-in-legal-oppression/664bcdf4-8aaf-475f-8ea7-eb597aee7ecd/.

40 **In 1661, a law:** "English running away with negroes," in Willie Lee Rose, ed., *A Documentary History of Slavery in North America* (Athens: University of Georgia Press, 1999), 18.

40 **In 1662, a landmark:** "Negro womens [*sic*] children to serve according to the condition of the mother," Rose, 19.

40 **As one encyclopedia:** General Assembly, "'Negro Womens Children to Serve According to the Condition of the Mother' (1662)," *Encyclopedia Virginia*, August 17, 2021, https://encyclopediavirginia.org/entries/negro-womens-children-to-serve -according-to-the-condition-of-the-mother-1662/.

40 **In 1667, the Virginia:** "An act declaring that baptisme [*sic*] of slaves doth not exempt them from bondage," Rose, 19.
41 **Legalized murder of oppressed:** "An act about the casuall [*sic*] killing of slaves," William Waller Hening, *The Statutes at Large: Being a Collection of All the Laws of Virginia, from the First Session of the Legislature, in the Year 1619* (Richmond: R. & W. & G. Bartow, 1823), 270.
41 **In 1680, Black people:** "An act for preventing Negroes Insurrections," Rose, 20.
41 **In Virginia, a man named Gabriel:** Douglas R. Egerton, *Gabriel's Rebellion: The Virginia Slave Conspiracies of 1800 and 1802* (Chapel Hill: University of North Carolina Press, 1993), 218. One of the men involved in the rebellion was owned by a distant member of the Leftwich clan; "Leftwich's Randolph" was the first to be tried and convicted of the rebellion, but was granted mercy.
41 **In 1682, the Virginia assembly:** "An act to repeale [*sic*] a former law making Indians and others free," Hening, vol. 2, 490–91; "An act for suppressing outlying Slaves," Rose, 20.
42 **The racial purity rules:** Arica L. Coleman, *That the Blood Stay Pure: African Americans, Native Americans, and the Predicament of Race and Identity in Virginia* (Bloomington: Indian University Press, 2013), 89–121.
42 **They were efficient:** Walter C. Rucker, *The River Flows On: Black Resistance, Culture, and Identity Formation in Early America* (Baton Rouge: Louisiana State University Press, 2008), 124.
42 **In 1690, the English:** Steven Mintz, "Historical Context: Facts about the Slave Trade and Slavery," History Resources, Gilder Lehrman Institute of American History, https://www.gilderlehrman.org/history-resources/teacher-resources/historical-context-facts-about-slave-trade-and-slavery#:~:text=The%20number%20of%20people%20carried,leaving%20Africa%20in%20slave%20ships.
42 **They declared that every:** The Virginia Slave Code Act, Hening, vol. 3, 447–63.
42 **In 1723, Black people:** Anti-Assembly Law, Hening, vol. 3, 126–34; Rose, 63.
42 **In 1724, even Black:** Emory G. Evans, "A Question of Complexion: Documents concerning the Negro and the Franchise in Eighteenth-Century Virginia," *The Virginia Magazine of History and Biography* 71, no. 4 (October 1963): 411–15.
43 **In 1774, fifty-eight:** See "Petition of Peaks of Otter Presbyterian Church, 1774." The Peaks of Otter Church was one of several Presbyterian congregations in the last half of the eighteenth century that paid for ministers by enslaving people; what Slowman and the others requested was fairly typical.
44 **In 1783, the church:** They vested ownership of the ten children in August 1783; the ownership is claimed by the Presbyterian Congregation of Peaks of Otter, Deed Book 7, 251, Bedford County Courthouse, Bedford, Virginia.
44 **One historian said that:** John Opie, "The Melancholy Career of 'Father' David Rice," *Journal of Presbyterian History (1962–1985)* 47, no. 4 (1969): 297, http://www.jstor.org/stable/23326162.
44 **Rice left the Peaks:** Rice's life, history, and legacy, like anyone's, is more complex than I can encapsulate in a few sentences. I do not mean to sanctify him, merely

to show that in a time and place where my ancestors lived, his choices diverged from theirs. See also, Andrew Lee Feight, "James Blythe and the Slavery Controversy in the Presbyterian Churches of Kentucky, 1791–1802," *The Register of the Kentucky Historical Society* 102, no. 1 (2004): 13–38, http://www.jstor.org /stable/23386345, and Kate Rivington, "In Its Midst: An Analysis of One Hundred Southern-Born Anti-Slavery Activists," *Australasian Journal of American Studies* 38, no. 1 (2019): 45–78, https://www.jstor.org/stable/26926688.

CHAPTER 5

46 **They passed an act:** The oath begins: "I swear and affirm that I renounce and refute all allegiance to George the third, king of Great Britain, his heirs and successors, and that I will be faithful and bear true allegiance to the commonwealth of Virginia." *An act to oblige the free male inhabitants of this State above a certain age to give assurance of allegiance to the same, and for other purposes* (Williamsburg: Printed by Alex: Purdie, Printer to the Commonwealth, 1777), Printed Ephemera Collection, Library of Congress, https://www.loc.gov/item/2020775037/.

46 **On August 9, 1777:** "A list of those that have taken and subscribed the Oath of Affirmation directed by an Act of General Assembly," unnumbered folder, Bedford County Courthouse, Bedford, Virginia.

46 **In November 1778:** Slowman swears to pay James Phillips a barrel and seven pecks of corn at three pounds per barrel in a case that would extend until July 1784; Judgments Folder 6/7, Bedford County Courthouse, Bedford, Virginia.

46 **Then, at some point:** "Ann, wife of Slowman Reese" relinquished her rights to lay future claims on land that had been her dowry—meaning it was free to sell. Either the record for the land sale was lost, or the sale took place off the books; either way, later court testimony indicates that the Reeses sold the land they had rented out; September 27, 1779, County Court Order Book 6, p. 256.

47 **One of those men:** The name actually reads "Howman Reese," a mistaken transcription since a handwritten *Sl* and *H* look similar on the court proceedings; Bedford County Court, Booklet 1, *Virginia Publick Claims: Bedford County*, compiled and transcribed by Janice L. Abercrombie and Richard Slatten (Athens, GA: Iberian Publishing Company, 1992), 2; this copy was found in the Bedford City/ County Museum, with great thanks to the librarians there.

47 **Better to try:** The plantation was named "Green Level," and it is now the site of the Avoca Museum. The impromptu court either did not keep written records, or they have been lost. They did, however, keep a record of who was accused and how long they were imprisoned. Details for the next few paragraphs are from "Colonel Charles Lynch," Avoca Museum, http://www.avocamuseum.org/col-charles -lynch.

48 **Jefferson personally wrote:** "From Thomas Jefferson to Charles Lynch, 1 August [1780]," Founders Online, National Archives, https://founders.archives.gov /documents/Jefferson/01-03-02-0602. Original source: *The Papers of Thomas*

Jefferson, vol. 3, June 18, 1779–September 30, 1780, Julian P. Boyd, ed. (Princeton: Princeton University Press, 1951), 523.

48 **The Virginia government:** This was not the first law of its kind; in October 1779, a bill introduced in the Virginia House of Delegates—the "Act to indemnify William Campbell, Walter Crockett, and others, concerned in suppressing a late conspiracy"— also provided retroactive legal cover for men who employed violence in putting down an insurrection; Hening, vol. 10, 195.

48 **Later, the vigilante:** There is some debate about whether the term "lynching" started at this moment in history. See Lakshmi Gandhi, "Tracing the Story of 'Lynch Mob,'" NPR, September 30, 2013, https://www.npr.org/sections/codeswitch /2013/09/30/227792122/tracing-the-story-of-lynch-mob.

CHAPTER 6

49 **He was quick:** From the transcription of court testimony for one of the trials when Slowman Reese and William Moon were suing and countersuing each other, which is also the testimony that provides his occupation as slave overseer; May 1786, "Reese vs. Moon," Chancery Case 1787–013, Bedford County Courthouse, Bedford, Virginia.

50 **Slowman leaned on almost all:** Uncovering the witness records was the point at which Sherry and I cracked open Sally Reese's past and proved her relationships not only with her father, for whom she was a witness multiple times, but also with her siblings, who themselves served as Slowman's witnesses. The order books generally provide the names of witnesses and stated how long they attended the trial. In early Virginia, whichever side called a witness had to pay them a fee. Presumably for a man in as much debt as Slowman was in, it was far cheaper to have a member of his household serve as a witness; there's certainly no way to know if Slowman ever paid Sally for her time. On this trial alone, Sally Reese attended the court for thirteen days in May and thirteen days in August 1786.

50 **In December 1786:** Summons issued for Edward McGraw and Edward Read to answer the charge of "Trespass Assault and Battery Two Hundred Pounds," December 30, 1786; unnumbered Judgments folder, Bedford County Courthouse, Bedford, Virginia.

50 **In the same court:** March 1787, Nancy Reese against the Commonwealth, Bastard Child, Order Book 9, p. 38, Bedford County Courthouse, Bedford, Virginia.

50 **Bastardy Bonds were:** Dominik Lasok, "Virginia Bastardy Laws: A Burdensome Heritage," *William & Mary Law Review* 9, no. 2 (December 1967): 402–29, https:// scholarship.law.wm.edu/wmlr/vol9/iss2/8.

51 **But the story:** Howard County Heritage Club book.

51 **That's how we:** Sherry Sorrels Finchum, "The Puzzle of Sarah 'Sally' Reese," *The Leftwich Heritage*, The Leftwich Historical Association 27 (Spring 2019): 40–48. I'm especially grateful to Sherry for her writing on the DNA research that proved Littleberry's parentage of the Reese ancestral line, as well as Shannon Reese and

Susan Allmond Redmond—two other researching "cousins"—whose early work led to that discovery. Shannon was particularly helpful in the early days when I was trying to piece together Sally's past, meeting often over Zoom with Sherry and me.

CHAPTER 7

52 **Over decades, the Leftwiches:** Walter Lee Hopkins, *Leftwich-Turner Families of Virginia and Their Connections* (Richmond: J. W. Fergusson & Sons, 1931), 18.

52 **The plantation of one:** Mary Leftwich Early married Joshua Early and lived on Trivium with their fourteen children, according to *The Leftwich Heritage*, The Leftwich Historical Association (Spring 1999): 16. Thomas Jefferson started visiting his land in Poplar Forest in 1809 and spent the next fourteen years designing an octagonal home and visiting three or four times a year for several weeks or months at a time.

53 **One local history book:** Ruth Hairston Early, *Campbell Chronicles and Family Sketches: Embracing the History of Campbell County, Virginia, 1782–1926* (Lynchburg: Bell Company, 1927); information from multiple Leftwich entries.

53 **In the years that:** June 13, 1778, "Littleberry & Fanny Hopkins. Francis Hopkins, Surety," William Wade Hinshaw, *Encyclopedia of American Quaker Genealogy, 1607–1943*, vol. 6 (Baltimore: Genealogical Publishing, 1994), 948.

54 **It is not the fact:** Many descendants of the Leftwiches share DNA results with descendants of families with the surname Gatewood, opening up the possibility that Littleberry's father, Augustine Leftwich Sr.—patriarch of the expansive, prolific clan—was the result of his mother's affair with a man who was not her husband. Tracking down and proving that parentage was beyond the scope of what I could do for this research, but it demonstrates the complexity of names and biological relations at a time without birth control or paternity tests. As I show in part 2, Littleberry's nephew, Robert Leftwich, in a letter to a family member, also insinuates he is not his father's biological son.

54 **The historians I spoke:** I am especially grateful to the following scholars who either provided me with interviews or connected me with experts who helped frame my inquiry: Kerri Mosely-Hobbs, Lisa Crutchfield, Lucien Holness, Dan Thorp, Peter Wallenstein, Donna Davis Donald, and Jessica Taylor.

54 **After William's birth:** It is unclear whether William was definitely Littleberry's and Sally's first child together, but it seems likely. The later 1831 bill of sale of Wolf Creek (details provided below) shows a list of Sally's children, and William's name was given first, which is why we assume he is the oldest; some of the children do not have birthdates as clear as William's, which we can prove because the 1850 census gives his age as fifty-eight. Littleberry's and Sally's children, in what we assume is their birth order, were William (1792–1852), Robert (1794–1877), Meaky (about 1795–about 1843), Martha "Patsy" (1796–1897), Featherston (about 1798–after

1865), James (1800–1888), Parthenia (about 1804–1871), Nancy (about 1805–1838), Wilkerson (1807–1899), and Fleming (1810–1870).

54 **During those years:** He became an ensign in 1793 and then a lieutenant in 1794, though his promotions came at a much slower pace than both his older and younger brothers'; Hopkins, 318.

54 **That was a known:** See especially Annette Gordon-Reed, *Thomas Jefferson and Sally Hemings: An American Controversy* (Charlottesville: University Press of Virginia, 2000) and Gordon-Reed, *The Hemingses of Monticello: An American Family* (New York: W. W. Norton, 2008).

54 **When I first:** In this research, I am especially indebted to Sherry's expertise on mitochondrial DNA research; together with Shannon Reese, Sherry and I shared our DNA research with a descendant of Sally's through a purely matrilineal line— Sally's daughter's daughter, etc.—whose age made her a closer descendant of Sally's than Sherry or I am. Her mitochondrial DNA results helped us prove—by comparing it to results that Sherry already had—that Sally's female line had only European ancestry, proving that Sally could not have been biracial. We discovered this fact while we were together in Bedford County, and it helped shape our archival research.

54 **Revolutionary-era Virginia:** See especially John D'Emilio and Estelle B. Freedman, *Intimate Matters: A History of Sexuality in America* (New York: Harper & Row, 1988).

54 **One historian I spoke:** Peter Wallenstein at Virginia Tech University especially informed my understanding of the cultural constraints and mobilities of Revolutionary-era Virginia, and in confirming that the relationship between Littleberry and his legal and common-law wives was unusual.

55 **This could not have:** January 6, 1794, Order Book 10, p. 284, Bedford County Courthouse, Bedford, Virginia.

55 **Jordan's charges were:** (1799–1803), Order Book 12, pp. 26–27, Bedford County Courthouse, Bedford, Virginia.

55 **There are other records:** December 28, 1797, Criminal Records Folder 1700–1799, Bedford County Courthouse, Bedford, Virginia.

55 **They never married:** Though determining the parentage of Sally Thornhill and exact birth dates of her children was outside the scope of my research for this book, it is possible that she is related to the family of Richard Thornhill who owned land next to Littleberry's. Her children were Catherine, Marshall, Elizabeth, Permelia, and Addison Thornhill.

56 **With two babies:** December 25, 1811, "Littleberry & Frankey Halley. Wm. Leftwich, Surety," Hinshaw, 949.

56 **Littleberry, black sheep:** Seventeenth- and eighteenth-century laws in the Virginia Commonwealth rewarded white men for raping Black women since any children that were born only increased the enslavers' wealth because those children were considered property. While I cannot know for sure what Littleberry's

relationship was like with the people he enslaved, his propensity for open sexual relationships and multiple children born out of wedlock, whom he acknowledged in his will, makes it seem likely to me that he would not have held moral compunctions against assaulting the women he enslaved. If he did, like so many other white men in power in those years, it could not have been a consensual "relationship" because the women he enslaved had no rights, freedom, or agency. In Littleberry's will, he refers to "Bowser's wife, Betsy, and *her* children Narcissy and Tener" (emphasis mine). Possibly Betsy had been widowed and Bowser was raising another man's children; possibly they were Bowser's children and the lawyer called them only Betsy's since in the eyes of Virginia law, enslaved Black children were— like Sally's kids—legal bastards even when their fathers were known. Or possibly, Littleberry raped Betsy and she bore him two children, which he later bequeathed to his last wife.

57 **But when he died:** Dated May 30, 1823, and recorded June 23, 1823, Will Book 5, p. 419, Bedford County Courthouse, Bedford, Virginia.

57 **Sally's acreage was "on the Northeast:** Deed Book 28, p. 368, Bedford County Courthouse, Bedford, Virginia.

57 **Ann and Slowman Reese:** The last mention of Ann in the archival records that we found was the deed where her land was sold, September 27, 1779, County Court Order Book 6, p. 256; the last mention of Slowman was an agreement with William Moon, in an unnumbered folder, October 18, 1803, Bedford County Courthouse, Bedford, Virginia. We assume that Ann died in the 1780s and Slowman in the early 1810s but cannot confirm their death dates.

CHAPTER 9

64 **He got married:** Their oldest daughter was Minerva, a name that does not seem to have a family precedence on either side of their family, and then the rest of the children are John, Jordan, Sloman, Sarah, and Nancy.

65 **When they finally sold:** May 14, 1831, deed of sale, Deed Book 22, p. 368, Bedford County Courthouse, Bedford, Virginia.

65 **In 1845, the year:** John O'Sullivan, "Annexation (1845)," *United States Magazine and Democratic Review* 17, no. 1 (Washington, DC: Langtree and O'Sullivan, July–August 1845), 5–10.

PART 2: ROBERT LEFTWICH (1778–1826)

71 **I had an ignorant:** Eugene Barker, ed., *The Austin Papers*, vol. 1 (Washington, DC: Government Printing Office, 1924), 207–12.

CHAPTER 10

76 **After a lifetime of trying:** The total amount is 1,459,155 acres; from Malcolm D.

McLean, "Robertson's Colony," Texas State Historical Association, https://www
.tshaonline.org/handbook/entries/robertsons-colony.

CHAPTER 11

77 **Long before Robert Leftwich:** Many of the historical details in parts 2 and 3
come from a number of works, primarily from the groundbreaking book Andrew
J. Torget, *Seeds of Empire: Cotton, Slavery, and the Transformation of the Texas Bor-
derlands, 1800–1850* (Chapel Hill: University of North Carolina, 2015); also from
Stephen Harrigan, *Big Wonderful Thing: A History of Texas* (Austin: University of
Texas Press, 2019); Timothy Anna, *Forging Mexico: 1821–1835* (Lincoln: Univer-
sity of Nebraska Press, 1998); Philip Russell, *The History of Mexico: From Pre-
Conquest to Present* (New York: Routledge, 2001); Donald E. Chipman, *Spanish
Texas, 1519–1821* (Austin: University of Texas Press, 1992); Randolph B. Camp-
bell, *Gone to Texas: A History of the Lone Star State* (Oxford: Oxford University
Press, 2003); Hodding Carter with Betty W. Carter, *Doomed Road of Empire: The
Spanish Trail of Conquest* (New York: McGraw-Hill, 1963); D. W. Meinig, *Impe-
rial Texas: An Interpretive Essay in Cultural Geography* (Austin: University of Texas
Press, 1969); Lewis W. Newton and Herbert P. Gambrell, *A Social and Political
History of Texas* (Dallas: Southwest Press, 1932); Roy R. Barkley and Mark F.
Odintz, eds., *The Portable Handbook of Texas* (Austin: The Texas State Historical
Association, 2000); among many others.

79 **In 1810, revolutionaries:** See Jesús F. de la Teja, ed., *Tejano Leaders in Mexican
and Revolutionary Texas* (College Station: Texas A&M University Press, 2010);
Gerald E. Poyo, *Tejano Journey, 1770–1850* (Austin: University of Texas Press,
1996); Arnold De León, *War Along the Border: The Mexican Revolution and Tejano
Communities* (College Station: Texas A&M University Press, 2012); Phyllis McKen-
zie, *The Mexican Texans* (College Station: Texas A&M University Press, 2004);
Guillermo Brenes Tencio, "Miguel Hidalgo a la luz del arte: iconografía del héroe
nacional padre de la patria mexicana (siglos XIX y XX)," *Káñina* 34, no. 2 (2012);
and Heriberto Frías and José Guadalupe Posada, *Miguel Hidalgo y Costilla, padre
de la Independencia* (Mexico City: Maucci Hermanos, 1900).

79 **Mexico also enslaved:** My thinking in these paragraphs was especially informed
by Alice Baumgartner, *South to Freedom: Runaway Slaves to Mexico and the Road to
the Civil War* (New York: Basic Books, 2022). In 1820, there were an estimated ten
thousand enslaved people in Mexico—mostly owned by the few dozen legal
Anglo landowners in Texas.

80 **Eli Whitney patented:** Note that I do not say Whitney "invented," only that he
patented the cotton gin. There have long been disputes about Whitney's role in the
invention, including historians who recorded rumors at the time that Whitney
obtained the idea from enslaved people, including a man named Sam. For more
about the complicated provenance of the cotton gin, see Monroe N. Work, ed.,
Negro Year Book: An Annual Encyclopedia of the Negro, 1914–1915 (Tuskegee: The

Negro Year Book Publishing Company, 1914), 283; and Angela Lakwete, *Inventing the Cotton Gin: Machine and Myth in Antebellum America* (Baltimore: John Hopkins University Press, 2003).

82 **Moses Austin journeyed:** He built a small community and ran a mine that was profitable for more than ten years; he'd obtained permission in 1798 to mine lead on land controlled by Spain in what is now Missouri. After the market cratered in the late 1810s, Austin went bankrupt and the community dispersed. See *D. B. Moses Austin: His Life* (San Antonio: Trinity University Press, 1987), and James Alexander Gardner, *Lead King, Moses Austin* (St. Louis: Sunrise Publishing Company, 1980).

83 **A grifter from Holland:** See Richard W. Moore, "Bastrop, Baron de (1759–1827)," Texas State Historical Association, https://www.tshaonline.org/handbook/entries/bastrop-baron-de.

83 **That summer, the political:** See José María Tornel y Mendívil, and Carlos María de Bustamante, *Fastos militares de iniquidad, barbarie y despotismo del gobierno español, ejecutados en las villas de Orizava y Córdoba en la guerra de once años, por causa de la independencia y libertad de la nación Mexicana* (Mexico City: Impreso por I. Cumplido, 1843); Timothy Anna, *Forging Mexico: 1821–1835* (Lincoln: University of Nebraska Press, 1998); Luis A. Canela Morales, and Héctor Strobel, eds., *Los Tratados de Córdoba y la consumación de la Independencia: bicentenario de su conmemoración, 1821–2021* (Mexico City: Instituto Nacional de Estudios Históricos de las Revoluciones de México, 2021); and C. I. Archer, "Royalist Scourge or Liberator of the Patria? Agustín de Iturbide and Mexico's War of Independence, 1810–1821," *Mexican Studies* 24, no. 2 (August 2008): 325–61.

84 **On September 27, 1821:** Dennis N. Valdés, "The Decline of Slavery in Mexico," *The Americas* 44, no. 2 (1987): 167–94, https://doi.org/10.2307/1007289.

CHAPTER 12

86 **There are also three:** Malcolm D. McLean, ed., *Papers Concerning Robertson's Colony in Texas*, 19 volumes (Fort Worth: Texas Christian University Press, 1974–1993).

87 **He married his wife:** Brent H. Holcomb, *Marriages of Bute and Warren Counties, North Carolina 1764–1868* (Baltimore: Genealogical Publishing Co., 2004), 102.

87 **One letter, about:** November 18, 1806, letter from Robert Leftwich to Joel Leftwich, Collection 00423-z, Joel Leftwich Papers, 1779–1843, University of North Carolina at Chapel Hill Library, Southern Historical Collection.

88 **Grandison was born:** The 1860 Federal Census makes it likely that his birth date was in 1811, which differs from what many family historians seem to think (namely, that Grandison was born in 1820).

88 **Several of Robert's cousins:** Meaky Reese Campbell got married in Logan County, Kentucky, in 1814 and lived in Russellville in 1820; Nancy Reese Beard lived in Kentucky from the late 1820s to early 1830s.

88 **Robert was doing well:** McLean, vol. 2, 32–34.

88 **According to later court:** I want to acknowledge the possibility that Robert was the father of Polly's children, but there is no way to prove their paternity; if he was, then the story is much darker than the one I have told. The court documents are twenty-four-page legal documents for a suit Grandison Leftwich later filed against Martin Parmer in Warren County, Mississippi: Grandison W. G. I. Leftwich Papers, May 19, 1830, 2E565, Natchez Small Manuscripts Collection, Briscoe Center for American History, University of Texas at Austin (hereafter referred to as the Grandison Leftwich Deposition).

88 **In the 1810s, Robert:** McLean, vol. 2, 34.

88 **In January 1819:** McLean, vol. 2, 33.

89 **On November 6, 1819:** McLean, vol. 2, 34–36; I added the totals of the five indenture documents McLean lays out.

89 **The lists included:** Ibid.

90 **In the letter, he:** The full quote is a run-on sentence that has puzzled professional and family historians; Robert states, "I was brought into this world without a father who had lived before me to give me aid and without the disposition to do so I am, I suppose, considered by him the black sheep of his flock as he has done more for every other child he has, but if being so is a crime I certainly should not be accountable for that which is beyond my control," Hopkins, 237.

90 **Three weeks later:** The deed was filed in Logan County Courthouse on April 27, 1820, McLean, vol. 1, 295–96.

91 **It was not uncommon:** One better known example is in 1796, when Thomas Jefferson sent a ten-year-old named Phill Hubbard from Jefferson's Poplar Forest estate to Monticello to work in the nailery; the child was allowed to visit his family at Christmastime. I'm in no way sugarcoating what Jefferson did by acknowledging that Hubbard was able to return home on occasion; it is not and never has been acceptable to separate children from their families. But knowing that Jefferson's separation of a family retained some relational ties still (in this instance, at least) makes Augustine's act even colder. From "Phill," "The Enslaved People of Poplar Forest: Slave Biographies," Poplar Forest website, https://www.poplarforest .org/learn/thomas-jeffersons-life-and-times/the-enslaved-people-of-poplar -forest/slave-biographies. See also Barbara J. Heath, *Hidden Lives: The Archeology of Slave Life at Thomas Jefferson's Poplar Forest* (Charlottesville: University of Virginia Press, 1999), and Isaac Jefferson, *Memoirs of a Monticello Slave: As Dictated to Charles Campbell in the 1840's by Isaac, One of Thomas Jefferson's Slaves*, ed. Rayford W. Logan (Charlottesville: University of Virginia Press, 1951).

91 **In Robert's March 1820:** March 7, 1820, letter to Joel Leftwich, Hopkins, 238.

92 **His business partners:** Unless otherwise noted, the facts in this section come from McLean, vols. 1 and 2, and from Denise Shoulders, "The Birth of Texas in Russellville, Logan County," in the *News-Democrat & Leader*, parts 1, 2, and 3, April 22, May 31, and June 7, 2022, https://www.franklinfavorite.com/russellville

/news/article_bde2408d-0060-5b11-9408-7b0af29379cb.html. Throughout this book, whenever I name a figure in contemporary currency, I have used this consumer price index inflation calculator: https://www.officialdata.org.

CHAPTER 13

93 **On March 6, 1822:** Unless otherwise noted, details in this chapter are also from McLean, vols. 1 and 2.

93 **On that same day:** *The Weekly Messenger*, Russellville, Kentucky, March 2, 1822, 4.

94 **It is unclear whether:** McLean, vol. 1, 368.

95 **In the few days before:** The source is his February 19, 1823 letter, McLean vol. 2, 92–93. He actually says "fascinate," but it's clearly a misspelling.

96 **By giving the money:** McLean, vol. 2, 40.

96 **On March 8:** Details in this section from McLean, vol. 1, liv–lv.

97 **During their delay:** "Letter from Thomas Reilly to J. H. Hawkins," Mexico, April 26, 1822. Barker, *Austin Papers*, vol. 1, 499.

97 **As it turned out:** Torget, 69.

97 **The letter designed:** Details and quotes in this paragraph and the next are from a May 11, 1822 letter from Col. Andrew Erwin published in the *Nashville Clarion*, July 9, 1822, 3.

98 **Erwin and Robert rode:** In my favorite quote, Erwin describes a kind of delicious food the villagers gave them which "they called pan"—though, to be fair, everyone who speaks Spanish calls bread . . . the Spanish word for bread.

98 **They reached the capital:** Details in this paragraph: "Letter from Austin to Hawkins," [About May 1, 1822], Barker, *Austin Papers*, vol. 1, pp. 504–5 and McLean, ed., *Introductory Volume: Robert Leftwich's Mexico Diary and Letterbook, 1822–1824* (Arlington: University of Texas at Arlington Press, 1968), 106–7, 128–29; hereafter referred to as "Diary."

99 **As one historian:** McLean, vol. 1, lx.

CHAPTER 14

100 **A group bribed:** McLean, Diary, 186–87, 191–92.

100 **The delegates had to:** McLean, Diary, 192.

100 **He was one of:** Details in this paragraph from McLean, Diary, 245, and 308.

101 **"Such is this uncertainty":** McLean, Diary, 193.

101 **By the end of the summer:** Details in this paragraph from Torget, 70.

101 **As Austin put it:** Torget, 73.

101 **In October 1822:** McLean, Diary, 369.

101 **While the Texas Association:** McLean, vol. 1, lxiii.

101 **Iturbide sent Robert:** McLean, Diary, 369–70.

101 **Iturbide had tension:** Santa Anna's faction were anti-imperialist republicans fed up with Iturbide's lavish spending and contentious ruling style. They delivered a

proclamation in Veracruz on December 2, 1822 that the country was a republic and declaring an end to Iturbide's reign.

102 **The law mandated:** Torget, 74.

102 **Robert decided to get:** Torget focuses on the gradual end of slavery, but most Texas historians describe the law as the beginning of the official role of legal empresarios. McLean's description in vol. 2 is typical: "This law invited immigrants of Roman Catholic faith to settle in Mexico, provided for the employment of agents, called *empresarios*, to introduce families in units of 200" and "defined the privileges and certain limitations of immigrants and empresarios," 41.

102 **The country was:** McLean, Diary, 414–15.

102 **In mid-February:** McLean, Diary, 418, and Gregg Cantrell, *Stephen F. Austin: Empresario of Texas* (New Haven: Yale University Press, 1999), 125–26.

102 **Robert wrote the Texas:** McLean, Diary, 420.

102 **And he thought:** McLean, vol. 2, 93.

103 **Robert had not officially:** On March 14, one official told Robert even if he had gotten a grant under Iturbide, it would "not be valid as the law had been past [*sic*] by a body illegally." Exhausted by trying to get a straight answer, Robert wrote, "I coud. [*sic*] not but admire the plain and candid manner in which he had given his opinion." McLean, Diary, 469–70.

103 **He switched sides:** McLean, Diary, 472.

103 **Austin's grant arrived:** Cantrell, 126–27.

103 **Possibly at the behest:** Torget, 76; he also lent five hundred to six hundred dollars to Austin.

104 **For people who:** They also argued with economic terms—bringing in enslavers would mean steep losses to Mexican ranchers who were already in Texas if Anglos changed the scope of the region's economic output. And they agreed that, if slavery were outlawed outright, there would be immediate economic repercussions for many people who relied on enslaved people to generate their wealth—many of those people had powerful connections in the turbulent government. But whether or not it was costly or difficult, it was a matter of integrity for leaders who cut their teeth on a Mexican Revolution with grand ideas about the rights of lower-class people. Whatever moral dilemmas their neighbor to the north wanted to embroil themselves in, those who held this position in Mexico continually asserted that slavery was wrong and they felt they might as well embed that truth into the very constitution of their new country.

104 **Robert, who enslaved:** My thoughts in this section were particularly informed by Torget, 78–79. According to Cantrell, Austin wrote one of his closest friends in Mexico, "There are two obstacles that slow down emigration to this province and the entire nation. . . . One is the doubt that exists if slavery is permitted and the other is Religion," 159.

105 **And on October 4:** The empresarios' interpretation of that law would become increasingly important as tension built between Texian colonists and the Mexican government over the next decade. As Cantrell put it, "Congress passed a vaguely

worded decree prohibiting the slave trade, but Austin and most Mexican officials interpreted it as not banning the importation of slaves by their owners. In fact, emigrants would be allowed to bring their slaves to Texas for many years. Similarly, Catholicism remained the established religion in Mexico, but neither Seguín nor Austin could see any problem with Protestantism as long as it was practiced discreetly," 161.

107 **From New Orleans:** McLean, vol. 2, 324–27, 335.

107 **He told the assembled:** Details for the next few paragraphs mostly from McLean, vol. 2, 57–58.

108 **A group led by Sterling:** McLean's books, *Papers Concerning Robertson's Colony in Texas*, are the most thorough records of the large land grant, but there are many other sources, including too many online databases to list; Robertson eventually served as empresario in 1835 and brought over six hundred families to Texas. The land would also be claimed by Stephen F. Austin as part of his larger grant; I found this source especially helpful for insight into how the land was understood in the 1830s: David B. Edward, with an introduction by Margaret S. Henson, *The History of Texas: Or, the Emigrant's, Farmer's, and Politician's Guide to the Character, Climate, Soil and Productions of That Country: Arranged Geographically from Personal Observation and Experience* (original edition, 1836; reprint, Austin: The Texas State Historical Association, 1990). Though the dispute over whether Austin actually controlled the land or whether it rightfully belonged to other owners is outside the scope of this project, I want to acknowledge that discussion by many Texas historians.

108 **Robertson and the other:** Details in this and the following paragraphs are from Robin Navarro Montgomery, *Historical Montgomery County: An Illustrated History of Montgomery County, Texas* (San Antonio: Historic Publishing Network), 15.

CHAPTER 15

109 **A distant relative:** C. W. Smith, "Our Family's Man in Mexico," Ancestry.com (family story), June 5, 2016, https://www.ancestry.com/mediaui-viewer/collection/1030/tree/163595542/person/302196598566/media/1250b8a0-17b4-48a7-8a29-7514b6b108ef?_phsrc=tQL2&usePUBJs=true&galleryindex=1&albums=pg&showGalleryAlbums=true&tab=0&pid=302196598566&sort=-created.

110 **The few extant:** From Vivian Gornick, *The Situation and the Story: The Art of Personal Narrative* (New York: Farrar, Straus and Giroux, 2002). Gornick defines the "inviolable self" as "some core being at the center in whose company we breathe free; with whom we feel neither isolated nor exiled nor bent out of shape; something we call our real selves. . . . It is the 'I' existentialists had in mind when they spoke of 'becoming,' the one that in our time is called authentic," 92–93. I'm especially grateful to my students Molly Bilinski, Kate Ekanem-Hannum, and Mandy Pennington for the excellent discussion that informed my thinking on this idea.

113 **Thomas Jefferson—who lived:** See Gordon-Reed, *The Hemingses of Monticello*,

especially 300–301, and Fred Kaplan, *His Masterly Pen: A Biography of Jefferson the Writer* (New York: Harper, 2022).

CHAPTER 16

115 **While he was in:** McLean, vol. 2, 62–63.

115 **Along the trip:** McLean, vol. 2, 513.

117 **He was called that:** Thomas Parmer, *Fifty-Five Years Ago in the Wilderness; Or the Old Ringtail Panther of Missouri* (Dallas: Dallas Daily Commercial Book and Job Rooms, 1874), 3.

117 **When his horses:** My thinking in this section was especially influenced by the work of Smith in the unpublished "Our Family's Man in Mexico"—I have independently verified his work with my own research and reporting, but want to acknowledge my debt to his interpretation of Robert's relationship with Parmer and the Beans.

117 **When Polly arrived:** See Jack Jackson, *Indian Agent Peter Ellis Bean in Mexican Texas* (College Station: Texas A&M University Press, 2005) and P. E. Bean, *Memoir of Col. Ellis P. Bean, written by himself, about the year 1816*, ed. W. P. Yoakum, with a postscript by Mattie Austin Hatcher (Houston: Book Club of Texas, 1930).

117 **According to some:** Smith, "Our Family's Man."

117 **While there, Robert:** McLean, vol. 2, 596–97.

118 **Within the first months:** See Robert Lawrence Gunn, "Connecting Borderlands: Native Networks and the Fredonian Rebellion," in *Ethnology and Empire* (New York: New York University Press, 2020), 114–44; and John Henry Brown, *The Fredonian Rebellion* (Houston: Union National Bank, 1930).

119 **Court documents would later:** Details and quotes in this paragraph are from the Grandison Leftwich Deposition.

120 **Mere weeks after:** Torget, 97.

120 **Bean suggested that:** Eugene C. Barker, *The Life of Stephen F. Austin, Founder of Texas, 1793–1836: A Chapter of the Westward Movement of the Anglo-American People* (New York: Da Capo Press, 1968), 234.

120 **Through his connections:** See especially Burrough, Bryan, Tomlinson, 30.

121 **It occurred recently:** Greg Abbott, @GregAbbott_TX. 2023. "I've announced a $50K reward for info on the criminal who killed 5 illegal immigrants Friday. Also directed #OperationLoneStar to be on the lookout. I continue working with state & local officials to ensure all available resources are deployed to respond." Twitter, April 30, 2023, 4:15 p.m., https://twitter.com/GregAbbott_TX/status/1652783731290013696?s=20.

121 **They eventually secured:** See Torget, 97–113.

121 **Two months after:** McLean, vol. 2, 75–77.

122 **As one historian wrote:** W. B. Bates, "A Sketch History of Nacogdoches," *The Southwestern Historical Quarterly* 59 (July 1955): 491–97.

122 **There are no details:** See especially Smith.

123 **Through a series:** Grandison Leftwich Deposition.
123 **At some point, Grandison:** By 1850, when the first Tennessee Slave Schedule came out, a "G. Leftwich" in Maury County, Tennessee, enslaved one young woman, who was twenty-two. Her name was not given. She was too young to be Polly, and no one else was in their household. "United States Census (Slave Schedule), 1850," NARA microfilm publication M432, National Archives, FamilySearch, http://FamilySearch.org.

PART 3: PERRY REESE (1818–1836)

125 **"All new States:** Clifford Hopewell, *Remember Goliad: Their Silent Tears* (Austin, Texas: Eakin Press, 1998), 14.

CHAPTER 17

129 **I was interviewing:** I am especially indebted to Chris Kelley for this conversation.
129 **I pulled out:** Ben Kiernan, *Blood and Soil: A World History of Genocide and Extermination from Sparta to Darfur* (New Haven: Yale University Press, 2007), 335–38.
129 **The summaries from:** I am deeply grateful to Tim Seiter, a scholar doing groundbreaking work resituating and recovering the history of the Karankawa people; through our conversations and an early manuscript of his brilliant dissertation, I learned critical information that corrects the myths of the Karankawa people. I also learned a great deal from Alexander Joseph Perez, *Karankawa Kadla—Mixed Tongue: Medicine for the Land & Our Peoples* (North Charleston: Palmetto Publishing, 2021). And, though she is mentioned in text as well, I could not have written this section without the openness and generosity of Chiara Sunshine Beaumont.
130 **As a witness reported:** Robert S. Weddle, Mary Christine Morkovsky, Patricia Galloway, eds., and Anna Linda Bell, trans., *LaSalle, the Mississippi, and the Gulf: Three Primary Documents* (College Station: Texas A&M University Press, 2000). See also Tim Seiter, "La Salle's Doomed 17th Century French Colony on the Texas Gulf Coast," July 16, 2021, https://www.timseiter.com/la-salle/.
130 **The settlers wrote letters:** As Seiter pointed out in our correspondence, there were instances of friendly relationships between the Karankawa people and various colonizing groups, but even those relatively benign encounters were still couched in the desire to dominate their land and oppress their people. See also Albert S. Gatshet, *The Karankawa Indians, The Coast People of Texas* (Cambridge: Peabody Museum of American Archeology and Ethnology, 1891) and Seiter, "Historiography of the Karankawa Indians," May 11, 2020, Karankawas.com, https://karankawas.com/2020/05/11/historiography-of-the-karankawa-indians/.
131 **If my teacher taught:** Adrian N. Anderson, Ralph A. Wooster, Jeanie R. Stanley, and David G. Armstrong, eds., *Texas and Texans* (Dallas: Glencoe Publishing, 1987), 104.
132 **One other seventh-grade:** Willoughby, 71.

132 **Himmel calls it:** Kelly F. Himmel, *The Conquest of the Karankawas and the Tonka-was, 1821–1859* (College Station: Texas A&M University Press, 1999), 49.

CHAPTER 18

134 **The emotional center:** Comanche National Museum and Cultural Center, "Photograph of distinguished Penateka Chief Tosahwi," Facebook, December 3, 2018, https://www.facebook.com/ComancheMuseum/posts/born-in-the-early -1800s-tosahwi-was-a-prominent-penateka-comanche-he-was-known-a /10155681758378204/.

134 **The original photograph:** "Spectacular Cabinet Card of Comanche Chief To-sawa," [Tosawhi or White Knife] by W. S. Soule, Fort Sill, ca. 1875.

136 **Second, that they:** Whether the Karankawas ever practiced cannibalism is a matter of some debate that I want to acknowledge here, but that does not justify their treatment at the hands of the colonizers who committed genocide against them. As Seiter told me, "There is enough primary source evidence to prove that the Karankawas, as with nearly every other group in Texas, practiced a very limited cannibalism too. Evidence of the Karankawas' cannibalism ceases beginning in the eighteenth century. Even so, white colonizers latched on to the notion of cannibalism as a means to justify their extermination of Karankawas." Message to the author, June 22, 2023.

136 **Perez is their:** His introduction was especially helpful to me in understanding how the Karankawa people retained their stories over generations.

136 **Many of them show:** Erin Douglas, "The Karankawa Were Said to Be Extinct. Now They're Reviving Their Culture—and Fighting to Protect Their Ancestors' Land," *The Texas Tribune*, October 4, 2021, https://www.texastribune.org/2021 /10/04/karankawa-corpus-christi-texas-artifacts/.

CHAPTER 19

138 **Stephen F. Austin encountered:** Throughout this book in the narrative of Stephen F. Austin, I relied on these sources and others: James S. Fishkin, *Stephen F. Austin* (New Haven: Yale University Press, 2000); Sallie Glasscock, *Dreams of an Empire: The Story of Stephen Fuller Austin and His Colony in Texas* (San Antonio: The Naylor Company, 1951); Eugene C. Barker, *The Life of Stephen F. Austin*; Barker, ed., *The Austin Papers*, vols. 1–3 (vols. 1–2, Washington: Government Printing Office, 1924; vol. 3, Austin: University of Texas Press, 1926); Jim McIntire, edited with an introduction by Robert K. DeArment, *Early Days in Texas: A Trip to Hell and Heaven* (Norman: University of Oklahoma Press, 1979); Noah Smithwick and Nanna Smithwick Donaldson, ed., *The Evolution of a State, or Recollections of Old Texas Days* (Austin: University of Texas Press, 1983); and Carleton Beals, *Stephen F. Austin: Father of Texas* (New York: McGraw-Hill, 1953), among other sources.

138 **He wrote, "The country":** Cantrell, 95.

139 **Of the Karankawa people:** "Journal of Stephen F. Austin on His First Trip to Texas, 1821," *The Quarterly of the Texas State Historical Association* 7, no. 4 (April 1904): 304–5.

139 **Austin wrote:** Himmel, 55.

140 **The clashes between:** "Texian" is the term that Anglos in Texas used for themselves until around 1850. Herbert Fletcher, "Texian," Texas State Historical Association, https://www.tshaonline.org/handbook/entries/texian.

141 **As the tension between:** August 1823 letter, in Mike Cox, "A Brief History of the Texas Rangers," *The Texas Ranger Hall of Fame and Museum*, 2018, https://www.texasranger.org/texas-ranger-museum/history/brief-history/.

141 **One of the colonists said:** Kiernan, 336; details in this section from Kiernan unless otherwise noted.

141 **As the old colonizer:** A. J. Sowell, *History of Fort Bend County: Containing Biographical Sketches of Many Noted Characters* (Houston: W. H. Coyle, 1904).

142 **On October 3, 1825:** Barker, *Austin Papers*, vol. 2, 1220.

143 **Eyewitnesses reported that:** J. W. Wilbarger, *Indian Depredations in Texas* (Austin: 1889).

143 **The historian of global genocide:** Kiernan, 15.

143 **One of the later settlers:** Kiernan, 338.

143 **By 1832, at a ceremony:** Ibid.

143 **By 1836, Anglo historians:** Kiernan, 338.

CHAPTER 20

145 **On September 15, 1829:** Torget, 142.

146 **Austin had convinced:** Cantrell, 204.

146 **Based on most of:** Torget, 152; Curtis Bishop, "Law of April 6, 1830," Texas State Historical Association, https://www.tshaonline.org/handbook/entries/law-of-april-6-1830.

147 **He wrote letters:** Cantrell, 223.

148 **In June 1830:** These ideas come especially from Torget, 153–59.

148 **A Virginia-born lawyer:** Richard Ellis to Austin, Alabama, January 30, 1830, "Sons of Dewitt Colony, Slavery Letters," http://www.sonsofdewittcolony.org/slaveryletters2.htm.

149 **The person who:** Essentially, Fisher argues, in order to make money as quickly as possible, these economic migrants will do whatever's easiest, whatever makes the most sense—even if it's illegal, even if they know it's inhumane—because it's logical to want to make money; Torget, 154.

151 **1834, slave-harvested:** Torget, 159.

151 **Cotton prices went up:** Torget, 157.

151 **The ensuing population boom:** Cantrell, 247.

151 **The Anglo population:** Torget, 157.

151 **After terse exchanges:** See Robert E. Davis, ed., *The Diary of William Barret*

Travis, August 30, 1833–June 26, 1834 (Waco: Texian Press, 1966); Archie P. Mc-Donald, *Travis* (Austin: Jenkins Publishing Company, 1976); and Martha Anne Turner, *William Barret Travis: His Sword and His Pen* (Waco: Texian Press, 1972).

152 **The rebellion led:** For more of the political context around Federalism, Centralism, and the political wrangling in Mexico, see *Manifiesto que el ciudadano Anastasio Bustamante dirige á sus compatriotas como general en gefe del ejército de operaciones sobre Tamaulipas y demas departamentos de oriente* (Mexico City: Impreso por I. Cumplido, 1839); Catherine Andrews, *Entre la espada y la constitución : el general Anastasio Bustamante, 1780–1853* (Tamaulipas, Mexico: Universidad Autónoma de Tamaulipas, 2008); and Carlos María de Bustamante, *El gabinete mexicano durante el segundo periodo de la administracion del exmo. señor presidente D. Anastasio Bustamante, hasta la entrega del mando al exmo. señor presidente interino D. Antonio Lopez de Santa-Anna* (Mexico City: J. M. Lara, 1842).

152 **He only believed it:** Torget, 164.

154 **They were loud:** John Myers, *The Alamo* (Lincoln: University of Nebraska Press, 1948), 122.

154 **Austin reported on what:** Cantrell, 311.

155 **Weeks later, War Party:** Cantrell, 312.

CHAPTER 21

157 **He was the:** Because Slowman's birth records are probably in Dinwiddie County, one of Virginia's "burned counties," it is impossible to know the exact relation between Drury and Sally. It is likeliest that Drury is Slowman's nephew, making him Sally's first cousin, but he might also be Slowman's great-nephew, or no relation (though, from my extensive research, I think it is likeliest that they are first cousins). I want to acknowledge the research gap that I was unable to fill here.

158 **For each three-month:** "Categories of Land Grants in Texas," The Texas Land Grant Office, https://www.glo.texas.gov/history/archives/forms/files/categories-of -land-grants.pdf.

159 **On October 3:** *Selma (AR) Free Press*, October 3, 1835, 2.

159 **The story that:** Torget says it best: "The role that slavery played in the secession of Texas from Mexico has been a source of both consensus and conflict among scholars. Most historians argue that slavery played no significant part in bringing on the Texas war and see the onset of the war instead as an almost inevitable clash of cultures between Americans and Mexicans. . . . A handful of dissenting historians, however, particularly those who study Mexico, have argued the opposite, claiming that slavery played a central—perhaps defining—role in the outbreak of the revolution." However, both approaches "focus on slavery as an end in itself for the colonists, rather than placing the institution within the large context of what slavery was meant to support: the agricultural and economic development of Texas. In so doing, both miss how slavery was embedded in broader economic, social, and political changes sweeping across the territory during those crucial

years, as tensions surrounding slave-based agriculture in Texas became part of larger battles raging in Mexico over state sovereignty and federalism. Adopting a wider perspective, indeed, reveals how a complex tangle of cotton, slavery, and Mexican federalism—rather than any single factor—produced the fights that eventually led to the Texas Revolution," 140.

159 **Perry must have read:** *Selma (AR) Free Press*, October 3, 1835, 2; other notations in this section come from the *Selma Free Press* in various editions in 1835.

160 **In October 1835:** The paper said that in Texas, Crockett "would have ample field to distinguish himself, and to render that province some essential service." *Selma (AR) Free Press*, October 31, 1835, 2.

160 **Newspapers throughout Alabama:** Claude Elliott, "Alabama and the Texas Revolution," *The Southwestern Historical Quarterly* 50, no. 3 (1947): 315–28.

160 **One editor at another:** *Macon (GA) Weekly Telegraph*, October 29, 1835, 2.

160 **The articles about:** There are a number of sources that I relied on for details about the Texas Revolt (or Revolution) in part 3, primarily Bryan Burrough, Chris Tomlinson, and Jason Stanford, *Forget the Alamo: The Rise and Fall of an American Myth* (New York: Penguin, 2021); General Antonio Lopez de Santa Anna, D. Ramon Martinez Caro, General Vicente Filisola, General José Urrea, and General José María Tornel, *The Mexican Side of the Texan Revolution [1836]* trans. Carlos F. Castañeda (Austin: Graphic Ideas, 1970); Adrienne Caughfield, *True Women & Westward Expansion* (College Station: Texas A&M Press, 2005); William C. Davis, *Lone Star Rising: The Revolutionary Birth of the Texas Republic* (New York: Free Press, 2004); Davis, *Three Roads to the Alamo: The Lives and Fortunes of David Crockett, James Bowie, and William Barret Travis* (New York: Harper Collins, 1998); and Andrés Tijerina, *Tejanos and Texas Under the Mexican Flag, 1821–1836* (College Station: Texas A&M University Press, 1994), among many others.

161 **A few years earlier:** Edward A. Lukes, "Dewitt, Green (1787–1835)," Texas State Historical Association, https://www.tshaonline.org/handbook/entries/dewitt-green.

161 **Before this time:** *Selma (AR) Free Press*, October 31, 1835, 3.

162 **On October 31:** Ibid.

162 **The Mexican forces:** *Selma (AR) Free Press*, October 3, 1835, 2.

162 **Perry signed up:** For further reading on James Fannin, the Battle of Goliad, and the later battles of the Texas Revolution (including the Battle of San Jacinto), see Hopewell, *Remember Goliad*; Abel Morgan, *An Acount [sic] of the Battle of Goliad and Fanning's [sic] Massacre: and the Capture and Imprisonment of Abel Morgan* (Paducah: Littlefield Fund, 1847); Roger Borroel, *The Texan Revolution of 1836: A Concise Historical Perspective Based on Original Sources* (Chicago: La Villita Publications, 2002); William C. Binkley, ed., *Official Correspondence of the Texas Revolution, 1835–1836*, vols. 1–2 (New York: D. Appleton-Century, 1936); Jack C. Butterfield, *Men of the Alamo, Goliad, and San Jacinto* (San Antonio: The Naylor Co., 1936); Francisco Becerra as told to John S. Ford, *A Mexican Sergeant's Recollections of the Alamo & San Jacinto* (Austin: Jenkins, 1980); and Alwyn Barr, *Texans in Revolt: The Battle for San Antonio, 1835* (Austin: University of Texas Press, 1990);

and Brian Kilmeade, *Sam Houston and the Alamo Avengers: The Texas Victory that Changed Everything* (New York: Penguin, 2019); and Mary L. Scheer, *Women and the Texas Revolution* (Denton: University of North Texas Press, 2012), among other sources.

165 **As they waited:** Information in this section from "Goliad Letters," Sons of Dewitt Colony, http://www.sonsofdewittcolony.org/goliadletters2.htm.

165 **In his military diary:** Patricia Roche Herring, "Tucsonense Preclaro (Illustrious Tucsonan): General José C. Urrea, Romantic Idealist," *The Journal of Arizona History* 34, no. 3 (1993): 307–20, http://www.jstor.org/stable/41696026.

165 **Fannin was a literal pirate:** Torget, 170.

167 **As one soldier:** John M. Niles, *History of South America and Mexico: Comprising Their Discovery, Geography, Politics, Commerce and Revolutions* (Hartford: H. Huntington, 1839), 331.

167 **Or they shot:** The bullets missed the men writing the report and so they escaped immediately; later survivor reports from the three sites told similar stories, of bullets that missed their marks or misfired or Mexican soldiers unwilling to shoot unarmed enemies at such a short range. See especially William Simpson, Zach T. Broos, and Dillon Cooper, "Communicated," *True American*, New Orleans, Louisiana, May 16, 1836, 2.

168 **A few months:** *Selma (AR) Free Press*, July 30, 1836, 3.

169 **Within weeks, the narrative:** It was eighteen minutes in some reports.

CHAPTER 23

172 **Of all of the periods:** Details in this section come from several sources, including James L. Haley, *Sam Houston* (Norman: University of Oklahoma Press, 1992); John H. Williams, *Sam Houston* (New York: Simon & Schuster, 1994); Stephen L. Moore, *Last Stand of the Texas Cherokees: Chief Bowles and the 1839 Cherokee War in Texas* (Garland: RAM Books, 2009); George Lankevich, ed., *The Presidents of the Republic of Texas: Chronology-Documents-Bibliography* (Dobbs Ferry: Oceana Publications, 1979); H. Yoakum, *History of Texas from Its First Settlement to Its Annexation to the United States in 1846*, vol. 2 (New York: Redfield, 1855); H. W. Brands, *Lone Star Nation* (New York: Doubleday, 2004); Fane Downs, *The History of Mexicans in Texas, 1820–1845* (Lubbock: Texas Tech University Press, 1970); William Ransom Hogan, *The Texas Republic: A Social and Economic History* (Norman: University of Oklahoma Press, 1946); Asa Kyrus Christian, *Mirabeau Buonaparte Lamar* (Austin: Von Boeckmann-Jones, 1922); Marshall de Bruhl, *Sword of San Jacinto: A Life of Sam Houston* (New York: Random House, 1993); Madge Thornall Roberts, *Star of Destiny: The Private Life of Sam and Margaret Houston* (Denton: University of North Texas Press, 1993); and Marquis James, *The Raven: A Biography of Sam Houston* (New York: Bobbs-Merrill, 1929), among many other sources.

172 **The constitution was:** There was a preamble, an outline of how power would be

divided in the states, information about term limits (which were short, one to two years), and a convoluted amendment process.

172 **But in Section 9:** Burrough, Bryan, and Tomlinson, 111.

172 **Slaves cannot be freed:** Even Black people who were not "slaves for life" were automatically enslaved in Texas under the same provision: "No free person of African descent, either in whole or in part, shall be permitted to reside permanently in the republic, without the consent of Congress." *Constitution or Form of Government of the State of Texas: Made in General Convention, in the Town of San Felipe de Austin, in the Month of April, 1833* (New Orleans: Office of the Commercial Bulletin, 1833), 19, Earl Vandale Collection, Dolph Briscoe Center for American History, University of Texas at Austin.

173 **An 1836 report:** "During the summer of 1836 President Jackson sent Henry M. Morfit, a State Department clerk, as a special agent to Texas to collect information on the republic's population, strength, and ability to maintain independence. In August, Morfit filed his report. He estimated the population at 30,000 Anglo-Americans, 3,478 Tejanos, 14,200 American Indians, of which 8,000 belonged to civilized tribes that had migrated from the United States, and a slave population of 5,000, plus a few free Blacks." Details in this paragraph from Joseph M. Nance, "Republic of Texas," Texas State Historical Association, https://www.tshaonline .org/handbook/entries/republic-of-texas.

174 **Throughout his time:** Though it's outside the scope of my argument to delve more deeply into Houston's policies toward indigenous people in Texas, I want to recognize the truth that these issues are complicated, and that even "friendly" encounters among colonizing groups and the people who lived on the land before them are still steeped in oppression. Houston certainly had better relationships with indigenous people than his successors, but that does not mean that there were not gross injustices that occurred under his reign too. See the books mentioned above about Houston's life and early presidency.

175 **Even accounting for:** John Nova Lomax, "The Problem with Mirabeau Lamar," *Texas Monthly*, September 17, 2015, https://www.texasmonthly.com/the-daily-post /the-problem-with-mirabeau-lamar/.

175 **Internally, Texas was:** Details in the new few paragraphs from Torget, 181, 190–91, 204–6, 208–9, and 227.

177 **In a November 1845:** Torget, 249.

177 **The brief, fierce war:** For further reading about Tejanos in Texas, the after effects of the Mexican-American War, and Latinidad along the southwest border from the days during and after the Republic of Texas into the first half of the twentieth century, see Martha Menchaca, *Naturalizing Mexican Immigrants: A Texas History* (Austin: University of Texas Press, 2011); Joseph Wheelan, *Invading Mexico: America's Continental Dream and the Mexican War, 1846–1848* (New York: Carroll & Graf, 2007); Philip R. N. Katcher, *The Mexican-American War, 1846–1848* (London: Osprey Publishing, 1976); Arnoldo De León, *The Tejano Community, 1836–1900* (Albuquerque: University of New Mexico Press, 1982); Bruce A. Glasrud and

De León, eds., *Bibliophiling Tejano Scholarship: Secondary Sources on Hispanic Texans* (Alpine: Sul Ross State University, 2003); and Douglas E. Foley with Clarice Mota, Donald E. Post, and Ignacio Lozano, *From Peones to Politicos: Class and Ethnicity in a South Texas Town, 1900–1987* (Austin: University of Texas Press, 1988), among many other sources.

178 **One newspaper editorial:** *El Diario De Hogar,* November 19, 1910, in Monica Muñoz Martinez, *The Injustice Never Leaves You: Anti-Mexican Violence in Texas* (Cambridge: Harvard University Press), 36.

PART 4: SAM HOUSTON REESE (1859–1899)

179 **On the western side:** Hubert Howe Bancroft, *The Work of Hubert Howe Bancroft: Popular Tribunals,* vol. 1 (San Francisco: The History Company Publishers, 1887), vii.

179 **"[The feud members'] ideas":** James C. Kearney, *No Hope for Heaven, No Fear of Hell: The Stafford-Townsend Feud of Colorado County, Texas, 1871–1911* (Denton: University of North Texas Press, 2018), 158.

CHAPTER 24

183 **Beginning in 1860:** Further reading about the Civil War: John C. Waugh, *One Man Great Enough: Abraham Lincoln's Road to Civil War* (New York: Harcourt, 2007); William E. Gienapp, *Abraham Lincoln and Civil War America: A Biography* (Oxford: Oxford University Press, 2002); Michael P. Johnson, ed., *Abraham Lincoln, Slavery, and the Civil War: Selected Writings And Speeches* (Boston: Bedford/St. Martin's, 2001); Vitor Izecksohn, *Slavery and War in the Americas: Race, Citizenship, and State Building in the United States and Brazil, 1861–1870* (Charlottesville: University of Virginia Press, 2014); Elizabeth Ann Regosin and Donald Robert Shaffer, eds., *Voices of Emancipation: Understanding Slavery, the Civil War, and Reconstruction through the U.S. Pension Bureau Files* (New York: New York University Press, 2008); Earl J. Hess, *The Civil War in the West: Victory and Defeat from the Appalachians to the Mississippi* (Chapel Hill: University of North Carolina Press, 2012); William S. Kiser, *Illusions of Empire: The Civil War and Reconstruction in the U.S.-Mexico Borderlands* (Philadelphia, Pennsylvania: University of Pennsylvania Press, 2022); Rev. Santiago Tafolla, auth., Carmen Tafolla and Laura Tafolla, eds., Fidel L. Tafolla, trans., *A Life Crossing Borders: Memoir of a Mexican-American Confederate / Las memorias de un mexicoamericano en la Confederación* (Houston: Arte Público Press, 2010); Debbie M. Liles and Angela Boswell, eds., *Women in Civil War Texas: Diversity and Dissidence in the Trans-Mississippi* (Denton: University of North Texas Press, 2016); Nicholas Keefauver Roland, *Violence in the Hill Country: The Texas Frontier in the Civil War Era* (Austin: University of Texas Press, 2020); Ralph A. Wooster and Robert Wooster, eds., *Lone Star Blue and Gray: Essays on Texas and the Civil War* (Denton, Texas: Texas State Historical Association, 2015); among other sources.

184 **Had they stayed:** Abraham Lincoln wrote, "My paramount object in this struggle
is to save the Union, and is not either to save or to destroy slavery. If I could save the
Union without freeing any slave I would do it, and if I could save it by freeing all the
slaves I would do it, and if I could save it by freeing some and leaving others alone I
would also do that." From August 22, 1862, letter to Horace Greeley, "The Restoration
of the Union the Paramount Object," Gerhard Peters and John T. Woolley, eds.,
"The American Presidency Project," https://www.presidency.ucsb.edu/node/342162.

185 **Texas saw relatively:** "18. The Battle of Sabine Pass," Edward T. Cotham, ed., *The
Southern Journey of a Civil War Marine: The Illustrated Note-Book of Henry O. Gusley*
(Austin: University of Texas Press, 2006), 173–75, and Edward T. Cotham, *Sabine
Pass: The Confederacy's Thermopylae* (Austin: University of Texas Press, 2010).

186 **In fact, many Texans:** In this section, I'm especially indebted to my conversations
with James Kearney, who also referenced the work of his co-writer (now deceased)
on *No Fear*, James Smallwood. Also, Smallwood's essay from Kenneth Howe, ed.,
The Seventh Star of the Confederacy: Texas during the Civil War (Denton: University
of North Texas Press, 2011), along with others in the collection.

186 **By some estimates:** "A Proclamation on Juneteenth Day of Observance, 2022,"
The White House, June 17, 2022, https://www.whitehouse.gov/briefing-room
/presidential-actions/2022/06/17/a-proclamation-on-juneteenth-day-of-observance
-2022/.

187 **On June 19, 1865:** For more about Juneteenth and Reconstruction-era politics
both nationally and in Texas, see Francis Edwards Abernethy, ed., *Juneteenth Texas:
Essays in African-American Folklore* (Denton: University of North Texas Press:
1996); Deborah Willis and Barbara Krauthamer, *Envisioning Emancipation: Black
Americans and the End of Slavery* (Philadelphia: Temple University Press, 2013);
Kidada E. Williams, *I Saw Death Coming: A History of Terror and Survival in the
War against Reconstruction* (New York: Bloomsbury Publishing, 2023); Lerone
Bennett Jr., *Black Power USA: The Human Side of Reconstruction, 1867–1877* (Bal-
timore: Penguin, 1969); Matthew Lynch, ed., *Before Obama: A Reappraisal of Black
Reconstruction Era Politicians, Vol. 1: Legacies Lost, the Life and Times of John R.
Lynch and His Political Contemporaries* (Santa Barbara: Praeger, 2012); Bruce E.
Baker and Brian Kelly, eds., *After Slavery: Race, Labor and Citizenship in the Re-
construction South,* with an afterword by Eric Foner (Gainesville: University Press
of Florida, 2013); Eric Foner, *Reconstruction: America's Unfinished Revolution,
1863–1877* (New York: Harper & Row, 1988); Henderson Hamilton Donald, *The
Negro Freedman: Life Conditions of the American Negro in the Early Years After
Emancipation* (New York: Cooper Square Publishers, 1971); Ira Berlin, Barbara J.
Fields, Thavolia Glymph, Joseph P. Reidy, and Leslie Rowland, eds., *Freedom: A
Documentary History of Emancipation, 1861–1867* (Cambridge: Cambridge University Press, 1985); LaWanda Cox and John H. Cox, *Reconstruction, the Negro, and
the New South* (Columbia: University of South Carolina Press, 1973); Carol
Faulkner, *Women's Radical Reconstruction: The Freedman's Aid Movement* (Philadel-
phia: University of Pennsylvania Press, 2004); Frank McGlynn and Seymour

Drescher, eds., *The Meaning of Freedom: Economics, Politics, and Culture After Slavery* (Pittsburgh: University of Pittsburgh Press, 1992); and Mary Farmer-Kaiser, *Freedwomen and the Freedmen's Bureau: Race, Gender, & Public Policy in the Age of Emancipation* (New York: Fordham University Press, 2010), among many other books.

187 **Juneteenth marked the end:** An opinion article that shaped my thinking about the importance of Reconstruction, among many other sources, was Henry Louis Gates Jr., "How Reconstruction Still Shapes American Racism," *Time*, April 2, 2019, https://time.com/5562869/reconstruction-history/; Gates quotes Foner, whom he calls "the leading historian of the era," as saying, "'The issues central to Reconstruction—citizenship, voting rights, terrorist violence, the relationship between economic and political democracy—continue to roil our society and politics today, making an understanding of Reconstruction even more vital. . . . Achievements thought permanent can be overturned and rights can never be taken for granted.'" See also Eddie Glaude, *History Is US*, podcast, six episodes, June 2022, C13 Originals, Shining City Audio, and Jon Meacham Studio.

189 **Under the Black Codes:** "The 1890s Black Codes," Texas State Library and Archives Commission, https://www.tsl.texas.gov/exhibits/forever/endofanera/page2.html.

190 **The Texas State Police:** Andrew Weber, "Why Texas' First Attempt at a Statewide Police Force Was a Crooked, Bloody Mess," KUT Radio, April 22, 2015, https://www.kut.org/austin/2015-04-22/why-texas-first-attempt-at-a-statewide -police-force-was-a-crooked-bloody-mess.

190 **In that one year:** Texas had 323 murders, 195 more than the next closest contender; *Texas Department of Public Safety: 65th Anniversary* (Nashville: Turner Publishing, 2003), 17.

190 **The Texas legislature:** "An Act to Regulate the Keeping and Bearing of Deadly Weapons," April 1871. See John Sayles and Henry Sayles, *Early Laws of Texas: General Laws from 1836 to 1879* (St. Louis: The Gilbert Book Co., 1888).

190 **From the 1860s:** C. L. Sonnischen, *I'll Die before I'll Run: The Story of the Great Feuds of Texas* (New York: Harper & Bros., 1951), 7.

191 **Counties became like:** Throughout this section, I am especially grateful to James Kearney, who shared his insights into this time period through many conversations, emails, and his writing.

192 **Of the ten deadliest:** Saeed Ahmed, "4 of the 10 Deadliest Mass Shootings in Modern US History Have Taken Place in Texas," CNN, August 4, 2019, https://www .cnn.com/2019/08/03/us/texas-el-paso-walmart-shooting-among-deadliest-trnd /index.html.

193 **One historian of Texas:** Sonnischen, 7.

CHAPTER 25

195 **An entry from:** From "Kinion W. Reese," Frank W. Johnson, Eugene C. Barker, and Ernest William Winkler, *A History of Texas and Texans* (Chicago: American Historical Society, 1916), 1712.

CHAPTER 26

196 **When I emailed:** James Kearney, *No Hope for Heaven, No Fear of Hell: The Stafford-Townsend Feud of Colorado County.*

197 **As one historian:** Sonnischen, 324.

197 **He had seen firsthand:** James C. Kearney and William H. Clamurro, *Duty to Serve, Duty to Conscience: The Story of Two Conscientious Objector Combat Medics during the Vietnam War* (Denton: University of North Texas Press, 2023).

CHAPTER 27

199 **Lillian Reese's book:** John Walter Reese and Lillian Estelle Reese, *Flaming Feuds of Colorado County* (Salado, Texas: Anson Jones Press, 1962). The history of the publisher has everything to do with the tone of the book: it began in 1859, when its founders spent five hundred dollars to buy 585 copies of Anson Jones's ranting memoir of grievances, *Memoranda and Official Correspondence Relating to the Republic of Texas.* Jones was the last president of Texas and he had died at his own hand the year before. His widow did not want his huge pile of books about his life; the founders sold those copies and then published other niche, opinionated books of Texas history for the next century. In 1962, that included Lillie Reese's poorly edited, highly dogmatic book about the Colorado County feud.

200 **The Stafford and Townsend:** Sion Bostick, one of the three scouts who captured Santa Anna, married Susan Townsend a few years later.

200 **Because of Bob Stafford:** The Townsends settled in Texas in 1831, and the patriarch of this particular branch of the family was Spencer Townsend. As oral tradition in the family has it, Spencer was a murderer many times over before the Texas Revolution was over—his brother only convinced Spencer to stop murdering imprisoned Mexican soldiers by begging him. He was gone from the area for a long time after shooting a man in the back. His reputation for violence was well known in the area. In 1867, Spencer's oldest son, Stapleton, was accused of horse stealing. When a posse confronted Stapleton as a horse stealer, Stapleton tried to flee. The posse killed him. They shot him while he ran away. Because his death seemed unnecessary, law enforcement charged five members of the posse with manslaughter. The trial did not start for four years. In March 1871, the five members of the posse that killed Stapleton were found guilty and sentenced to two years in the state penitentiary. However, two days after the trial ended, the defense asked for a new trial—apparently the state had not fully entered witness testimony that would exonerate their clients. The court granted the new trial, and in July 1871, a witness testified that he had visited Stapleton on his deathbed and that Stapleton had said that he could not verify his killer's identities since he was running away. The court exonerated the men charged with manslaughter and they went free because of the new testimony. That witness was Bob Stafford. Five months after the trial, Bob, his brothers Ben and John, and their cousin ran into Stapleton's cousin, Sumner, on the streets of Columbus

(Kearney, 54). Sumner had already had run-ins with the Staffords over land and cattle. Within minutes, the men began shooting at each other; court documents later reveal that it was Ben and Richard who fired shots on the Stafford side, four Staffords against one Townsend. Four days after the shooting, all five men were arrested. Later county court rulings fined the Stafford brothers and their cousin for their parts in the shootings, though not Sumner Townsend. December 1871 is the date most scholars point to as the first act of hostility between the families that endangered the public.

201 **By 1860, 306 white:** Eighth Census of the United States (1860), Schedule F, Slave Schedule for Colorado County, Texas, in Kearney, "The Black Vote," unpublished chapter draft. Details in this section from Kearney's published and unpublished writing, as well as the Colorado County Tax Records and my own research.

CHAPTER 28

205 **Light was only elected:** Reese, 30.
205 **Lillie calls Larkin:** Ibid.
206 **According to Lillie:** Reese, 33.
206 **Bob asked, "Larkin":** Ibid.
208 **Within two years:** Kearney, 12–19.
208 **In 1890, Light:** Lillie said that Sheriff Townsend was disqualified, and then her father came in, but Kearney's more trustworthy account makes Reese Townsend's deputy until 1894; Kearney, 61, Reese, 38.
208 **And then, four years:** Kearney, 64.
209 **He was quiet:** In the book, when he and Walter disagreed on something, Sam spoke in "that low, gentle, firm voice, which was characteristic of the Reese men." When Walter finally opened up to his father, Sam "smiled one of those rare, understanding smiles," and then told his son, "'My boy, you are a man. I'm proud of you and appreciate your confidence and integrity,'" Reese, 51–52.
209 **Lilly framed even:** Reese, 48.
210 **By her account:** Reese, 77.

CHAPTER 29

212 **The next morning:** Interview with James Kearney, March 9, 2022.
214 **Kearney's interview with Goep:** All "Goep" quotes are from John Goeppinger, interview by Charles Kearney and James C. Kearney, multiple dates, Colorado County, 1972.

CHAPTER 30

218 **Burford beat Reese:** "In the general election of November 1898, Will Burford received 1,952 votes, Sam Reese 1,391, and a third candidate, James Shropshire, 871," Kearney, 77.

218 **According to Kearney:** Kearney, 78.

220 **There were several:** Kearney, 80–81.

220 **The new deputy:** Kearney, 81. A former cellmate and mutual friend of Jim Coleman was in town.

220 **A second bullet:** Kearney, 83.

220 **As Lillie writes:** Reese, 81–83.

221 **Captain Bill McDonald:** For further reading about McDonald, see "Chapter 14: Captain Bill to the Rescue," in Doug J. Swanson, *Cult of Glory: The Bold and Brutal History of the Texas Rangers* (New York: Viking, 2020), 235–46.

221 **McDonald met with:** Kearney, 85.

221 **Clements and another deputy:** Kearney, 86, Goep transcription.

222 **Reese family members:** Kearney, 87–88.

222 **A little before:** Kearney, 88–89.

222 **Two Townsend men:** Those men were Step Yates and Jim Townsend.

223 **The records for:** All information in these sections come from the Tax Assessment Roll of Colorado County for the years 1874, 1879, 1880, 1881, 1882, 1884, 1892, 1893, and 1894.

224 **The Townsend men:** Details for the next few sentences are from *The Houston Post*, May 19, 1899, 5.

224 **Three days after:** *The Houston Post* (May 20, 1899), 5.

CHAPTER 31

225 **It was the conundrum:** Here's how Kearney put it after one of many times when killers got off without a punishment: "The grand jury convened in September and, once again, no-billed all the participants in the street fight. The action was emblematic of the almost schizophrenic reflex within the community to the shoot-out: on the one hand, the citizens were willing to do away with city government, but, on the other hand, they refused to hold anyone accountable before a court of law," 133.

226 **On the first:** Details for the next several paragraphs are from Kearney, 104–5.

226 **As in every other:** Kearney, 108–9.

227 **Newspapers around the country:** *Las Vegas (NM) Daily Optic*, January 16, 1900, 1.

227 **In statements that:** *The Daily Times*, Davenport, Iowa, January 16, 1900, 1.

228 **In 1891, the Texas:** See Garna L. Christian, *Black Soldiers in Jim Crow Texas, 1899–1917* (College Station: Texas A&M University Press, 1995); Bruce A. Glasrud and Debbie M. Liles, eds., *African Americans in Central Texas History: From Slavery to Civil Rights* (College Station: Texas A&M Press, 2019); Jason A. Gillmer, *Slavery and Freedom in Texas: Stories from the Courtroom, 1821–1871* (Athens: University of Georgia Press, 2017); and Ari Berman, "Texas's Voter-Registration Laws Are Straight out of the Jim Crow Playbook," *The Nation*, October 10, 2016, https://www.thenation.com/article/archive/texasss-voter-registration-laws-are-straight-out-of-the-jim-crow-playbook/.

228 **The conservative Democratic Party:** Kearney, 121.

228 **They planned what:** Kearney, 122.
228 **The violent extremism:** "The Hollow Men," T. S. Eliot, *Poems 1909–1925* (London: Faber & Gwyer, 1925).
228 **In July 1906:** Kearney, 128.
229 **The one person:** Kearney, 130–31.
229 **Law enforcement officers:** Bill Stein, "Colorado County Protects Womanhood: The Murder of Geraldine Kollmann and the Subsequent Lynching of the Accused," *The Southwestern Historical Quarterly* 108, no. 4 (2005): 440–66, and "Nov. 12, 1935: Mob of 700 White People Lynches Two Black Teenagers in Colorado County, TX," calendar.eji.org, https://calendar.eji.org/racial-injustice/nov/12#:~:text=On%20November%2012%2C%201935%2C%20a,in%20the%20mob%20was%20punished. http://www.jstor.org/stable/30240422.

CHAPTER 32

231 **Coleman—who had:** Kearney, 137–39.
233 **Journalist Ann Jones:** Ann Jones, *War Is Not Over When It's Over: Women Speak Out from the Ruins of War* (New York: Picador, 2011).
234 **He named his series:** "Consider the Lily: The Ungilded History of Colorado County," Nesbitt Memorial Library, https://www.columbustexaslibrary.net/local-history-and-genealogy-material/history-of-colorado-county/consider-the-lily-the-ungilded-history-of-colorado-county.
235 **Kearney draws that phrase:** From Kearney, email to the author, March 23, 2002: "Sophocles, 'Ode to Man' (ll. 332–33, *Antigone*): πολλὰ τὰ δεινὰ κοὐδὲν ἀνθρώπου δεινότερον πέλει."

PART 5: J. C. REESE, (1881–1930)

237 **West Texas is the most:** "Annual C. of C. Meet Big Success," *The Abilene (TX) Daily Reporter*, March 3, 1920, The Portal to Texas History.
237 **A lot of people:** Alisha Janette Taylor, dir., *A Legacy Unearthed*, 1:15:38, Taylor Made Studios, premiere sponsored by the Curtis House Cultural Center and Carl Spain Center at the Paramount Theatre, Abilene, Texas, July 23, 2022.

CHAPTER 33

241 **I was miserable:** My thinking in this chapter was formed through several conversations with Alisha Taylor, Jerry Taylor, Doug Foster, Tryce Prince, Jason Fikes, Randy Reese, Jim Reese, Dwayne Holden, and Jack Reese, among others. It is worth noting that everything I know about the racist history of ACU revealed in this chapter comes from people who were employed by or attended the university; many in this community are as deeply invested in rooting out their racist past as I am, if not more so.

CHAPTER 34

250 **Still, the campaign:** Details in this section from Tracy Shilcutt, David Coffey, and Donald S. Frazier, *Historic Abilene: An Illustrated History* (Abilene: The Abilene Preservation League, 2000).

251 **Jumanos, and then:** There is very little information about the indigenous people who lived in West Texas, so my sources are limited. I am aware that, without an accurate historical background, I could be repeating some of the same mistakes that Beaumont and others identified as happening when historians and scholars discussed the Karankawa people. If that is the case, the mistakes are my own. See *Frontier Texas: History of a Borderland to 1880* (Abilene: State House Press, 2004).

252 **In the "Trade":** Shilcutt, Coffey, and Frazier, 21.

252 **They even developed:** Shilcutt, Coffey, and Frazier, 27.

253 **One leader in town:** Ibid.

255 **It was the closest:** See Jeff W. Childers, Douglas A. Foster, and Jack Reese, *The Crux of the Matter: Crisis, Tradition, and the Future of Churches of Christ* (Abilene: Abilene Christian University Press, 2002).

257 **The origin of each:** Hiram W. Evans, "The Klan's Fight for Americanism," *North American Review* 223 (March 1926): 38–39.

CHAPTER 35

258 **Texas Tech University:** Ku Klux Klan (Amarillo, Texas): An Inventory of Its Records, 1921–1925 and undated, S1381.1, Southwest Collection, Special Collections Library, Texas Tech University.

258 **In Dallas around:** "What happened was when the Klan started, the first people they would recruit are people in the upper echelon—economic elites, business elites, etc.—and they'd work their way down because it was a pyramid scheme. People would get a percentage of membership fees." From Robin Young, "In the 1920s, 1 in 3 Eligible Men in Dallas Were KKK Members," Here & Now, November 6, 2019, https://www.wbur.org/hereandnow/2019/11/06/ku-klux-klan-dallas-texas.

259 **Officially, the revived:** Details about the Ku Klux Klan in Texas come from these and other sources: Norman LeRoy Murphy, *The Relationship of the Methodist Church to the Ku Klux Klan in Texas, 1920–1928* (Austin: University of Texas, 1971); Charles C. Alexander, *Crusade for Conformity: The Ku Klux Klan in Texas, 1920–1930* (Houston: Texas Gulf Coast Historical Association, 1962); Patricia Bernstein, *Ten Dollars to Hate: The Texas Man who Fought the Klan* (College Station: Texas A&M University, 2017); Linda Gordon, *The Second Coming of the KKK: The Ku Klux Klan of the 1920s and the American Political Tradition* (New York: Liveright, 2017); David Mark Chalmers, *Hooded Americanism: The History of the Ku Klux Klan* (Durham: Duke University Press, 1987); Michael Newton, *White Robes and Burning Crosses: A History of the Ku Klux Klan from 1866* (Jefferson, North Carolina: McFarland & Company, Inc., 2014); Timothy Egan, *A Fever in the Heart-*

land: The Ku Klux Klan's Plot to Take Over America, and the Woman Who Stopped Them (New York: Viking, 2023); and Wyn Craig Wade, *The Fiery Cross: The Ku Klux Klan in America* (New York: Simon & Schuster, 1986).

260 **When covering a Klan:** Untitled article, *The Abilene (TX) Daily Reporter*, May 25, 1921, The Portal to Texas History.

260 **One article in the:** "A Ku Klux in Africa," *The Abilene (TX) Daily Reporter*, October 30, 1921, The Portal to Texas History.

260 **In August 1921:** "List of Those Who Signed Petition for Employing Whites," *The Abilene (TX) Daily Reporter*, August 17, 1921, The Portal to Texas History.

261 **On November 16:** "Over $5,600.00 Raised for the Salvation Army," *The Abilene (TX) Daily Reporter*, November 16, 1921, The Portal to Texas History.

262 **A week later, the newspaper:** "White-Robed Klansmen to Parade the Streets of Abilene Thursday Evening," *The Abilene (TX) Daily Reporter*, November 23, 1921, The Portal to Texas History.

262 **The Friday morning:** "Silent Marchers Parade Streets," *The Abilene (TX) Daily Reporter*, November 25, 1921, The Portal to Texas History.

263 **In their write-up:** "Birth of a Nation," *The Abilene (TX) Daily Reporter*, December 11, 1921, The Portal to Texas History.

263 **What I found so:** See also Richard Brody, "The Worst Thing about 'Birth of a Nation' Is How Good It Is," *The New Yorker*, February 1, 2013, https://www.newyorker.com/culture/richard-brody/the-worst-thing-about-birth-of-a-nation-is-how-good-it-is.

263 **As Roger Ebert famously:** Roger Ebert, "The Birth of a Nation (1915) Movie Review," rogerebert.com, https://www.rogerebert.com/reviews/great-movie-the-birth-of-a-nation-1915.

263 **The movie relies:** D. W. Griffith and Thomas Dixon, *The Birth of a Nation*, Triangle Film Corporation, 1915.

267 **April 1922 was:** Quotes in the following few paragraphs from "Grand Jury Is Still at Work" and "Klansmen Tells Object of Order," *The Abilene (TX) Daily Reporter*, April 19, 1922, The Portal to Texas History.

269 **On Wednesday, April 26:** "Hamlin Cut Off by Flood Which Damages a Lake," *The Abilene (TX) Daily Reporter*, April 26, 1922, The Portal to Texas History.

269 **On May 31:** "Chief Clinton's Condition Grave," *The Abilene (TX) Daily Reporter*, May 31, 1922, The Portal to Texas History.

269 **One of the things:** "The Memorial," *The Abilene (TX) Daily Reporter*, June 7, 1922, The Portal to Texas History.

CHAPTER 36

271 **Later, witnesses would:** "Orders Thorough Probe of Slaying," *The Abilene (TX) Daily Reporter*, September 18, 1922, The Portal to Texas History.

271 **Davis told the:** Quotes in the next few paragraphs are from "Official Inquiry into

Death of Negro Here Saturday," *The Abilene (TX) Daily Reporter,* September 11, 1922, The Portal to Texas History.

273 **Ely was obviously:** "Orders Thorough Probe of Slaying."

275 **The crowd was:** "Knights of Ku Klux Klan Visit A.C.C.," *The Optimist,* November 9, 1922, The Portal to Texas History.

CHAPTER 37

276 **The university president:** I'm especially indebted to Jason Fikes and his stellar article here, "Jesse P. Sewell, White Supremacy, and the Formative Years of Abilene Christian College," *Restoration Quarterly* 64, no. 3 (2022): 170–81.

276 **According to the student:** "Gospel Meeting Is Closed Sunday Eve," *The Optimist,* November 9, 1922, The Portal to Texas History.

277 **The newspaper later:** "Knights of Ku Klux Klan Visit A.C.C."

278 **Enclosed was twenty-five dollars:** John C. Stevens, *No Ordinary University: The History of a City Set on a Hill* (Abilene: Abilene Christian University Press, 1998), 56.

278 **The question might:** Fikes, 171. Also, according to Fikes, "When the Klan heard Sewell speak about returning to the primitive gospel or about the ancient order of things, they believed they had found an ally with whom they shared much in common . . . they offered their gift and were received with respect. . . . When given clear opportunities to choose a more challenging way—either by publicly refuting the Klan or engaging in more humanizing relationships with persons of color— the administration chose the easier, broader path," 181.

278 **A similar scene:** "Ku Klux Endorse Revival Meeting at A.C. College," *The Abilene (TX) Daily Reporter,* November 7, 1922, The Portal to Texas History.

279 **That's when this:** My memory was confirmed by Fikes's research as well. In an endnote to the Sewell article, Fikes points to an apology that Royce Money—then the president of ACU—issued in November 1999, what the university called a "formal apology on behalf of its board, administration, faculty and staff" to Southwestern Christian College, a historically Black college; the apology was then repeated to the ACU community in 2000. The university's description of the audio, which is still online, is that Money "confessed that ACU acted in prejudiced and discrim- inatory ways toward African-Americans, particularly by denying their admission for almost the first full sixty years of the school's existence." See Royce Money, "The Apology," February 2000, https://digitalcommons.acu.edu/historical_audio _video/8/. I was there when Dr. Money repeated his apology at ACU. Though the response by the university was probably not perfect—I was too young to fully know how it played out—it was a watershed moment for me and I imagine many others. In many ways, I can trace the origins of this book back two decades to those months on campus when I learned at a formative time in my young life that people of faith and integrity speak the truth even when it's hard; those are values I learned at ACU and hold to this day.

CHAPTER 38

280 **Of the local:** Details in the next several paragraphs from Stevens, chapter 3, "Moving the School," 85–159, and from the John F. Worley Directory Company, Abilene City Directory, 1926.

281 **By 1927, Texas:** Bob Garcia-Buckalew, "The Backstory: When Texas Governors Fought the Ku Klux Klan and Won," kvue.com, March 5, 2022, https://www .kvue.com/article/news/history/the-backstory-texas-governors-fought-ku-klux -klan-won/269-efa1a3f1-f623-45a4-96b8-276b728a4ed6.

282 **As the college paper:** "Business Men in Banquet at A.C.C. Thurs. Evening," *The Optimist*, November 25, 1926, The Portal to Texas History.

283 **As a local historian:** Stevens, excerpt from *No Ordinary University*, in *ACU Today* (Spring 1998): 15.

283 **They wanted to:** "Eighty Thousand of Original Cost Is Reported as Raised," *The Optimist*, September 22, 1927, The Portal to Texas History.

283 **The first building:** "J.C. Reese Starts Work on First Building in A.C.C. Addition," *The Optimist*, April 19, 1928, The Portal to Texas History.

284 **Between Clause III:** My source for these deeds is Doug Foster, a retired professor of the university, who found them in the Abilene Christian University archives with the caption "Copies of selected pages from Carl Cheatham's Abstract of the Property at 1618 Cedar Crest Drive formerly a part of the old Hashknife Ranch." Email to the author, September 20, 2020.

CHAPTER 39

285 **"Redlining" is the word:** For further reading, see "The Fair Housing Act," Civil Rights Division, June 22, 2023, https://www.justice.gov/crt/fair-housing-act-1; Michael Jones-Correa, "The Origins and Diffusion of Racial Restrictive Covenants," *Political Science Quarterly* 115, no. 4 (2000): 541–68, https://doi.org/10.2307/2657609; Bruce Mitchell, "HOLC 'Redlining' Maps: The Persistent Structure of Segregation and Economic Inequality," NCRC, March 8, 2022, https://ncrc.org/holc/; and Mae M. Ngai, "Nationalism, Immigration Control, and the Ethnoracial Remapping of America in the 1920s," *OAH Magazine of History* 21, no. 3 (2007): 11–15, http://www.jstor.org/stable/25162123.

285 **In 2022, the US:** "Racial Differences in Economic Security: Housing," U.S. Department of the Treasury, December 6, 2022, https://home.treasury.gov/news/featured -stories/racial-differences-in-economic-security-housing#:~:text=In%20the %20second%20quarter%20of,households%20of%20any%20other%20race.

286 **In a documentary:** Taylor, *A Legacy Unearthed.*

286 **In *A Legacy*:** *A Legacy Unearthed*, 13:00.

286 **Only a few:** "The Big Floods," *The Abilene (TX) Daily Reporter*, May 26, 1974, The Portal to Texas History.

287 **Effie Brewster, the first:** *A Legacy Unearthed*, 30:00–40:00.

287 **He founded the:** *A Legacy Unearthed*, 1:08, and Greg Jaklewicz, "History Is in the House: Penns Leads Effort to Present, Preserve Abilene's Black History," *Abilene (TX) Reporter-News*, July 19, 2020, https://www.reporternews.com/story/news /local/2020/07/18/abilene-black-history-community-andrew-penns-preserve -present/5415247002/.

287 **The Treasury Department's:** "Redlining Was Outlawed in 1968. Here's How the Practice Is Still Hurting Black Americans.," CBS News, https://www.cbsnews .com/news/wealth-gap-black-americans-redlining/.

288 **That they would:** According to Fikes, "Abilene Christian University would not exist today without the support of supremacists in its earliest days. The administration received these funds with open arms, placed them in the bank at interest; consequently, the college enjoyed prosperity. Its graduates found jobs, raised families, started churches, and improved their social standing. . . . Every inheritor of this legacy should readily recognize the tangled, complex, and even scandalous origin of the benefits that they have received. There are no exemptions," 181.

289 **Those family stories:** See Jack R. Reese, *At the Blue Hole: Elegy for a Church on the Edge* (Grand Rapids: Eerdmans, 2021), as well as *The Crux of the Matter*.

289 **They worked with others:** Loretta Fulton, "'Precious Cargo': Soil Honors Everett Grover, Black Man Killed in Abilene in 1922," *Abilene (TX) Reporter-News*, May 24, 2019, https://www.reporternews.com/story/life/faith/2019/05/24/soil-honors -everett-grover-black-man-killed-abilene-1922/3768311002/.

PART 6: FRANK PROBST (1905–1990)

297 **The story of the:** Swanson, *Cult of Glory*, 5.

297 **I imagine one:** James Baldwin, *Notes of a Native Son* (New York: Beacon Press, 1955), 91.

CHAPTER 41

301 **The Rangers were:** Beginning with two novels, Alfred W. Arrington, *The Rangers and Regulators of the Tanaha; or, Life among the Lawless. A Tale of the Republic of Texas* (New York: R. M. De Witt, 1856) and Jeremiah Clemens, *Bernard Lile; An Historical Romance Embracing the Periods of the Texas Revolution and the Mexican War* (Philadelphia: J. B. Lippincott & Co., 1856). See also *Captain Jeff, or Frontier Life in Texas with the Texas Rangers* (Colorado, Texas: Whipkey Printing, 1906) and Bruce A. Glasrud and Harold J. Weiss, eds., *Tracking the Texas Rangers: The Twentieth Century* (Denton: University of North Texas Press, 2013).

301 **There have been:** "Rangers in Pop Culture," Texas Ranger Hall of Fame and Museum, February 27, 2018, https://www.texasranger.org/texas-ranger-museum /researching-rangers/rangers-in-pop-culture/.

302 **One journalist called:** Sean O'Neal, "Walkers and Lone Rangers: How Pop Culture Shaped the Texas Rangers Mythology," *Texas Monthly*, November 16, 2022,

https://www.texasmonthly.com/arts-entertainment/how-pop-culture-shaped
-texas-rangers-myth/.

303 **I was surprised:** "Escorted Ginger," *The Victoria (TX) Advocate*, September 25,
1942, 4.

304 **The saving the cat:** "Ranger Rescues Cat," *Beeville (TX) Bee-Picayune*, December
31, 1959, 4.

CHAPTER 43

310 **In 1939, according:** U.S. Census Bureau, April 5, 1940, Three Rivers, Live Oak,
Texas, *1940 United States Federal Census*, Sheet No. 3A, lines 27–29, Ancestry.com,
https://www.ancestry.com/imageviewer/collections/2442/images/m-t0627
-04095-01215?pId=156794986.

311 **They were serving:** Retrieve Prison Farm was originally a plantation that, in 1860,
was one of the largest in Texas; the state bought the plantation in 1918 and prisoners took over the work of enslaved people on the "prison farm" until the 1990s. See
Joe Holley, "Former Texas Inmate's Story Proves to Be a Page Turner," *Houston
Chronicle*, May 25, 2018, https://www.houstonchronicle.com/news/houston-texas
/houston/article/Former-Texas-inmate-s-story-proves-to-be-a-page-12944916.php.

312 **It merited only:** "Live Oak County Patrolman Kills Escaped Convict," *Beeville
(TX) Bee-Picayune*, February 27, 1941, 10.

314 **Ennis had already been:** "Youth Killed, Officers Hurt in Altercation," *Beeville
(TX) Bee-Picayune*, April 1, 1943, 1.

314 **When Uncle Frank:** *Beeville (TX) Bee-Picayune*, 1943–1945.

CHAPTER 44

316 **His mentor was:** For more about Alfred Allee, see Swanson, "The Melon Harvest," *Cult of Glory*, 359–76.

316 **Despite the fact:** As I mentioned in the Author's Note, the Rodriguez family
prefers the term "Hispanic" over other terms, so it is the word I will use in part 6.
During World War I, US and British intelligence released reports about enemy
plots to turn Mexican citizens and Mexican Americans against the US, including
a political manifesto discovered in 1915 in the nearby city of San Diego, Texas, that
showed German efforts within Mexico and other Central American countries to
forge anti-US alliances in the region. See McCollom, *The Last Sheriff in Texas*, 38.

317 **But like it had:** According to McCollom, in the elections from 1922 to 1932, "The
community was split. Those were the years of the Ku Klux Klan. When they were
over, people preferred to erase them from the county history," 46.

317 **The local paper:** "Negro Is Killed in Jail When He Grabs for Sheriff's Gun,"
Beeville (TX) Bee-Picayune, January 18, 1945, 1.

318 **He and Ennis:** Quotes from the following few sentences are from "Kiwanis Club,"
Beeville (TX) Bee-Picayune, March 1, 1945, 2.

318 **They were bitterly:** Quotes and details in this section from coverage in *The Victoria (TX) Advocate*, from jury selection to acquittal, January 15–20, 1946; "State Rests in Vail Ennis Murder Case in Victoria Court," *Beeville (TX) Bee-Picayune*, January 17, 1946, 1; as well as interviews with the Rodriguez family and McCollom, 16–21.

320 **The first was:** See especially a description of Ennis's Hudson in 2006, Rob Johnson, *The Lost Years of William S. Burroughs* (College Station: Texas A&M University Press), 118–34.

324 **But a neighbor:** "Letters to the Editor: Remembers deadly Ennis shooting," *Beeville (TX) Bee-Picayune*, March 11, 2003, 5 and 14.

324 **As one writer:** Swanson, 365.

325 **Allee was himself:** Swanson, 364.

325 **One case would:** "Allee v. Medrano," U.S. Reports, vol. 416, October Term 1973, https://tile.loc.gov/storage-services/service/ll/usrep/usrep416/usrep416802/usrep416802.pdf.

325 **Though he would:** José Ángel Gutiérrez in Swanson, 365.

325 **Uncle Frank was:** "State Rests," *Beeville (TX) Bee-Picayune*, January 17, 1946, 2.

CHAPTER 45

326 **More than a thousand:** McCollom, 19.

326 **While they waited:** Details in this paragraph from the *Beeville (TX) Bee-Picayune*, December 27, 1945, December 17, 1946, and September 8, 1945.

326 **He told the press:** Ches Evans, "Despite Murder Trial, Ouster Suit, Sheriff Will Seek Reelection," *The Victoria (TX) Advocate*, January 16, 1946, 1.

327 **Around 4:30 p.m.:** "State Rests in Vail Ennis Murder Case in Victoria Court," *Beeville (TX) Bee-Picayune*, January 17, 1946.

329 **It certainly did:** Much of McCollom's focus in *The Last Sheriff in Texas* is on the narrative of Ezell's efforts—along with other community members—to oust Ennis from office; in this section, I'm deeply indebted to McCollom's excellent work.

CHAPTER 46

331 **Then he told:** McCollom, 2.

332 **On November 24, 1947:** "Texas: Hellbent Sheriff," *Time* 50, no. 21, November 24, 1947, 30.

CHAPTER 47

335 **In September 1946:** Ad, *Beeville (TX) Bee-Picayune*, September 26, 1946, 19.

CHAPTER 48

340 **But those kinds:** McCollom, 213.

342 **As the *Beeville*:** Ad, *Beeville (TX) Bee-Picayune*, February 21, 1952, 7.

342 **That same day:** Ibid.

343 **As one scholar:** Brent M. S. Campney, "Police Brutality and Mexican American Families in Texas, 1945–1980," *The Annals of the American Academy of Political and Social Science* 694 (March 2021): 108–21.

343 **More than two thousand:** The crowd number is from McCollom, 227; the census information is from "1950 Census of Population: Preliminary Counts," U.S. Department of Commerce, Bureau of the Census, Series PC-2, No. 43 (September 14, 1950), https://www2.census.gov/library/publications/decennial/1950/pc-02/pc-2-43.pdf.

343 **One witness later:** Elias Chapa, in McCollom, 227.

344 **One witness said:** Adam Gonzales, in McCollom, 228–29.

344 **The headline the next:** "Political Rally Last Night Was Largest in Quarter of Century," *Beeville (TX) Bee-Picayune*, July 24, 1952. See also McCollom, 226.

344 **Old-timers knew:** McCollom, 234.

344 **In November 1952:** "Landslide Vote Cast in Nation," *Beeville (TX) Bee-Picayune*, November 6, 1952, 1.

345 **In response, Lucy:** "Former Sheriff Not a Hero," *Beeville (TX) Bee-Picayune*, March 15, 2003, 5A.

345 **A few months:** "Letters to the Editor: Ennis killed grandfather," *Beeville (TX) Bee-Picayune*, June 11, 2003, 5A.

CONCLUSION

349 **"Here, in time":** Pádraig Ó Tuama, *Being Here: Prayers for Curiosity, Justice, and Love* (Grand Rapids: Eerdmans, 2023), 135.

353 **According to the UN:** "The Justice and Reconciliation Process in Rwanda," Outreach Programme on the Rwanda Genocide and the United Nations, March 2014, https://www.un.org/en/preventgenocide/rwanda/assets/pdf/Backgrounder %20Justice%202014.pdf.